Liberty, right and nature is a vibrant and powerful contribution to the recently renewed debate over natural rights and natural rights language.

Closely examining traditional histories of the subject, which place the origins of individual rights squarely within the voluntarist tradition, Annabel Brett argues persuasively that in order to understand the development of the concept we need to look at the way in which the Latin language of *ius* functioned in a wide range of philosophical contexts. Deploying an enormous array of primary sources, many of them previously ignored, Dr Brett traces the range of the terminology of rights within the scholastic tradition from the thirteenth-century poverty controversy to the works of the sixteenth-century neo-Thomistic 'School of Salamanca'. A final chapter considers the consequences of this investigation for the rights theory of Thomas Hobbes. Dr Brett's analysis covers a panoply of theological and legal sources, and should prove indispensable to all those working in the field of mediaeval and early modern moral and political philosophy.

IDEAS IN CONTEXT

LIBERTY, RIGHT AND NATURE

IDEAS IN CONTEXT

Edited by QUENTIN SKINNER (*General Editor*)
LORRAINE DASTON, DOROTHY ROSS and JAMES TULLY

The books in this series will discuss the emergence of intellectual traditions and of related new disciplines. The procedures, aims and vocabularies that were generated will be set in the context of the alternatives available within the contemporary frameworks of ideas and institutions. Through detailed studies of the evolution of such traditions, and their modification by different audiences, it is hoped that a new picture will form of the development of ideas in their concrete contexts. By this means, artificial distinctions between the history of philosophy, of the various sciences, of society and politics, and of literature may be seen to dissolve.

The series is published with the support of the Exxon Foundation.

A list of books in the series will be found at the end of the volume.

LIBERTY, RIGHT AND NATURE

Individual rights in later scholastic thought

ANNABEL S. BRETT

University of Cambridge

CAMBRIDGE
UNIVERSITY PRESS

PUBLISHED BY THE PRESS SYNDICATE OF THE UNIVERSITY OF CAMBRIDGE
The Pitt Building, Trumpington Street, Cambridge, United Kingdom

CAMBRIDGE UNIVERSITY PRESS
The Edinburgh Building, Cambridge CB2 2RU, UK
40 West 20th Street, New York NY 10011–4211, USA
477 Williamstown Road, Port Melbourne, VIC 3207, Australia
Ruiz de Alarcón 13, 28014 Madrid, Spain
Dock House, The Waterfront, Cape Town 8001, South Africa

http://www.cambridge.org

First published 1997
Reprinted 2000
First paperback edition 2003

A catalogue record for this book is available from the British Library

Library of Congress Cataloguing in Publication data
Brett, Annabel S.
Liberty, right and nature: individual rights in later scholastic thought / Annabel S. Brett.
p.   cm. –(Ideas in context; 44)
ISBN 0 521 56239 2 (hardback)
1. Human rights – History. 2. Natural law – History.
3. Scholasticism. I. Title. II. Series.
JC571.B683   1997
323.44´01 – dc20   96–15357   CIP

ISBN 0 521 56239 2 hardback
ISBN 0 521 54340 1 paperback

Transferred to digital printing 2003

For my parents

Contents

Acknowledgements

This book has been several years in the making, and during that time I have incurred more debts of gratitude to individuals and institutions than I can hope to mention here. I would like to begin by acknowledging the material support, firstly of the British Academy, and secondly of Gonville and Caius College, Cambridge, which provided me, as an Unofficial Fellow, with an ideal working environment for three years. I would also like to acknowledge the helpfulness of the staff of the Rare Books Room of Cambridge University Library.

It is a pleasure to have here another opportunity of thanking my supervisor, Quentin Skinner, for all his unfailing encouragement and kindness, without which I could never have completed this research. I am also very much indebted to Anthony Pagden for his consistent interest in the project. I owe special thanks to George Garnett, who first introduced me to the history of political thought, and who has offered an acute comment at timely intervals ever since; and to Shelley Lockwood, who has patiently discussed assorted arguments with me for several years now, with her own particular clarity.

This book has benefited from the comments of several scholars, to whom I am deeply grateful, especially James Burns, Alan Cromartie, John Ford, Steve McGrade and Brian Tierney, who all spent time reading and commenting on various chapters, and saved the work as a whole from a number of errors and failings of consistency. For those that remain they cannot be held in any way responsible. I would also like to thank the anonymous reader from Cambridge University Press for many constructive suggestions, and my copy-editor, Karen Anderson Howes, for all her attentive and patient help in making it more readable.

Finally it remains for me to thank again all my family and friends for their affection and forbearance; and most especially my parents, to whom this book is dedicated.

Notes on the text

Where available, I have used modern critical editions of all mediaeval and early modern works cited. Where such have not been
available, I have used the first edition where possible, and where not,
the earliest possible subsequent edition.

TRANSLATIONS

All translations are my own unless otherwise indicated: I have
aimed for literal accuracy rather than elegance. The reader's
attention is drawn to the following particular points of translation:
firstly, the Latin term 'ius', as the authors were themselves aware,
can cover the senses of both 'law' and 'right'. It is part of the
argument of this book that they used it with a high degree of self-
consciousness and precision. Hence, I have not hesitated to render
it as 'right' either where it is clearly attributed to a subject
('subjective right') or where it is equivalent to the 'iustum', 'the
right thing' ('objective right'). Where it is evidently used in the same
sense as 'law', 'lex', I have translated it as such. There remain,
however, a few cases in which 'ius' bears an objective sense of 'right
ordering' or 'right ordination', which lies between 'iustum' and
'lex': and in these cases I have occasionally rendered this as 'right',
although other translators have preferred 'law'. Secondly, with
regard to 'proprius' ('proper to oneself', 'one's own'): I have
rendered this as 'proper', to preserve the overtone of 'proprietas',
'property'. Thirdly, I have usually translated the Latin 'civitas' as
'city', in the sense of the civic or political unit, close to the sense of
'respublica' as 'commonwealth'.

For all quotations of any length I have given the original Latin without altering spelling and punctuation where practicable. Where there are errors in the original I have indicated the fact without correcting it.

PROPER NAMES

I have used the appellation which is most usual: so Thomas Aquinas, but Jean Gerson. Where neither Latin nor vernacular is more usual, I have generally preferred the Latin form, as being the one used by the authors themselves.

Introduction

This book was originally conceived as a study of the political theory
of the Dominican 'School of Salamanca' or 'second scholastic': that
group of sixteenth-century Spanish theologians (and, to some extent,
the jurists who worked alongside them) whose works take the form of
commentaries on the juridical and legal aspects of Aquinas' *Summa
theologiae*.[1] While the general outlines of their political teaching are
well known as an episode in European intellectual history,[2] there
continues to be some debate over their juridical philosophy – their
philosophy of right – and over the aspects of their political philosophy which flow from that. In broad terms, the issue lies between
those who hold that the School represents a return to an authentic
Thomist–Aristotelian theory, depending on the notions of natural
law and of right as the object of justice ('objective right'), and those
who argue that, although on the surface these Spanish neo-Thomists
may appear faithful to Aristotle and Aquinas, in reality they thought
of right as a faculty or liberty of the individual ('subjective right'),
and that their political theory is based on such rights and is a
forerunner of Hobbes'.[3]

[1]   The terms 'School of Salamanca' and 'second scholastic' usually apply to the entire period
of sixteenth-century Spanish scholasticism, from Vitoria to Suárez. They therefore span
both the early Dominican period and the later, Jesuit-dominated stage, when the movement
had ceased to be centred on the University of Salamanca. However, the Jesuit continuation
of work of the School is a study in its own right. In this book I concentrate on the early
period from the mid-1520s to the mid-1560s, and I use the term 'School of Salamanca' to
refer to the Dominican theologians at the College of San Esteban in Salamanca, and the
jurists who worked there and were influenced by or responded to their work.
[2]   For an excellent general analysis of the School in the context of the European debate, see
Q. R. D. Skinner, *The foundations of modern political thought*, vol. II (Cambridge 1978), pp. 135–
73; for their works in terms of the discovery of the New World, see the fundamental study
by A. R. D. Pagden, *The fall of natural man: The American Indian and the origins of comparative
ethnology* (Cambridge 1982). See also D. Ferraro, *Itinerari del volontarismo. Teologia e politica al
tempo di Luis de León* (Milan 1995), esp. chapter 5 for a fresh overall account of the School's
intellectual project.
[3]   For the proponents of these positions, see the references below, chapter 4, nn. 2 and 3. In

It soon became clear that these conflicting views were not isolated judgements but were bound in with a whole story of the genesis of the modern notion of individual rights. Any attempt to resolve the problem, and thereby to reassess the political theory of the School of Salamanca, would demand a reconsideration of that history from its foundations.

Subjective right as an element of modern linguistic usage functions in many different ways. W. N. Hohfeld famously isolated eight usages of the term 'right' as applied to the individual.[4] Within moral-philosophical discourse, rights are generally seen either as 'liberty-rights' ('active rights'), independent licences of action, or as 'claim-rights' ('passive rights', 'rights of recipience'), which are dependent for their existence on the obligations of others.[5] Again, the former type of rights can be seen as constituting an area wherein the individual and her choice are sovereign;[6] but it is also possible to conceive of using a claim of this kind of right to do that which we are under obligation to do.[7]

So the language of rights today is fluid between several different senses of the term. However, the history of subjective right has not been written in a way that reflects the pluralistic nature of the

---

between there is a third, less fully developed, opinion which holds that, although the Spaniards did have a notion of individual rights, they understood such rights as conditioned by natural law, and their theory has therefore more of a Lockeian cast. This interpretation has been put forward for the case of Suárez by James Tully, *A discourse on property: John Locke and his adversaries* (Cambridge 1980), pp. 66–8, and in *An approach to political philosophy: Locke in contexts* (Cambridge 1993), pp. 103–7. Tully does not, however, consider the earlier School of Salamanca, with which I am concerned in this study.

[4] W. N. Hohfeld, *Fundamental legal conceptions* (New Haven 1919); and see the discussion in J. Finnis, *Natural law and natural rights* (Oxford 1980), pp. 199–201.

[5] See D. D. Raphael, 'Human rights', *Aristotelian Society Supplements* 39 (1965), 205–18, esp. pp. 206–7. Raphael divides subjective rights into 'rights of recipience' and 'rights of action', equating the latter with Hobbes' right to life, which is a liberty: 'the right of action itself is *a liberty*' (p. 210; italics in the original; see also by the same author, 'Obligations and rights in Hobbes', *Philosophy* 37 (1962), 345–52, esp. pp. 348–9).

[6] See H. L. A. Hart, 'Are there any natural rights?', first printed in *Philosophical Review* 64 (1955), 175–91, reprinted in A. Quinton (ed.), *Political philosophy* (Oxford 1967), 53–66.

[7] Cf. D. Lyons, 'The correlativity of rights and duties', *Noûs* 4 (1970), 45–55, p. 45: 'It is generally supposed that an "active" right essentially involves an element of choice in the sense that one cannot have a right to do something without having the right to refrain ... [This is false, for] one can sometimes support one's claim of a right to do something by showing that one has a positive obligation to do it.' It might be argued that such a right is not truly subjective, since it has objective content. But the point about a right belonging to an individual is not only or necessarily that her actions are indifferent; it is also that her action can be justified in terms of herself and not merely in terms of her relations with others. Hence a right to do something to which we are obliged is a subjective right in an important sense.

present concept. The plurality of concepts of subjective right today has been recognised largely through attention to the way the term 'right' – as attributed to the individual – functions as an element in the languages of legal, moral and political discourse. But although historians such as Brian Tierney and James Tully are now writing the history of right as a history of language – a history of the usage of the Latin term *ius* – the subject is still largely shaped by attempts to locate an origin for the idea of subjective as opposed to objective right.

Objective right is conceived as right in the sense of the object of justice, that at which justice aims and with which it deals: the *dikaion* of Aristotle's *Ethics*, the *ius* of classical and Byzantine Roman law.[8] It is the just portion which is due between persons, rather than something belonging to the person herself. This objective sense of *ius* was transmitted to mediaeval discourse through the study of the Roman law and the recovery of Aristotle's *Ethics*, the doctrines concerning justice of which were adapted by Thomas Aquinas as the basis of his analysis. Largely through the standing of Aquinas as *the* exponent of a mediaeval philosophical outlook,[9] objective right has been taken as part of the high mediaeval achievement of synthesising classical and Christian heritages into rationalist philosophies of universal order. Hence the origin of subjective right is attributed to Thomism's traditional opponents, the voluntarists and nominalists of the late thirteenth and fourteenth centuries who are widely portrayed as the destroyers of the Thomist synthesis, initiators of a philosophy

---

[8] I follow the vast majority of commentators in understanding the Aristotelian *dikaion* in an objective sense. For the view that Aristotle sometimes understands *dikaion* in a subjective sense, see F. D. Miller, *Nature, justice and rights in Aristotle's 'Politics'* (Oxford 1995). Although it is widely agreed that the *ius* of Roman law is objective rather than subjective, many accept that at points the language of the Roman law hesitates on the brink of the subjective sense; for example H. Coing, 'Zur Geschichte des Begriffs "subjektives Recht"', in Coing, F. H. Lawson and K. Grönfors (eds.), *Das subjektives Recht und der Rechtschutz der Persönlichkeit* (Frankfurt a. M. 1959). Others go further and assert that the Roman law can properly be said to have the concept of subjective right, e.g. G. Pugliese, '"Res corporales", "res incorporales" e il problema del diritto soggettivo', in *Studi in onore di V. Arangio-Ruiz*, vol. III (Naples 1953), 223–60. His argument depends to a large extent on the idea that a concept can be in use even if it is not elaborated as such: for a critique of this notion of an unelucidated concept of rights, see the remarks in R. Dagger, 'Rights', in T. Ball, J. Farr and R. Hanson (eds.), *Political innovation and conceptual change* (Cambridge 1989), 292–308, pp. 296–8.

[9] See Brian Tierney, 'The origins of natural rights language: Texts and contexts, 1150–1250', *History of Political Thought* 10 (1989), 615–46, p. 616, who speaks of 'the fallacy, widespread among modern jurists and philosophers who are not medieval specialists, that if an idea is not found in Aquinas it is not a medieval idea at all'.

of individualism and the *esprit laïque*.[10] This perspective is bound up with the traditional story of later scholasticism as a struggle between *antiqui* and *moderni*, and further with the broader story of the advent of 'modernity' out of the putative 'communitarianism' or 'holism' of the mediaeval Western world, with all the passions that story has inspired.[11]

Supporting this general philosophical or 'partisan' history[12] – still very much alive – of subjective right, however, there are more specific arguments for the association of subjective right with the voluntarist tradition. The first focuses on the difference between objective right and subjective right in terms of their relation to the notion of law.[13] It is argued that the point about objective right – in Aristotle, classical Roman law and Aquinas – is that it is conceptually independent of the notion of law as the rule of actions. Right is an objective thing (*res, chose*) and it has nothing to do with the possibility of actions. By contrast, subjective right as 'une *qualité* du sujet, une de ses *facultés*, plus précisément une franchise, une liberté, une possibilité d'agir'[14] is dependent on the notion of law. It is the invention of William of Ockham, who first characterised *ius* as a *potestas* ('power')

---

[10] The prominent exception to this generality is the recent work of Brian Tierney, who in a series of important articles questions the whole idea that subjective right is a late mediaeval (post-Aquinas) development and refuses to subscribe to the starkly dualistic picture of 'subjective' opposed to 'objective' right. He locates the origin of the philosophical idea of natural right in a modern sense in the canonistic of the twelfth century. For discussion of this thesis, see below, esp. chapter 2, pp. 83–7.

[11] This traditional picture of the distinction between the middle ages and modernity is, of course, now being abandoned for a more nuanced view which sees elements of recognition of the individual within the group-oriented society of the middle ages: see the remarks by A. Black, 'The individual and society', in J. H. Burns (ed.), *The Cambridge history of medieval political thought, c. 350–c. 1450* (Cambridge 1988), 588–606, and his account of mediaeval 'civil society' in *Guilds and civil society in European political thought from the twelfth century to the present* (London 1984), pp. 32–43. The Gierkean perspective is still an important force, however, as witness for example L. Dumont, *Essays on individualism* (Chicago 1986), pp. 62–6, who argues that Ockham's theory of individual rights is part of his refusal to recognise the universal reality of the group (p. 64, n. 7; see the discussion below, pp. 50–1).

[12] I borrow the phrase from Alasdair MacIntyre in his book, *Three rival versions of moral enquiry: Encyclopaedia, genealogy and tradition* (London 1990), p. 151. Unlike Tierney, MacIntyre wants to keep the traditional picture of subjective right originating in the fourteenth century as part of his argument for a break in Western philosophy after the death of Aquinas. I do not suggest, of course, that the present argument is not also 'partisan'.

[13] This is the highly influential view of the French legal historian Michel Villey. See his classic article, 'La genèse du droit subjectif chez Guillaume d'Ockham', *Archives de la philosophie du droit* N.S. 9 (1964), 97–127; and *Leçons d'histoire de la philosophie du droit*, 2nd edn (Paris 1962), chapter 11, section 11.

[14] Villey, 'La genèse du droit subjectif', pp. 99–102; quotation from p. 101; italics in the original.

of the individual subject, and it is associated with his inability to think of the juridical order in terms other than that of the individual, her actions and the law which commands them.[15]

Relatedly it is argued that it is the conception of law in the voluntarist tradition which is required to ground a subjective understanding of right.[16] Voluntarists understand law as the will of the legislator, laid upon individuals who are free or have liberties in so far as they are not commanded by such a legislative will – ultimately, that of God. The freedom of the individual apart from the law, a conceivably absolute latitude of action, is the individual's subjective right. If, by contrast, the individual is understood to be directed towards certain actions of her nature as such, as on a rationalist conception of law, then there is no such subjective latitude of action which could constitute subjective right. Connectedly, just as in the voluntarist tradition it is the supremacy of the will the intellect which ensures the freedom of God, so in human beings too, it is the exercise of their will which makes them free. Rights as faculties of the individual serve this freedom and its expression.

In a rather different vein, but again connectedly, a third argument for the origins of subjective right focuses not on the question of law but on the notion of *property*, and depends on that element of the modern language of rights which sees right as the property of the individual, and likewise property as the paradigmatic right.[17] Subjective right is that domain of individual sovereignty wherein the individual's will is her right. The origins of this notion are said to be found in the equivalence of *dominium* and *ius* in early Franciscan poverty tracts and in subsequent late mediaeval literature. Here it is understood to be linked with the subjectivity of early Franciscan philosophy, which posits a radical disjunction between the individual

[15] See further below, chapter 3.
[16] See M. Bastit, *La naissance de la loi moderne. La pensée de la loi de saint Thomas à Suárez* (Paris 1990), p. 21. See also the important work of Noel Malcolm, 'Thomas Hobbes and voluntarist theology', unpublished Ph.D dissertation, Cambridge 1983, Pt. II, pp. 139ff. I do not wish to question the thesis that Hobbes' understanding of law owes much to voluntarist theology. But I shall develop the suggestion (below, chapter 6) that it is renaissance Roman law, rather than the theological voluntarist tradition, which provides the fundamentals of Hobbes' notion of right.
[17] This is the argument of Paolo Grossi in his two fundamental articles, '*Usus facti*. La nozione di proprietà nell'inaugurazione dell'età nuova', *Quaderni fiorentini* 1 (1972), 287–355, and 'La proprietà nel sistema privatistico della seconda scolastica', in Grossi (ed.), *La seconda scolastica nella formazione del diritto privato moderno. Incontro di studi* (Milan 1973), 117–222. To some extent it is also the thesis of Richard Tuck, *Natural rights theories: Their origin and development* (Cambridge 1979), chapters 1 and 2. See below, chapter 1.

subject and the world of things, and contrasts with the philosophy of Aquinas wherein the individual is *inquadrato nell'universo*,[18] embedded in a universal order.

These arguments differ from each other at important points. But together they form an impressive consensus: subjective right, in its true or at least most significant sense, is the corollary of a voluntarist theology which conceives it as that area, defined by the law, in which the individual may act at will, as free and sovereign proprietor. From its origins in Franciscan discourse, this conception of right is said to be developed in the writings of Fitzralph, Wyclif, Gerson and Summenhart, and to be expressed definitively by Hobbes as the heir of this theological tradition. It is in terms of this concept that members of the early School of Salamanca, both theologians and jurists, are analysed as either positing a theory of individual rights or not.

However, although this general theory concerning subjective right and its origin may be convincing in the abstract, in practice it faces several difficulties. If we are not looking for the origin of an idea, but enquiring after the specific languages of right available in late mediaeval discourse, then we must translate the above argument into terms of vocabulary. Here it becomes the thesis that the language of *ius* as *facultas* or *potestas*, or the language of *ius* as *dominium*, signifies a notion of right as indifferent liberty or sovereignty. The problem then is that this does not fit the texts to which it is supposed to apply.

One of the clearest signs of this is the fact that for almost all of the voluntarist authors generally cited in the story of subjective right, *ius* as a faculty, power or dominion is predicable of animals and even of inanimate entities, which by the same authors are consistently denied liberty. This feature has tended either to go unremarked or to have been dismissed, but its prominence suggests that it was not as irrelevant as historians have implied. Moreover, rights as *potestates* or *facultates* of an individual entity – including man – can be seen by these authors as operating in accordance with the law, not as being a liberty granted by the law. In the unique instance – that of Conrad Summenhart – in which the vocabulary of *ius* is associated with the liberty of man left over by the ten commandments, this is for

---

[18]   The phrase is Grossi's in '*Usus facti*'.

Summenhart not the nature of right in general, but a very specific type of right. Hence it is not straightforwardly the case that the appearance of *ius* characterised as a *facultas* or *potestas*, or as *dominium*, implies the concept of rights outlined in the arguments above, nor can we necessarily talk in terms of a language of right as indifferent liberty in the late mediaeval period. A different approach is needed.

This book, therefore, is not an attempt to find the origin for the, or any, modern concept of subjective right. What I try to do instead is to recover the variety of the senses of the term *ius* as employed to signify a quality or property of the individual subject in late mediaeval and renaissance scholastic discourse. The reassessment of *ius* in a subjective sense entails that its relation with the notion of objective right be reconsidered: I therefore attempt to assess the precise understanding of objective right held by authors of this period. To escape the grip of the philosophical history of subjective right sketched earlier, I try to get behind the categories of voluntarist, nominalist, realist and the like, which have too often shaded over into explanatory factors, and concentrate instead on the nature of the literature in which *ius* is used in a subjective sense, taking into account the constraints of genre within scholastic literary production.[19]

The first three chapters of this book are therefore devoted to the period between c. 1250 and c. 1525. The argument proceeds roughly chronologically, with departures from this basic scheme where considerations of genre override those of temporal proximity. In chapter 1, I examine the equation between *dominium* and right, trying to pin down the sense of this equivalence in its various contexts in late mediaeval literature. Chapter 2 considers fourteenth-century developments, from Ockham through to Gerson, in connecting nature, natural agency and right. Here *ius* in a subjective sense is incorporated into a universe governed by natural law, sometimes

[19] My concern is therefore primarily with identifying the different languages (idioms or rhetorics) of rights within late mediaeval and renaissance discourse, i.e. with that side of intellectual history wherein the historian tends to become an 'archaeologist', revealing and tracing buried seams of language. For archaeology in this sense, see J. G. A. Pocock, 'The concept of a language and the *métier d'historien*: Some considerations on practice', in A. Pagden (ed.), *The languages of political theory in early modern Europe* (Cambridge 1987), 19–28. In so far as I have charted developments or mutations within these languages, my focus has been on the intellectual context which provided the immediate orientation for the authors involved. I have not discussed in detail wider issues of political, social and economic milieu. My concern has been rather with the relations between texts, with exposing the ways in which, and the extent to which, these books 'speak of other books', and in so doing lay down their distinctive 'ways of speaking'.

with explicitly Thomist references. I suggest that this understanding of subjective right is profoundly distinct from that considered in chapter 1. In chapter 3 I trace the development of the notion of objective right in mediaeval discourse, charting in particular the changes within the Thomist position which bring early sixteenth-century Thomist authors close to a Gersonian position on rights such as that held by Jacques Almain.

With this background in place, in chapters 4 and 5 I come to consider the early School of Salamanca. I argue that once we are in a position to appreciate the different notions of subjective right current in late mediaeval and renaissance scholasticism, the picture with regard to these authors becomes more nuanced and at the same time clearer. I suggest that Vitoria, still working basically within a late mediaeval framework of understanding inherited from his days at the University of Paris, hesitates between two late mediaeval senses of subjective right in two different works. I then contend that the work of his pupil Soto constitutes an attempt to reconcile these two senses as part of a larger political project to harmonise the demands of the organic natural commonwealth with those of individual liberty.

A more accurate picture of Soto's doctrine of subjective right enables us to reassess the work of his contemporary, the jurist Fernando Vázquez. Vázquez is usually seen as holding the voluntarist notion of subjective right, either together with his theologian contemporaries or in opposition to them, depending on the perspective of the historian. But the reassessment of the late mediaeval language of subjective right permits us to understand that Vázquez's theory of rights not only bears no simple relation of either opposition or identity to those of Vitoria and Soto, but also cannot be assimilated to any of the theological traditions of right developed during the course of the later middle ages. Vázquez's work, combating (as we shall see) the specifically political use of the notion of right by Soto, employs a sense of right based on legal rather than theological sources, which constitutes a radical alternative to those of the theologians.

This is the end of the story about the early School of Salamanca. But by this point enough has been said to make it a story not just about sixteenth-century scholasticism, but about the whole trajectory from the Franciscans to Hobbes. A final chapter therefore considers the effect of placing Hobbes' notion of natural right as liberty not within a theological discourse, but within the legal tradition originating with Fernando Vázquez.

This study is therefore a history of the early language of rights. But political theorists today are still grappling with the heritage of that language: still at odds over what rights imply and what they do not, and over the political significance of appealing to them. Much of the present debate presupposes, in one form or another, the particular philosophical or partisan history outlined above. To appreciate some of the complexities of early rights language may help to provide a new perspective on some of the difficulties it encounters.

I

Right and liberty: the equivalence of dominium *and* ius

In the history of subjective right, a great amount of importance has in recent years been attached to certain texts and bodies of texts which posit an equivalence between the Latin terms *dominium* and *ius*. First of all it is said that in this equivalence we have the 'origin' of the modern subjective right in its most radical (and therefore strongest and most significant) form, in which it is preeminently associated with liberty, with property and with a certain idea of sovereignty.[1] Secondly, this conclusion is extended to the discussions of *ius* in a whole range of *moderni* who are thought to be part of the same theological current. It has resulted from this that almost all late mediaeval authors – such as Ockham and Gerson – who treat *ius* subjectively are assimilated to the tradition which equates *ius* with *dominium*.[2]

---

[1] So, for example, Richard Tuck in *Natural rights theories*, esp. chapter 1. Tuck uses the distinction between 'active rights' and 'passive rights', and sees the equivalence of *dominium* and *ius* in mediaeval texts as signalling an 'active rights' theory, a theory of rights as liberties and sovereignties, which is also a strong theory of rights as property. For problems with this view, see B. Tierney, 'Tuck on rights: Some medieval problems', *History of Political Thought* 4 (1983), 429–41, p. 431. The same sort of point is made in a slightly different way by Paolo Grossi in his two articles *'Usus facti'* and 'Proprietà'. Grossi sees in the equivalence of *dominium* and *ius* in the Franciscan texts of the thirteenth-century poverty controversy the articulation of a distinctive notion, based in a voluntarist theology of the supremacy of the will, of subjective personality and subjective liberty distinguished from the objective external world by its relation of *dominium* over it. Grossi argues that in this voluntaristic notion of *dominium-ius* as a 'strumento potestativo della libertà del singolo' ('Proprietà', p. 124), 'l'interscambiabilità tra libertà e proprietà, *leit motiv* di tutte le correnti individualistiche dell'età moderna, è qui già pienamente posta' ('Proprietà', p. 135). I cannot agree with Grossi's extension of his conclusions, but the following account of Franciscan theology owes a great deal to his sensitive and convincing analysis of these texts.

[2] Thus for both Tuck and Grossi, subjective right as dominative sovereignty constitutes, as Grossi puts it, 'uno strumento interpretativo ricorrente nelle mani degli *homines novi* della speculazione post-medievale da Occam a Fitzralph, da Wycliff a Gerson' (*'Usus facti'*, p. 313). This view is widely accepted, for example by James Burns in a recent article 'Scholasticism: Survival and revival', in Burns (ed.), *The Cambridge history of political thought, 1450–1700* (Cambridge 1991), 132–55, p. 141, who speaks of a '"Gersonian" position' on subjective right (i.e. that right and *dominium* are equivalent).

In this chapter I question these results. A close examination of the texts involved suggests that it is anachronistic to talk of the equivalence of *ius* and *dominium* as the beginning of a modern subjective rights theory. Secondly, it appears that the equivalence of *ius* and *dominium* is far from being the universal outlook in the moral theology of the later middle ages – not even among authors who can be said to have had a notion of 'subjective right'. We shall see that after its initial expression in the peculiar circumstances of the thirteenth-century poverty controversy, it is restricted to a particular genre, the literature on cases of conscience.

MENDICANT POVERTY AND THE EQUIVALENCE OF *DOMINIUM* AND *IUS*

A language of *dominium* and right as equivalent notions is first found systematically elaborated in the texts of the mendicant poverty controversy in the middle of the thirteenth century, the course of which strengthened and developed the assumptions implicit in the Rules of the two mendicant religious orders, particularly that of the Franciscans.[3]

The Order of Friars Minor, founded by St Francis of Assisi in 1209, was the most successful and influential of a series of poverty movements which proliferated in the late middle ages.[4] Poverty as a

---

[3] For an account of the attack on the mendicant orders and their concept of poverty mounted by the secular clergy at the University of Paris, see M. Bierbaum, *Bettelorden und Weltgeistlichkeit an der Universität Paris. Texte und Untersuchungen zum literarischen Armuts- und Exemtionsstreit des 13. Jahrhunderts (1255–1272)* (Münster i. W. 1920). For the dating of the various tracts of the controversy, see P. Glorieux, 'Les polémiques "contra Geraldinos"': Les pièces du dossier', *Recherches de théologie ancienne et médiévale* 6 (1934), 5–41, and A. Teetaert, 'Deux questions inédites de Gérard d'Abbeville en faveur du clergé séculier', in *Mélanges Auguste Pelzer* (Louvain 1947), 347–87. Although by the beginning of the fourteenth century the scholastic language of poverty, *dominium* and right had become principally the preserve of Franciscan theologians – employed both in the quarrel within the Order between the Spirituals and the community, and by some of the Franciscan polemicists in their defence of mendicant poverty against the attacks of Pope John XXII – it is important to remember that up until the end of the thirteenth century the Franciscans made common cause with the Dominicans in defending mendicant poverty against the secular clergy. Despite the subsequent theological differences between the Orders, the idea of a sharp division between Franciscan and Dominican 'worldviews' remains an inconvenient tool of analysis in the present literature and the subsequent genres we shall be looking at in this chapter (cf. the arguments of the Dominican Hervé de Nédellec against the Franciscans in the early fourteenth century: below, chapter 2, pp. 54–6).

[4] The literature on movements of religious poverty in general, and on St Francis and the Franciscans in particular, is immense. For a brief overview, see J. Coleman, 'Property and poverty', in J. H. Burns (ed.), *The Cambridge history of medieval political thought c. 350–c. 1450* (Cambridge 1988), 607–48; and M. D. Lambert, *Franciscan poverty* (London 1961).

salvific ideal was principally based on the depiction of the life of Christ in the New Testament, but its meaning as a voluntary practice involved senses of poverty which had developed during the course of the middle ages. 'Poverty' was seen not merely to involve the absence of *divitiae*, riches (although this was certainly one of the senses of the term). It had in addition a sense as an antonym of *potentia* or *potestas*.[5] The *pauper* was the *servus* or *subditus*, the subject of the *dominus* or *potens*, the person of superior might. He was also the impotent, the socially insignificant or less significant, he who required protection against the power of lords.[6] Poverty thus came to have in addition a juridical dimension in the sense of absence of legal standing. It was the opposite of *dominium*, which signified the relation of power over other objects and persons, defensible in law and consequently yielding standing in law. It is in this context that *dominium* comes to be equivalent to *ius*, as we see in the radical Spiritual Peter John Olivi's *Quaestio quid ponat ius vel dominium*.[7] Right or *dominium* is the relation of power or authority over other persons or things, which the pauper lacks.[8]

The rule of St Francis – in both of its formulations – stipulated poverty or absence of *dominium* in this widest sense. The brothers were to be among the humble, *minores*, having nothing, as Chapter VII of the *Regula bullata* exhorted:

Let the brothers appropriate nothing to themselves, neither house nor place nor any thing. And like pilgrims and strangers in this present world, serving God in poverty and humility, let them go trustingly forth to beg for alms, nor should they be ashamed, for the Lord for us made himself a pauper in this world.[9]

---

[5] See K. Bösl, 'Potens und pauper. Begriffsgeschichtliche Studien zur gesellschaftlichen Differenzierung im frühen Mittelalter und zum "Pauperismus" des Hochmittelalters', in *Alteuropa und die moderne Gesellschaft. Festschrift für Otto Brünner* (Göttingen 1963), 60–87.

[6] See F. Margiotta Broglio, 'Ideali pauperistici e strutture temporali nella canonistica del secolo XIV. Notazioni ed appunti per una edizione del "Liber Minoritarum" di Giovanni da Legnano', *Studia gratiana* 14 (1967), 369–436, p. 371.

[7] Ed. by F. Delorme, 'Question de P. J. Olivi, *Quid ponat ius vel dominium* ou encore *De signis voluntariis*', *Antonianum* 20 (1945), 309–30, p. 318. For Olivi's thought in the context of the debate on poverty, see D. Burr, 'Poverty as a constituent element in Olivi's thought', in D. Flood (ed.), *Poverty in the middle ages* (Werl i. W. 1975), 71–8.

[8] It should be remarked here that for Olivi and for the Franciscan discourse here considered in general, *dominium* and therefore *ius* and *potestas* fall into the formal category of relation, as defined in Aristotle's *Categories* (wherein one of the examples given is *dominus* or *despotes*): Aristotle, *Categoriae et liber de Interpretatione*, ed. by L. Minuo-Paluello (Oxford 1949), p. 20, 6b28–30.

[9] *Regula II Fratrum minorum (Regula bullata)*, in *Opuscula sancti patris Francisci Assisiensis. Edita cura et studio P.P. collegii St. Bonaventurae* (Quaracchi 1904), 63–74, p. 68: 'Fratres nihil sibi

But for the Minorites, outward poverty was only the expression of a more important inward poverty, 'poverty of the spirit'.[10] The basic command of both Rules was that the brothers live 'in obedience, in chastity and with nothing proper to themselves', and obedience was interpreted as internal poverty, in being the renunciation of one's own proper will: the ultimate form of 'having nothing proper'.

This feature is very clear in the work of the Franciscan John Pecham (d. 1292). Pecham was committed to maintaining the doctrines of the Fathers and of Bonaventure against the new Aristotelianism, and he wrote a *Tractatus de anima* which emphasised the freedom of the will as the completion of human life.[11] In his *Tractatus pauperis* of c. 1270, he argued that

He only perfectly abnegates himself who fully renounces his own proper will. For the will is in a man's power to such an extent, that it cannot be extorted by anyone else. A man can therefore offer God no sacrifice so pleasing as to cut off from himself that which is supremely his own, that is, *dominium* of his own proper will ... This is the obedience which annihilates all of a man, keeping nothing of the human to himself, so that the obedient man does not live himself, but Christ in him.[12]

The primary *dominium* of man is that which he has over his own will: a *dominium* so inherent in any individual that no one but that individual himself may take it from him. This *dominium*, moreover, is precisely constitutive of humanity; if a man renounces it, he annihilates himself as a human being or as human being *simpliciter*. *Dominium* of external goods is secondary and presupposes this primary *dominium*, as we see in Thomas Aquinas' contribution to the mendicant defence, the

---

approprient, nec domum nec locum nec aliquam rem. Et tanquam peregrini et advenae in hoc saeculo, vadant pro eleemosyna confidenter, nec oportet eos verecundari, quia dominus pro nobis se fecit pauperem in hoc mundo.'

[10] This point is well brought out in K. Eβer, 'Die Armutsauffassung des Hl. Franziskus', in Flood, *Poverty in the middle ages*, 60–70.

[11] For Pecham's opposition to the new learning, see E. Gilson, *La philosophie au moyen age*, 2nd edn (Paris 1944), pp. 488–9; for his tractate *De Anima*, see E. Stadter, *Psychologie und Metaphysik der menschlichen Freiheit. Die ideengeschichtliche Entwicklung zwischen Bonaventura und Duns Scotus* (Munich, Paderborn and Vienna 1971), 86–143.

[12] John Pecham, *Tractatus pauperis*, ed. by A. G. Little, in C. L. Kingsford, A. G. Little and F. Tocco (eds.), *Pecham de paupertate* (Aberdeen 1910), 13–90, Chapter x, p. 31: 'Ille enim solus perfecte se abnegat qui proprie voluntati plene renunciat. Voluntas enim ita in hominis potestate est, quod a nullo extorqueri potest. Nullum igitur tam suave holocaustum potest offeri Deo sicut a se prescindere illud quod summe suum est, dominium scilicet proprie voluntatis ... Hec est obedientia, totum hominem adnihilans, nihil sibi de humano reservans, ut vivat obediens non ipse sed Christus in ipso.' The determining text is Paul, Epistle to the Galatians II, 20: 'vivo autem iam non ego, vivit vero in me Christus'.

tractate *De perfectione spiritualis vitae*.[13] Arguing that 'for the perfection of charity, a man must not solely reject external goods, but also in some way relinquish himself', Aquinas asserts that:

the more a thing is naturally the object of desire, the more perfectly it is despised for the sake of Christ. Now nothing is more desirable to man than the liberty of his proper will. For it is by this that he is a man and master [dominus] of other things, by this that he can use and enjoy them, by this even that he masters his own actions. So that just as the man who relinquishes riches, or persons conjoined to him, denies their being; so he who foregoes the authoritative judgement [arbitrium] of his proper will, by which he is master of himself, denies his own being.[14]

If a man relinquishes *dominium* of his will, he is incapable of *dominium* of anything else.

The notion that *dominium* of one's own will is liberty and is constitutive of humanity as such antedates the recovery of Aristotle's *de Anima*, resting on the neoplatonic notion of the reflexivity of the two spiritual powers of intellect and will, which was transmitted to mediaeval theology principally via Augustine's work *De trinitate*[15] and the Latin translation of the anonymous Arabic *Liber de causis*.[16] Both of these sources differentiate between material or corporeal, and immaterial or spiritual, powers in the ability of the latter to reflect upon themselves, that is to constitute themselves as their own object or to be self-determining.[17] Rationals, that is all creatures endowed with reason, are distinguished from all the rest of creation through

---

[13] Edited in *Sancti Thomae de Aquino. Opera omnia iussu Leonis XIII P. M. edita, cura et studio Fratrum Praedicatorum*, vol. XLI, parts B–C (Rome 1969), 67–111. The tract was composed towards the end of 1269. For the intervention of Aquinas in the poverty controversy, see the profoundly illuminating study of Yves Congar, 'Aspects ecclésiologiques de la querelle entre mendiants et séculiers dans la seconde moitié du XIIIe siècle et le début du XIVe', *Archives d'histoire doctrinale et littéraire du Moyen Age* 36 (1961–2), 35–151.

[14] *De perfectione spiritualis vitae*, Chapter XI, p. 79: 'quanto aliquid magis naturaliter amatur, tanto perfectius contemnitur propter Christum. Nihil enim est homini amabilius libertate propriae voluntatis; per hanc enim homo est et aliorum dominus, per hanc aliis uti vel frui potest, per hanc etiam suis actibus dominatur. Unde sicut homo dimittens divitias vel personas coniunctas, eas abnegat; ita deserens propriae voluntatis arbitrium, per quod ipse sui dominus est, se ipsum abnegare invenitur.'

[15] St Augustine, *De trinitate libri XV*, vol. I, Books I–XII, ed. by W. J. Mountain (Turnholt 1968), Book IX, Chapters II–VI, esp. Chapter III.

[16] *Liber de causis*, ed. by A. Pattin, *Tijdschrift voor Filosofie* 28 (1966), 90–203, pp. 162–8. The work, commonly attributed in the middle ages to Aristotle, is in fact a ninth-century Arabic work heavily based on Proclus' *Elementatio theologica*, translated into Latin in the twelfth century by Gerard of Cremona.

[17] See J. Korolec, 'Free will and free choice', in N. Kretzmann, A. Kenny and J. Pinborg (eds.), *The Cambridge history of later medieval philosophy: From the rediscovery of Aristotle to the disintegration of scholasticism, 1100–1600* (Cambridge 1982), 629–41, p. 631, and the references there.

the possession of spiritual powers, whose characteristic of reflexivity is the foundation of liberty and *dominium*. Thus, when Bonaventure asks 'Whether freedom of judgement (*liberum arbitrium*) be only in those creatures which have reason, or whether it be also in brute animals',[18] he replies:

We should say, that without doubt freedom of judgement is found only in rational substances. And the reason for this is assumed from both the 'freedom' and the 'judgement' components. From the component that is 'freedom', as follows: for freedom is opposed to servitude. So that that power alone is said to be free, which has full *dominium* as much with respect to its object, as with respect to its own proper act. But a power which has this *dominium* resulting from its freedom with respect to its object, is one which is not restricted to a certain kind of desirable object.[19]

Of such a kind, according to Bonaventure, is the will in rationals: because it is reflexive, it operates freely and with *dominium*. In contrast, those potencies which are 'tied to matter' have no possibility of reflexion.[20] Thus brute beasts, which are excluded from spirituality, have no internal liberty or *dominium*.[21]

The having of *dominium* is thus separated from irrational and therefore unfree nature, where 'unfree' has the sense of 'externally determined'. Bonaventure phrases the distinction as between rational (free) nature and irrational (unfree) nature: but it is also set in terms of a contrast simply between the natural and the free, for example in the psychological work of the early fourteenth-century Dominican Durand de Saint-Pourçain. Arguing that there is no distinction between the will and the intellect, Durand asserted that 'every non-

[18] John of Fidanza, St Bonaventure, *In secundum sententiarum commentarius*, in *Opera omnia edita cura et studio pp. collegii a S. Bonaventura*, vol. II (Quaracchi 1882), Distinction 25, pt. 1a, a. unicus, Q. 1: 'Utrum liberum arbitrium sit in solis habentibus rationem, an etiam sit in animalibus brutis.'

[19] Ibid., in conc.: 'Respondeo: Dicendum, quod absque dubio liberum arbitrium reperitur in solis substantiis rationalibus. – Et ratio huius sumitur tum ex parte libertatis, tum ex parte arbitrii. Ex parte libertatis: libertas enim opponitur servituti. Unde illa sola potentia dicitur esse libera, quae dominium habet plenum tam respectu obiecti, quam respectu actus proprii. Illa autem potentia dominium habet ex libertate respectu obiecti, quae non est arctata ad aliquid genus appetibilis.'

[20] Ibid.: 'Sed nunquam aliqua potestas ... super seipsam reflectitur, quae sit alligata materiae.' Bonaventure goes on to suggest that only reason – *ratio* – is not 'tied to matter and corporeal substance'. However, in the next question he insists that 'tam ratio quam voluntas sit nata super se reflecti' (q. 2, in conc.). Here, it is the will which is the primary example of a reflexive potency.

[21] Ibid., Q. 1, in conc.: 'In brutis autem animalibus, etsi aliquo modo sit reperire dominium respectu actus exterioris, quia bene refrenant aliquando, sicut patet in animalibus domesticis; respectu tamen actus proprii interioris, videlicet appetitus, dominium non est.'

cognitive virtue is drawn to its object naturally and not freely'. This is evident from the fact that

every free agent must be able to have a view of its own act ... a subject is free because it has a free power. If, therefore, having judgement of one's own act is of the essence of freedom, that power by which man is free must have judgement of its own act, which can belong to nothing but a cognitive power.[22]

Nature is opposed to freedom in operating necessarily and without reflexive awareness.

This is the philosophy of the soul which lies behind the traditional elucidation of the words of Genesis in commentary on the second book of Peter Lombard's *Sentences*, which considers God's creation of the world, and specifically his creation of man. In Bonaventure's exposition,

all sensible animals are made for the sake of man. And this is insinuated by the Philosopher, when he says 'In a certain way, we are the highest end of all those things that are.' And Scripture too conveys this in a far more excellent way, when it says: Let us make man in our image and likeness, and let him be over the fishes of the sea etc. For because man is capable of reason, therefore he has freedom of judgement [libertatem arbitrii] and it is his nature to dominate the fishes.[23]

Man's spirituality, his reflexivity which means he can dominate his own actions, is that whereby he is made in the image of God, and can therefore have a *dominium* analogous to that of God over inferior creation.

The passages we have been discussing equate internal liberty, property in oneself, power over oneself, *dominium* of oneself. *Dominium* of externals, the consequence of the spiritual state, is similarly equated with external liberty, property and power. These equiva-

---

[22] Durandus a Sancto Porciano, *In quattuor sententiarum libros questiones* (Paris 1508), In primum, Dist. 3, 2a pars, Q. iv, B: 'omnis virtus non cognoscens fertur in suum obiectum naturaliter et non libere ... patet quia omne agens libere habet videre de actu suo (alioquin non imputaretur ei) et per eandem potentiam per quam est liberum habet huiusmodi iudicium: quia potentia non est libera ex hoc quod est in supposito libero ... sed suppositum est liberum quia habet potentiam liberam. Si ergo de ratione libertatis est habere iudicium sui actus necesse est quod illa potentia per quam homo est liber sit iudicativa sui actus quod non potest convenire nisi potentie cognitive.'

[23] St Bonaventure, *In II sent.*, Dist. 15, a. 2, Q. 1, p. 383: 'omnia sensibilia animalia facta sunt propter hominem. Et hoc insinuat Philosophus, cum dicit: "Summus finis nos quodam modo omnium eorum quae sunt." Insinuat etiam Scriptura multo excellentius, cum dicit: Faciamus hominem ad imaginem et similitudinem nostram, et praesit piscibus maris etc. Quia enim homo rationis capax est, ideo habet libertatem arbitrii et natus est piscibus dominari.'

lences are clear in Chapter x of Pecham's *Tractatus pauperis*, which discusses the external aspect of *fratres nihil sibi approprient*. Pecham begins by arguing from a text of Augustine that the church, and thus the secular clergy who make up the church, does indeed have its wealth as proper to itself – that is, it has *dominium* of its goods: 'that the church has *dominium* of these objects in a certain way is proved by Augustine, "On the words of the Lord, concerning Luke", where he says that to dominate is to enjoy a proper power'.[24] The notion of power recurs throughout Pecham's attempt to illuminate precisely what is involved in Minorite poverty: 'for this is to possess, that is to hold something in one's power'.[25] Thus a Minorite can take things into his hands, but he cannot take them possessively into his hands:

I say ... that the possessive reception of money is forbidden the Friars Minor; which is [thus] received at that time when with the heart it is understood, that *dominium* is transferred from another, so that it is subject to the full power of the brother, so that he may use it fully and at whim ... Whoever receives in this way, is not a Minorite brother, into whose *dominium* nothing can be transferred, even if – perish the thought – it be poured into his lap.[26]

The true Minorite brother is in a position of complete impotence with regard to external goods. Furthermore, as for Aquinas, *dominium* or possession, together with power, is for Pecham associated with liberty. Stressing the peculiar distinction of the Friars Minor from other *religiosi* in that unlike the latter, the Minorites have no property even in common, he asserts that 'They cannot ... have common moveables nor immoveables immoveably in the title of their community, nor can they dominate objects freely having them completely in their power. For the houses in which they live belong freely to their patrons.'[27] The

---

[24] Pecham, *Tractatus pauperis*, Chapter x, p. 34: 'quod horum rerum alico modo habeat ecclesia dominium, probatur, dicente Aug. de Verbis Domini super Luc.: Dominari, inquit, est propria potestate gaudere. Clerici autem habent pro tanto huiusmodi possessiones in propria potestate, quod possunt sibi de eis in omnibus sufficienter providere, ablatas repetere, nec multo plus querunt homines secundum seculum prudentes in divitiis.'

[25] Ibid., p. 35: 'Hoc enim est possidere quod est in posse suo tenere.'

[26] Ibid., pp. 40–1: 'Dico ergo quod prohibetur minoribus receptio possessaria pecunie; que tunc recipitur, cum corde sic admittitur, ut dominium ab alio transferatur, ut potestati plene fratris subiciatur, ut ea plene ad libitum ... utatur ... quicunque sic recipit, frater minor non est, in cuius dominium nulla res transire potest, etiam si, quod absit, gremio infundatur.'

[27] Ibid., p. 36: 'Non ergo possunt habere communia mobilia vel immobilia communitati sue immobiliter intitulata, nec possunt dominari res libere omnino habendo in sua potestate. Domus enim quas inhabitant sunt patronum libere sicut ille quas patroni inhabitant, sicut dicit declaratio regule: salvo locorum dominio illis ad quos noscitur pertinere.'

Minorite who has renounced the freedom of his will necessarily
foregoes the freedom of other objects.

This aspect of the absence of dominative will is the crucial part of
the mendicant proof of non-ownership. But Franciscan theologians
had in addition to show that their position of renunciation of all
property or *dominium* in person and in common was legally possible:
if the Minorites had no *dominium* or property in the things they used
of necessity in order to stay alive, were they not acting illegally in
that use?

The Franciscans' basic argument was that use was different from
dominium, and that one could have use without *dominium*. A certain
minimal use is necessary for sustaining mortal life, and the voluntary
pauper 'is sustained from what is not his own, i.e. proper to himself,
but from what is another's, which has however been justly and
piously placed at his disposal by another for his sustenance',[28]
without the *affectus* of the *dominus* towards that which is his own and
which constitutes his external being. If that thing has been given by a
dominus towards that use, then the Minorite may legitimately make
use of it without any pretension to its *dominium*.

It is important that it was open to the Franciscans to deny *dominium*
but to admit a right of using. However, Franciscan theologians
repudiated the idea of having any *ius in rebus* as strongly as they
resisted the idea of *dominium*: for to them, to have right was equally to
adopt the same appropriative attitude to the things of this world, the
worldly existence and pride that was forbidden them in their Rule.
Ius as much as *dominium* involved the ability to claim in court: it
equally gave the legal standing that was the opposite of true *humilitas*.
Although Bonaventure did distinguish between *proprietas, possessio* and
ususfructus,[29] the important distinction for him is between all these
three and *simplex usus*. For him, *ius, dominium* and *proprietas* are all the
same in being the appropriative relation towards external goods, *ius
seu proprietas*, opposed to the simple use which the Minorites *de
necessitate vitae* could not and did not renounce.[30]

28 St Bonaventure, *Apologia pauperum*, in *Opera omnia*, vol. vii, Opusculum xi, pp. 272–3. For
the notion that temporal *dominium* involves spiritual *affectus* towards the things dominated,
see ibid., p. 322: 'Evangelica vero paupertas, pro eo quod ad aeterna sublevat, tanquam ea
quae in caelis totaliter thesaurizat, perfecte ipsam profitenti suadet omnibus temporalibus
debere nudari quantum ad affectum atque dominium, et arcta sustentatione necessitatis
esse contentum quantum ad usum.'
29 Ibid., p. 312: 'intelligendum est, quod circa res temporales quatuor sit considerare, s.
proprietatem, possessionem, usumfructum et simplicem usum'.
30 Cf. ibid., p. 313: 'sic quicquid datur congregationi Minorum Fratrum in ius, dominium et

In 1279 Pope Nicholas III intervened in the continuing controversy with the bull *Exiit qui seminat*.[31] Elaborating on Bonaventure's statement, Nicholas distinguished five different possible relationships to temporal goods: *proprietas, possessio, ususfructus, ius utendi* and *simplex usus facti*.[32] By incorporating the specification 'of fact' into the last, he cast the issue as one of the separation between the realms of fact (*factum*) and right (*ius*): Franciscan activity is *de facto*, juridically indifferent, whereas activity on the part of persons holding the other four relations is *de iure*, juridically significant. In avoiding any mention of *dominium* as a specific relationship, he implicitly acknowledged an equation of *ius* and *dominium* in the sense of that position which is opposed to a simple *de facto* relationship.

However, it is not clear that this was the same understanding of the equivalence as that of the likes of Bonaventure and Pecham. For them, right and *dominium* were the same in being appropriative stances towards the things of this world: a liberty, a free power, a property. By contrast, *ius* and *dominium* as equated in the *Exiit* carry only the sense of being distinct from *factum*. The text of the *Exiit*, while suggesting that *possessio, ususfructus* and *ius utendi* are all *dominium* in the sense of derogating from Minorite poverty, nevertheless does not assert that they are all examples of *proprietas*: rather, it expressly differentiates them from it. And in Franciscan discourse after the *Exiit* there seems to be less talk of *ius seu proprietas*. For Peter Aureol, the *dominium* that is equivalent to *ius* is only '*dominium* of a kind', *dominium aliquod*.[33] Similarly we find Bonagratia of Bergamo clarifying the Franciscan position by saying that the Minorites have use of fact, 'just as a horse has the use of fact of the oats it eats, nor does it have *dominium* of any kind ... [the Minorite] does not have any kind of *dominium*, nor any property, but only use of fact, which gives

proprietatem summi pontificis et Romanae ecclesiae transit; praecipue cum ipsi Fratres ius seu proprietatem rei alicuius sibi acquirere nulla ratione intendunt.'

[31] Text in *Corpus iuris canonici*, ed. by A. Friedberg, vol. II (Leipzig 1879; reprinted Graz 1959), Liber sextus decretalium, V. 12. 3, cols. 1109–21.

[32] Ibid., col. 1113.

[33] Peter Aureol, *Quaestio De usu paupere*, ed. by E. Longpré, 'Le Quolibet de Nicholas a Lyre, OFM', *Archivum Franciscanum Historicum* 23 (1930), 42–56, p. 53: 'Licet habens usum in re habet dominium aliquod, quia habet ius in usu, tamen utens rebus nullum ius habet, sed habet usum qui dicitur tantum simplicis facti usus.' The tract was written in 1311–12. The attribution to Nicholas of Lyra is false: see the details in A. Teetaert, 'Pierre Auriol', in *Dictionnaire de théologie catholique* 12 (Paris 1933), 1809–1881; M. Damiata, *Guglielmo d'Ockham. Povertà e potere*, vol. I, *Il problema della povertà evangelica e francescana nel secolo XIII e XIV. Origine del pensiero politico di Guglielmo d'Ockham* (Florence 1978), p. 215.

no right in the using'.[34] The implication of these later texts is that *dominium* as equated with *ius* is reduced to a broad notion of a juridical as opposed to a factual or *de facto* hold on an object. It derogates from Minorite poverty but it does not have the overtone of property.

THE EQUIVALENCE OF *IUS* AND *DOMINIUM* IN THE ROMAN LAW TRADITION

In this seeming moderation of the force of *dominium* in so far as it is equivalent to *ius*, post-*Exiit* Franciscan discourse appears to be following developments in contemporary commentary on the Roman law. Since the beginning of the thirteenth century, commentators of the *Corpus iuris civilis* had begun the process of crediting with a sort of *dominium* those who had heretofore been simple users, if long-term or in perpetuity, of land belonging properly to a *dominus*.[35] That is, the holder of what was before only a *ius in re* was now seen as holding *dominium* of a kind. This has been seen, yet again, as an 'origin' of modern subjective right in its radical or 'active' sense.[36] Behind this lies the assumption that because a user was granted to have *dominium* 'of use', *dominium utile*, he was therefore seen to have *dominium* in the same sense as the principal *dominus*, the holder of *dominium directum* with its connotation of ultimate superiority and authority.

However, the evidence does not bear out this view. Although the holder of *dominium utile* and 'natural possession' (the physical reten- tion of the land) is often said to have the stronger *dominium*, in the sense that his *dominium* is preferred in cases of dispute to that of the holder of *dominium directum*, nevertheless it is the holder of *dominium*

---

[34] Bonagratia of Bergamo was the companion of William of Ockham and Michael of Cesena at the imperial court during the struggle with John XXII in the 1330s. See Bonagratia de Bergamo, *Tractatus de paupertate Christi et apostolorum*, ed. by L. Oliger, *Archivum Franciscanum Historicum* 22 (1929), 292–335 and 487–511, p. 511: 'sicut equus habet usum facti avene quam comedit, nec habet aliquod dominium ... nec ad momentum habet dominium aliquod, nec aliquam proprietatem, nec ius utendi, sed simplicem facti usum, qui nichil iuris tribuit in utendo'.

[35] The classic discussion of this subject is E. Meynial, 'Notes sur la formation de la théorie du domaine divisé (domaine direct et domaine utile) du XIIe au XIVe siècles dans les romanistes', in *Mélanges Fitting* (Montpellier 1908), 409–61. See also Coleman, 'Property and poverty', pp. 611–16.

[36] Tuck, *Natural rights theories*, pp. 15–17. Grossi ('*Usus facti*', p. 318) argues to the contrary that the mediaeval jurists' multiplication of *dominia* signifies 'mortificazione della proprietà – appartenenza e subordinamento dell'istituto proprietà ai fenomeni esterni'. For doubts upon the relevance of *dominium utile* to the question of the 'origin of subjective rights', see Tierney, 'Tuck on rights', p. 440.

directum who is the *superior dominus* and who has ultimate authority. When the thirteenth-century jurist Marino da Caramanico argues for the supreme authority of the king of Sicily despite the fact that the kingdom is a papal fief, although he uses the argument that the king as holder of *dominium utile* is *potior*, his main strategy in proving the supremacy of the king in the rule of Sicily is to argue that the king has both *dominium directum* and *dominium utile*. It is *dominium directum* which conveys superiority or sovereignty.[37]

Closely related to the division of *dominium* into *directum* and *utile* is its division into a broad and a narrow sense of the term.[38] During the course of the thirteenth century the question had been discussed of the relation between usufruct and *dominium*; specifically, following two contradictory loci in the Digest, whether usufruct could be said to be a 'part of *dominium* [pars dominii]'.[39] It was explained that usufruct was indeed a part of *dominium* in the sense of a component, but not in the sense of being a species of the genus *dominium*. However, the most important of the post-Glossators, Bartolus of Sassoferrato, made the innovation of arguing that usufruct was indeed a species of the genus *dominium*, but for Bartolus, this broad, generic notion of *dominium* comprehends within it a narrower notion of *dominium*, *dominium plenum* or 'full *dominium*', which is equally a

---

[37] Marino da Caramanico, Proem to the *Liber constitutionum* of Frederick II, ed. as Appendix in F. Calasso, *I glossatori e la teoria della sovranità*, 3rd edn (Milan 1957), 175–205, pp. 192–4: 'Posito tamen quod diceretur ecclesiam temporalem iurisdictionem non sic a se totaliter abdicasse, cum directum dominium et civilis possessio regni apud eam remanserit, non est ius quia rex, qui est feudatarius, est utiliter dominus et naturaliter possidet et sic sive de dominio sive de possessione agatur rex est potior et prefertur ... habendo respectum ad universitatem regni, sine dubio papa est superior dominus, et quando de toto regno seu quota pars eius controversia fieret, ad ipsum cognitio pertinet. In singulis vero regni corporibus apud ecclesiam nichil prorsus remansit, sed totum et integrum dominium et possessio sunt translata in dominum regem ... In his ergo corporibus singulis solus rex est dominus superior et supremus et omnia iura maioris dominii pertinent sibi soli.' For the changing sense of the term *superior* from the basic sense of being *super*, above, in a hierarchy, to the sense of 'sovereign' (*superanus*), see Calasso in the same work, p. 44, n. 11.

[38] See the fundamental article by H. Coing, 'Zur Eigentumslehre des Bartolus', *Zeitschrift der Savigny-Stiftung für Rechtsgeschichte (Römische Abteilung)* 70 (1953), 348–71. For a more recent and summary consideration, see K. Seelmann, *Die Lehre des Fernando Vázquez de Menchaca vom 'dominium'* (Cologne and Graz 1979), pp. 39–43, and the remarks in R. Feenstra, 'Der Eigentumsbegriff bei Hugo Grotius im Licht einiger mittelalterlicher und spätscholastiker Quellen', in O. Behrends (ed.), *Festschrift für Franz Wieacker zum 70. Geburtstag* (Göttingen 1978), 209–34, pp. 211–12, who suggests that the all-important text of Bartolus (below, n. 41) may be corrupt.

[39] The two loci are D. 7, 1, 4: 'Usus fructus in multis casibus pars dominii est, et exstat, quod vel praesens vel ex die dari potest'; and D. 50, 16, 25: 'Recte dicimus eum fundum totum nostrum esse, etiam cum usus fructus alienus est, quia usus fructus non dominii pars, sed servitutis sit ut via et iter' (cited in Seelmann, *Vázquez*, p. 40, n. 12).

species of generic *dominium*.[40] Generic *dominium* he sees as equivalent to any incorporeal right: 'in the broadest sense it can be the term for any incorporeal right, as I have *dominium* of an obligation; for example of usufruct'.[41] This broad sense of *dominium* stands in contrast with a narrower sense, which is defined as 'the right of perfectly disposing of a corporeal object, unless it be prohibited by the law'.[42] For Bartolus, then, it is clearly the narrow notion of *dominium*, *dominium plenum*, the sense in which it is not equivalent to *ius*, which carries the connotation of liberty and sovereignty.

An interesting point arises from Bartolus' formulations, however. It would appear that for Bartolus, *dominium* in its broad sense as an incorporeal right (of any kind) is equivalent to *dominium* of an incorporeal right. (Indeed, the question of whether an incorporeal right could be the object of *dominium* was, along with the question of the specific relationship between *dominium* and right, part of what necessitated the redefinition of *dominium* to include a wider sense: for while the Roman law generally suggested that *dominium* was only properly of corporeal things (e.g. at D. 7, 1, 4), one particular text suggested that *dominium* could still be of incorporeals.)[43] But this *dominium* that one can have of a right does not appear to be *dominium* in the narrow sense of 'perfect disposition', for this sense is expressly limited to *res corporales*. Thus although Bartolus could be construed here as positing some modern-looking notion of property of rights, this does not in fact appear to be the case. It seems that for Bartolus, the *dominium* in *dominium* of right is still only *dominium* in the broad sense of *dominium* as right.

DOMINIUM AND IUS IN THE CASUISTRY OF CONSCIENCE

The adoption of a broad sense of *dominium* as right and of its related idea of *dominium* of right is the characteristic feature of the teaching on *dominium* of the literature concerned with cases of conscience.

Since the early twelfth century, with the practice of confession

---

[40] Seelmann, *Vázquez*, pp. 39–40.
[41] Cited in Coing, 'Eigentumslehre', p. 349: 'et potest appellari largissime pro omni iure incorporali: ut habeo dominium obligationis ut puta ususfructus'. And again ibid: 'omnis enim qui habet aliquod ius in re potest recte dicere ego habeo dominium illius iuris'.
[42] Cited in ibid., p. 352: 'ius de re corporali perfecte disponendi nisi lege prohibeatur'.
[43] D. 7, 6, 3: 'Qui usumfructum traditum sibi ex causa fideicommissi desiit in usu habere tanto tempore, quanto, si legitime eius factus esset, amissurus rem fuerit, actionem ad restituendam eam habere non debet: est enim absurdum plus iuris habere eos, qui possessionem dumtaxat usus fructus, non etiam dominium adepti sunt.'

reformed and made compulsory, a specific literature of handbooks had evolved providing the knowledge necessary for the informed assessment of sin. These ranged from the very simple to massive and juristically sophisticated tomes which were evidently composed more for the already learned than for poor and ignorant local clergy.[44] All of them discuss in more or less detail the nature of *dominium* and its objects, either (in the alphabetically organised *Summae*) under the heading of *Dominium*, or in the discussion of interpersonal morality and contracts. To these specifically designated *Summae confessorum* or *Summae de casibus conscientiae*, however, there can be added two cognate genres. One of these is the literature broadly termed 'On contracts' (*De contractibus*) which, in both academic and practical form, functioned as examinations of and guides to morality in the practice of business and commerce. The other is the examination of the sacrament of penance in commentary on Book IV, Distinction 15 of Peter Lombard's *Sentences*. Here, the dictum *non dimittitur peccatum nisi restituitur ablatum* provided an opportunity for writing a tract on restitution and thus indirectly on theft and fraud.[45] All of these

---

[44] For a survey of this literature from its origins in the twelfth-century humanist redefinition of penance as a private rather than public act of making good (which demanded that the confessor priest be able to assess the personal quality of the fault), to the enormous and juristically highly sophisticated final products of the genre in the early sixteenth century, see P. Michaud-Quantin, *Sommes de casuistique et manuels de confession au moyen âge (XIIème–XVIème siècles)* (Louvain 1962). See further the fundamental series of articles by Johannes Dietterle, 'Die Summae confessorum (sive de casibus conscientiae) von ihren Anfängen bis zu Silvester Prierias', *Zeitschrift für Kirchengeschichte* 24 (1903), 353–74, 520–48; 25 (1904), 248–72; 26 (1905), 59–81; 27 (1906), 70–83, 166–88; 28 (1907), 401–31, and the article by Leonard E. Boyle, 'Summae confessorum', in *Les genres littéraires dans les sources théologiques et philosophiques médiévales. Actes du Colloque international de Louvain-la-Neuve, 25–7 mai 1981* (Louvain-la-Neuve 1982), 227–37. There are interesting suggestions in C. Bergfeld, 'Katholische Moraltheologie und Naturrechtslehre', in H. Coing (ed.), *Handbuch der Quellen und Literatur der neueren europäischen Privatrechtsgeschichte*, vol. II/I (Munich 1977), 999–1033, for the importance of this confessionary literature in the development of the natural rights theories. Bergfeld does not, however, consider the genre as related to the contract literature and commentary on *Sentences* IV, 15.

[45] Book IV of the *Sentences* considers the sacraments of the church, one of which is penance (treated in Distinction 14), and the question is raised whether it is possible for a man to make satisfaction to God for his sins (Distinction 15). The phrasing of Lombard's text generated immediate controversy over whether or not restitution of unjustly possessed goods was a part of satisfaction or not; Thomas Aquinas answered in the negative, that restitution was distinct from, and preliminary to, satisfaction. The issue of what material to discuss in commentary on IV, 15 split Thomists from Scotists and nominalists right up until the end of the genre. The neo-Thomist Domingo de Soto made his point forcefully: 'Indeed, we have added this third conclusion [that restitution is not a part of satisfaction] not just in order to clarify the nature of satisfaction, but also to demonstrate how foreign to the issue in hand is any consideration or debate concerning restitution. Therefore, even if the Master of the Sentences [Lombard], paying insufficient attention to the order of things,

literatures have a strongly juridical tone, using doctrines from both
canon and Roman law.

The *Summae confessorum* are exclusively the preserve of the two
mendicant preaching Orders, the Dominicans and the Franciscans,
and in their elaborate form particularly of the latter, connected with
their activity as preachers and confessors in the rapidly developing
urban economies of late mediaeval Europe and especially Italy.[46]
The literature on contracts, by contrast, is dominated by secular
university masters. Those who elected to write on restitution at
Sentences IV, 15 are either Franciscans following (as we shall see)
Scotus, or secular masters, often of broadly 'nominalist' philosophical
tendencies, following the Scotist tradition on this locus: those of
'realist' persuasion follow Aquinas in distinguishing restitution from
satisfaction and treating only of the latter. These facts of authorship
have strengthened the hand of those who want to argue that the
convertibility of *dominium* and *ius* is the modern notion of subjective
right as liberty and property, and was, appropriately, put forward
and developed by nominalist and voluntarist theologians, for whom
subjective right is the corollary of a theology of liberty and the will.

These facts ought, however, to be treated with a little more
caution. To begin with, we have very little textual evidence concerning moral theology in Dominican or broadly 'realist' circles
throughout the fourteenth and fifteenth centuries. We have very little
idea of what might have been taught in the Dominican *studia* or by
Dominicans engaged in practical preaching activity. Various decrees
of the Order indicate that Aquinas' *Summa theologiae* was from an
early date being widely used as the textbook of theology, and he had
early been commended to members of the Order as the authority on
doctrinal questions. Dominicans following Aquinas' *Summa theologiae*

---

may have mixed up restitution with satisfaction, offering a handle to his interpreters to
write a long tract on restitution, we however are not going to make any mention of it. For it
is a matter pertaining to the subject of justice, about which we have said more than enough
in Book IV of our "On justice and right".' See Domingo de Soto, *In quartum sententiarum
librum commentarii* (Salamanca 1566–79), vol. I, Distinction 19, Q. 1: 'De quidditate, et
necessitate satisfactionis'.

[46] There is a large literature on this connection. See among many others L. K. Little, *Religious
poverty and the profit economy in medieval Europe* (London 1978). For a reading of these texts in
their socio-economic milieu, see G. Todeschini, ' "Oeconomica franciscana". Proposte di
una nuova lettura delle fonti dell'etica economica medievale', *Rivista di storia e letteratura
religiosa* 12 (1976), 15–77 and 13 (1977), 461–94; Todeschini, *Un trattato di economia politica
francescana: Il 'De emptionibus et venditionibus, de usuris, de restitutionibus' di Pietro di Giovanni Olivi*
(Rome 1980); and the articles collected in O. Capitani (ed.), *Una economia politica nel medioevo*
(Bologna 1987). Here as throughout, however, my concerns are primarily intertextual.

or commentary on the *Sentences* would not posit any equivalence of *dominium* and *ius*, as there was none to find in their chosen authority. However, the fact that Dominican academic activity does not involve itself with the question of the equivalence of *dominium* and *ius* does not exclude the possibility that it might have been common in more practice-orientated teaching. On this point concrete textual evidence is scarce. But in so far as the question of the equivalence is discussed in Dominican confessionary literature, we have one rejection (Antoninus, who nevertheless expounds a subjective notion of right, albeit a different one) and one acceptance (Mazzolini da Prierio). It is a little too easy to say that (therefore) Mazzolini was part of a late mediaeval nominalist and voluntarist 'current'. Substantively, there is no evidence that the equivalence of *dominium* and right is an expression of theological voluntarism or nominalism. This notion only serves to enthrone in the history of rights the sort of dichotomy between *moderni* and *antiqui* on the issue of 'individualism' or 'subjectivism' which it has been the effort of recent scholarship on scholasticism in general to overthrow.

What is distinctive about the casuistic moral system, however, and what differentiates it (as we shall see) not only from the moral theology of Aquinas but also from that of other Franciscans, Scotists and 'nominalists' is the analysis of civic society in terms of a series of relations of *dominium-ius*, and its corollary in a radically attenuated notion of the role of civil law – whether seen as a deduction from the natural law of reason, or as the will of the prince – in civic morality. The law of society – the civic law – is nothing other than the rule determining distinct *dominia*, and justice is assigning to each what is his own. This law does not function to direct personal conduct, but to fix persons and things in relations of *dominium* and servitude to one other. Legality consists in respecting the distinction between that which is one's own (*suum*) and that which is another's (*alienum*). Correspondingly, all illegality falls under the broad heading of *furtum*, theft.

Given the limitation, in this literature, of the analytical category for the morality of social actions to *dominium* alone, it was evident that *dominium* must be made to cover a very wide range of relationships to other objects and persons. It is here that we find the source of the adoption by the science of casuistry of the equivalence between *dominium* and *ius*. It was also fuelled by the explicit concern of writers on practical morality not to overburden the consciences of ordinary believers to the point where they might feel that Christianity was too hard a faith to bear and might abandon it altogether. This had the consequence of allowing cases of *dominium* where previously none had been allowed: most significantly, in incorporeal rights. As we saw in discussing the Roman law, the concepts of *dominium* of rights and of rights as *dominia* are very closely related. In the casuistic they are both elements of an understanding of society and commerce which is radically divergent from that of Aquinas, in that instead of focusing on actions and the law which regulates them, it reifies those actions into the objects of *dominium-ius*. But the fact that it is not a Thomist understanding does not mean that there is any necessary connection between an emphasis on the will rather than the reason of God, and the equivalence of *dominium* and *ius*, nor that external *dominium*-right can therefore be interpreted as an expression of the will and liberty of the subject. In the course of what follows I shall try to establish these conclusions more fully.

Dominium *and* ius *in the literature on cases of conscience to c. 1460*

The *Summae confessorum* consider the question of *dominium* in their treatment of the nature of theft. The first *Summa* of the kind is the *Summa de poenitentia et matrimonio* of the thirteenth-century Catalan Dominican Raymund of Peñafort, written (in its second and fuller version) in 1234.[47] Considering the topic *De furtis*, Raymund slightly altered the original Roman law text to define theft as 'the fraudulent seizure of a thing that belongs to another, moveable and corporeal, against the will of the *dominus*, for the sake of making profit; either of the thing itself, or of its use or its possession'.[48] Raymund's source text does not specify that the *res* should be *aliena*, and Raymund goes

---

[47] It is possibly somewhat contentious to describe Raymund's work as the first *summa de casibus*: Leonard Boyle has argued that it is false to draw a sharp distinction, either between the *summae* and the earlier manuals for confessors, or between the *summae* and the later sixteenth- and seventeenth-century works of casuistry. However, I share the view of Michaud-Quantin and others that the *summae* are sufficiently stylistically similar to constitute them a genre in their own right. See the exchange between Boyle and Thomas Tentler in C. Trinkaus and H. A. Oberman (eds.), *The pursuit of holiness in late medieval and renaissance religion* (Leiden 1974), 103–37.

[48] Raymund of Peñafort, *Summa de poenitentia et matrimonio cum glossis Ioannis de Friburgo* (Farnborough, Hants. 1967; facsimile of Rome 1603 edn), Book II, tit. 6, p. 219: 'Furtum est contrectatio rei alienae, mobilis, corporalis, fraudulosa, invito domino, lucrifaciendi gratia, vel ipsius rei, vel etiam usus eius, possessionisve.' The original Roman law definition at D. 47, 2, 1, 3 reads: 'Furtum est contrectatio rei fraudulosa lucrifaciendi gratia vel ipsius rei vel etiam usus eius possessionisve.'

on to explain what he means. ' "A thing that belongs to another" is added for this reason, because theft is not committed in a thing which is fully one's own. I say "fully", because if another had a right in that thing, for example a creditor ... a lender, a business-partner, or other such person, then the *dominus* in furtively withdrawing that thing from a person of that kind would commit theft.'[49] Raymund implies that a *res* in which a person apart from the *dominus* has a *ius* is to that extent *alienum*, i.e. the *res* of another *dominus*, which is what entails that the original *dominus* commits theft in abstracting it. The right-holder is thus implied to hold *dominium* of a kind.

The *Raymundina* hesitates, however, over whether there can be *dominium* of rights, the position that for Bartolus in the fourteenth century was the corollary of the notion that *dominium* and right coincide in a broad sense. Raymund deduces from his Roman law source that theft cannot occur in incorporeals. But he also agrees with that source that not only the *res* itself, but also its use or possession may be the object of theft. As we saw in discussing Bartolus,[50] at least one Roman law locus – and one that particularly impressed mediaeval jurists, leading precisely to Bartolus' theory of broad *dominium* – treats usufruct, at least, as an incorporeal right and as an object of *dominium*. The gloss of the Dominican John of Freiburg clarifies Raymund's *incorporalia* as 'actions and servitudes', but interestingly not as 'rights', *iura incorporalia*. Thus it is possible that Raymund, or at least his interpreter, has some notion that there can be *dominium* in use.

This suggestion is continued within the Italian tradition of *Summae de casibus*, beginning with that of the Franciscan Astesanus d'Asti (*Summa astesana*) dating from about 1317. The *Astesana* discusses theft in Book I, considering the seventh of the ten commandments, 'Thou shalt not steal.' Astesanus is unusual among authors of the casuistic in basing his analysis not principally on Raymund but on the discussion of the thirteenth-century Franciscan Alexander of Hales, who posits that the term 'theft' can be taken in three ways: strictly, generally and interpretatively. 'Strictly, it names the seizure of another's *res*, without the knowledge and against the will of the

---

[49] *Summa de poenitentia*, Book II, tit. 6, p. 219: 'Rei alienae ideo apponitur, quia non committitur furtum in re plenissime propria. plenissime dico, quia si alius haberet in re illa ius, puta creditor ... vel commodatarius, vel socius, vel similia alia persona, dominus furtive surripiens alicui tali personae committeret furtum.'
[50] Above, pp. 20–2 and n. 54 below.

dominus: nor do we need to say (as some want) "of another's moveable res", because this is understood in the term "seizure": for an immoveable *res* cannot be seized.' However, 'In a general sense theft is the term for any illicit usurpation of a *res* belonging to another.'[51] Astesanus' broad and the narrow senses of theft can be seen as corresponding to the wide and the narrow senses of *dominium* distinguished by the Roman lawyers and ultimately by Bartolus.

The genre of *Summae de casibus* underwent towards the end of the fourteenth century a period of stagnation which lasted for almost a century. However, the end of the fifteenth century and the beginning of the sixteenth saw a final flowering of the literature, producing two highly elaborate and influential works, both written by Italians and both adopting an alphabetic format. The first of these is the *Summa angelica* of the Franciscan Angelus Carletus de Clavasio, written c. 1462 but first published at Chiavasso itself in 1486.[52] Under the entry *Furtum* we find the following: 'Theft is properly the fraudulent seizure of another's mobile and corporeal *res* against the will of the *dominus* done with the intention of gaining riches: either of the *res* itself; or of the use of the *res*; or of the possession [of it].'[53] Angelus follows Raymund in affirming that there can therefore be no theft in immobiles and in incorporeals like actions and servitudes.

However, he goes on, 'I ask whether he who usurps only the use or the possession is a thief? I reply that he is ... for example he who uses a *res* that has been deposited or a *res* that has been accommodated for another use, and situations of this kind; and he is bound to restore the estimated value of that use.'[54] There is a strong implication, here again, that there can be *dominium* in use and possession.

---

[51] Astesanus de Asti, *Summa de casibus conscientiae* (Nuremberg 1482), Book I, tit. 32: 'Proprie dicitur contrectatio rei aliene ignorante domino contra suam voluntatem: nec oportet aliud addere ut dicatur (sicut quidam volunt) rei aliene mobilis. quia intelligitur nomine contrectationis ... Communiter dicitur furtum omnis illicita usurpatio rei aliene.' The change of noun from *contrectatio*, with its implication of physical handling, to *usurpatio*, is significant.

[52] Along with Michaud-Quantin, Dietterle and Bergfeld, see Mario Viora, 'La "Summa angelica"', *Bollettino storico-bibliografico subalpino* 38 (1936), 443–51, for an account of Clavasius' background and career, and the circumstances of composition of the *Summa*. Clavasius is also the author of a tract *De contractibus* and another *De restitutionibus*, first printed in 1768 and 1771 respectively. I have not been able to consult these works, but their existence is another indication of the links between the genres which I have been suggesting.

[53] Angelus de Clavasio, *Summa angelica* (Nuremberg 1488), fol. 115v: 'Furtum proprie est contractio rei aliene mobilis corporalis fraudulosa invito domino facta animo lucrandi: sive ipsius rei: sive usus rei: sive possessionis.'

[54] Ibid., fol. 116r: 'Utrum ille qui solum usum vel possessionem usurpat sit fur? Respondeo

But when Angelus comes to the entry *Dominium*, he adopts a definition very close to the narrow sense of *dominium* offered by Bartolus, viz. that '*Dominium* is the right of having, possessing, using, enjoying and disposing of a certain thing at the pleasure of the will; or according to a particular determinate mode defined by some kind of superiority or authority.'[55]

The *Angelica* is explicitly taken to task for its confusion over *dominium* in the last great product of the genre, the Dominican Sylvester Mazzolini da Prierio's alphabetical *Summa summarum*, called the *Sylvestrina*, and first published in 1515. Before considering this work, however, we need to look at the literature on contracts and conscience at the Northern universities of the late fourteenth and fifteenth centuries.

Dominium, ius *and Augustinianism in the literature on contracts and restitution at the Northern universities*

The decisive text for the contract literature's understanding of the formation and nature of civic society is the treatise on restitution of the Franciscan Johannes Duns Scotus (c. 1265–1308) at Book IV, Distinction 15 of his Oxford commentary on the *Sentences* (the *Opus oxoniense*). Scotus is apparently the first to use the locus specifically to write a tract on the nature of restitution, and his analysis became the base text of the subsequent literature adopting this mode of discourse. Scotus' second *quaestio* on this Distinction asks 'Whether whoever has taken or detains something that belongs to someone else is in such a way bound to restore it that he cannot do penance without such restitution'.[56] Scotus here contends that the question cannot be answered without establishing 'whence the *dominia* of *res* are distinct in such a way that this is called mine and that yours; because this is the foundation of all injury committed in seizing hold of another's *res*, and consequently of all justice in restoring it'.

---

quod sic ... sicut utens re deposita vel commodata ad alium usum et huiusmodi. et tenetur ad restutionem estimationis ipsius usus.'

[55] Ibid., fol. 87v: 'Dominium est ius habendi possidendi. fruendi et utendi ac disponendi de aliqua re pro libito voluntatis. vel secundum aliquem determinatum modum a quadam superioritate vel auctoritate diffinitum.'

[56] Johannes Duns Scotus, *Opera omnia editio nova. Juxta editionem Waddingi ... a patribus franciscanis de observantia accurate recognita*, vol. XVIII, *Quaestiones in quartum librum sententiarum a d. 14a usque ad 22am* (Paris 1894), Dist. 15, Q. 2, p. 255: 'Utrum quicunque iniuste abstulit, vel detinet rem alienam, teneatur illam restituere ita quod non possit vere poenitere absque tali restitutione.'

Scotus' mode of approaching the question introduces a consideration of the human dynamic from an original state where individual
control over particular objects was unknown to the present situation
where it constitutes the norm. But it is Scotus' peculiar formulation
of this process which is so important. Scotus holds that originally
everything was in common by the law of nature or divine law.[57] But,
he continues, 'my second conclusion is that that precept of the law of
nature about having everything in common was revoked after the
Fall, and with reason' – with reason because the strong began to
oppress the weak in the satisfaction of their own avarice.[58] 'The third
conclusion is that after the revocation of that precept ... and the
consequent concession of a licence of appropriating and distinguishing common things, the actual distinction did not happen
through the law of nature nor the divine law ... It follows that the
first division of *dominia* happened by some positive law.'[59] Scotus goes
on to argue that the division was just if the law which divided was
just; he elaborates on the conditions for a just law, that it be rational
and promulgated by someone in legitimate authority. He divides
legitimate authority into paternal and political: paternal authority is
legitimate because it is a precept of the natural law which has never
been revoked; political authority is legitimate because it proceeds
from the consent of the people constituting a community.

Although Scotus does not use the language which equates *ius* and
dominium, the political ideas here formulated constitute leitmotifs of
the tradition which does. Scotus does not envisage the immediate

---

[57] Ibid., p. 256: 'lege naturae vel divina, non sunt rerum distincta dominia pro statu
innocentiae, imo tunc omnia sunt communia'. Scotus appeals to the authority of Gratian's
Decretum, D. 8, c. 1, and the citations of Augustine contained therein: 'Quo iure defendis
villas ecclesiae divino an humano? ... iure divino dei est terra et plenitudo eius. Jure ergo
humano dicitur haec domus mea est: haec villa mea est. hic servus meus est', and 'Tolle
iura imperatorum: quis audet dicere: haec villa mea est?' (originally in the commentary
super Iohannem); together with the canon *Dilectissimis*, a letter from Ps.-Clement IV asserting
that common use of all things ought to obtain among men, and did so in the state of
innocence, each man occupying only what he needed for his preservation and sustenance:
'Communis enim usus omnium, quae sunt in hoc mundo, omnibus hominibus esse debuit.
Sed per iniquitatem alius hoc dixit esse suum, et alius istud, et sic inter mortales facta est
divisio.'

[58] In this contention he distances himself radically from Aquinas and his followers, for whom
individual *dominia* are a deduction from the law of nature, which remains in being,
immutable in constituting the order of God's creation (which, as the object of divine
volition and intellection, is part of God himself).

[59] Ibid., p. 265: 'Tertia conclusio, quod revocato isto praecepto legis naturae de habendo
omnia communia, et per consequens concessa licentia appropriandi et distinguendi
communia, non fiebat actualis distinctio per legem naturae, nec per divinam ... Ex hoc
sequitur quod aliqua lege positiva fiebat prima distinctio dominiorum.'

succession of one law upon another, but two disjunctive states of *dominium*, one of everything in common, the other of distinct *dominia*, under the natural law and the positive law respectively. Both orders of *dominium* are dependent on the will of the legislator expressed in law; conversely, the full extent of the law is the definition of *dominia distincta*.[60] In between there is a legal vacuum wherein there was no ordination of *res* but simply a fluid situation of *de facto* appropriation. In this situation, fraught with danger and misery for the weak, it is human agency which imposes and undertakes to defend a new order. The civic environment, the city, is simply the state of the existence of *dominia distincta*, and the civic power is for the maintenance of that state. I shall henceforth call this complex of ideas 'neo-Augustinianism': Scotus' treatment of *Sentences* IV, 15 constitutes it, and (as we shall see) the other genres which treat of restitution, as a locus for the exposition of an Augustinian political theory whose primary political concern is justice understood as the just assignation of *dominia distincta*.

This Augustinianism is patent in the *Tractatus de contractibus* of the late fourteenth-century secular master Henry Totting of Oyta, probably written while Henry was at the University of Vienna, c. 1384–90.[61] The vast majority of the *questiones* concern the justice or otherwise of the practice of establishing revenues (*redditus*) in property or persons, i.e. a fixed income from an original material good. Henry opens his treatise with the opening words of the Book of Wisdom: 'Diligite justitiam qui iudicatis terram',[62] and the Proem develops the theme of justice as the principal virtue, useful, bringing of

---

[60] See the late thirteenth-century *Communiloquium sive summa collationum* of Johannes Gallensis, like Scotus a Franciscan at Oxford. The second part discusses the various 'mutual bindings' (*colligationes*) which ensure that the commonwealth coheres as one body. In the table of contents at the beginning of the work we find the following: 'Secunde partis que est de colligatione multiplici membrorum ad invicem sunt distinctiones novem. quarum prima est de colligatione ordinali vel legali que est dominorum ad servos et econverso' (the point is repeated in the Prologue to the *Secunda pars*). That is, the legal order embraces nothing but *dominia* (although John makes no mention of *dominia* over things). See Johannes Gallensis, *Communiloquium sive summa collationum* (Wakefield 1964; originally printed by Jordanns de Quedlinburg, Strasburg 1489). For Gallensis himself, see A. G. Little, *The grey friars at Oxford* (Oxford 1892), pp. 143–51.

[61] Henricus de Oyta [Henry Totting of Oyta], *Tractatus de contractibus* (Paris 1506), Dubium secundum: 'Utrum redditus pecuniarum vel aliarum rerum sc. bladi vini sc. rationabiliter constitutos in aliqua re vel persona aliquis emere possit licite pro pecunia vel pro pecuniis.' For details of Henry Totting's life and works, see A. Lang, *Heinrich Totting von Oyta. Ein Beitrag zur Entstehungsgeschichte der ersten deutschen Universitäten und zur Problemgeschichte der Spätscholastik* (Münster i. W. 1937).

[62] Wisdom i, 1.

salvation and necessary, 'as Augustine shows ... saying take away justice and what are kingdoms but great robberies'.[63]

Henry's purpose, however, is to establish the ideal in order that he might better lament the depravity of his own times, when the rulers are no longer upright and the people have consequently fallen into a state of evil:

in Psalm 24 [it says], 'There is not absent from their broad avenues usury and fraud' ... and in truth these evils within the Christian people have grown and gained strength to such an extent that from their excessive cultivation and multiplication they are reputed just and licit by many. And those who do not dare to say openly that usury and fraud are licit, colour them with multiple dye, as in various exchanges and contracts which they falsify under the title of just and licit purchase and sale.[64]

To put an end to this lamentable situation, Henry intends to treat of justice in certain common contracts, 'in which are hidden doubts even for the wise, and many dangers for the souls of men ... enquiring as far as our strength may permit ... what in such affairs is to be observed and what to be avoided'.[65] The contract literature is clearly shown here to be closely connected with the casuistic of the summaries for confessors: both are concerned with the practical care of the soul.

Henry's work demonstrates the connection of this Augustinian politics, wherein justice regulates a vast mesh of interlocking *dominia*, with the notion that it is possible to have *dominium* of rights. The question of whether it was licit not merely to establish but also to purchase revenues had been a vexed question since the late thirteenth century. We can trace the debate back to the work of the Belgian master at the University of Paris, Godfrey of Fontaines. The fourteenth Question of his fifth Quodlibet examines the question 'Whether it be licit to purchase revenues for life and to receive from the purchased revenues beyond the initial capital'.[66] According to

---

[63]   Henry Totting, *Tractatus de contractibus*, Proem, sig. aii r.
[64]   Ibid., Proem, sig. aiii v: 'et in psalmis 24. non deficit de platheis eius usura et dolus ... et revera hec mala in christiano populo adeo creverunt / et sic invaluerunt ut ex nimia eorum assiduatione et multiplicatione quasi iusta / et licita a multis reputentur. Et qui usuram et dolum dicere manifeste non audent esse licita multiplici fuco ea colorant prout in variis commutationibus et contractibus quos sub titulo licite. et iuste emptionis et venditionis confingunt.'
[65]   Ibid.: 'De quibusdam contractibus communiter homines usitatis et currentibus quibus latent dubia etiam apud sapientes. et multa animarum pericula videamus investigando ut poterimus quid ... in eis sit observandum quidve fugiendum seu vitandum.'
[66]   Godfrey of Fontaines, *Quodlibet V*, ed. in M. de Wulf and J. Hoffmans, *Les quodlibets cinq, six*

Godfrey, the problem is that it seems that this is not a case of licit purchase and sale, principally because it does not appear to be an exchange of one thing for another ('commutatio rei ad rem'). God-frey's response to the problem demonstrates the practical tendency of this literature: the condemnation of the practice would be 'contrary to common usage everywhere: therefore I do not dare to judge such contracts illicit. And therefore to show in what way the said contract might be licit, we have to show how in fact there is a contract of purchase in this case.'[67]

This requires of Godfrey that he redefine the possible object of sale and purchase, which is the nub of the problem. On Aristotelian ethical economics, man needs certain objects for his physical conve-nience. The original mode of exchange is of such extraneous and material goods for other items of this kind. Money is introduced as a means of facilitating exchange; but it is solely the medium of exchange, and cannot naturally and therefore licitly constitute a *res* in itself (that is, one of the termini – *extrema* – of the contract of sale and purchase).[68] The purchase of revenues appears to be a case of buying money, and therefore to constitute illicit commerce. To ground his argument against this conclusion, Godfrey's strategy is twofold. First he establishes that incorporeal objects are, 'according to the law', as much *res* as are corporeal objects, and both can equally be sold (which means, implicitly, that both are equally the object of *dominium*).[69] In the second place he posits the distinction of the right from that to which is the right:

And therefore it seems that in the matter in question it may be said that a revenue for life, whether in money, or in any other *res*, is a right of taking money or some such other *res*; and that it is something incorporeal distinct from the corporeal *res* itself. Therefore, although money in itself is not a *res* capable of purchase, nevertheless the right of taking money can be sold; and just so, the right of bringing an action for a certain amount of money can be sold. For although the right of bringing an action for a certain amount of money be not bought except for the sake of that money,

---

et sept de Godefroid de Fontaines (Louvain 1914), Q. 14, p. 63: 'Utrum licitum sit emere redditus ad vitam et recipere de redditibus emptis ultra sortem.'

[67] Ibid., p. 65: 'quod est contra communem usum ubique terrarum; ideo non audeo iudicare illicitos contractos predictos. Et ideo ad ostendendum quomodo possit esse licitus dictus contractus, declarandum est quomodo est ibi vere contractus emptionis.'

[68] Aristotle, *Politica*, ed. by W. D. Ross (Oxford 1957), 1258a38f.

[69] Under 'incorporeals' he mentions the right of inheritance, the right of action (in court) and servitudes both personal and real; he has already implicitly included usufruct.

nevertheless because the right is not formally the money (albeit it may be so potentially), it can therefore be bought.[70]

Godfrey's solution is adopted verbatim by Henry. The refinement of the notion of *res* brings incorporeal objects into the web of *dominia* that constitutes civil society, allowing these authors to analyse a far greater range of economic practices as free from the prohibition on usury and thus as safe in conscience.

The later fifteenth century: the work of Conrad Summenhart

All the features on the literature on contracts and cases of conscience which we have looked at so far are taken up and systematised by the fifteenth-century Tübingen theologian Conrad Summenhart in his monumental *Septipertitum opus de contractibus pro foro conscientiae atque theologico*, which has rightly been taken as the high point of the literature which equates *dominium* and *ius*.[71] Summenhart is therefore taken as *par excellence* the late mediaeval philosopher of rights as liberties.[72] In this section I shall suggest that the account of *dominium* and right in the *Septipertitum opus* principally shows how far this discourse has deviated from the original Franciscan equation of right and *dominium* in liberty and spirituality; and that Summenhart arrives at a notion of liberty in the spaces left over by the law only when he begins to step out of his analytic framework of *dominium* and right.

Summenhart's treatise adopts the traditional stance of the contract literature in its reluctance to be over-strict in the morality of human affairs. His Prologue follows much the same pattern as Henry of Oyta's Proem, considering first the ideal of justice and moving on to the author's intention in such circumstances:

And so ... we must travel a royal road: so that we do not curve to the right, lest in being too fine and acute, we draw blood, and pierce the consciences

---

[70] Ibid., p. 65: 'Ergo videtur quod possit dici in proposito quod redditus ad vitam, sive in pecunia sive in quocunque re alia, sit ius quoddam percipiendi pecuniam vel talem rem; et est quid incorporale aliud ab ipsa re corporali. Quamvis ergo pecunia secundum se non sit emibilis, tamen ius percipiendi pecuniam vendi potest; sic etiam ius agendi ad certam pecunie quantitatem vendi potest. Quamvis enim ius agendi ad certam quantitatem pecunie non ematur nisi propter ipsam pecuniam, tamen quia non est ipsa pecunia formaliter, licet in virtute, ideo emi potest.'

[71] For Summenhart in the context of late scholastic theology and the discussions on *dominium*, see Burns, 'Scholasticism: Survival and revival', p. 138 and pp. 145–6.

[72] E.g. by Grossi, 'Proprietà', p. 123: 'il teologo tubingense, educato a Parigi ... traduce in termini più rigorosamente tecnici le premesse generali delle correnti volontaristiche': Tuck, *Natural rights theories*, pp. 27–8.

of weaker brothers; nor to the left, so that we justify the iniquitous. Jean Gerson ... reports that his mentor [Pierre d'Ailly] said once, that in the case of human contracts which, presupposing sin, are natural and necessary, one should not lightly reprove or restrict them or reduce them to the depravity which is usury.[73]

Summenhart emphasises the utilitarian aspect of his work, the aim of which is to help ordinary Christians to live the good life; he repeats the humanistic polemic of the early fifteenth-century chancellor of the University of Paris, Jean Gerson, against those theologians who inappropriately take off into flights of logic, metaphysics and even mathematics, ignoring the nature of their audience, and deservedly earning for themselves the names of 'sophists, windbags and fantastics'.[74]

Summenhart, then, is very much the heir of Gerson's approach to practical moral theology, and of his humanist vision of a personal Christian ethic of the good life. It is not in this sense, however, that we find Summenhart's name coupled with that of Gerson, either in other late scholastic authors or in modern histories of political thought. In the neo-Thomist tradition stemming from the sixteenth-century authors of the Dominican School of Salamanca, Gerson and Summenhart are invariably treated together as *moderni* or *neoterici* (authors of suspect nominalist philosophical tendencies), and as equally positing the equivalence of *ius* and *dominium*; and this judgement has also been approved in modern histories of rights theories.[75] These later interpreters give the offending text of Gerson as Lectio III of his *De vita spirituali animae*: as we shall see, however,[76] this is not a work of practical but of speculative and academic theology, nor does

---

[73] Conradus [Conrad] Summenhart, *Septipertitum opus de contractibus pro foro conscientie atque theologico* (Hagenau 1515), Prologus, sig. Eiii r: 'Regia itaque via in primis eundum est: ut non declinetur ad dexteram: ne nimis emungendo: sanguinem eliciamus: et conscientias infirmorum fratrum percutiamus. neque ad sinistram: ita ut iniquum iustificemus. Refert Joa. Gerson cancell. parisiensis preceptorem suum cardinalem cameracensem dixisse: quod super contractibus humanis que presupposito peccato sunt naturales atque necessarii: non debet leviter reprobatio fieri seu restrictio vel ad usurariam pravitatem reductio.'

[74] Ibid., sig. Eiii v: 'Horum theologorum cancell. Paris. in sermone domenice. xix. post Pentec. dicit verbosam sophisticam et loquitatem esse et ad chimericam inquit mathematicam esse redactam. Cur insuper (inquit) ob aliud appellantur theologi nostri temporis sophiste et verbosi: imo et phantastici? nisi quia relictis utilibus intelligibilibus pro auditorum qualitate: transferunt se ad nudam logicam et metaphysicam / aut etiam mathematicam ubi et quando non oportet.'

[75] Thus Tuck, *Natural rights theories*, pp. 27–8, writes that Summenhart 'took Gerson, quite rightly, to have implied that all *iura* are *dominia*, that the categories of *ius* and *dominium* are identical'.

[76] Below, chapter 2, pp. 81–6.

Gerson anywhere in it posit the equivalence of *ius* and *dominium*. It is
certainly true that it is this text which Summenhart principally uses
in order to form his own definition of *dominium* as equivalent to *ius* in
Tract I of the *Septipertitum opus*. However, throughout the first Tract,
what is striking about Summenhart's use of Gerson is how often he
feels obliged to criticise Gerson's pronouncements, and the amount
of work he has to do to bring the theory of the *De vita spirituali animae*
in line with his own position: that all right is *dominium* because the
notion of theft applies equally to both.

The first Question of the first Tract of the *Septipertitum opus* asks,

whether the two descriptions of right and the one of *dominium* be by the
master well and masterfully posited; by whom it is said: Right is a proximate
power or faculty accruing to something according to the dictate of primary
justice. And again. Right is a proximate power or faculty accruing to
something according to the dictate of right reason. *Dominium* however is a
proximate power or faculty of drawing other things into one's own faculty
or licit use according to statutes or laws rationally laid down.[77]

Summenhart begins by equating the two descriptions of right with *ius*
as taken in its second regular sense (it being in its first equivalent to
lex, 'law'): 'In the second way right is taken as the same thing as
power, as we take it when we say that a father has right over his son
and the king over his subjects ; and that men have right in things and
in their possessions, and even sometimes in persons, as in slaves.'[78]
Summenhart derives this second sense from a particular locus of the
Roman law, where the right of persons is divided into (in Summenhart's terms) the 'right of paternal power', and the 'right of *dominium*
with respect to one's own'.[79] We can see how this suits Summenhart's

---

[77] Summenhart, *Septipertitum opus*, Tract I, Q. I, sig. Eiv v: 'Utrum due descriptiones iuris et
una descriptio dominii sint a magistri bene ac magistraliter posite: quibus dicitur. Ius est
potestas vel facultas proprinqua conveniens alicui secundum dictamen prime iustitie. Et
item. Ius est potestas vel facultas propinqua conveniens alicui secundum dictament recte
rationis. Dominium autem est potestas vel facultas propinqua assumendi res alias in suam
facultatem vel usum licitum secundum iura vel secundum leges rationabiliter institutas.'
Summenhart later gives the definitions of right as taken respectively from the thirteenth
Consideration of Gerson's *De potestate ecclesiastica*, and the third Lectio of his *De vita spirituali
animae*. These texts are discussed below, chapter 2, pp. 81–7.
[78] Summenhart, *Septipertitum opus*, Tract I, Q. I, sig. Eiv v: 'Alio modo accipitur ius ut idem est
quod potestas quo modo accipitur cum dicimus patrem habere ius in filium / regem in
subditos. et homines habere ius in rebus et possessionibus suis. et etiam in personis
aliquando. puta in servis.'
[79] The locus is I. I, 8, which Summenhart interprets characteristically expansively: 'Sequitur
de iure personarum alia divisio. nam quaedam personae sui iuris sunt, quaedam alieno iuri
subiectae sunt: rursus earum, quae alieno iuri subiecto sunt, aliae in potestate parentum,
aliae in potestate dominorum sunt.'

purposes, for it yields a sense both of 'power' and of 'right' which is exclusively over or towards other things or persons, enabling him both to characterise right as a relation, and to bring Gerson's description of right as a power into his own description of right as a relation:

Right in the second sense is a relation, that is, a habitual condition with respect to something [habitudo: 'habitude']: founded in him who is said to have right, and terminating in the thing over which or in which he has right (as the remote terminus), and in the action which he is able to perform upon or concerning that thing (as the proximate terminus).[80]

Summenhart wants to argue that right is a relation because this facilitates its assimilation with *dominium*, his whole purpose as a contributor to the genres of contract and conscience literatures being to give a firm theoretical grounding to the basic equivalence between right and *dominium*.

'Second supposition: taking right in the second way it is the same as *dominium* and truly and universally is predicated of *dominium*, in such a way that all *dominium* is *ius* in the second sense ... because for someone to be *dominus* of a thing is formally for him to have right in that thing or over that thing.'[81] Summenhart acknowledges that the equation does not work the other way round if one takes *dominium* in its strict sense, which for Summenhart is the sense proper to civil law, for then it will not be true that all *ius* is *dominium*:

taking *dominium* properly, it connotes beyond the account of right, superiority as well ... If therefore *dominium* were taken strictly in this way: then they would be the same, but not convertibly, because *ius* would apply more widely; and in consequence not all right would be *dominium*. For an inferior has right over a superior, because a superior is often bound to an inferior ... but nevertheless we would not properly concede that an inferior has *dominium* over a superior.[82]

---

[80] Summenhart, *Septipertitum opus*, sig. Eiv v: 'Ius secundo modo est relatio. s. habitudo fundata in illo qui dicitur habere ius. et terminata in rem in quam vel in qua habet ius tanquam ad terminum remotum: et ad actionem. quam habet exercere in talem rem vel circa eam tanquam ad terminum proprinquum.'

[81] Ibid.: 'Secunda suppositio: capiendo ius secundo modo idem est quod dominium. et vere et universaliter predicatur de dominio. sic quod omne dominium est ius secundo modo ... quia aliquem esse dominus alicuius rei est formaliter eum habere ius in illa re. vel in illam rem.'

[82] Ibid., sig. Ev r: 'Nam appropriate capiendo dominium: connotat ultra rationem iuris etiam superioritatem ... Si igitur ita stricte accipiatur dominium: tunc essent idem: sed non convertibiliter: quia ius esset in plus. et per consequens non omne ius esset dominium. Nam inferior habet ius in superiorem: quia superior tenetur inferiori in multis ... Et tamen proprie non concederemus inferiorem habere dominium in superiorem.' Summenhart is

Summenhart concludes, however, that the wider sense in which *dominium* is convertible with right is valid,

because whoever has right in a thing: if that thing were snatched from him or carried off by stealth against his will, the taker would be said to have committed theft. And if so, then the taker seized possession of another's *res* against the will of the *dominus* – the consequence holds from the definition of theft. And in consequence, he who had right in that thing: could in some sense be said to be the *dominus* of that thing.[83]

Here we can see Summenhart making explicit the assumption of the casuistic literature in the question of theft: the right-holder is a *dominus* because furtive seizure of the *res* in which he has a right counts as theft. But we can also see that this right which is equivalent to *dominium* has nothing to do with 'superiority', the 'moral sovereignty' his modern interpreters want.

Summenhart's considerations concerning Gerson's definitions give him, therefore, a threefold equivalence: of *ius*, *dominium* and *potestas*, all belonging to the category of relation. As we saw at the beginning, the term 'power' (*potestas*) is used frequently in a non-technical sense in the early Franciscan discourse, where it is associated with *ius* and *dominium*. By the late fifteenth century, however, with the development of Aristotelian science and a technical language of agency (particularly in commentaries on Aristotle's *de Anima*), such an association of *potestas* with *relatio* was linguistically problematic – at least for an author of Summenhart's synoptic ambitions. This is demonstrated by his immediate move to demonstrate in technical terms that *potestas* and *posse* are relationships, by a reference to current theory concerning the *de Anima*:

Note ... that just as is wont to be said in respect of the book 'On the soul', that a potency [potentia] or power [potestas] of the soul is taken in two ways: firstly, materially or fundamentally, for a reality of the soul which elicits acts, in which sense a potency of the soul is an independent entity and

---

indebted to the mid-fifteenth-century *Summa* of the Florentine Dominican Antonino Pierozzi (Sant'Antonino; Antoninus Florentinus) for his characterisation of the stricter sense of *dominium*. This latter sense, however, is the only sense of *dominium* Antoninus was prepared to acknowledge, explicitly rejecting any sense in which *dominium* and *ius* were equivalent. Because of this, and because of the Thomistic influences on his *Summa*, he is treated below, chapter 3, pp. 107–11.

[83] Summenhart, *Septipertitum opus*, sig. Ev r: 'quia quicunque habet ius in re: si ei surriperetur vel subtraheretur res illa eo invito surripiens diceretur furtum commississe. et si sic. ergo surripiens contrectavit rem alienam invito domino. tenet consequentia per diffinitionem furti. Et per consequens ille qui habuit ius in ea re: poterit aliquo modo dici dominus illius rei.'

not a relation ... Secondly, formally ... and thus it is a disposition [habitus] of the soul founded in such a reality; and the soul has this 'habitude' towards its object and towards actions which it can produce with respect to the object; and in this way a potency is a relation. Similarly here, power or faculty should not be understood ... as any absolute entity ... because right and *dominium* are formally relations; but as a 'habitude'.[84]

Summenhart's rhetoric of 'as is wont to be said' would not have impressed a knowledgeable contemporary, for the thesis to which he refers was in fact the subject of intense debate in the literature on the *de Anima*.[85] We can, however, find texts which come close to Summenhart's account. For example, John of Jandun argues that: 'With regard to the question, we should briefly understand that this name potency is sometimes taken as the potent subject, sometimes for the immediate principle of operation (passive or active), and sometimes for the respect towards, and ordination to, an act.'[86] John

---

[84] Ibid.: 'Nota tamen quod sicut circa librum de anima / dici solet. Potentia seu potestas anime capitur dupliciter. Uno modo materialiter seu fundamentaliter pro realitate anime elicitiva actuum quomodo potentia anime est res absoluta et non relatio ... Alio modo formaliter ... et sic est habitus anime fundata in tali realitate quam habitudinem habet anima ad obiectum et ad actus producibiles a se circa obiectum. et sic potentia est relatio. Ita hic non debet capi potestas vel facultas ... pro aliqua entitate absoluta ... quia ius et dominium formaliter sunt relationes; sed debet capi pro habitudine ut dictum est.'

[85] We find the discussion in two questions invariably raised in all the commentaries: on Book I, Chapter I, whether the potencies of the soul are defined by their objects and their acts; on Book II, Chapter II, whether the soul is distinct from its potencies. Regarding the first of these questions, Scotists object that the Thomists are in fact saying that a potency is a relation. See the early seventeenth-century Franciscan Hugo Cavellus' *Supplementum ad quaestiones Io. Duns Scoti...in libros de anima*, Sect. 19, 'Whether potencies be distinguished by acts or objects?', in Scotus, *Quaestiones super libris Aristotelis de anima*, ed. by Cavellus (Lyons 1625): 'We should say that potencies are not intrinsically distinguished by acts and objects, thus Scotus ... And the reason is, that every being which is the principle of an operation, is such a principle, because it is in itself a being of that nature in itself ... otherwise potencies would be relations, because these alone are defined by their habitude towards another thing.'
    The second question involves the nominalists as well, and is the problem which principally generates the thesis Summenhart finds so convenient. Thomists argued that the potencies of the soul are really distinct from the soul itself, Scotists that they are formally so, and nominalists of Ockham's stamp that the soul simply is its potencies, with no distinction either real or formal. However, there is a fourth opinion, which holds that in some sense the potencies are simply the soul, but that they are distinct 'in so far as the potencies add on top of it [the soul] a certain mode, or a certain relation to an act: for the soul *qua* intellective is said to have a relation to intellection, and in so far as it is volitive, to volition'. See Michael Zanardus O. P., *Commentaria cum quaestionibus in tres libros Aristotelis de anima* (Venice 1616), Book III, Question 39: 'Whether the potencies of the intellective soul be really distinct from the soul', reciting the opinion of Henry of Ghent and Durand Saint-Pourçain. Summenhart's interpretation is in this latter tradition.

[86] Ioannes de Ianduno [John of Jandun], *Super libros Aristotelis de anima* (Venice 1561), Book II, Q. 9: 'An potentiae animae sint realiter idem cum ipsa anima: Ad quaestionem intelligendum est breviter, quod hoc nomen potentia aliquando sumitur pro subiecto

thus admits a definition of a potency as (a) the soul; (b) a principle of operation distinct from the soul; (c) a relation to an act. It seems clear that it is this *via media* which Summenhart appropriates, for nowhere else in the commentary literature on the *de Anima* do we find the concept of relation applied to potencies – in fact, quite the opposite. But he introduces in addition his own important differentiation between the proximate and remote termini of the relation, which allows him to convert a theory about the relationship of potency to act to one about the relationship of potency to object.

In this way, Summenhart can assimilate the *ius* characterised by Gerson as a power of acting to the relation over persons or things which is *dominium*. But by assimilating *dominium* to the potency (in one sense) of the literature on the *de Anima*, he transforms it from the mark of rational nature into a neutral quality which can be predicated of all created beings in so far as they are capable of any kind of action which affects other creatures.[87] From being, in the early mendicant discourse, the presupposition of action in its strong sense as independent and willed activity, it becomes a category able to explain what for that discourse was mere motion, like the horse's eating of its hay – losing entirely its association with liberty. *Dominium-ius* is for Summenhart as much a category of natural science as it is of human and human civic agency. Hence Summenhart posits twenty-three subdivisions of *dominium* which between them account for the entire range of creation, from inanimate bodies, through animals to rationals.[88] Again it is clear that Summenhart's *dominium* in its aspect as convertible with right has none of the associations of liberty and 'sovereignty' with which it has been latterly imbued.

We turn now to the political corollaries of Summenhart's theoretical position, beginning with his critique of the traditional idea of the division of *dominia*. Answering the question, 'Whether the *dominia* of things were at one time not distinguished', Summenhart argues that it is indeed the case that, at some time, some *dominia* were not

---

potente, aliquando sumitur pro principio immediato operationis activo vel passivo, aliquando pro respectu et ordine ad actum.'

[87] Jean Gerson had arrived at the same position with regard to *ius*: he had argued that every created nature has as much right as it has being. But Gerson had not assimilated *ius* to *dominium*. Gerson in the *De vita spirituali animae* is writing too much in the old tradition of Aquinas and Bonaventure to dislodge *dominium* from its position as a category predicable only of rational nature. See below, pp. 86–7.

[88] Summenhart, *Septipertitum opus*, Tract I, Q. 6, sig. Gii r–Giii v.

distinct (i.e. proper to individual persons), and that such *dominia* are even today indistinct, if they still exist at all; but some *dominia* were never indistinct, and are not so today. 'It is proved: because civil *dominia* understood as involving appropriation ... were never indistinct; because it was never the case that someone had civil *dominium* of a thing of which everyone else had *dominium* ... because this involves contradiction.'[89] Civil *dominia* – *dominia* under the civil law – are, precisely, distinct *dominia*: there is no sense in asking if they were ever indistinct, because indistinct *dominia* are not civil *dominia*. If civil *dominia* were ever indistinct, they were not *civil dominia*. Rather, the question 'should be understood as concerning *dominia* diverse in species, but the same in sharing the generic rationale of *dominium*, thus, that at one time there were no civil *dominia* of things involving appropriation: but afterwards, at human ordination, there began to ordained civil *dominia* involving appropriation'.[90] Civil polity is completely coincident with distinct *dominia*, and the civil law is nothing but the law determining the appropriation of *dominia*.[91]

However, Summenhart's reduction of activity within the civil state to the mesh of distinct *dominium-ius* wavers when he comes to considering the nature of free human activity in the question, 'Whether it be licit for any individual man ... to constitute for another in himself or in his person a revenue of any useful thing'.[92] This is the occasion for a full-scale treatment of the idea that a person has *ius* and *dominium* over himself. Having conceded that to constitute a revenue in oneself is to oblige oneself to another person,

[89] Ibid., Q. 8, Gviii v: 'Probatur. quia civilia dominia accepta cum appropriatione ... nunquam fuerint indistincta. quia nunquam sic fuit / quod quis haberet tale dominium civile unius rei / quod illius eiusdem rei omnes alii haberent dominium ... quia hoc implicit contradictionem.'

[90] Ibid., Corollarium: 'sed debet intelligi de dominiis diversis in specie, eisdem tamen in ratione generica dominii. quia s. cum ut olim nulla erant dominia rerum civilia existentia cum appropriatione: postea ceperunt humana ordinatione ordinari civilia dominia existentia cum appropriatione.'

[91] Cf. Tract I, Q. 10, 'Utrum distinctio dominiorum fuerit facta per legem naturalem vel humanam': 'On a sane understanding of the title of the question, the question involves no difficulty: because it is certain that the distinction of *dominia* is only according to the civil and human law. It is proved, because a sane understanding of the title of the question is: through what law were civil *dominia* established or made. But this question involves no difficulty: because the response is clear from the terms of the question. For by the very fact that the title of the question concerns civil *dominia*, it is obvious from the description and proper rationale of civil *dominium*, that they were thus made according to no law if not human law; and not according to natural law, for then they would be natural *dominia*; and not according to divine law, for then they would be divine *dominia*.'

[92] Tract IV, Q. 54, sig. Kkiv v: 'Utrum licet alicui homini singulari: et etiam communitati hominum: in se vel sua persona constiture alteri redditum alicuius rei utilis.'

Summenhart has to face both legal and theological arguments against the possibility: legally, that a free man cannot be obliged, and more particularly cannot be bought and sold (for he is outside human commerce), and therefore cannot oblige or dispose of himself; theologically, that man is not *dominus* of himself, and therefore cannot dispose of himself or make anyone else *dominus* of himself. Summenhart's reply is that it is true that no one is *dominus* of himself to the extent that he can destroy his limbs without legitimate cause; but not to the extent that he cannot oblige himself and his limbs to honest work or useful function for another. 'If a man did not have right over himself or his body in this way, vain would be the title in the "Institutes" "Concerning those who are of their own right": of which kind are the free. Whence also God gave man power over himself and his person, as it says in Ecclesiasticus 15: He left him – viz. man – in the hands of his own counsel.'[93] Summenhart adduces in addition Scotus on the *Sentences*: 'albeit man of his creation may be bound to God in all that he is able to do, nonetheless God does not exact so much from man: on the contrary, he dismisses him to his liberty, as long as he obeys the ten commandments'.[94]

Here Summenhart introduces a notion of negative liberty which is very close to elements of the modern language of rights. This liberty is not in the equivalence of *dominium* and *ius* by itself: liberty is the *ius* and *dominium* man has over himself. It operates in the spaces left over by the laws, as Summenhart further clarifies by his introduction of the Roman law definition of liberty: 'for if [man] is free, he has the faculty of doing whatever he likes, unless it be prohibited by force or right: as is clear from the definition of liberty' (D. 1, 5, 4: 'Libertas est naturalis facultas eius quod cuique facere libet, nisi si quid vi aut iure prohibeatur').[95] But this notion strains his overall analysis of rights as relations: for while liberty so defined may be a relation over oneself,

---

[93] Ibid., sig. Kkvi r: 'Unde si homo non haberet ius super se / vel suum corpus modo dicto: tunc inanis esset titulus in inst.: de his qui sunt sui iuris: cuiusmodi sunt liberi. Unde et homini dat deus potestatem super se et persona sua. prout dicit Eccl. xv. Reliquit illum. s. hominem. in manu consilii sui.'

[94] Ibid.: 'et Sco. in iv. d. 26. q. i. invalidando quandam rationem cuiusdam doctoris: qui volebat ponere quod mutuam translationem corporum / que fit in contractu matrimoniali: congruum fuit a deo approbari: eo quod corpora illa sunt dei: et sic non deberent contrahentes ea sic transferre sine approbatione domini: dicit. quod licet homo ex creatione teneatur deo in omnibus que potest: tamen deus non tantum exigit ab homine: immo dimittit eum libertati sue / solummodo ut servet precepta decalogi.'

[95] See Tract 1, Q. 1, 5a conc., where Summenhart is arguing that the soul in so far as it is will has *dominium* in its own inferior potencies, and 'similarly liberty is a certain species of right and the free man has this right in himself, viz. of doing what he pleases. So that right is

with regard to the external world it is a faculty of action, rather than a relation; and it is limited by a law which is not simply assignatory of *dominia*, but commands actions. Thus on the one hand Summenhart sees *dominium* of oneself as a distinct *dominium* which forms part of the civil establishment, which is coincidental with *dominia distincta*; on the other, he sees it as a power of action in some sense outside the civil law of distinct *dominium*, for he goes on to speak of practices whose doing (*fieri*) the law prohibits, but once done (*factum*), ratifies.[96] Summenhart fails to assimilate liberty entirely to his schema of the manifold ordination of thing to person and person to person which constitutes *dominium* and right, to the extent that he is obliged ultimately to hint at a connection between liberty and *de facto* activity.

Coda: the equivalence of ius and dominium in the early sixteenth century

Summenhart's *Septipertitum opus* became enormously influential from the moment of its publication, an influence which can be seen in two important texts of the early sixteenth century. The first of these is the commentary on *Sentences* IV, 15 of John Mair, master at the Collège de Montaigu in Paris. Just as Summenhart had brought the Scotist history of the distinction of *dominia* from commentary on *Sentences* IV, 15 into the contract literature with its concept of the equivalence of *ius* and *dominium*, so Mair brings this equivalence into the *Sentence*-commentary tradition on restitution. Mair opens his discussion in the manner common to the locus: restitution presupposes distinct *dominia*, and therefore we must enquire how this distinction came about (Mair does not adopt Summenhart's views on the absurdity of the question).[97] He goes on to employ his nominalist metaphysics to found the thesis that *ius* and *dominium* are equivalent, in a piece of language more than worthy of Rabelaisian satire:

Following the nominalists we should say, that *dominium* of a thing, is either that thing itself or the possessor of that thing . . . And thus this proposition: I

---

defined in the "Institutes" "On the right of persons" para. 1 as "the natural faculty of that which it pleases anyone to do, unless it be prohibited by force or right".'

[96] Tract IV, Q. 54, sig. Lli r: 'Unde notandum quod multa disponuntur in legibus: in quibus dicitur hoc vel hoc non posse fieri: que tamen non disponunt nisi super invaliditate illius facti: sed non propter hoc prohibent illud factum. immo quod plus est econtra nonnulla prohibentur in iure humano: que tamen facta tenent / licet fieri non debuerint.'

[97] Johannes Major [John Mair], *In quartum Sententiarum* (Paris 1519), Distinction 15, Q. 10, fol. 109v.

have *dominium* of this horse, will be equal to this: I am *dominus* of this horse
... Let the same be said about a *usuarius* or a *usufructuarius*. From which it
follows that the *dominium directum* of a certain thing is the *dominium utile* of
another. Secondly it follows: that usufruct is use, and similarly the use of a
thing is the propriety of the same. Which propositions can easily be
deduced in expository fashion: so that it being demonstrated perhaps: here
is the propriety of this horse: and here is the use of this garden; the
conclusion to be inferred from those premisses yields this: use is propriety.[98]

The point appears to be that because relations, for a nominalist, are
none other than the persons or things related,[99] right and *dominium*
coincide in the being of the *terminus*, whereas on a Scotist metaphysics
of relation (such as Summenhart professes) the *termini* would be said
to have two different relations. Mair appears to realise that the point
is not without difficulty, for he reopens the matter at the end of the
Question, dismissing abstract metaphysics 'to some degree' and
affirming that,

Whoever has right in a thing can be said to be the *dominus* of that thing ...
as the usuary has *dominium* of use, and the usufructuary *dominium* of usufruct.
Which is clear from this sign, that if I take a thing from a usuary, I am said
to commit theft, and the injury which is theft. Therefore what I do is to take
away another's thing against the will of the *dominus*; therefore in some way
he is called a *dominus* in an extended sense of the term.[100]

This assertion is taken over almost word for word from
Summenhart,[101] and clearly demonstrates the continuing confusion

---

[98] Major, *In quartum Sent.*, D. 15, Q. 10a, fols. 109v–110r: 'Nominales insectando dicere
oportebit: quod dominium rei, vel est res ipsa vel rem ipsam possidens ... Et sic ista
propositio: ego habeo dominium huius equi: valebit hanc: ego sum dominus huius equi ...
Eodem modo de usuario et usufructuario dicatur. Ex quo sequitur quod dominium
directum alicuius rei est dominium utile alterius. Secundo sequitur. quod usufructus est
usus: similiter usus rei est proprietas eiusdem. quae propositiones facile deduci possunt
expositorie: ut forte demonstrato: hic est proprietas huis equi: et hic est usus huius horti
conclusio inferenda ex illis praemissis hanc infert. usus est proprietas.'
[99] See Ockham's pronouncements on relations in his discussion of the question of God's
relation to his creatures, in Guillelmus de Ockham [William of Ockham], *Quaestiones in II
librum Sententiarum I–XX*, in *Opera philosophica et theologica. Opera theologica V* (St Bonaventure,
N. Y. 1981), Q. 1, p. 9: 'relatio realis nihil aliud positivum dicit reale nisi extrema relata et
non aliquam habitudinem vel rem mediam inter correlativa ... Eodem modo relatio
rationis nihil dicit nisi ipsa extrema relata praecise et nihil quomodocunque medium inter
extrema.'
[100] Ibid., fol. 103v: 'Quicunque habet ius in re potest dici dominus illius rei ... ut usuarius
habet dominium usus. et usufructurarius habet dominium ususfructus. quod patet a signo.
si ab usuario rem auferam, dicor facere furtum, et iniuriam furti. ergo tollo alienum invito
domino. ergo aliquo modo vocatur dominus extenso vocabulo.' Mair acknowledges the
narrow sense of *dominium*, defined as Summenhart defines it.
[101] See above, n. 83. It is not likely to be Mair's mis-statement, as a theologian, of Bartolus
himself, as Seelmann suggests, *Vázquez*, p. 85.

between having *dominium* in a right, and right and *dominium* being equivalent.

The second text that is important for a consideration of sixteenth-century developments is the entry *Dominium* in the alphabetical *Summa summarum* of Mazzolini da Prierio. The 'Summary of summaries' is Mazzolini's own title: he intended it to be a comprehensive handbook of practical moral theology, and he opens by giving a list of his authorities, which include 48 theologians, 113 jurists and 18 Summistae.[102] The entry for *Dominium* constitutes a reply to the *Summa angelica* using Conrad Summenhart, but also a development of Summenhart himself using the *Summa angelica*. The *Angelica* under the entry *Dominium* had failed to make any reference to a wider as well as a narrower sense of *dominium*. Under the entry *Dominium* Mazzolini explicitly contrasts the wide sense of *dominium*, in which '*Dominium* . . . is the same thing as right. So that he who has right in a thing, has *dominium* in the thing; and he who has right in the use of a thing, has *dominium* in that use, and vice versa', with *dominium* as defined by the *Angelica*. But Mazzolini not only posits the wide sense as a sense which is valid for civil law: he refuses to recognise the narrow sense:

I say, that *dominium* according to Thomas [Aquinas][103] . . . always imports potency, so that *dominium* is the same as *posse*, and is twofold just as is *posse*: viz. [firstly] *dominium* or *posse iuris* . . . and this is the same thing as right, and

---

[102] Michaud-Quantin, *Sommes de casuistique*, p. 103. Michaud-Quantin remarks upon the diversity of authors which Mazzolini saw as appertaining to the tradition in which he was writing, and comments, 'Il semble difficile d'en donner une description plus précise que celle-ci: Un sommiste est pour Sylvestre de Prierio (ou tout autre de ses contemporains) un auteur chez qui il rencontre la solution de problèmes de morale pratique tels que ceux qu'il se pose, et auquel il prête des intentions analogues aux siennes . . . Il se confirme par là que cette science de la morale pratique apparait à ceux qui l'enseignent et en écrivent les traités comme une discipline à part qui possède ses spécialistes.' The genres we have been following constitute a specialist literature and their analysis of morality in terms of *dominium-ius* is peculiar to them.

[103] The locus to which he refers is *De potentia Dei*, Q. 7, a. 10, ad 4, where however Aquinas (discussing the name *Dominus*) does not equate *dominium* with *potentia* or anything like it, but distinguishes between potency and the order which follows as a result of it. The passage of Aquinas is quoted in Jaime Brufau Prats, 'La noción analógica del *dominium* en Santo Tomás, Francisco de Vitoria y Domingo de Soto', *Salmanticensis* 4 (1957), 96–136 (now reprinted in J. Brufau Prats, *La escuela de Salamanca ante el descubrimiento del nuevo mundo* (Salamanca 1989), 11–47), p. 107, n. 3: 'Hoc nomen, Dominus, tria in suo intellectu includit, scilicet potentiam coercendi subditos, et ordinem ad subditos qui consequitur talem potestatem, et terminationem ordinis subditorum ad dominum; in uno enim relativo est intellectus alterius relativi.' For further consideration of Aquinas' view of the notions of power and relation and the connection between them, see below, chapter 2, n. 88.

does not pertain to an inferior: so that the son in so far as he has right against his father, is his superior, and acts against him for food.[104]

That the son is not the superior of his father and therefore cannot properly be said to have *dominium* in his father was Summenhart's argument, as we saw, for acknowledging a narrower sense of *dominium*. Mazzolini refuses to accept it: everyone with a right is to that extent a superior.

This does not, however, mean that a right is a freedom. Mazzolini's most important development from Summenhart is to move liberty expressly out of the sphere of right and posit it firmly in the *de facto*. For Mazzolini, apart from *dominium* or *posse iuris*, there is in addition '*dominium* or *posse facti*, and this is twofold, viz. free, and in this sense man alone among inferiors has *dominium* of his actions; and not free, and thus the elements dominate each other in turn'.[105] Man's control of his actions is not a right, because it is not *dominium iuris*: it is *de facto* control. That Mazzolini conceives this human control over actions specifically as liberty is clear from an implicit reference to Angelus' entry (and his own, which is exactly the same) *Liber*, which contains the phrase, 'He does not have free *dominium* over his action, who when he wishes to exercise it, is impeded in some way.'[106] Whereas Summenhart's liberty was a natural right or *dominium* which he was forced to imply operated *de facto* with regard to civic right, thus disturbing his argument that it *is* a civic right or *dominium* and throwing into confusion his carefully constructed

---

[104] Sylvester Mazzolini da Prierio, *Summa summarum quae sylvestrina nuncupatur* (Strasburg 1518), fol. 127v: 'Ego vero dico quod dominium secundum Thomam ... semper importat potentiam. unde dominium est idem quod posse: et est duplex sicut et posse. sc. dominium: vel posse iuris ... et est idem quod ius: nec inferiori convenit: ut sic imo filius ut habet ius in patrem est superior: et agit contra eum ad alimenta.' The term *superior* here appears to bear its hierarchical sense rather than the sense of 'sovereignty': see above, n. 37, for the distinction.

[105] Ibid.: 'dominium vel posse facti: et hoc est duplex. scil. liberum: et sic solus homo inter inferiora habet dominium sui actus et non liberum: et sic elementa invicem dominantur vicissim'.

[106] *Summa angelica*, fol. 181v: 'liberum dominium non habet quis super actum qui quando vult illum exercere impeditur aliqualiter'. For this sense of 'free' as 'unimpeded' the *Angelica* refers the reader to two loci in the commentary of the famous early fifteenth-century canon lawyer Nicolaus de Tudeschis (Panormitanus) on the third book of the Decretals, both of which explicitly elucidate the sense of 'free' as 'not requiring the consent of another', and one of which implies the specific sense of 'unimpeded'. The relevant loci are the commentary on Decretals 3, 18, 2: 'of the signification of this word free, is that there is not demanded the consent of another'; and on Decretals 3, 28, 6: 'it would not be a free burial if it were impeded even for a time. For of the signification of this word "free", is that the consent of no one is required.' See Nicolaus de Tudeschis, *Super tertio decretalium* (Lyons 1534), fols. 135v and 86v.

hierarchy of right, Mazzolini removes liberty entirely from the sphere of right (including natural right) and locates it in the *de facto* along with that *dominium* which is over slaves.[107] Both are free in the sense that they cannot be impeded in their exercise: paradoxically, they share the sphere of the *de facto* with the *dominium* of the wholly necessitated.

Mazzolini's work proved indeed to be the summary to end all summaries. Luther threw the *Angelica* on the fire at Wittenberg in 1520, and the Catholic Counter-reformation never revived the genre in its monumental, juristically elaborate form, concentrating rather on small and increasingly humanistic manuals of personal penitence. Although a literature on contracts continued to survive into the sixteenth century, the day of the commentary on the *Sentences* was also to a large extent over. With one very prominent exception, the Spaniard Francisco de Vitoria who is discussed in chapter 4, the formal equivalence of *dominium* and *ius* disappears from the scholastic discussion of moral theology along with the disappearance of its customary loci.[108]

As we saw, the original equivalence between *dominium* and *ius* in the Franciscan poverty literature did indeed link property and liberty with right as a quality of the rational subject. Liberty is that *dominium* whereby man is made in the image of God and set above irrationals in the neoplatonic hierarchy of *dominia*; it is not negative and indifferent, but a positive dignity of man as a spiritual rather than a natural being. However, the development of the equivalence of *dominium* and right in the casuistic, under strong influence from contemporary study of the Roman law, had two results. Firstly, *dominium* in its aspect as equated with right became diluted in sense to signify a basic notion of juridical hold over another person or object, losing the association with liberty and property which was reserved to *dominium* in a strict sense which was not equivalent to right. Secondly and in parallel, *dominium* became the category of analysis

---

[107] Mazzolini, *Summa summarum*, fol. 127v: 'A *dominus* ... is said to be he who has *dominium* and is divided into the *dominus* by right – viz. he who juridically holds *dominium* – and by fact; and this latter into the free *dominus* – viz. he who is said to be *dominus* with regard to a slave; and the unfree – viz. in regard to that which is susceptible to his action.'

[108] There remain certain isolated survivals of the literature: for example, Martin Ledesma's Commentary on the Sentences, which posits the formal equivalence of *dominium* and right in the traditional locus of Book IV, Dist. 15: Martin Ledesma, *Secunda quartae* (Coimbra 1560).

not merely for spiritual beings but for all nature, which was similarly perceived as a series of *dominia*. Thus *dominium-ius* was confirmed in its distance from any notion of liberty.

The result was a problem over the nature of human liberty, which could not be made to fit into the scheme of the hierarchy of *dominium*-right. The *dominia* or rights of this hierarchy are not negative freedoms of action: they are positive ordinations in a universal scheme which begins with God. Where Summenhart, uniquely in this literature, wanted to introduce a notion of negative liberty, he had to step out of his framework of *dominium-ius*; Mazzolini explicitly removed liberty from the sphere of right. Liberty is not properly a *ius* as *they* conceived it, although – as seen by Summenhart as the liberty of action left over by the laws – it might be coming very close to something that we might want to call a right.

It results from this survey, therefore, that the course of the literature on cases of conscience, and the equivalence of *dominium* and *ius*, did not bequeath to the scholastics of the sixteenth century a language of *ius* as sovereignty or freedom of indifferent choice. This is not to say that it was of no significance in affecting their own language. As we shall see, Francisco de Vitoria took from Summenhart the language of *dominium-ius* as the tool of analysis for social morality. But rather than using it in the sense of the casuistic, or understanding it as an indifferent faculty, he fused it again with the ancient overtones of spirituality, reflexivity and liberty which it had held in the early mendicant discourse, of which Thomas Aquinas himself was a part; and expressly distanced himself from the characteristic development of the casuistic literature, which is the extension of *dominium-ius* to all nature.

2

Our just nature: subjective right in the fourteenth century

In the last chapter we explored a particular tradition of discourse concerning the term *ius* or 'right', in which right was equated with *dominium*. In that discourse, any independent sense of *ius* is absorbed in the sense of *dominium* seen as a relation of control or power. In this chapter we turn to consider the fourteenth-century development of a concept of subjective right, and of subjective natural right, independent of the notion of *dominium*.

The fourteenth century has often been associated with the 'birth' of subjective right because of the work and influence of William of Ockham and his philosophical nominalism. Nominalism and the critique of universal realities have been seen as operating in parallel in metaphysics and in moral and political philosophy, producing works which militate equally against the great philosophical systems of the thirteenth century and against such entities as 'society' and 'the church'. This view has been strengthened by the picture of later mediaeval philosophy as the story of two *viae*, *moderna* and *antiqua*, nominalist and realist, perennially and necessarily at odds with each other, where the latter stands for the grand scholastic tradition and the former for innovation and modern subjectivism.[1]

This traditional picture is now challenged in two ways. Firstly, work has been done on the content of late mediaeval nominalism to suggest that it was not the monolithic and unremittingly destructive movement it has been made out to be.[2] This applies primarily to the fifteenth century, but has implications for the fourteenth. Secondly, the relevance to the fourteenth century of the idea of the quarrel

[1] See the portrait of this traditional view in W. J. Courtenay, 'Nominalism and late medieval religion', in Trinkaus, *Pursuit of holiness*, 26–59, at pp. 26–31.
[2] In particular, the researches of Heiko Oberman have been effective in changing the picture, especially his fundamental work, *The harvest of medieval theology* (Cambridge, Mass. 1963). However, Oberman is only a part of a general revision of perspective; see Courtenay, 'Nominalism and late medieval religion', pp. 32ff.

49

between *viae*, the *Wegestreit*, has been questioned.[3] It is argued that
the fixation with delineating the *Wegestreit* in the fourteenth century
has distorted the history of scholasticism in that period by obscuring
the presence of other philosophical schools, notably the Augustinian.[4] Finally, the practice of characterising fourteenth- and early
fifteenth-century authors as either nominalist or realist has given way
to a recognition of the many intellectual strands which feed into their
work.[5] All of these ideas are current in the history of scholastic
philosophy in general. The present analysis attempts to transfer some
of these insights to the specific history of subjective right.

WILLIAM OF OCKHAM AND THE TRANSFORMATION OF FRANCISCAN DISCOURSE

William of Ockham was once regarded as the source of the doctrine
of subjective natural rights through his elucidation of *ius* as a *potestas*
of the individual.[6] His emphasis on the individual as the source of
right was argued to be the moral and political corollary of his
metaphysical nominalism.[7] Recently, however, with the exposure of

---

[3] See Neal Ward Gilbert, 'Ockham, Wyclif and the "Via moderna"', in *Antiqui et moderni.
    Traditionsbewußtsein und Fortschrittsbewußtsein im spälen Mittelalter* (Berlin and New York 1974),
    85–125.
[4] Ibid., pp. 120–1. In 1925 Franz Ehrle remarked on the key position the Augustinian school
    appeared to hold and suggested that this was the one whose further illumination would do
    most for our assessment of the fourteenth-century scholastic: Franz Ehrle, *Der Sentenzenkom-
    mentar Peters von Candia des Pisaner Papstes Alexanders V* (Münster i. W. 1925), p. 265. But the
    extent and nature of philosophical Augustinianism in the fourteenth century is still not
    enough studied, despite A. Zumkeller's important work, 'Die Augustinerschule des
    Mittelalters: Vertreter and philosophisch-theologische Lehre', *Analecta augustiniana* 27–8
    (1964–5), 167–262, and other works detailed in W. J. Courtenay, 'Nominalism and late
    medieval thought: A bibliographical essay', reprinted in Courtenay (ed.), *Covenant and
    causality in medieval thought* (London 1984), essay XI.
[5] This is particularly true of Jean Gerson; see below, p. 77.
[6] See Georges de Lagarde, *La naissance de l'esprit laique au déclin du moyen âge*, vol. VI, *Ockham: La
    morale et le droit*, 1st edn (Paris 1946), p. 164; Villey, 'La genèse du droit subjectif'.
[7] This thesis, supported by Lagarde and Villey, was widely criticised, for example by J. B.
    Morrall, 'Some notes on a recent interpretation of William of Ockham's political
    philosophy', *Franciscan Studies* 9 (1949), 335–69, who suggests that the linkage between
    Ockham's politics and general philosophy is a product of the neo-Thomist revival (p. 338).
    Such criticism led Lagarde, in a second edition of 1962, to modify his position, retaining
    only the idea that Ockham's political and ecclesiological stances were decisively influenced
    by his logical theory. Nevertheless Michael Wilks in *The problem of sovereignty in the later middle
    ages: The papal monarchy with Augustinus Triumphus and the publicists* (Cambridge 1963)
    consciously adopted Lagarde's first ideas as a 'corrective' to the position of Morrall (pp. 88–
    96, esp. p. 88, n. 1). For the overall fortunes of the notion see H. Junghans, *Ockham im Lichte
    der neueren Forschung* (Berlin and Hamburg 1968), pp. 262–75; for a formal critique of the
    entire project, see C. Zuckerman, 'The relationship of theories of universals to theories of

the language of *ius* as *potestas* in earlier Franciscan tracts,[8] and with
the increased attention now paid to the canonists' subjective usage of
the term *ius*,[9] Ockham has ceased to be regarded as an innovator in
this respect and currently occupies no particular position in the
history of subjective right.

In this section I shall defend the idea of Ockham's originality in his
usage of *ius*. I shall argue that Ockham's understanding of *ius* as a
potestas is not the same as that of the earlier Franciscan literature. *Ius*
in Ockham is integrated into a quite different philosophy of agency,
one which does not use the dichotomy between nature and spirit and
one which therefore need not assimilate *ius* to liberty or to *dominium*
in the strong sense. Ockham develops a notion of subjective natural
right connected with the objectively rational order or law of nature
(the objective *ius naturale*) and based on the Aristotelian categories of
potency and act. As A. S. McGrade has remarked, it is indifferent in
this context that Ockhamist nature is dependent on the divine will.[10]
Rational nature, as it actually is, functions without constant reference
to the liberty of God; and natural morality and right are similarly
independent notions. Because Ockham is, at one level, a voluntarist,

---

church government in the middle ages: A critique of previous views', *Journal of the History of
Ideas* 36 (1975), 579–94. The idea that there is a fit between Ockham's subjective conception
of rights and his logic has, however, recently been defended by A. S. McGrade, 'Ockham
and the birth of individual rights', in P. Linehan and B. Tierney (eds.), *Authority and power:
Studies in medieval law and thought presented to Walter Ullmann on his seventieth birthday* (Cambridge
1980), 149–60; and many scholars are still sympathetic to the idea that there must be some
connection between Ockham's philosophical and polemical activity, for example H. S.
Offler, who writes that 'it would be silly to suggest that around about the year 1328
Ockham's brain underwent some sort of drastic leucotomy' ('The "influence" of Ockham's
political thinking', in W. Vossenkuhl and R. Schönberger (eds.), *Die Gegenwart Ockhams*
(Weinheim 1990), 338–65, p. 345). Studies adopting this approach include J. Miethke's
hermeneutic study of Ockham's thought, *Ockhams Weg zur Sozialphilosophie* (Berlin 1969), and
A. S. McGrade's earlier work, *The political thought of William of Ockham* (Cambridge 1974).

[8] See above, chapter 1. Grossi's work caused Villey to revise his earlier thesis: see M. Villey,
'La promotion de la loi et du droit subjectif dans la seconde scolastique', in Grossi, *Seconda
scolastica*, 53–71, p. 54.

[9] In a series of recent articles, Brian Tierney has argued for the origins of subjective right in
the twelfth-century canonistic. For this view in the context of a critique of Villey's thesis, see
Brian Tierney, 'Villey, Ockham and the origin of individual rights', in J. Witte and F. S.
Alexander (eds.), *The weightier matters of the law: Essays on law and religion* (Atlanta 1988), 1–31,
and 'Origins of natural rights language'. For a detailed consideration of the position of the
latter article, see below, n. 142. See also Tuck, *Natural rights theories*, p. 23.

[10] McGrade, *Political thought of Ockham*, pp. 175–6: 'the issue of God's wilfulness in relation to
natural law is of only marginal bearing on Ockhamist political thought, since Ockham's
appeals to *ius naturale* in his political writings are based on its rationality (in explicit contrast
with positive law). Hence, the possibility that natural law is itself positive at some higher
level is not of direct concern to us.'

it does not follow that this affects his notion of a natural subjective right.

With the promulgation of the bull *Exiit qui seminat* in 1279, the Franciscan Order seemed to have won its battle against the seculars. During the following years it was to be preoccupied with divisions within the Order over the issue of *usus pauper*.[11] For the Franciscan community, one was a pauper if one had nothing: it was indifferent whether one made use of the things of others richly or miserably. The Spiritual wing, in contrast, argued that it was part of poverty to use minimally the things of others. As Grossi pointed out, the Spiritual position completely overturned the metaphysics of the traditional Franciscan view of poverty.[12] But in so doing it did not create a new language of right; moreover, the victory of the community over the Spirituals ensured the absolute imposition of the language of the former.

However, just as the Franciscan Order had weathered the storm over the Spirituals, it faced a new challenge from the very quarter to which it had traditionally looked for defence: the papacy.[13] In 1322 John XXII reopened the debate on Franciscan poverty with the bull *Quia nonnunquam*, going on to condemn the Minorite position in a series of bulls culminating in the *Quia vir reprobus* of 1328, which denounced the *Appeal* (*Appellatio*) of the Franciscan general Michael of Cesena (written from the imperial court after his flight from Avignon in 1328, and directed against the whole series of papal bulls). It was this bull which provoked Ockham, then with Michael at the imperial court, to his hastily penned first contribution to the anti-papal polemic, the *Opus nonaginta dierum* (henceforth *OND*) of c. 1332, a blow-by-blow refutation of the offending *Quia vir reprobus*.

The vituperative, but rambling and repetitive, attack which is the text of the *Quia vir reprobus* (henceforth *QVR*) involves three main

---

[11] The controversy has been examined in detail in many works, but for briefer overviews, see Gordon Leff, *Heresy in the later middle ages*, 2 vols. (Manchester 1967), vol. 1, pp. 51–166; Marino Damiata, *Problema della povertà*, esp. chapter 8 for an account of the Spirituals and their arguments.

[12] Grossi argued that the whole point of Franciscan doctrine was to make an absolute distinction between the subject and the objective, material world. To suggest that poverty involved a material aspect, as the Spirituals did, was to confound the two worlds of subject and object again: '*Usus facti*', p. 345; and see also above, chapter 1, n. 1.

[13] For an account of the persons and texts concerned, Damiata, *Problema della povertà*, chapters 9 and 10.

arguments.[14] The first constitutes an assault on the Franciscan position that Minorites are in a state of absolute poverty because they have no *dominium*: they have nothing which can be called their own, *proprium* or *suum*. John uses the Roman law to argue that in things which are consumed in use – food, drink and vestments being the examples – usage cannot be separated from *dominium*. If, therefore, the Franciscans use things – and they can hardly deny that they eat, drink and clothe themselves – then they have *dominium* of at least these necessary items. Hence they are not absolute paupers.

The second point of John's attack denies the Franciscan claim that because they are absolute paupers with regard to earthly things – they have nothing – they are in the state of perfection in which were the Apostles, who gave up all they had and followed Christ. The pope holds rather that 'the perfection of evangelical poverty consists more in the soul, in that the soul does not cling to those earthly things with love, than in the lack of earthly things'.[15] The emphasis on poverty as a spiritual more than a temporal matter had always differentiated the Dominican defence of poverty from that of the Franciscans, and here the pope – more a lawyer than a theologian – is leaning on Dominican theology with the authority of Aquinas behind it. John does not care to linger long on the point.

Thirdly, John presses his argument with a focus on the notion of using. Michael had posited a distinction between a licence of using and a right of using – the Franciscans having the former without the latter; a distinction which the pope contends is impossible:

that heretic [Michael] will admit that he, to whom a licence of using a certain thing is conceded, uses that thing either justly, or unjustly, or neither justly nor unjustly. If he says that he uses it unjustly, he agrees with the decree in question [John's bull *Quia quorundam*], which intends that he who uses without right, uses unjustly. If he says that he uses justly, it follows in consequence that he does so with right: because what occurs justly, occurs also with right ... But if he says that he ... uses neither justly nor unjustly, this is false. For it is impossible for any individual human act to be indifferent, that is, neither good nor bad, neither just nor unjust. For since an act is said to be human, which proceeds from a deliberation of the will,

[14] The text of the *QVR* is reproduced in sections at the head of each chapter of the text of the *OND*, in J. G. Sikes and H. S. Offler (eds.), *Guillelmi de Ockham. Opera politica*, vols. I and II, 2nd edn (Manchester 1963), 292–858. All subsequent references to the *QVR* apply to the text as given in this edition.

[15] *OND*, Chapter 22, p. 467, 2–4: 'Perfectio siquidem paupertatis evangelicae plus consistit in animo, ut scilicet amore istis temporalibus non adhaereat, quam in carentia temporalium rerum.'

and which in consequence takes place for the sake of a certain end, which is recognised to be the object of the will, it follows that if the end of the act is good, then the act itself is good; if indeed the end is bad, then the act itself is bad.[16]

I have quoted this passage at length because of its vital importance in terms of the progress of the debate. For Michael, the demonstration that the Franciscans have no right is all part of the demonstration that the Franciscans have no *dominium*, have nothing – for the Franciscan position is that *dominium* and right coincide. John knows that if he can demonstrate that the Franciscans have a right, he has defeated their thesis that they have nothing. But this time he does not focus directly on the notion of having a right, but argues backwards from the moral quality of actions. The primary focus is not on *having* but on *doing* – specifically, on *using*. The issue is no longer the question of relation to an external object or person, but the question of subjective action: in answer to which question John draws on canonistic sources to posit the thesis that 'justly : unjustly' equals 'with a right : without a right'.[17] He then expands the point to constitute a more generally moral argument: that the opposition between 'just' and 'unjust' coincides with that between 'good' and 'bad', which exhausts the universe of possible human actions. The debate on Franciscan poverty thus became a debate over human agency.

John's focus on specifically *human* agency was sharply aimed, a point of attack he may well have derived from the formal response (*responsio*) by the Dominican Hervé de Nédellec to the question put

---

[16] Ibid., Chapter 65, p. 573, 1–13: 'iste haereticus dicet quod iste, cui utendi re aliqua licentia est concessa, iuste re illa utitur, aut quod iniuste, aut quod nec iuste re illa utitur nec iniuste. Si dicat quod iniuste, concordat utique cum constitutione praedicta, quae vult quod qui sine iure utitur, utatur iniuste. Si dicat quod iuste utitur, sequitur per consequens quod et iure: quia quod iuste fit, et fit iure ... Si autem dicat quod ille, cui est licentia utendi concessa, nec iuste utatur nec iniuste, hoc falsum est. Impossibile est enim actum humanum individualem indifferentem esse, id est nec bonum nec malum, nec iustum nec iniustum. Cum enim actus humanus dicatur, qui ex deliberata voluntate procedit, et per consequens qui fit propter aliquem finem, qui quidem obiectum noscitur voluntatis, oportet quod si finis actus sit bonus, quod et ipse actus sit bonus; si vero finis sit malus, oportet quod actus sit malus.'

[17] In a recent article, Brian Tierney examines the decretalist origins of John's pronouncement. The source is *Decretales*, 5, 40, 12: 'Ius dictum est a iure possidendo. Hoc enim iure possidetur quod iuste.' Tierney contends that it was John's innovation to interpret a text in which *ius* holds the objective sense of 'law' in the subjective sense of 'a right' in order to challenge the Franciscan case. See B. Tierney, '"Ius dictum est a iure possidendo": Law and rights in *Decretales*, 5. 40. 12', in D. Wood (ed.), *The church and sovereignty, c. 590–1918: Essays in honour of Michael Wilks* (Oxford 1991), 457–66.

forward in the bull *Quia nonnunquam*, of whether it would be heretical to say that Christ and the apostles possessed nothing singly or in common. Nédellec was the general of the Dominican Order and a friend and counsellor of John's.[18] His text in many respects forms an interesting contrast with that of John and shows the extent to which John had moved the debate on by employing argumentative strategies from the canon law. Nédellec's attack is still firmly set within the limits of the thirteenth-century language of poverty elaborated in chapter 1, keeping *dominium* as the axial category. But he makes a point of moral philosophy which John would take up and which Ockham could not disregard. Nédellec's strategy is to accept the old Franciscan dichotomies between *dominium* and poverty, and then to argue that absolute poverty is impossible for a human being as a rational creature.

Nédellec begins by exposing the Franciscan position on absolute poverty faithfully. But he goes on to declare:

> To the contrary is the argument that whoever uses an object, either uses it as his own or as belonging to another. If he uses it as his own, therefore he has a right of some kind in it, because we say 'This is mine', 'This is yours', to the extent that you and I have a right of some kind in that object. But if he uses it as belonging to another, then he acts unjustly, and in consequence just or licit use is inseparable from *dominium*.[19]

The target of Nédellec's attack is one of the foundations of the Franciscan Community's (and hence Michael of Cesena's) position as laid out in their 'Declaration on the subject of poverty in use' of 1309/10, directed against Ubertino of Casale and the Spirituals.[20] Here the Community declares that he who vows poverty 'uses [whatever object he uses] as not his own but as belonging to another'. For the Community, to use a thing 'as another's' is neither

---

[18] Damiata, *Problema della povertà*, p. 325.

[19] Hervaeus Natalis [Hervé de Nédellec], *De paupertate Christi et apostolorum*, ed. by J. G. Sikes, *Archives d'histoire doctrinale et littéraire du moyen âge* 11 (1937–8), 209–97, p. 235: 'In contrarium est quod omnis qui utitur re aliqua, aut utitur illa ut sua aut ut aliena. Si utitur ea ut sua, ergo aliquod ius habet in ea, quia sic dicimus: "Hoc est meum", "Hoc est tuum", in quantum ego et tu habemus aliquod ius in tali re. Si autem utitur ea ut aliena, tunc iniuste agit, et per consequens usus iustus vel licitus est inseparabilis a dominio.' Nédellec is making effectively the same point as John in the passage quoted above, p. 53. But the basic difference is profound, for Nédellec still analyses right action in terms of *dominium*.

[20] The *Declaratio Communitatis super materiam de usu paupere* is edited in A. Heysse, 'Ubertini de Casali opusculum "super tribus sceleribus"', *Archivum Franciscanum Historicum* 10 (1917), 103–74, pp. 116–22.

just nor unjust, for such use is completely extra-juridical. Nédellec sums up their view thus:

> in the case of him, who is capable of use but not of *dominium*, use is separated from *dominium*: but someone can be capable of use and not *dominium*, therefore etc. The major proposition is evident. The proof of the minor is taken not only from children and animals, but even from others, viz. men having the use of reason, because a man through a vow may make himself incapable of *dominium* in things, but no one can make himself incapable of use, for otherwise he would die of hunger and cold, therefore.[21]

But he replies in denying the possibility of extra-juridicality to those capable of reason; the action of one who is capable of the licit and the illicit, the just and the unjust, can never escape the qualification of 'just' or 'unjust', 'nor does it seem to me that anyone ought to make himself incapable [of the just and the unjust] by any vow whatsoever'. It is immoral for a rational creature to make itself like an irrational.[22]

The debate played out in the pages of the *De paupertate Christi et apostolorum* contains the classic features of traditional discourse on poverty: the explicit equation of *dominium* and *ius*; the enormous weight carried by the distinction between *suum* and *alienum*; the comparison of men without *dominium* to animals. John in the *QVR* reformulated Nédellec's attack in terms of personal right and not of *dominium*. *Usus facti* – the thesis of the extra-juridicality of Minorite acts – was attacked as a mode of action rather than as a mode of relation towards external goods. Human beings cannot act neutrally. In the face of this attack the author[23] of the *OND* had two options.

---

21 Natalis [Nédellec], *De paupertate Christi*, p. 235: 'in eo, qui est capax usus et non dominii, separatur usus a dominio, sed aliquis potest esse capax usus et non dominii, ergo etc. Maior patet. Probatio minoris non solum de pueris et brutis, sed etiam de aliis, s. de hominibus habentibus usum rationis, quia homo per votum potest se facere non capacem dominii in rebus, sed nullus non potest se facere non capacem usus, alioquin moreretur fame et frigore, ergo etc.'

22 Ibid., p. 244: 'nec videtur mihi quod aliquis talis debeat se facere non capacem per quodcunque votum iuris'. Cf. Bonagratia's comparison of the Minorite using external goods with a horse eating its oats: above, p. 20, n. 34.

23 The question how far Ockham can be regarded as the 'author', in a strong sense, of the *OND*, is currently debated. In the Prologue to the *OND*, Ockham explicitly asserted that 'since not a few take it upon themselves to attack many of the things asserted in the decree *Quia vir reprobus* ... I have considered that their reasons should be inserted in the present work, so that, once the allegations of both sides have been understood, the truth itself may shine forth more brightly.' This has led to debate among scholars as to how far any of the arguments can be said to be Ockham's own. On the one hand is the persuasion that the author must have a viewpoint which he intends to express in a given work. Lagarde and

He could insist on the synonymity of *ius* and *dominium* and argue the old Franciscan case. Or he could attempt to answer the pope on his own ground, by positing a sphere of human action which is not criminal but not strictly 'right' either. If he chose the former course, he could not adequately respond to the pope's point about action: for the duality of the Franciscan system left him no middle ground to argue for *human* agency without *dominium*. But if he chose the latter, he had to overturn a fundamental constituent of the Franciscan position: for the Minorites had argued that the actions of the Franciscan with regard to temporals are *not* properly human.

Many of the difficulties of the *OND* spring from the fact that Ockham is trying to juggle the two options. Ideally he must posit a theory of human agency which does not undermine the validity of the old Franciscan linguistic formulae, but which can at the same time answer John's ultimate point about moral action. At times the *OND* seems to speak purely the language of the old mendicant tracts.[24] However, it will be my contention that although the old Franciscan linguistic strategies are still present in the *OND*, the

Villey have little hesitation in speaking of 'Ockham' and in attributing the arguments of the *OND* to him as author. Marino Damiata, in his recent major work on Ockham, argues that while the *OND* undoubtedly puts forward the views of the whole group of dissident Minorites at the imperial court, nevertheless the text 'reflects' the thought of Ockham, who has left the 'imprint' of his personality even on a work which may be said to be the *opinio communis* of that group (*Problema della povertà*, p. 397). But on the other hand is the fact that Ockham never departs from the formula 'his [John XXII's] opponents say that ...'. In a recent article Sten Gágner has argued the case for taking Ockham seriously when he declines 'authorship' of given propositions: S. Gágner, 'Vorbemerkungen zum Thema "dominium" bei Ockham', in *Antiqui et moderni*, 293–327. Citing as exemplary Tierney's approach in his article 'Ockham, the conciliar theory and the canonists' (*Journal of the History of Ideas* 15 (1954), 40–70), wherein Tierney exposes the canonist origins of several statements previously unhesitatingly attributed to Ockham himself, Gágner argues that we shall never know what 'Ockham thought' until studies similar to Tierney's have been undertaken over the whole corpus of Ockham's polemic writings.

My own standpoint is that just as the *QVR* uses a number of different arguments against Franciscan poverty, so Ockham in the *OND* employs a series of different argumentative strategies to rebut the pope. There is no reason why we should assume that all these strategies are compatible with each other and form a coherent 'thought' or 'theory' – any more than we must say that the *QVR* constitutes a theoretical unity. It is reasonable to assume that they have different sources. However, my contention is that just as the *QVR*, amid a myriad different legal formulations, makes one very important point concerning human agency, so the *OND*, amid a myriad hackneyed arguments in defence of Franciscan poverty, makes one very important answer. This answer can be shown to feed off other strands of the mediaeval scholastic, and no doubt there are many more than I have recognised. But the strategy of the response belongs to the person who wrote the *OND* – Ockham, who can be said to be the author of the language of rights contained therein.

[24] For example, at Chapter 61, p. 562, lines 158–9, where *ius* is said to be *suum* because it can be stolen and recovered in a court of law.

interest lies in Ockham's response to the implicit challenge of John's equating of the good and the bad with the just and the unjust: that is, John's theory of human agency. Frequently in the course of the *OND*, Ockham affects surprise at John's audacity, as a lawyer – a mere scientist of legislation – in putting forward what was effectively a general theory of human action. But his text acknowledges the shift in the focus of the debate.[25] As we shall see, Ockham draws upon his superior resources as a philosopher to demonstrate the relation of right to the natural agency of Aristotelian science and the moral agency of a Scotist-influenced moral philosophy.

Responding to the need both to protect the old Franciscan arguments and to posit a new theory of agency, Ockham begins his second chapter with a series of definitions of terms, in which his first move is effectively to redefine *usus facti*. *Usus facti* is here defined as 'the act of using an external object, for example to inhabit, to eat, to drink, to ride, to put on clothing and the like';[26] 'every act, which any person may exercise with regard to an external object, such as eating, drinking, dressing, writing, reading in a book, riding and the like, is called use of fact'.[27] (It is further emphasised that when *usus* appears on its own, it too means the simple act of using.) What Ockham does in this definition of use is to isolate something which is the pure activity in itself, the *actus* of natural (Aristotelian) science. But in terms of official Franciscan discourse since the resolution of the *usus pauper* issue, this move constitutes a *redefinition*: because such a neutral act is precisely what is impossible on the theory of the community. If we look again at the community's 'Declaration on the subject of poverty in use', we find them facing the objection that poverty cannot be a purely negative thing, but must have 'a use and an act' (*usus et actus*); and what can be the use and act of poverty, if not 'poverty in use' (*usus pauper*), as the Spirituals have always urged? The response of the community is that the 'positive extrinsic act' of

---

[25] This feature of the *OND* has been remarked by other scholars as the basic weakness of what is overall an unimpressive defence: 'Ockham was fighting on the pope's ground' (Tuck, quoting Gordon Leff, *Natural rights theories*, p. 23). It is more apt to say that Ockham was trying to reground the pope's arguments and to show that that ground did not justify the absolute dichotomy in human agency that the pope was positing. It is not a weakness, but the source of the philosophical importance of the *OND*.

[26] *OND*, Chapter 2, p. 300, 99–100: 'actus utendi re aliqua exteriori, sicut inhabitare, comedere, bibere, equitare, vestem induere et huiusmodi'.

[27] Ibid., p. 301, 122–5: 'omnis actus, quem exercet aliquis circa rem extrinsecam, sicut comedendo, bibendo, vestiendo, scribendo, legendo in libro, equitandi et huiusmodi, vocatur usus facti'.

poverty is to use everything not as one's own but as another's.[28] The act of using is not neutral to the *dominus* and the *pauper*, because the former uses things as his own, the latter as if they are another's. As we saw in chapter I, to treat things as one's own was for the Franciscans equivalent to having the will to dominate them: the Minorite, having surrendered his own proper will, must use things without any act of will. This latter act coincides with *usus facti*: the non-juridical act of him who has no juridical position. *Usus facti* excludes *dominium* and *ius*.

By neutralising *usus facti*, Ockham maintains outward continuity with the Franciscan thesis. He can say, with them, that *usus facti* is separable from *dominium*, because as the pure exterior act of using, it is separable from any personal attribute of the subject.[29] Again, maintaining specious continuity with the Franciscan tradition, Ockham attributes this pure exterior act, neither just nor unjust, to animals, the mad, children: that is, to irrationals.[30]

Ockham does not immediately do anything with his neutralised *usus*. It is not his purpose to equate the purely exterior act with the act of the Minorites in using external goods. Having isolated this act in theory, he is concerned rather to show that the Franciscans' use of fact is *licit* use of fact. In practice, Ockham accepts John's point that there must be something distinctive about an act committed by a rational being: that no rational with the use of reason can commit a morally unqualified act. For the case of rationals, he accepts the dichotomy between licit (morally good) acts and illicit (morally bad) acts. If he is to save the Franciscan case, therefore, he must demonstrate that within the range of licit acts there are both just acts and acts which are not just but which are not unjust either. His response in terms of moral philosophy has two strands.

One strand focuses on the act itself, combining Aristotle's analysis of the just act in *Ethics* v with a basically Scotist analysis of the morally good act in order to deny the simple coincidence between the just act and the good act. In Chapter 60, Ockham puts his case as follows:

---

[28] *Declaratio Communitatis*, in Heysse, 'Ubertini de Casali opusculum "super tribus sceleribus"', p. 119: 'Contra predicta sic obicitur: Sicut frater Minor vovet castitatem, sic et paupertatem; set non est castitas sine usu et actu; set usus paupertatis non potest esse nisi pauper usus ...

Dicendum, quod ... actus voventis paupertatem est nolle in effectu proprium ... Et ad hoc sequitur actus extrinsecus positivus quem habet vovens paupertatem circa quamlibet rem qua utitur, quia utitur re ut non sua set ut alterius.'

[29] *OND*, Chapter 58, p. 551, 114–20. [30] Ibid., Chapter 41, p. 524, 65ff.

Fourthly the *impugnatores* exhibit the difference between just use and licit use. For this distinction to become clear it is necessary to know that the noun 'justice' can be understood in three ways. In one way it is understood as a certain particular virtue distinct from the three other cardinal virtues ... according to which a man acts justly towards another. In the second way, justice is understood as a certain general virtue, which is called legal justice, which ordains all the acts of the virtues to the common good. In a third way, justice is understood as the due ordination of an act to reason or to another operation, and in this sense according to some it is called justice taken metaphorically.[31]

If justice is taken in the first sense (the sense, it is implied, in which John understands it), then 'there are many human acts which are licit and meritorious, but which are not just, such as the acts of chastity, courage, mercy, liberality, and many others'. Similarly in the second sense: for not all virtuous acts are covered by the law which is ordained to the common good. The only sense of justice in which the just act coincides with the licit or morally good act is the third sense (manifestly not the sense John has in mind): 'and in that sense every licit act is just, because it is good and consonant with true reason'. Thus Ockham defends Michael's point that there are acts which are neither just nor unjust in John's sense of 'justice' as civil juridicality, but yet without having to approximate such acts to those of irrationals.

In the above passages, Ockham defines the morally good (licit) act as one that is ordained 'to reason or another operation' and as 'consonant with true reason'. These albeit brief remarks suggest a position on the morality of actions closer to that of Scotus than to Ockham's own conclusions on the subject, or which at least corresponds to only one aspect of Ockham's theory. Scotus had asserted that 'the convergence [convenientia] of the act with right reason is that, to posit which identifies the act as good';[32] 'it is necessary to the

---

[31] Ibid., Chapter 60, pp. 556–7, 119–29: 'Quarto isti impugnatores ostendunt differentiam inter usum iustum et usum licitum. Ad cuius evidentiam est sciendum quod nomen "iustitiae" tripliciter accipi potest. Uno modo accipitur pro quadam virtute particulari distincta ab aliis tribus virtutibus cardinalibus ... secundum quam homo iuste operatur ad alterum. Secundo accipitur iustitia pro quadam virtute generali, quae vocatur iustitia legalis, quae omnes actus virtutum ordinat ad bonum commune. Tertio accipitur iustitia pro debita ordinatione actus ad rationem vel aliam operationem, et ita secundum quosdam vocatur iustitia metaphorice sumpta.'

[32] Johannes Duns Scotus, *Opera omnia*, vol. x, *Quaestiones in primum librum sententiarum a d. 14a usque ad 48am* (Paris 1893), Dist. 17, Q. 3, p. 55: 'convenientia actus ad rationem rectam, est qua posita, actus est bonus'. Scotus' theory of the morality of action is discussed by Etienne Gilson, *Jean Duns Scot. Introduction à ses positions fondamentales* (Paris 1952), chapter ix, pt. iii, 'Volonté et moralité'.

goodness of a moral act, that the complete dictate of right reason should precede it: to which right dictate it should conform as the measured to the measure'.[33] This moral goodness of an act is an accidental quality, 'as if it were some kind of ornament of that act, comprising the sum of its due proportion to all those things to which an act should be proportioned ... according as right reason dictates that they should accompany the act'.[34] It is something over and above the basic substantial act itself.[35]

Ockham had criticised Scotus for placing too much emphasis on the relation to right reason as the essential feature of the morally good act.[36] His own analysis involved the notion that the will must contain rectitude in itself and have right reason for its own object, employing his critique of the notion of relation to combat the reality of Scotus' *respectus ad rectam rationem*.[37] He did not abandon entirely the Scotist terminology of conformity, but insisted that the morally good act is a neutral act performed in conformity with right reason,

---

[33] Scotus, *Opera omnia*, vol. x, *Quaestiones in primum librum sententiarum*, p. 67: 'est necessarium ad bonitatem actus moralis, quod eam praecedat dictamen completum rationis rectae, cui recto dictamini conformetur tanquam mensuratum mensurae'.

[34] Ibid., p. 55: 'ita bonitas moralis actus est quasi quidam decor illius actus includens aggregationem debitae proportionis ad omnia, ad quae debet actus proportionari ... ut ista dicantur a recta ratione debere convenire actui'. Scotus stresses that the relevant right reason is *in* the operating subject: 'si ille [actus] non est secundum rectam rationem in operante, puta si ille non habeat rectam rationem in operando, non est bonus actus' (ibid.).

[35] See Scotus' analysis of acts of the will in the second book of the same commentary, *Opera omnia*, vol. xi, *Quaestiones in secundum librum sententiarum a d. 3a usque ad 14am* (Paris 1893), Dist. 7, Q. unica, 'Utrum mali angeli necessarie volunt male', p. 386. Scotus distinguishes between the natural goodness of an act of volition, and its moral goodness, which has three levels: 'dico quod ultra bonitatem naturalem volitionis, quae competit sibi inquantum est ens positivum, quae etiam competit cuicumque enti positivo, secundum gradum suae entitatis magis et minus, praeter illam est triplex bonitas moralis, secundum ordinem se habens; prima dicitur bonitas ex genere; secunda potest dici bonitas virtuosa sive ex circumstantia; tertia bonitas meritoria, sive bonitas gratuita, sive bonitas ex acceptatione divina in ordine ad praemium'. The *bonitas ex genere* of an act of volition results 'ex hoc quod ipsa transit super objectum conveniens tali actui secundum dictamen rectae rationis, et non solum quia est conveniens tali actui naturaliter ut Sol visioni' (ibid.). The *bonitas virtuosa* belongs to an act of will 'ex hoc, quod ipsa elicitur a voluntate cum omnibus circumstantiis dictatis a recta ratione, debere sibi competere in eliciendo ipsam' (ibid.). The moral goodness of actions in I, 17, 3 thus comprehends both the first and the second of the *bonitates* here enumerated; suggesting that the basic substantial act is seen as naturally good with the goodness that belongs to every thing that is in so far as it is. See also the discussion of this article in A. Wolter, *Duns Scotus on the will and morality* (Washington, D. C. 1986), 48–51.

[36] See Miethke, *Ockhams Weg*, p. 308.

[37] For Ockham on relations see above, p. 44, n. 99. The principal locus for the critique of Scotus' notion of rectitude as a relation is Quodlibet III, Q. 15, 'Utrum rectitudo actus et deformitas differant a substantia actus' (edited in *Quodlibeta septem*, vol. ix, *Opera theologica* (St Bonaventure, N. Y. 1980), 257–62). For the will which must have right reason as its object, see p. 260. The doctrine is analysed by McGrade, *Political thought of Ockham*, pp. 189–96.

not a neutral act plus conformity to right reason.[38] In the *OND*, however, Ockham concentrates, like Scotus, on the simple conformity of the act to right reason. His redefinition of *usus facti* as the pure *actus* in existence as an act corresponds to the neutral act (hence the importance for him of revising the old Franciscan understanding of the term); *licitus usus facti* is this basic act which is in conformity to right reason – the morally good act. In this strand of his reply, therefore, Ockham draws on a basically Scotist moral philosophy to respond to the arguments of the pope concerning good and bad human action.

In his other strand, however, Ockham develops the notion of a right as a subjective potential of human action. It is here that his originality becomes clear. After concentrating on the licit act, he introduces the notion of a licit potential. As the licit act of the first strand is based on the Aristotelian notion of an act, qualified as consonant with right reason, so Ockham in the second uses the Aristotelian notion of potential for an act to base a concept of a licit power. This licit power is what Ockham will argue a right to be.

If we go back to the series of definitions which opens the work, we see that Ockham's second definition, after that of *usus facti*, is that of *usus iuris*, which is said to have various significations as to its precise extent. However, 'In whatsoever way "usus iuris" might be taken, it is always a right of some kind, and not an act of using ... [the term] "iuris" is added to differentiate from "usus facti", which is an act.'[39] Thus a right is something which is not an act or an actuality. This is confirmed when Ockham moves on to his fourth definition, that of *ius utendi*. 'Fourthly they explain what is the right of using, saying that the right of using is a licit power of using an extrinsic object, of which no one should be deprived against his will without culpability on his part and without reasonable cause; and if he should be [so] deprived, he can bring an action against the person who deprives him in

---

[38] See William of Ockham, *Quaestiones in librum tertium sententiarum (Reportatio)*, in *Opera theologica*, vol. VI (St Bonaventure, N. Y. 1982), Q. 11, pp. 386–8; and Quodl. III, Q. 15, p. 261: 'rectitudo actus non est aliud quam ipse actus qui debuit elici secundum rectam rationem'. Ockham distinguished between acts which are necessarily virtuous, and acts which are contingently virtuous, the latter being capable of being first upright or good and then morally vicious, or vice versa, according to whether they are accompanied by an act of the will following right reason (pp. 259–60).

[39] *OND*, Chapter 2, p. 302, 149–54: 'Qualitercunque ergo accipiatur usus iuris, semper est ius quoddam, et non est actus utendi ... additur autem "iuris" ad differentiam usus facti, qui est actus.'

court.'[40] A right is a form of power in the Aristotelian sense of a potential for an action. Against the jurists, Ockham argues that the right of using necessarily belongs to all those who have any right in anything whatsoever: 'The right of using ... belongs to him who has pure use[41] and also to him who has usufruct, and not only to them, but it often belongs to him who has "dominium" and the property of a thing.'[42] The *ius utendi* is thus the basic juridical attribute justifying personal activity.

The *ius utendi* is, then, as Villey rightly stressed in his early articles, a subjective power of action. It is not a relation of control over things, as was *ius* for the earlier Franciscans. Moreover, the category of a licit power directed towards action gives Ockham the genus for his two definitions of *dominium*. Ockham replaces *dominium* with right as the axial analytic category: '*dominium* is the principal human power of vindicating and defending a temporal thing in a human court'; more precisely, '*dominium* is the principal human power of vindicating a temporal thing in court, and of treating it in every way, which is not prohibited by natural law'.[43]

---

[40] Ibid., p. 302, 155-7: 'Quarto exponunt quid est ius utendi, dicentes quod ius utendi est potestas licita utendi re aliqua extrinseca, qua quis sine culpa sua et absque causa rationabili privari non debet invitus; et si privatus fuerit, privantem poterit in iudicio convenire.'

[41] The term here is *usus nudus*, which signifies the right of use alone, i.e. as distinct from usufruct, which is the right of using and enjoying the fruits thereof. *Usus nudus* is what is possessed by the *usuarius*, whereas *ususfructus* belongs to the *usufructuarius*. It is important to be clear that *usus nudus*, being a juridical entity, and thus a right or power, is distinct from *usus facti*, which is the pure act of using.

[42] *OND*, pp. 174-6: 'Ius ergo utendi competit habenti usum nudum et etiam habenti ususfructum, et non solum illis, sed saepe competit habenti dominium et proprietatem rei.'

[43] Ibid., Chapter 2, p. 306, 320-1: 'Dominium est potestas humana principalis vendicandi et defendendi in iudicio rem aliquam temporalem'; and p. 308, 391-3: 'Dominium est potestas humana principalis rem temporalem in iudicio vendicandi, et omni modo, quod non est a iure naturali prohibitus, pertractandi.' The general definition of *dominium* is probably taken from Chapter 12 of Discourse II of Marsilius of Padua's *Defensor pacis*: '[dominium] significat stricte sumptum potestatem principalem vendicandi rem aliquam ... que siquidem *ius* alicuius dicitur, quoniam iuri primo modo dicto conformis' (*Defensor pacis*, ed. by R. Scholz (Hanover 1932), p. 270, para. 13). Marsilius' 'first sense' of right is the sense in which it is identical with *lex* in its proper sense as the command (*preceptum*) of the legislator. *Dominium* as a power in accordance with *lex* is a species of right in Marsilius' second sense: 'Dicitur autem ius secundo modo de omni humano actu, potestate vel habitu acquisito, imperato, interiori vel exteriori, tam immanente quam transeunte in rem aliquam aut in rei aliquid, puta usum aut usumfructum, acquisicionem, detencionem seu conservacionem aut commutacionem ... conformiter *iuri* dicto secundum primam significacionem' (p. 269, para. 10). Although Marsilius therefore appears to be the source for Ockham's positing of *dominium* as a species of subjective right, it is nevertheless clear that Marsilius thinks of subjective *ius* in a very different way. For Marsilius, this *ius* is primarily an act (all his examples are of actions), whereas for Ockham, this would exclude it from the category of

Ockham thus characterises *ius* or subjective right as a *potestas licita*, not a *potestas iusta*. In his treatment of *actus*, as we saw, he had been very careful to distinguish between the just and the licit – this was his whole point. An act can be licit without being strictly just. But in treating of *potestas* the just and the licit are wholly confused. This confusion comes to the fore in his treatment of *ius naturale*.[44]

In Chapter 61, Ockham divides *ius utendi* into natural and positive.[45] Positive *ius utendi* is *ius utendi* as we have seen it defined above. It is a '*licit* power', *potestas licita*, but it is clearly strictly just in the sense of juridical. It is what the Minorites *lack*. However, this strict juridicality applies not only to human positive rights, but also to the natural right of using, which 'is common to all men, because it is held by nature, and not by any subsequent convention'.[46] No human being can be without this right: 'the life of mortals cannot be without natural right, because no one can renounce such a right'.[47] However, although every person has this right all the time, he does not have it *at* all times: he only has it in practice at the time of extreme necessity, when on the authority of this right he may use anything that he needs to sustain his life.[48] That this natural right is a right in the same strong sense as a positive right is clear from the fact that Ockham, for one particular circumstance, allows the argument

---

ius. Marsilius' account of *ius* belongs in fundamentals to the Aristotelian analysis as developed by Gerald Odo and John Buridan (Marsilius and Odo were contemporaries at the University of Paris between 1313 and 1315), stretched to include *dominium* as a *potestas*, whereas Ockham's is an entirely new strategy. For Odo and Buridan, see below, chapter 3, pp. 97–102.

[44] See W. Kölmel, 'Das Naturrecht bei Wilhelm Ockham', *Franziskanische Studien* 35 (1953), 39–85, pp. 43–4. According to Kölmel, Ockham uses the term *ius* both for 'positive, streitbare Rechtsatzung' and for the simple 'Fähigkeit, ein Verzehrgut zu verbrauchen, eine: "potestas licita utendi"'. He consequently argues that the term *potestas* must change its sense from its use in the phrase *potestas licita utendi* to its use in the phrase *potestas principalis vendicandi . . . rem* (the definition of *dominium*), asserting that in the latter it means not mere 'Fähigkeit' but 'Gerichtsfähigkeit'. He concludes that it is inconsistent that Ockham calls the *potestas licita utendi* a *ius* at all: 'Deshalb bleibt die Definition Ockhams als "potestas licita utendi" als "ius aliquod utendi" reichlich verschwommen.' My account of the confusion is slightly different: Ockham equivocates not over the word *potestas* alone, but over the whole phrase *potestas licita utendi*: the fundamental equivocation being over the term 'licit'. But I am in agreement that in its second sense (as the power possessed by a Minorite) it does not mean what Ockham says that he means by *ius* at all.

[45] *OND*, Chapter 61, p. 559, 34–5: 'ius utendi est duplex. Quoddam enim est ius utendi naturale; aliud est ius utendi positivum.'

[46] Ibid., p. 559, 36–7: 'Ius utendi naturale commune est omnibus hominibus, quia ex natura, non aliqua constitutione superveniente, habetur.'

[47] Ibid., Chapter 60, p. 556, 93–4: 'iure enim naturali non potest carere vita mortalium, quia tali iuri nullus renuntiare potest'.

[48] Ibid., Chapter 61, p. 559, 37–44.

that the Minorite brothers must have some kind of right in what they use, because they have a natural right.[49] He holds that at a time of extreme need, the brothers do have a right of use like anyone else – the natural right of use. But, given that the Minorites are not permanently in a state of extreme necessity, they have no such right of use in the things that they use at other times, but only a *licentia utendi*, which is not a *ius* in any sense: 'The brothers have a licence of using things for times other than that of extreme necessity; but they have no right of using whatsoever except in a time of extreme necessity; therefore a licence of using is not a right of using.'[50] Outside extreme necessity they use things by licence, not by right, not even by natural right. To argue otherwise would be to concede the pope's point.

Thus Ockham uses the term *potestas licita* for right in the strict sense, be it natural or positive (both of which the Minorites, outside extreme necessity, *lack*). But it is clear that he also wants to use the notion of *licita potestas utendi* as the power by which Minorites use things outside extreme necessity. We should expect him, therefore, to develop a second understanding of the term as the power to perform an *actus licitus* or *consonans rationi rectae* (which the Minorites *have*) – a power which would be not strictly just, but only licit. And these expectations appear to be fulfilled as, in Chapter 4, he asserts that 'for use of fact to be licit, the general licit power of using is sufficient ... the general licit power of using, is the power of using, which God after or before the Fall gave to the whole human race in the persons of our first parents ... with the existence of such a power of using, use of fact can be licit'.[51] 'If, therefore', Ockham goes on, 'there should be some consumable thing, which is in no one's *dominium*, the general power of using suffices for this, that someone should licitly use it, if there is no other impediment.'[52]

Ockham elaborates on this 'general power' in Chapter 14. According to Ockham in this chapter, God in creating man gave him two things. Firstly, he gave him *dominium* over all the other creatures

---

[49] Ibid., p. 561, 116–33.

[50] Ibid., 130–7: 'Fratres habent licentiam utendi rebus pro alio tempore quam pro tempore necessitatis extremae; sed non habent quodcumque ius utendi nisi pro tempore necessitatis extremae; ergo licentia utendi non est ius utendi.'

[51] Ibid., Chapter 4, p. 333, 197–202: 'quod usus facti sit licitus, sufficit licita potestas utendi communissima ... licita potestas utendi communissima est potestas utendi, quam Deus in primis parentibus post peccatum vel ante toti humano generi dedit ... stante tali potestate utendi, potest usus facti esse licitus'.

[52] Ibid., 203–5.

of the world. Ockham is careful to stress, against John, that this was not any kind of proprietorial right over the rest of creation, but rather the power of ruling and governing it without encountering its resistance. Secondly, God gave to man and to all other animals a power of using certain things.[53] While original *dominium* was lost with the Fall, whereupon man had to subdue the world by force, the power of using external objects remained with him.[54]

As we have seen, according to Ockham in Chapter 4 this power makes use of fact licit. However, Ockham is principally concerned not with the situation of using unclaimed objects – the Minorites do not wander around the world, making use of things that belong to no one – but with the situation that the Minorites are actually in by law, that of using goods which belong to others and have been placed at their disposal. The problem for him is to explain why a Minorite can licitly use things which belong to others, but a thief cannot.[55] Ockham's response is that in the case of the thief, there is an impediment to the power of using of such goods – viz. the fact that they belong to another – which is what makes his action illicit.[56] He specifies, however, that in the case of extreme necessity there is no impediment for anyone.

The problem with this response is that the power to use goods in extreme necessity is, by Ockham's own argument, the strict *ius naturale*. It *justifies* such use, it does not make it merely *licit*. Hence if, outside extreme necessity, the Minorites through the licence of the owners use the goods of others by the same power that they would use such goods without such licence in extreme necessity, then that use takes place by right – it is *justified* – and is not simply use of fact.

The same problem is abundantly clear in Chapter 65, where Ockham, by way of clarification, introduces a further two categories *ius poli* ('right of heaven') and *ius fori* ('right of the forum').[57] For

---

[53] Ibid., Chapter 14, p. 432, 92–4: 'Praeter istud autem dominium, fuit data ipsis [primis parentibus] et animantibus terrae potestas utendi quibusdam rebus determinatis'; p. 433, 125–6: 'illa enim potestas data fuit aliis animalibus, quibus non fuit datum dominium'.

[54] Here in Chapter 14 this power is described simply as *potestas utendi*, and is common to all animals: by emphasising this latter characteristic, Ockham is stressing its *natural*ness and its distance from any power, such as the power of ruling the rest of creation, which belongs only to the *spiritual* state of original innocence. But in Chapter 4 this power is described as *licita potestas utendi*, belonging only to the human race: here, by contrast, Ockham is pursuing his main strategy of reply to John, which – as we saw above – turns on the recognition of a distinction between human and animal activity.

[55] Ibid., Chapter 4, p. 334.   [56] Ibid.

[57] The distinction is Augustine's, incorporated by Gratian into the *Decretum* (C. 17, Q. 4, c. 43). The notion of *ius poli* was appealed to in the text of the *Exiit* and in Ubertino of Casale's

Ockham these are categories of both objective and subjective right. In the objective sense, *ius fori* is 'the just thing, which is constituted out of an explicit pact or ordinance human or divine', and *ius poli* 'natural equity, which without any human or even purely positive divine ordinance is consonant with right reason, whether it be consonant with purely natural right reason, or with right reason understood from those things, which are divinely revealed to us'.[58] In the subjective sense, '*ius poli* is nothing other than a power conforming to right reason; *ius fori* is a power originating in an agreement, sometimes conforming to right reason, sometimes not'.[59] *Ius poli* – objective or subjective – includes both *ius naturale* ('every natural right pertains to *ius poli*'), and *ius divinum* (because it includes further all things that are consonant with revealed right reason).[60]

Subjective *ius poli* is thus the *potestas licita* which corresponds to the *actus licitus* of the first strand of Ockham's reply to the pope: a *potestas consonans rationi rectae*. But it is also clear throughout these passages that Ockham assimilates *ius poli* to *ius naturale* as the power by which all individuals can make use of things in the state of extreme necessity.[61] It is enabled to be actualised in an act of using by the

---

response to the *Quia nonnunquam*, which had asserted that Christ and the apostles 'had temporal goods by natural right, which by some is called the *ius poli*, for the sustaining of nature'. The passage is quoted in Miethke, *Ockhams Weg*, p. 369, n. 83.

[58] *OND*, Chapter 65, pp. 573–4, 40–1: 'iustum, quod ex pactione seu ordinatione humana vel divina explicita constituitur'; p. 574, 76–9: 'aequitas naturalis, quae absque omni ordinatione humana et etiam divina pure positiva est consona rationi rectae, sive sit consona rationi rectae pure naturali, sive sit consona rationi rectae acceptae ex illis, quae sunt nobis divinitus revelata'. The equivalence between *ius poli* and *aequitas naturalis* is found in the *Glossa ordinaria* to C. 17, Q. 4, c. 43 (Miethke, *Ockhams Weg*, p. 480, n. 182), the author of which, Johannes Teutonicus, had also connected *aequitas naturalis* with the *ius naturae* (see below, p. 86, n. 142). *Aequitas naturalis* is implied to constitute the second mode of objective *ius naturale* at *Dialogus*, III, II, iii, 6 (text reedited in H. S. Offler, 'The three modes of natural law in Ockham: A revision of the text', *Franciscan Studies* 37 (1977), 207–18): 'Aliter dicitur ius naturale, quod servandum est ab illis, qui sola equitate naturali absque omni consuetudine et constitutione humana utuntur.' This is the *ius naturale* which orders human actions after the fall but still in the pre-political state, which is clearly the sense required for the *OND*. See McGrade, *Political thought of Ockham*, 177–85 for a sensitive analysis of the *Dialogus* text.

[59] *OND*, Chapter 65, p. 579, 273–6: 'Ius autem poli non est aliud quam potestas conformis rationi rectae absque pactione; ius fori est potestas ex pactione aliquando conformi rationi rectae, et aliquando discordanti.'

[60] Ibid., p. 575, 80–1.

[61] Ockham's amalgamation of *ius poli* and *ius naturale* in Chapter 65 is clear from such phrases as 'naturale et poli' (line 229); 'ius poli sive naturale' (line 231). See the discussion in Miethke, *Ockhams Weg*, pp. 491–3 and n. 221.

licentia of the *dominus*, which removes the prohibition on using things that belong to others outside the state of extreme necessity.[62]

Thus Ockham in the end has no clear reply to the pope, for he has failed to isolate a *potestas licita* which would be a power to perform acts which are licit in the sense of consonant with right reason, but not strictly just. However, despite the fact that the understanding of a *potestas* consonant with right reason as a (natural) right does not quite serve Ockham's purposes in the *OND*, this notion would be enthusiastically taken up at the beginning of the new century by the French theologian Jean Gerson to define right in general. His target in so doing was those who exploited Ockham's notion of subjective right to support the notorious thesis that *dominium* is founded in grace: Richard Fitzralph and John Wyclif.

SUBJECTIVE RIGHT AND ONTOLOGICAL STATUS: 'JUST BEING'
IN THE AUGUSTINIANISM OF RICHARD FITZRALPH
AND JOHN WYCLIF

With the *De pauperie salvatoris* of Richard Fitzralph, bishop of Armagh, written between 1351 and 1356, the debate on mendicant poverty reached its culmination.[63] Fitzralph, originally an Oxford theologian of moderate Augustinian tendencies,[64] was resident at Avignon and moving in the circles of the papal curia from 1337, where anti-mendicant sentiment was still vigorous and where he could have encountered the *OND* as a specific target of attack.[65] Here he would certainly have come into contact with the theory of papal plenitude of power based on the thesis that *dominium* is founded on justifying grace, most famously associated with the Augustinian

---

[62] *OND*, p. 578, 218–27.

[63] See James Doyne Dawson, 'Richard Fitzralph and the fourteenth-century poverty controversies', *Journal of Ecclesiastical History* 34 (1983), 315–44, for the mid-fourteenth-century anti-mendicant sentiment in England and Avignon, and for details of the continuing controversy over the ecclesiastical status – and, particularly, the privileges – of the friars after the death of Ockham in 1349. For a detailed account of the life and writings of Fitzralph, see K. Walsh, *A fourteenth-century scholar and primate: Richard Fitzralph in Oxford, Avignon and Armagh* (Oxford 1981).

[64] See Leff, *Richard Fitzralph, Commentator of the Sentences: A study in theological orthodoxy* (Manchester 1963), and Walsh, *Fitzralph*, pp. 51ff. for a more positive assessment of Fitzralph's theological merits.

[65] It appears for example that the curialist Lawrence of Arezzo in the 1340s knew of it: see Offler, '"Influence" of Ockham's political thinking', n. 96.

Giles of Rome.[66] This doctrine had been used again in 1325 by William of Cremona to attack Marsilius of Padua.[67] William's work is probably the direct source of Fitzralph's ideas.

The *De pauperie salvatoris* consists of seven books, the first five asserting the thesis that *dominium* depends on grace, the last two attacking the privileges of mendicant friars. The nature of the connection between the two parts has long been debated.[68] What seems certain, however, is that the dialogue engages directly with the *OND*, criticising that work's separation of original *dominium* from the natural right of using, and then going on to ground original *dominium*, and therefore the right of using, in grace.

Fitzralph opens this work with the argument that to consider poverty as a state of privation, we must first discuss that of which it is a privation, namely, wealth or *dominium*.[69] The first *dominium* is that of God, from which all other *dominia* descend. God is *dominus* because he created, governs and preserves all things: 'all things are of him, and through him, and in him'.[70] As *dominus* of all, God is in the position of giver towards his creatures: God gives his essence, that creatures might be (*essent*); his goodness, that they might be good; his power, that they might be powerful; his beauty, that they might be beautiful; his life, or rather him being life – *immo se vitam* – that they might live. To sentient creatures he communicates himself as sense, to rationals as reason; and to dominant rationals he communicates *dominium*.[71]

In the second book Fitzralph considers *dominium humanum*. He takes as his starting point the first book of Genesis, where God gives

---

[66] See Walter Ullmann, *Mediaeval papalism: The political theories of the mediaeval canonists* (London 1949), chapters IV and V, for the origins of the doctrine; Wilks, *Problem of sovereignty*, for Giles of Rome and the papal publicists. A. Gwynn, *The English Austin friars in the time of Wyclif* (Oxford 1940), part II, chapter 4, suggests the importance of Fitzralph's stay in Avignon in the development of his ideas.

[67] The *Refutatio* or *Reprobatio errorum*, dated by Wilks to 1327 (*Problem of sovereignty*, p. 558), by Gwynn to 1325 (*English Austin friars*, pt. II, 4).

[68] Aubrey Gwynn (*English Austin friars*) suggests that the two discussions are connected by the thesis that through the abuse of their privileges, the mendicants have lost any right to them in the face of God. Walsh (*Fitzralph*) thinks of the work as partly an exercise in clarifying the author's own thoughts (p. 388), and argues that Fitzralph composed the first five books as a papal publicist in Avignon, and the last five as a practical administrator in his diocese of Armagh. Dawson, however, argues that the aim of the work is to reconcile the two sides in the quarrel over poverty. He finds that Fitzralph accepts the Minorite thesis of a natural *dominium* distinct from civil *dominium*, and that the thesis of *dominium* dependent on grace is irrelevant to Fitzralph's main argument. But this does not explain the amount of space Fitzralph devotes to developing that thesis.

[69] Fitzralph, *De pauperie salvatoris I–IV*, ed. by R. Lane Poole as Appendix to Wyclif, *De dominio divino* (London 1890), Book I, Chapter I.

[70] Ibid., Chapter IV.   [71] Ibid., Chapter XX, pp. 309–10.

man *dominium* over the things of the earth, and his analysis forms a reply to Ockham's corresponding discussion in *OND*, Chapter 14. Fitzralph defines Adam's *dominium* as 'the mortal right or original authority of possessing naturally things by nature subject to him in conformity with reason, and of fully using or treating them'.[72] He carries over from Ockham both *ius* as the genus of *dominium* and the notion of conformity with reason, but, unlike Ockham, he treats the right of using as part of original *dominium*. The natural power of man to use the rest of creation cannot be separated from his superiority as a rational, whereby he is *dominus* and made in the image of God.

Fitzralph expands his critique in elucidating the terms of the definition. When John goes on to ask why Richard used the word 'authority' or 'right', Richard replies that

Authority or right pertains only to a rational creature; power or faculty belongs to irrationals of their first institution; since, in accordance with the words of Genesis quoted above, "That they might be to you as food, and to all the animals", the animals of the earth ... have in their natural way a congenital and irreprehensible faculty.[73]

This is the passage used by Ockham in Chapter 14 of the *OND* to distinguish the natural *potestas utendi* from the *dominium originale* of Adam. In this chapter, Ockham refers only to 'power' and not to 'right', and suggests that this power belongs equally to humans and to other animals (even though when referring to the situation after the Fall, he consistently speaks of the natural *right* of human beings to use the rest of creation, and never credits animals with right as opposed to simple power).[74] Fitzralph in reply distinguishes human from animal use from the outset. Humans have an authority or right to do what animals only have a power to do.

Animal power is 'congenital' and 'of their institution': there cannot be an animal without this power. Similarly, the right which is original *dominium* is said to be essentially consequent on 'our just nature'.[75] The nature of man was created by God just, that is, in a

---

[72] Ibid., Book II, Chapter II, p. 335 : 'Videtur ita posse describi, quod Ade dominium fuit racionalis creature mortale ius sive auctoritas originalis possidendi naturaliter res sibi natura subiectas conformiter racioni, et eis plene utendi sive eis tractandi.'

[73] Ibid., Chapter IV, p. 338: 'Auctoritas seu ius soli racionali convenit creature; potestas sive facultas irracionabilibus competit ex sua institucione primaria; quoniam iuxta supra posita verba de Genese, *Ut sint vobis in escam, et cunctis animantibus*, animalia terre ... suo naturali modo habent congenitum irreprehensibilem facultatem.'

[74] See above, p. 66 and n. 54.

[75] Fitzralph, *De paupere salvatoris*, Book II, Chapter V, p. 340.

state of justifying grace.[76] Quoting Genesis i. 26–8 to the effect that God created man in his image and likeness, Fitzralph distinguishes between *ymago*, which signifies man's 'conformity of nature', and *similitudo*, which signifies his 'conformity in virtue', which latter includes justice (in the sense of grace). He argues that God saw that his creation was very good: 'but who can say that a man is very good and perfect, who does not possess charity, which is the bond of perfection ... ?'[77] At first sight this appears a Thomist point: grace is the perfection of man's nature. But Fitzralph's argument is in fact the other way round: the nature of man is to be perfect, that is, in a state of grace. He who is not in a state of grace or charity, through mortal sin, does not properly have the nature of man: 'Adam in disobeying lost all the virtues which he had, and even his rational soul, which he bound over to death, which truly is called perdition ... in sinning he incurred the first death of body and similarly of soul, whose life is God.'[78] Human nature is just nature, or it simply is not; and that inherent justice is the title of all human *dominium*.

Fitzralph's overall position is clear, but his language of justice and right is to some extent confused. He had generally held that *dominium* was a species of *ius*, so that *ius* itself cannot be a title of right or *dominium*:[79] the title to original *dominium* is rather original justice. However, he was capable of referring to right as the cause of *dominium*[80] and to rights and *dominia* as accruing 'by right or title extrinsically acceding',[81] so that right is the ground or foundation of *dominium* and tends to coincide with justice itself. This latter notion was taken up by Fitzralph's notorious successor in the argument concerning *dominium* and grace, John Wyclif.[82]

---

[76] Ibid., Chapter vi.

[77] Ibid., Chapter vii, p. 346: 'Si enim cuncta opera Dei in suis gradibus fuerunt valde bona, sic homo erat valde bonus in sua specie, ut in suis speciebus cetere creature: set quis potest dicere hominem valde bonum aut perfectum, qui non possidet caritatem, que est vinculum perfectionis ... ?'

[78] Ibid., Chapter xi, p. 353: 'Adam omnes virtutes quas habuit perdidit delinquendo, et animam racionalem similiter, quam obligavit ad mortem eternam, que veraciter perdicio appellatur ... eciam peccando incurrebat mortem primam corporis et anime similiter, cuius vita est Deus.'

[79] Ibid., Book iii, Chapter iii, p. 384.   [80] Ibid., Book i, Chapter xxvii, p. 321.

[81] Ibid., Book ii, Chapter v, p. 340.

[82] For a brief summary of Wyclif's career, see Leff, *Heresy*, vol. ii, pp. 494–500; A. Kenny, *Wyclif* (Oxford 1985), 1–5. How significant was the doctrine of *dominium* founded on grace for Wyclif's overall theory of authority, and the precise nature of the relationship of his work to that of Fitzralph, has been debated: see M. Wilks, 'Predestination, property and power: Wyclif's theory of dominion and grace', in G. J. Cuming (ed.), *Studies in church history*, vol. ii (London and Edinburgh 1965), 220–36; Leff, *Heresy*, vol. ii, p. 548, who argues

Wyclif's ideas are elaborated in the *De dominio divino* and the *De dominio civili*, which constitute the third book of his theological *Summa*, written in the late 1370s. Defining *dominium* in the *De dominio divino*, Wyclif, unlike Fitzralph, is prepared to contemplate at least a sense in which *dominium* can be predicated of irrationals and inanimates: 'according to the natural philosophers, every corporeal agent holds itself in *dominium* over its related passivity'.[83] However, 'more strictly and more pertinently to the mind of a political theorist [politici], a rational nature which holds preeminence over something subject to it, is said to be its *dominus*'.[84] Thus *dominium* is formally defined as 'preeminence with regard to ruling free acts', and as such it pertains to rationals alone: 'it does not follow from the fact that irrationals have the use of edibles that they have *dominium* over them'.[85]

This *dominium* falls into the category of relation (*relacio*): 'for "master" and "slave" (from the "Categories" and "Metaphysics" v) are said with regard to something, and in consequence that by which they are formally said to be these things is a relation'.[86] Wyclif stresses that as such, *dominium* is distinct from *ius*. 'For a man can have the same right to possess a thing without *dominium* of it, as he has having obtained *dominium*.'[87] *Dominium* is not the right, but presupposes the right as its foundation (*fundamentum*). It follows, Wyclif continues, that 'power' (*potestas*) is not the genus of *dominium*. For a power is independent of the existence of another being, whereas *dominium* depends for its existence on the existence of a

---

that Wyclif, unlike Fitzralph, treated the whole question of *dominium* as a moral question of justice. As we have seen, however, justice and the moral life was central to Fitzralph's argument as well.

[83] *De dominio divino libri tres*, ed. by R. Lane Poole (London 1890), Book I, Chapter I, p. 2: 'Sic enim secundum naturales omne agens phisicum se habet in dominio ad suum passum.'

[84] Ibid., p. 4: 'Strictius tamen et magis pertinenter menti politici dicitur natura racionalis que preest sibi subdito, eius *dominus*.'

[85] Ibid.

[86] Ibid.: 'quoad genus dominii, patet quod sit relacio ... nam dominus et servus (ex Predicamentis et quinto Metaphisice) dicuntur ad aliquid, et per consequens illud quo formaliter dicuntur huiusmodi est relacio'.

[87] Ibid., Chapter II, p. 8: 'Ex istis patet error quorundam putancium quod dominium dictum formaliter sit ius aliquod vel potestas. Nam homo potest habere idem ius ad rem possidendam cum privacione eius dominii; quod ius habebit nacto dominio.' Wyclif inveighs against the error of those who confuse the two, admitting however that '*dominium* is sometimes taken formally, as in the description ... above; sometimes causally or materially, for the subject or foundation or terminus of formal *dominium* ... For everyone who talks about *dominium* says that it is in general terms one of these four, viz. the relation, or the subject dominating, or the right in which *dominium* is founded, or the thing possessed': Chapter I, p. 6.

dominated. It is rather right which is assimilated to power as the foundation of *dominium*.[88]

Opening the *De civili dominio*,[89] Wyclif's first priority is 'to see if civil *dominium* presupposes natural *dominium* founded in grace'. He answers that it does: 'no one in a state of mortal sin has justice *simpliciter* to the gift of God ... whoever exists ultimately in a state of justifying grace does not merely have a right to, but in their substance *has* all the gifts of God'.[90] The state of substantively having, or *dominium*, presupposes a right to, or justice to, what is had.

Justice is to be in grace; and to be in grace is the only true being, 'because since [man] has being out of pure grace, in which being he is bound by the law of nature to continue in grace, when he loses the rule of this law, he does not remain a creature or possessing anything except equivocally'.[91] The mode of one's being determines the mode of one's possession: 'The sinner possesses things only in that way, in which he is, but howsoever he is, he is unjustly, therefore howsoever he possesses, he possesses unjustly.'[92] This is so because sin infects nature: if the life and thus the being of a man is unjust, then so is his every other operation, even sleeping or eating. Even his having body, soul, organs and all his other natural assets is unjust, on the Augustinian principle that 'sin is nothing and when they sin, men become nothing'.[93]

Grace or justice – justifying grace – is therefore the foundation of

---

[88] Ibid., pp. 8–9. This is a purely Thomist account of the category of relation. Every relation is founded on a potential which is distinct from that relation. The potential or power is part of the substance of an entity, which every relation presupposes; see Aquinas, *Summa theologiae* (*ST*), 1a, Q. 13, a. 7 in corp.: '*dominium* presupposes power, which is the divine substance'. The classic example of a relation founded upon a potential, which Wyclif uses, is fatherhood (*paternitas*); see Aquinas' discussion at *ST* 1a, Q. 16, a. 5: 'Utrum potentia generandi significet relationem, et non essentiam'. For an exhaustive account of the concept of relation in Aquinas and later Thomists, see A. Krempel, *La doctrine de la relation chez Saint Thomas* (Paris 1952).

[89] *De civili dominio*, ed. by R. Lane Poole (London 1885), Chapter 1.

[90] Ibid., Chapter 1, p. 1: 'oportet in primo videre si civile dominium presupponat dominium naturale fundatum in gracia ... Intendo itaque pro dicendis ostendere duas veritates ... prima, quod nemo ut est in peccato mortali habet iusticiam simpliciter ad donum Dei; secunda, quod quilibet existens in gracia gratificante finaliter nedum habet ius, sed in re habet omnia bona dei.'

[91] Ibid., p. 3: 'quia cum habet esse ex pura gracia, quo esse tenetur ex lege naturae continuare in gracia, dum perdit regulam huius iuris non manet creatura vel quidquam possidens nisi equivoce'.

[92] Ibid., p. 2: 'Peccator solum illo modo quo est possidet, sed qualitercunque est, iniuste est, ergo qualitercunque possidet, iniuste possidet.'

[93] Ibid., p. 3: 'Et inter alia hoc movet Augustinus, super Ioannem omelia prima, quod "Peccatum nihil est et nihil fiunt homines cum peccant." '

dominium, the *ius ad rem*, the prior disposition which is the necessary condition of subsequent *dominium*. This worthiness or justice is that by which a creature merits 'the kingdom and the grace of final perseverance': for 'no one can merit anything if he does not have a right to it'.[94] The full sense of 'right' in Wyclif is therefore merit, claim, worth or title: coinciding with grace, it is the creature's very mode of being or ontological status. Outside grace, there is only primary being (*esse primum*) and the natural good (*bonum naturae*). The just alone have secondary perfection (*perfeccio secunda*) and the good of grace (*bonum gracie*).[95]

Wyclif had discussed the themes of worth and merit in the *De dominio divino*. There he argued that on account of its retractability, every gift from God to a creature is in fact a loan.[96] That loan is the creature's possibility of acting meritoriously; and because this possibility is dependent on God, merit can never be condign but only congruent. A creature merits *de congruo* by serving God,

> and not in any way whatsoever in naturally wanting what is simply good, but by a deliberate act of will ... For a stone and every created substance naturally desires its own being, and in consequence to be good; nor from this sort of affection, since it is purely natural, is it to be morally praised or blamed. But, presupposing natural praise from the naturally good, a free creature, eliciting an act of the will, must rise up delighting in primary justice, and then merit and moral goodness follows natural goodness.[97]

The basic terms are taken from Scotus' analysis of the morality of acts of will in his consideration of whether evil angels necessarily will evilly,[98] where the natural goodness of such an act is distinguished from its moral goodness. But whereas Scotus had then distinguished within morally good acts of will between the *ex genere* good, the virtuous and the meritorious, Wyclif treats the class of morally good acts as coincidental with the meritorious.

The elision of the sphere of natural morality coincides with the elision of that of natural justice. Replying, in the *De civili dominio*, to the argument that sinners at God's pleasure have as much *esse* as the

---

[94] Ibid., Chapter II, p. 15: 'nemo meretur aliquid, nisi habuerit ius ad illud'.
[95] Ibid., p. 11.   [96] *De dominio divino*, Book III, Chapter IV, pp. 225–6.
[97] Ibid., p. 234: 'nec quomodolibet naturaliter volendo bonum simpliciter, sed volicione deliberativa ... Nam lapis et omnis creata substancia appetit naturaliter suum esse, et per consequens esse bonum; nec ex affeccione huiusmodi, cum sit pure naturalis, est laudanda moraliter nec culpanda. Sed presupposita laude naturali ex bono nature debet creatura libera, acto voluntatis elicito, insurgere prima iusticia delectando, et tunc sequitur meritum ac moralis bonitas naturalem.'
[98] See above, n. 35.

righteous, and therefore similarly at his pleasure possess external goods with as much justice as the righteous,[99] Wyclif responds by making a further distinction, between the senses of justice: 'for that which is just actively is one thing, but there is another which is just extrinsically or passively'.[100] In the first way, only that is just which has formally within it the virtue of justice. A thing can have this form either essentially (and the only thing of this kind is God), or accidentally, as do rational creatures existing in a state of grace. But in the passive mode of justice, all creatures are just, 'since the being, the just and the good are convertible *simpliciter*'.[101]

That being and the good are convertible is a doctrine in which both Aristotle and Augustine concurred and was a commonplace of the scholastic. But that these two are also convertible with *iustum* is something which Wyclif had to argue: 'Justice, which naturally and *per se* is consequent on [the existence of] a creature, is the goodness by which a creature conforms to the will of the first principle.' Since it is the will of the first principle – God – that every creature be (otherwise it would not be), 'every being ordained by God to be, is just to be'; 'every work of the primary Justice, which he continually fashions according to the exemplar of his volition, will be just'.[102] A just being is that which justly is; and as such, every creature is just. On this level, the just and the unjust are equally men and equally just; but it is, again, merely the natural justice of the stone. Nor does this justice constitute the *ius ad rem* which is the foundation of *dominium*: for the mode in which 'bits of wood and stones and other insensates' have their goods is merely *naturalis habicio*, natural having, and not any kind of *dominium*.[103]

Wyclif's work thus develops and elaborates Fitzralph's elucidation

---

[99] *De civili dominio*, Chapter III, p. 16.

[100] Ibid., p. 17: 'aliquid enim est iustum active, et aliquid ab extrinseco vel passive'.

[101] Ibid., p. 18: 'Secundo modo est omnis creatura iusta, cum ens iustum et bonum simpliciter convertuntur.'

[102] Ibid., p. 18. Wyclif is using the Augustinian principle that evil is convertible with that which entirely is not; anything which in any way is must be good. 'So that just as every bad nature is good (as is clear in Enchiridion 9 [Augustine, *Enchiridion*, XI, para. 4]), so too every unjust nature; because the actively unjust is the passively just, inasmuch as it is the work of the primary Justice: and therefore let it be conceded that as much the just as the unjust has, according to the primary existence of a creature, univocally as much the body as the soul, along with any other natural [being]': p. 19.

[103] Ibid., pp. 20–1: 'Cum enim quelibet creatura racionalis habet potestatem datam sibi ad habendum, optimo modo habendi in genere, quidquid habet; patet quod est multum culpandus si abutiur sua potestate, quiescendo in habicione pure naturali, ut habent ligna vel lapides aut alie creature insensibiles bona sua.'

of the distinctive quality of properly human actions through the notion of justice understood as grace and as ontological status. While the context of the poverty controversy and of the *ius utendi* has been left behind, Wyclif remains firmly within the same tradition of Augustinian discourse, with its underlying (if distorted) Scotism and its consideration, in defining the human, of the status of other levels of life: not the animals of Genesis, here, but the wood and stones that are the lowest level of natural life, and properly *nichil* with respect to real *esse*. As for Fitzralph, truly to be is to be in grace, and grace is right.

SUBJECTIVE RIGHT AND THE RESTABILISATION OF NATURAL BEING: AUGUSTINE, ARISTOTLE AND OCKHAM IN JEAN GERSON

The last section examined the appropriation of Ockham's terminology of subjective right to the Augustinian language of personal justice. The context was polemical and the positions extremist. However, parallel with the violent discourse of the publicists and polemicists, we find a tradition of Augustinianism at the universities, which owes little to Giles' notorious ideas about *dominium* and grace, and much to his theoretical work as a pupil and a critic of Thomas Aquinas. This pervasive moderate Augustinianism, combined with the ideas of Aquinas, Scotus and Ockham – the 'eclecticism' of the fourteenth and fifteenth centuries – could in the end find a reply to the extreme Augustinianism of Fitzralph and Wyclif on its own terms in the moral theology of Jean Gerson.

Born in 1363, Jean Gerson was the student of Pierre d'Ailly at the College of Navarre from the year 1387, succeeding d'Ailly as chancellor of the university in 1395.[104] He continued in close association with d'Ailly, active with him within the nascent conciliar movement and playing an important part at the Councils of Pisa and Constance. But he was also active as a preacher at Notre Dame, writing a large number of sermons and involved in pastoral care. In both of these capacities he strenuously opposed the doctrines of Wyclif and Hus.[105]

[104] For details of Gerson's life, see Johann Baptist Schwab, *Johannes Gerson, Professor der Theologie und Kanzler der Universität Paris* (Würzburg 1858). Schwab's remains the basic study of Gerson's life and works. See also J. B. Morrall, *Gerson and the great schism* (Manchester 1960), pp. 1–16.

[105] Gerson's opposition to Wyclif is suggested as a motive force for Gerson's doctrine of rights in the *De vita spirituali animae* by B. Tierney, 'Conciliarism, corporatism and individualism:

There is little doubt among historians of subjective right that Jean Gerson is a major figure in their story. This certainty has been partly produced by the later scholastic itself. For Domingo de Soto, for example, Gerson is the prime object of his critique for his errant doctrines of right.[106] Whether the second scholastic is regarded as recreating an essentially Thomist, objective doctrine of right, or on the contrary as perpetuating a subjective concept, attention has been focused on Gerson as a critical figure in the development of subjective rights.

Most of these interpretations – sixteenth-century and modern – are due to the distorting influence of Conrad Summenhart and his *Septipertitum opus*. They depend on the idea that Gerson assimilated *ius* to *dominium* as Summenhart said he did. They also rely on the familiar picture of later nominalism as subjective and destructive of rational order. However, not only has this picture been superseded in recent scholarship, as we have seen, by a more subtle picture of the movement; in addition, the characterisation of Gerson as a 'nominalist' – however defined – is no longer firm. Gerson tends now to be seen as drawing on several different strands of the late fourteenth-century theological heritage.[107]

This acknowledgement of eclecticism is highly relevant to the question of interpreting the *De vita spirituali animae*. This is the work in which Gerson sets out his elaboration of right most completely, and has been read equally as nominalist (in the tradition of d'Ailly), as Thomist and as a work of mystical theology – part of the same intellectual enterprise as his *De mystica theologia speculativa* and the

---

The doctrine of individual rights in Gerson', *Cristianesimo nella storia* 9 (1988), 81–111, pp. 102–5 and 107.

[106] See below, p. 149. As I shall argue, the critique was more properly directed against Summenhart.

[107] See the apposite remarks of D. Catherine Brown, *Pastor and laity in the theology of Jean Gerson* (Cambridge 1987), p. 79: 'Although he has most often been referred to as a nominalist, in both the older and the newer senses, Gerson has also been called anti-Occamist, realist, voluntarist, Bonaventurian, Augustinian, Thomistically inclined, and eclectic, while his mysticism has been labelled as Gersonism by one commentator.' She suggests that we join Gordon Leff in characterising the fourteenth and fifteenth centuries as marked by 'heterogeneity and consequent eclecticism' – enabling us to accept that different features of Gerson's texts may appear to have different or even opposing doctrinal sources. See G. Leff, *The dissolution of the medieval outlook: An essay on intellectual and spiritual change in the fourteenth century* (New York 1976), pp. 12–13; and see also Morrall, *Gerson and the great schism*, p. 20, who describes Gerson's system as 'something of a mélange', resulting from his desire to teach to his age 'the basic Christian truths of faith and practice' and his opposition to *vana curiositas* into things divine.

Notulae super quaedam verba Dionysii de caelesti hierarchia. In considering the issue, the detailed work on the precise nature of Gerson's mysticism undertaken by André Combes is illuminating.[108] Combes insists that Gerson's mystic theology is distinct from, and moreover an implicit critique of, the Netherlandish mysticism of Ruysbroeck and his *De ornatu spiritualium nuptiarum.*[109] Ruysbroeck suggested that the union with the divine – the return to God – which is the consummation of human being and the object of mystical meditation, is an evanescence and an absorption of man into the divine essence. For Combes, Gerson by contrast holds that the creatures return to God through the realisation, not the annihilation of their being (although properly speaking it is only man who effects the return by knowing and loving the rest of creation).[110] Combes stresses the Aristotelianism inherent in Gerson's interpretation of Dionysius.[111] Gerson's commentary on the *De Caelesti hierarchia* takes as its starting point Albert the Great's commentary on the same text, which interprets Dionysius' emanationism via the Aristotelian concept of the analogy of being, neutralising the essential Dionysian notions of descent and inferiority. This fusion of Pseudo-Denys with

---

[108] André Combes, *Jean Gerson commentateur dionysien. Les 'Notulae super quaedam verba Dionysii de Caelesti hierarchia'. Texte inédit* (Paris 1940). Combes regards the influence of d'Ailly and Ockhamism on Gerson as slight from the beginning. While James L. Connolly, *Jean Gerson: Reformer and mystic* (Louvain 1928), emphasised mysticism as the dominant note of Gerson's theological activity in his middle and later period, Combes (p. 427) argues that Gerson already by 1400 had dropped any direct concern with Ockhamist theses. As a Dominican and an admirer of Gilson, Combes' work takes on something of the character of a rehabilitation of a hero from the slur of being marked as a nominalist. See the apposite remarks by Christoph Burger, in his *Aedificatio, fructus, utilitas: Johannes Gerson als Professor und Kanzler der Universität Paris* (Tübingen 1986), part I, 'Zum Forschungsstand', on Gersonian scholarship in general and on Combes in particular. Despite the qualifications that must be imposed on Combes' conclusions, they appear to illuminate the enterprise of the *De vita spirituali animae* better than the account of the early Gerson as nominalist and mystic given by Oberman, *Harvest of medieval theology*, pp. 331–40.

[109] Combes argues that Gerson only began constructing his own system of mystical theology *after* coming into contact with Ruysbroeck's mysticism (*Gerson*, p. 451).

[110] 'L'homme, par ses opérations naturelles de connaissance et d'amour, est chargé de consommer le retour universel': Combes, *Gerson*, p. 438, citing in connection a passage from Gerson's *Sermo de die Jovis sancta* of 23 March 1402: 'Ab hoc igitur esse ydeali illud recte perhibetur egredi quidquid fit extrinsecus in esse suo reali, regredi autem non nisi creature rationali proprie datum est, quamquam velit Boecius omnia in suum regredi principium … Hoc fit dum motus inditos naturae suae custodiunt dumque vices indultas peragunt agendo paciendo movendoque.' See the discussion of Gerson's mysticism and the sermon 'A deo exivit' in S. Ozment, *Homo spiritualis: A comparative study of the anthropology of Johannes Tauler, Jean Gerson and Martin Luther* (Leiden 1969), pp. 49–58.

[111] See Combes, *Gerson*, p. 437: 'sa métaphysique comporte un physicisme aristotélicien où les natures sont conçues comme douées d'une permanence de soi indestructible'.

Aristotle is vital to Gerson's understanding of subjective rights. While remaining fundamentally within an Augustinian neoplatonic ontological framework, the peripatetic tradition with its emphasis on the real solidity of nature and its analysis of that nature in terms of power and act gives him the element he needs to combat the negativity of Fitzralph and Wyclif and to reincorporate Ockham's analysis into the discourse of right.

The *De vita spirituali animae* (henceforth *DVSA*), consisting of six lectures beginning from a text of Mark, is an early work of Gerson's, written in 1402.[112] In the opening Lectio, Gerson considers the Augustinian themes of sin and death familiar from Fitzralph and Wyclif. Positing four lives and four corresponding deaths of the soul (the natural, and the three stages of the life in grace), he says: 'We call the life of nature in the soul the purity of its essence with the integrity of its potencies.'[113] To the life of nature belong also gifts of God *gratis data*, that is, which do not bestow merit. But the 'death of nature' occurs 'through its total annihilation, or by the removal of those things which are due to its nature, or by the immission of contrary habits prohibiting the free exercise of this life, of which kind is original sin which is called the tinder of death'.[114]

This passage appears to be purely Augustinian: lack of grace destroys nature.[115] But Gerson in the *DVSA* in the end rejects the extreme Augustinianism which denies man any moral virtue outside grace. 'Let us add ... that it is impossible for the soul living the natural life alone, to effect its salvation ... But I do not want to deny that the soul might of its natural life act morally well, and, doing

---

[112] I have throughout used the edition of Palémon Glorieux: *Jean Gerson. Oeuvres complètes* (Paris 1961–), vol. III, *L'oeuvre magistrale*, pp. 113–202. For criticism of Glorieux's edition, see Burger, *Aedificatio*, pp. 7–9.

[113] *DVSA*, p. 115: 'Vitam naturae in anima dicimus puritatem suae essentiae cum integritate suarum potentiarum.'

[114] Ibid., p. 116: 'Nam est mors naturae quae fit seu per annihilationem ejus totalem, seu per immissionem contrariorum habituum prohibentium liberum exercitium hujus vitae, quemadmodum est peccatum originale quod fomes mortis dicitur.'

[115] This is paralleled in Gerson's other works, particularly in the sermons. A favourite passage of his is Ps. 48, 13: 'Et homo, cum in honore erat, non intellexit: comparatus est iumentis insipientibus, et similis factus est eis.' Human nature has bent down to animal nature; the soul has become curved, *anima curva, incurvata*, losing its original *rectitude*. See Louis B. Pascoe, *Jean Gerson: Principles of church reform* (Leiden 1973), chapter 6, section 3, 'Sin and the image'; Ozment, *Homo spiritualis*, pp. 67–8. In a recent work, Mark S. Burrows argues that this Augustinianism grew more severe in Gerson's writing after the Council of Constance: see Mark S. Burrows, *Jean Gerson and 'De consolatione theologiae' (1418)* (Tübingen 1991), esp. chapter 5.

what is in its power to do, dispose itself for the life of grace.'[116] While
Gerson's theology appropriates Augustinian language and moves
within the same realm of discourse, his position on nature with
regard to grace reflects the conviction of the positive ontological
stability of the world which marks his interpretation of Dionysius.

As the first Lectio continues, Gerson leaves the discourse of
scriptural and Augustinian rhetoric to return to a Scotist mode of
analysing the morality of external acts and of acts of the will. 'It is
probable that no act of a creature is *per se* and intrinsically good with
the goodness of morality or merit, or similarly bad, except with
respect to the divine reason and will';[117] 'all moral rectitude of the
very will results from its conformity or the conformity of its acts or
omissions to the divine law and its right reason'.[118] However, whereas
Scotus had specified that the relevant right reason inhered in the
agent subject, and Ockham in his analysis of *actus* had been unspecific,
Gerson argues that the right reason in question is the right reason of
God. This potentially allows all creatures, both rational and irrational,
moral goodness of action by way of 'conformity'. But Gerson escapes
this consequence by introducing differentiation into the notion of
'conformity': 'In the same act multiple rectitudes and goodnesses can
be concurrent: one of nature, another of morality *de genere*, another of
grace, another of glory; and this is according to the diverse modes of
considering that act to conform in multiple ways to the divine law or
goodness.'[119] Conformity with the divine will and reason is not the
exclusive quality of moral action. Although (as becomes clear in the
third Lectio) Gerson is here considering human acts alone, his divorce
of 'conformity to right reason' from specifically moral action will serve
him in attributing right to all creatures.[120]

---

[116] *DVSA*, pp. 116–17: 'Addamus rursus dicentes quod impossibile est animam sola vita
naturali viventem, operari salutem suam … Nolo tamen negare quin anima possit ex sua
vita naturali bene moraliter agere et, faciendo quod in se est, se ad vitam gratiae
disponere.'

[117] Ibid., pp. 123–24: 'Probabile est nullum actum creaturae de per se et intrinsece, esse
bonum bonitate mori aut meriti, aut similiter malum, nisi per respectum ad divinam
rationem et voluntatem.'

[118] Ibid., p. 124: 'Omnis rectitudo moralis ipsius voluntatis resultat ex conformitate ejus aut
suorum actuum vel omissionum ad divinam legem et ejus rectam rationem.'

[119] Ibid., p. 125: 'In eodem actu possunt concurrere multiplices rectitudines atque bonitates:
una naturae, alia moris de genere, altera gratiae, altera gloriae; et hoc est secundum
diversas habitudines considerandi eundem actum conformari multipliciter divinae legi seu
bonitati.' Gerson makes the Ockhamist point that there is no diversity in God and his laws,
but it is simply that we conceive the divine law differently according to God's different
relations to his creatures.

[120] Typically, Gerson also expresses his point in the Augustinian neoplatonic phraseology of

Having considered the moral quality of actions and the nature of law, Gerson moves on in the third Lectio to consider the subject of *ius*. 'We were hastening to respond to the principal issue by means of one sole conclusion after these explanations of terms; but a subject very close to the one we have been treating has claimed our attention and turned our steps aside.'[121] This subject is 'what is right', and its affinity with the subject of law is clear in Gerson's definition of the term: 'right is an immediate faculty or power pertaining to a thing according to the dictate of right reason. And thus the entire and final resolution of our subject ends at the dictate of right reason.'[122] As we saw, right reason is central to Gerson's elucidation of law; for Gerson, individual rights are consequent upon the law that governs those individuals.

Going on to elucidate the terms of the definition, Gerson confirms his assertion that his central concept is right reason: rights are being considered as a subset of 'things pertaining according to the dictate of right reason': ' "Faculty or power" is set down [in the definition], because many things pertain to individuals according to the dictate of right reason, which are not said to be their rights, like the penalty of the damned, and the punishments of those *in via*; for we do not say that someone has a right to his harm.'[123] Penalty, *poena*, was habitually considered in discussing the problem of evil, as in Gerson's *Notulae*: 'evil is tempered within the order of the universe as a whole. Note here that penalty is just in the way that evil is just.'[124] Within the overall order of the universe, penalty, like evil, is just – a just thing – but it is not a *right*. 'However it is not wholly alien to Holy Scripture that the things which divine providence ordains, be called rights, just as in I Kings it says that this will be the right of the king

Fitzralph and Wyclif. Just as conformity to 'the divine law and its right reason' yields the rectitude of the will, so 'nothing is true, nothing beautiful, nothing powerful, nothing desirable except in so far as they conform to the primary truth and beauty and power and sweetness ... the goodness of creatures and their truth and beauty and like things are not anything greater, with respect to intensity, together with God than God by himself ... It is clear therefore that in him we live, move and are': ibid., pp. 124–5.

121 Ibid., p. 141.

122 Ibid.: 'jus est facultas seu potestas propinqua conveniens alicui secundum dictamen rectae rationis. Itaque totalis et finalis resolutio materiae nostrae ad dictamen rectae rationis terminatur.'

123 Ibid.: 'Ponitur "facultas seu potestas", quoniam multa conveniunt secundum dictamen rectae rationis aliquibus quae non dicuntur jura eorum, ut poena damnatorum, et punitiones viatorum; non enim dicimus aliquem jus habere ad ejus nocumentum.'

124 Gerson, *Commentateur dionysien*, ed. by Combes, p. 31: 'malum contemperatur in ordine tocius universi. Hic nota quomodo malum iustum est pena est iusta.'

etc. And we say that demons have a right to the punishment of the damned.'[125] Gerson is clearly uneasy with the idea that demons, irreparably evil and therefore for whom nothing can be to their good, should be said to have a right in the strict sense of a faculty or power. The punishment of the damned is in no way to the advantage of the demon, who is equally condemned. It is closer to the ordination of God, the just thing, than to the positive right.

Gerson's next point refers to the same underlying issue. ' "Immediate" is set down because many things can pertain to an individual according to the dictate of right reason which according to the same dictate *de facto* do not pertain to him, as a person existing actually in mortal sin has the power or faculty of meriting eternal life, but not immediate.'[126] The term 'immediate' (*propinqua*) is familiar precisely from Scotus' discussion of whether damned angels have the power to will the good.[127] According to Scotus,

if the question is understood to concern that power, which is the differentiation of being – i.e. which is ordained to action – then it can be conceded [that they do have] with regard to a remote power ... but not with regard to an immediate power: because the former does not issue in an act unless all the impediments have been removed.[128]

Demons are,[129] and therefore they have some differentiation of being: but that being is so compromised by evil that the positive power for the realisation of their good has receded.

Gerson goes on to explain the term 'right reason' in the definition. He had previously emphasised that 'right reason and its dictate is firstly originally and essentially in God',[130] but 'participatively' in rational creatures alone. The language is very close to that of Thomas Aquinas in his treatise on the laws, where the participation

---

[125] *DVSA*, p. 141: 'Tamen non est penitus alienum a Scriptura Sacra quod ea dicantur jura quae divina providentia sapienter ordinat, sicut I Reg. dicitur quod hoc erit jus regis, etc. Et daemones dicimus habere jus ad punitionem damnatorum.'

[126] Ibid., pp. 141–2: 'Ponitur "propinqua" quoniam multa possunt alicui competere secundum dictamen rectae rationis que secundum idem dictamen de facto ei nequaquam conveniunt, ut existens actualiter in peccato mortali habet potestatem seu facultatem merendi vitam aeternam, non tamen proprinquam.'

[127] See above, p. 61, n. 35, and p. 74 for Wyclif's use of Scotus.

[128] Scotus, *Opera omnia*, vol. XI, *Quaestiones in secundum librum sententiarum*, Dist. 7, Q. un., p. 393: 'Si autem intelligitur de potentia quae est differentia entis, quae scilicet ordinatur ad actum, concedi potest de potentia remota ... non tamen potest concedi de potentia propinqua, quia illa non exit in actum nisi amotis omnibus impedimentis.'

[129] This is a tenet common to the entire scholastic, being derived from Ps.-Denys (*De divinis nominibus*, cap. 2): *manent naturalia*, what is natural to demons remains.

[130] *DVSA*, p. 141.

of rational creatures in the eternal law is the natural law.[131] Gerson goes on to speak of the higher part of reason in man as *synderesis*, which was often, especially in the early canonist texts, assimilated to the natural law or natural right. This latter assimilation is the basis of the recent suggestion that Gerson's theory of right should be placed in the tradition of the twelfth-century canonists, inspired by the humanist renaissance of that century, who saw subjective natural right as the faculty by which the soul discerns what is right.[132]

Whatever may be the case with Gerson's notion of natural right – which we shall consider below – there are difficulties in placing his notion of *ius* in general wholly within this tradition:

> Let us say therefore that every positive being has as much right thus generally defined as it has of being, and thus of goodness. In this way the sky has a right to rain, the sun to shine, fire to warm, the swallow to build its nest, and moreover whatsoever creature in all that which it can do well with its natural faculty. The reason for which is evident: since all such things pertain to them according to the dictate of divine right reason, otherwise they would never survive. Thus even the man who is a sinner has a right to many things and other creatures defective in their natures.[133]

Ius, per se, belongs not only to rationals, but to every creature in so far as it is. It is not a cognitive faculty but a potential for specific

---

[131] Aquinas, *ST* 1a2ae, Q. 91, a. 2. But the proximate source may be rather Henry of Langenstein, a close friend of Henry of Oyta: 'lex naturalis racionis volens perfectum dictamen est quodammodo exemplum vel transcriptio divine legis rationali creature participative communicata' (cited in W. Kölmel, 'Von Ockham zu Gabriel Biel. Zur Naturrechtslehre des 14. und 15. Jhdts', *Franziskanische Studien* 37 (1955), 219–59, p. 236, n. 79). Kölmel argues that we should read 'the law of natural reason willing the perfect dictate' rather than 'the natural law willing the perfect dictate of reason' – and thus that we are not here considering the natural law as such – on the basis of another formulation of Langenstein's: 'dictamen recte rationis naturalis vel legi naturaliter ei indite, et illa lex est ymago vel transcriptio quedam illius legis eterne'. This does not make obvious sense; it is possible that the dative *legi* is a misreading for the genitive *legis*, yielding 'the dictate of natural right reason or of the law naturally inherent in it [right reason]', on the authority of a citation in the same article from Henry of Oyta, 'quedam sunt leges naturaliter rationem indite, que sunt regula et mensura prima omnium actuum humanorum. Et hec dicuntur ius naturale que nunquam deficiunt' (p. 232, n. 67). Whatever the case, it appears that the close-knit group of Oyta, Langenstein and Gerson think of the dictate of natural human right reason as the natural law and part of the human cognitive faculties.

[132] Tierney, 'Origins of natural rights language'.

[133] *DVSA*, p. 142: 'Dicamus ergo quod omne ens positivum quantum habet de entitate et ex consequenti de bonitate, tantundem habet de jure sic generaliter definito. In hunc modum coelum jus habet ad influendum, sol ad illuminandum, ignis ad calefaciendum, hirundo ad nidificandum, immo et quaelibet creatura in omni eo quod bene agere naturali potest facultate. Cujus ratio perspicua est: quoniam omnia talia conveniunt eis secundum dictamen rectae rationis divinae, alioquin nunquam perstiterent. Sic homo etiam peccator jus habet ad multa sicut et aliae creaturae naturis suis derelictae.'

action – and it is in thus defining right that Gerson is able to make his point against both Fitzralph and Wyclif.[134] As we saw, Fitzralph had corrected Ockham by separating 'right or authority' from 'faculty or power', animals having merely the latter. Gerson in turn corrects Fitzralph: faculty or power is right. Wyclif had said that being, the just and the good are convertible, but only in the second mode of justice, which is the passive mode. Everything is just – has justice – in so far as, in simply existing, it inevitably conforms to the divine will; but only the predestined are just – have justice – in the active mode, which is right and title to all the things of the earth. In defining right as a potential for action, Gerson responds that all creatures, of their nature, are actively just, or have positive rights.

Thus, where Wyclif had combined the language of goodness, being and justice, but banished the term 'power', Gerson reinstates this latter element. Ockham is his obvious source. And yet, as we have seen, Gerson goes far beyond Ockham in his elaboration of the fundamental nature of a right. Ockham combined the language of right with that of power understood in its Aristotelian sense as a potential for action, but he did not make the connection with being. The source of that connection is the tradition which Gerson does *not* share with Ockham and d'Ailly, the Augustinian neoplatonism common equally to Fitzralph and Wyclif, combined with his own peculiar Aristotelianised mysticism derived from Albert the Great. That this is the case receives strong confirmation from a passage of Albert quoted by Combes in a different connection:

There remains the question of whence comes the diversity of types of soul, vegetable, sensible and intelligible? ... This question is swiftly solved, if it is considered with subtlety in what way the bestowals of natures proceed from the first cause. For all forms are bestowed by him who is the nature of the whole universe: but those which are more distanced from him, to that extent are deprived of their nobilities and goodnesses: and the less they recede, the more they are noble and have more powers of goodnesses [bonitatum potestates] and virtues ... This essence descending is deprived

---

[134] Brian Tierney, '*Ius* and metonymy in Rufinus', in R. Castillo Lara (ed.), *Studia in honorem eminentissimi Cardinalis Alphonsi M. Stickler* (Rome 1992), 549–58, emphasises the way in which mediaeval authors could slide over in their writing from one sense of a word to another, and could expect their readership to make the same connections; and so there could be an easy association between *ius* as an intellectual faculty and as a faculty for action. I want to suggest, however, that Gerson deliberately chose one particular sense of *ius* in order to be able to respond to Fitzralph's and Wyclif's understanding of the term.

of simplicity and power more and more ... as far as the furthest being, which receives the least differentiation of being and power.[135]

Differentiation of being, as we saw in Scotus' consideration of evil angels, is potential ordained to action: but this power is not morally neutral. Every being, in its aspect as an emanation from the first principle, is noble and good, and since that being in its differentiation is power, that power is its goodness. When Gerson says that a being has as much right, defined as a power of action, as it has being and goodness, he is appropriating Albert's peripatetic Dionysianism to the rights discourse of the fourteenth century.

Gerson more or less repeats his general definition of right in later works.[136] However, in the *DVSA* he stresses that although this is the basic definition of right, 'the term is understood more narrowly among *politici*, so that right is predicated only of those which belong to rational creatures in so far as they have the use of reason'.[137] Law in general is the *dictamen primae iustitiae* or *rectae rationis*; right in general is the faculty which belongs to an entity in accordance with this dictate.[138] But the narrower sense of the two terms is associated with that justice and therefore that right reason which is participated by rational creatures.[139] It is in relation to the justice or right reason of rational creatures that there are multiple laws, multiple rights and multiple *dominia*: 'Let us say that there are as many varieties of laws as there are modes in which rights vary according to the dictate of

---

[135] Albert the Great, *De intellectu et intelligibili*, I, i, 5, cited in Combes, *Commentateur dionysien*, Appendix V, pp. 490–1: 'Remanet ergo quaestio unde provenit animae generum diversitas, vegetabile, sensibile, et intelligibile? ... quaestio haec citius solvitur, si consideretur subtiliter secundum quem modum largitiones naturarum a prima causa procedunt. Omnes enim formae ab ipso (!) [sic] totius universitatis natura largiuntur: quae autem magis ab ea elongantur, eo magis nobilitatibus suis et bonitatibus privantur: et quominus recedunt, eo magis nobiles sunt et plures habent bonitatum potestates et virtutes ... Haec autem essentia descendens privatur simplicitate et potestate plus et in plus, sicut dicimus usque ad ultimum ens quod minimum accipit entis differentiam et potestatem.'

[136] *De potestate ecclesiastica* (henceforth *DPE*; in *Jean Gerson: Oeuvres complètes*, ed. by Glorieux (Paris 1965), vol. VI, 210–50), p. 242: 'right is a faculty or power pertaining to a thing according to the dictate of right reason. Further, this dictate is called law, because law is a rule having conformity to the dictate of right reason; the dictate of right reason and of first justice coincide in God synonymously'; *Definitiones terminorum theologiae moralis* (in *Oeuvres complètes*, ed. by Glorieux, vol. IX, 133–42), p. 134: 'Right is a faculty or power pertaining to someone according to the dictate of right reason.'

[137] *DVSA* p. 142: 'contractior tamen est ejus acceptio apud politizantes, ut jus dicatur solum de illis quae competunt creaturis rationalibus ut utuntur ratione'. In the *DPE*, more theoretically, he says that 'from this very broad understanding of [the terms] right and law ... there is a narrower descent to those which concern a rational creature in so far as it is rational': *DPE*, p. 243.

[138] Ibid., p. 242. [139] Ibid., p. 243.

participated justice. Therefore there are some laws properly divine, some properly natural, some positive or human; of which some are canonical or ecclesiastical, others are civil or political';[140] 'it remains to show how, out of right so described, there arise multiple ... polities and multiple jurisdictions and diverse dominations, kingdoms or empires'.[141] *Natural* law and consequent *natural* rights belong to rationals alone.[142]

Gerson's theory is thus very clearly distinguished from those authors we examined in chapter 1, who equated *ius* and *dominium*. He is not part of the tradition which produced Summenhart and Mazzolini. Nor is he responsible for positing a theory of rights as liberties. For Gerson as for the whole scholastic, liberty is a species of

[140] Ibid.: 'Dicamus praeterea tot esse legum varietates quot modis jura variantur secundum dictamen participatae justitiae. Propterea sunt quaedam leges proprie divinae, quedam proprie naturales, quaedam positivae vel humanae; quarum aliquae sunt canonicae vel ecclesiasticae, aliae sunt civiles vel politicae.'

[141] *DVSA*, p. 143: 'Nunc superest ostendere qualiter ex jure sic descripto multiplices, saltem secundum rationem, oriuntur politiae et multiplices jurisdictiones et diversae dominationes, regna vel imperia.'

[142] Thus Tierney (above, n. 132) is correct in arguing that a natural right in Gerson is a faculty to act in accordance with participated justice or *synderesis*. But this is not the canonists' doctrine, for unlike them, Gerson distinguished clearly between natural right and *synderesis*. From another text of Gerson's it appears clear that Gerson interpreted the canonistic *synderesis* which was equivalent to *ius naturale* in the sense of law or rule, not as a *ius* in the sense of a subjective right: Jean Gerson, *De passionibus animae*, in *Oeuvres complètes*, ed. by Glorieux, vol. IX, 1–25, p. 2: 'Therefore whatsoever natural being has its own certain inclinations ... in whatsoever thing God left a passion which is an assimilation or coaptation or pertinence, or an inclination or tendency towards him ... But this general inclination ... is called the natural appetite or affection, sometimes the weight of things, sometimes pull or tendency, sometimes innate love, sometimes law, sometimes rule, sometimes instinct, sometimes natural equity, sometimes the stable pact of things, sometimes the sense of nature.' The terms *instinctus, aequitas naturalis* and *sensus naturae* are canonistic in origin, and refer to man's innate reason which, for them, is *ius naturale*. See Gilles Couvreur, 'Les pauvres ont-ils des droits? Recherches sur le vol en cas d'extrême nécessité depuis la Concordia de Gratien (1140) jusqu'à Guillaume d'Auxerre (?1231)', *Analecta gregoriana* 111 (Rome 1961), who quotes Huguccio: 'ratio vel sensualitas scilicet ordo et instinctus nature' (p. 143, n. 453) and Johannes Teutonicus: 'ius ex tali natura proveniens dicitur naturalis equitas' (p. 151, n. 490). When Gerson says 'sometimes' instinct, natural equity and sense of nature, that 'sometimes' would therefore appear to have the sense of 'in the case of rationals'; Gerson in his enumeration shifts from terms which describe the right ordination of irrationals to their end, to terms which describe the right ordination of man to his end. But this ordination of rationals – the canonistic *ius naturale* – is equivalent to *lex* or *regula*: implying that Gerson understood the canonists' 'natural right' as coinciding with Aquinas' 'natural law', as the subjective faculty of a rational by which it naturally discerns and follows the right path, just as irrationals follow the right path without discernment. Gerson is very careful to avoid using the term *ius* in any but his own sense of active power in accordance with right reason. Subjective natural right is, for Gerson, a power in accordance with the natural right reason or natural law which is the natural justice of man – what the canonists, not he, called natural right.

dominium and pertains only to rationals capable of controlling their own acts.[143] That irrationals are not so capable does not prevent their having rights, which are just powers under the law. The *dominium libertatis* is related to natural *dominium* as a faculty consequent on the original institution of man: but it is not natural *dominium*, nor is it natural right. Natural right, like any right, is a power for specific action. Gerson cannot therefore be seen in any way as an antecedent to a theory of natural rights as liberties, nor can he be seen as positing a theory of rights in opposition to the law. Right is deduced from the existence of the law which determines the positive actions of all things that are. It was precisely this focus on the law and on being, understood in the Aristotelian sense as potential and act, which would enable elements of his view to be assimilated in the fifteenth century to the Thomistic current of argument on the nature of law and right.

[143] *DVSA*, p. 146.

3

Objective right and the Thomist tradition

In this third chapter we shall be concerned with the development of the notion of objective right in the later middle ages, both in works of Thomist moral philosophy and in commentary on Aristotle. The notion of right in the Thomist tradition was primarily determined by the account given by Aquinas in the 2a2ae of the *Summa theologiae*, an account he adapted from Aristotle in Book v of the *Nicomachean Ethics* (henceforth *NE*), in which he saw *ius* or right objectively as the *iustum*, the 'right thing', in a given situation. The history of the Thomist tradition of right therefore coincides to some extent with that of the tradition of objective right in general. It is important to stress, however, that the two are not coterminous. Besides the tradition embedded in commentary on the *Summa theologiae*, a non-Thomist literature of commentary on the *NE* flourished throughout the period of later scholasticism. Commentators of Franciscan and secular background reached interpretations which differed in fundamental aspects from that of Aquinas and can be understood as a critique of the Thomist analysis. The first part of this chapter is concerned with analysing the assumptions about objective right implicit in both Thomist and non-Thomist interpretations.

An appreciation of the divergences of the latter from the Thomist understanding is important because they illuminate the difficulties of the original Thomist view and thereby contribute to explaining the course of its elaboration within the Thomist tradition itself. In this we are not talking about supposed defections of Dominican writers to the subjectivist camp. Throughout the course of the fifteenth century, Dominican authors starting from explicitly Thomist premises explored the limits of that analysis in the course of responding to contemporary intellectual issues. The second part of this chapter considers the development of the Thomist tradition of objective right in the fifteenth century in the works of the leading Thomists of the period: Henry of Gorkum and Denis the Carthusian, Sant'Antonino of Florence, Cardinal Cajetan and Konrad Köllin. We shall see that the moral theology of Thomism, although tied originally to an objective conception of right, was nevertheless open to the second tradition of subjective rights discourse (examined in chapter 2), through the concern with nature and with law laid out in the 1a2ae of the *Summa theologiae*. In this context we shall examine the work of Jacques Almain.

OBJECTIVE RIGHT IN AQUINAS

The notion of right as the object of justice is laid out in Book v of Aristotle's *Nicomachean Ethics*, the full text of which became available to the Latin West with the translation completed by Robert Grosseteste in c. 1246–7. The ten books were swiftly incorporated in the curricula of Faculties of Arts.[1] The first detailed commentary on the text in its entirety was completed by Albert the Great at Cologne between 1248 and 1252, taking the form of an exposition of the text followed by Questions upon the subject matter. Albert's commentary initiated a tradition of commentary upon the *NE* that was to endure in a virtually unchanged format (except for the occasional sacrifice of the expository section) well into the seventeenth century.

The fifth book of the *NE* is a treatise on the virtue of justice. 'With regard to justice and injustice', the book begins, 'we have to examine what sort of actions they may concern, and what kind of mean is justice, and of what things the just is the mean ... We see everyone meaning by "justice" such a disposition, by which they are doers of just things and by which they act justly and want just things.'[2] The

---

[1] For a summary account of the introduction of the text to the Latin West and a brief survey of the subsequent commentary literature, see G. Wieland, 'The reception and interpretation of Aristotle's *Ethics*', in Kretzmann, Kenny and Pinborg, *Cambridge history of later medieval philosophy*, 657–72. Further details are in R. A. Gauthier and J. Y. Jolif, *L'Ethique à Nicomaque. Introduction, traduction et commentaire*, vol. 1 (Louvain 1958), pp. 74–85.

[2] Aristotle, *Ethica Nicomachea*, ed. by I. Bywater, Oxford 1894, 1129a3–9, p. 88. Aristotle's analysis of justice consciously follows the pattern of his analysis of all the virtues: virtue is a state of character, a habit or disposition which is a mean state between two opposing vices, which is such a mean because it aims at a mean between excess and deficit in the particular class of things with which it is concerned. See Book II in general, and the sixth chapter in particular, for the full statement of the doctrine.

Translated into Latin, the passage reads as follows: 'De iustitia autem et iniustitia intendendum, et circa quales sunt operationes, et qualis est medietas iustitia, et iustum quorum medium ... Videmus utique omnes talem habitum volentes dicere iustitiam, a quo operativi iustorum sunt, et a quo iusta operantur et volunt iusta.' The translation is question is the revised version of Grosseteste's translation, a fairly poor manuscript of

mediaeval exposition characterised the 'just thing', *dikaion* or *iustum*, as the 'object of justice', the *obiectum iustitiae*: that at which justice aims.[3] The Aristotelian analysis initially makes it clear that the object of justice is an action, a part of our daily practice. It is also clear that this action concerns or is towards another: it is peculiar to justice as distinct from all other virtues that it operates *ad alterum* rather than with regard to the subject of the action. Correspondingly, the second peculiarity of justice is that the mean at which it aims – its *obiectum* – is not constituted in relation to the subject,[4] but is objectively determined by the demands of equality in human transactions.

Aquinas' own analysis of right is found in the *Summa theologiae*, 2a2ae, Question 57, 'On right' ('De iure'), and Question 58, 'On justice' ('De iustitia').[5] Its place within the *Summa theologiae* is important. The whole of the *secunda pars* constitutes a treatment of what would soon be called 'moral theology', which is traditionally analysed as consisting in a 'speculative' and a 'practical' branch.[6] Aquinas' *secunda pars* is generally seen as belonging entirely to the former. But contemporaries seem to have thought of the 2a2ae as belonging to the latter: for the Dominican John of Freiburg, writing a *Summa confessorum* at the end of the thirteenth century, the 2a2ae is in great part 'moralis et casualis', 'moral and casuistic'.[7] Questions 57–79 of the 2a2ae can be seen as an attempt to treat all the topics belonging to the nascent casuistry of justice using the Aristotelian category of the *iustum*.

which was used by Thomas Aquinas for the basis of his exposition. It is reprinted in *Sententia libri ethicorum*, vol. XLVII, *Sancti Thomae de Aquino. Opera omnia iussu Leonis XIII P. M. edita cura et studio Fratrum Praedicatorum* (Rome 1969). For the question of authorship of the translation, see Gauthier and Jolif, *L'Ethique à Nicomaque*, vol. I, pp. 80–2.

3   See Aquinas, *Sententia libri ethicorum* v, Lectio prima, p. 265: 'dicit [Aristoteles] Et qualis medietas est iustitia et iustum, quod scilicet est obiectum iustitiae.'

4   E.g. the mean in the case of the virtue of temperance, for example, which is relative to the personal characteristics of the subject – certain physiques require more nourishment than others, and therefore what is indulgence for one is temperance for another. See *NE*, II, 6 for the famous example of the athlete Milo.

5   Aquinas had been involved in editing his master Albert the Great's lectures on the *NE* and, like him, had commented on the text. Unlike Albert, however, he had confined himself to the exposition of the text without appending any subsequent questions. His substantive conclusions on the text are rather to be found in these questions of the *Summa theologiae*.

6   See J. Theiner, *Die Entwicklung der Moraltheologie zur eigenständigen Disziplin* (Regensburg 1970) for this distinction in the course of a useful analysis of the tradition of moral theology since the early middle ages.

7   See Michaud-Quantin, *Sommes de casuistique*, p. 45; for further details, Leonard E. Boyle, 'The *Summa confessorum* of John of Freiburg and the popularization of the moral teaching of St Thomas Aquinas and some of his contemporaries', in Armand A. Maurer (ed.-in-chief), *St Thomas Aquinas, 1274–1974: Commemorative studies*, 2 vols. (Toronto 1974), vol. II, 245–68.

Aquinas' Aristotelianising intentions are clearly signalled by the fact that he opens his treatment not with a definition of the virtue itself but with a definition of its object, according to the principle of Aristotelian science that the identification of the object logically precedes that of the faculty or habit. As we saw, the object of justice, according to the *NE*, is the *iustum* or just thing. Aquinas' first move is to bring the *iustum* into line with more traditional ways of talking by employing a passage from the ubiquitous scholastic authority St Isidore of Seville. Isidore had said that '*ius* [right] is so called, because it is *iustum* [just, or the just thing, the right thing].'[8] The passage enabled Aquinas to identify the Aristotelian 'just thing' with 'right', concluding that 'it is manifest, that right is the object of justice'.[9] Right in this sense is an action: 'right or the just thing is a certain action which is equal in relation to another person according to a certain mode of equality'.[10] Aquinas' example is the recompense of the due wage for a service rendered.[11] The just thing or right is what justice requires that a subject do with regard to another in a given situation. It is in some sense an obligation or duty of that subject: doing the right thing is not a matter of personal choice.[12]

---

[8] Isidore of Seville, *Etymologiarum libri*, 2 vols., vol. I, *I–X*, ed. by W. M. Lindsay (Oxford 1911), v, 3.

[9] *ST*, 2a2ae 57, a. 1 in corp.: 'unde manifestum est, quod ius est obiectum iustitiae'.

[10] Ibid., a. 2 in corp.: 'jus sive justum est aliquod opus adaequatum alteri secundum aliquem aequalitatis modum'. G. Kalinowski, 'Le fondement objectif du droit d'après la "Somme théologique" de saint Thomas d'Aquin', *Archives de la philosophie du droit* 18 (1973), 59–75, p. 64, n. 1 correctly insists on the primacy in Aquinas of the sense of *iustum* as 'action juste'. John Finnis' translation and elucidation of the Thomist *iustum* as 'the fair' or 'the what's fair' is indifferent to whether the *iustum* is an action or a thing: see Finnis, *Natural law and natural rights*, p. 206. For Michel Villey, the sense of *iustum* as 'just action' is distinctly secondary to its sense as 'the just thing': M. Villey, 'Si la théorie générale du droit, pour saint Thomas, est une théorie de la loi', *Archives de philosophie du droit* 17 (1972), 427–31, p. 428; this is also the view of M. Bastit, *Naissance de la loi moderne*, chapter 5. All of these positions on the correct sense of *ius* in Aquinas are related to their authors' views on the relation between law and right in Aquinas; for this thorny question, see below, p. 95, n. 29.

[11] *ST*, 2a2ae 57, a. 1 in corp.

[12] The basic sense of 'right' in Aquinas is thus 'objective' as opposed to 'subjective'. This does not, however, mean that Aquinas never uses the term in a subjective sense: see J.-M. Aubert, *Le droit romain dans l'oeuvre de saint Thomas* (Paris 1955), pp. 90–1, where it is shown that Aquinas is prepared to use the term *ius* in the sense of a subjective *ius* of doing something: for example in the phrase, 'quasi habeat ius possidendi totum thesaurum' at *ST*, 2a2ae 87 a. 3. As the author remarks, 'Il aurait été étonnant que saint Thomas, qui a largement utilisé les sources juridiques, n'ait pas été influencé par le langage courant en ces matières' (ibid.). However, the scattered usage of the subjective construction of *ius* with the gerund does not affect the theoretical elucidation of *ius* as objective, which is indeed the sense that *ius* normally bears in Aquinas' text; nor does it necessarily imply a concept of subjective right as liberty.

Having established the nature of *ius* as the object of justice, Aquinas goes on in the next Question to consider justice itself.[13] According to the Aristotelian definition, justice is 'that whereby men are operative of just things'. Given the elucidation of the *iustum* as in some way due to another, Aquinas was able easily to assimilate the definition of the *NE* to that of the Roman law, 'the constant and perpetual will of rendering to each his right'. But the issue which he skirts in this attempt to reconcile his sources is that of the possessive pronoun 'his'. In Aristotle's text, the right thing is the right thing for a just man to do. But the legal definition suggests that right belongs to the recipient of the action. It is *his* right, *suum ius*: indeed, an almost equally common formulation of the definition, and one used by Aquinas in the course of the same Question,[14] speaks simply of 'his', *suum*. Aquinas is able to harmonise the two languages of right by exploiting the language of due (*debere, debitum*).[15] The right thing is due *from* the just man *to* another citizen. But he is thereby led to concede that the right thing may not always be an action but may sometimes be a *res*.[16] This enables him to cover topics such as restitution, which involve the notions of *dominium* and *suum*, in the same terms of *iustum* defined as the *obiectum iustitiae*.[17] As we shall see, future Thomists would make the shift in sense explicit.

The primary and theoretically important sense of *iustum* in Aquinas, however, remains that of 'just action'. In a. 4 of Q. 57, Aquinas moves objections against the Aristotelian notion that there is a *ius paternum*, 'father's right', and a *ius dominativum*, 'master's right', distinct from right in its usual sense, which is *ius politicum*, 'political right'. Aquinas replies with a faithful exposition of the Aristotelian text, that right or the just thing is determined *ad alterum*, with regard to another, but that 'other' could be other in two ways: 'In one way, which is *simpliciter* other, as what is altogether distinct [from the original]: as appears in two men, of whom one is not under the other, but both are under one prince of a city: and between such persons according to the Philosopher in Ethics v there is the just thing *simpliciter*.'[18] But, he goes on, 'in a second way something is said

---

[13] Ibid., Q. 58, a. 1.

[14] Ibid., a. 11: 'Utrum actus iustitiae sit reddere cuique quod suum est'.

[15] On the interpretation of the *iustum* as *debitum*, see Paul. M. Van Overbeke, 'Saint Thomas et le droit. Commentaire de IIa-II, Q. 57', *Revue thomiste* 55 (1955), 519–64, p. 529.

[16] *ST*, 2a2ae 58, a. 11 in corp.

[17] Ibid., Q. 62, a. 1 in corp. and ad 1.

[18] Ibid., Q. 57, a. 4 in corp.: 'Uno modo, quod simpliciter est alterum, sicut quod est omnino

to be other, not *simpliciter*, but as if it were something which belonged to [the original]'.[19] The latter mode describes the position of a son in relation to his father and a slave in relation to his master. Neither has independent existence, and therefore between them there is no right or right thing, properly speaking. Right is social, that part of social *activity* demanded by the virtue of justice, and has no place outside political society, which is the active realisation of the good of man. Doing the right thing is part of the living well which the city achieves, not the living secured by the household.[20]

After establishing that the right thing is between citizens alone, Aristotle had gone on to divide this proper sense of 'right' – the specifically *political* 'just thing' – further into natural (*phusikon*) and conventional (*nomikon*): natural as that which always has the same force and is not a matter of opinion, and conventional as that which is originally juridically indifferent.[21] In his own consideration of the point, 'Whether right be appropriately divided into natural right and positive right',[22] Aquinas follows Aristotle closely, dividing *ius* into *naturale* and *positivum*, understood respectively as that which is just *ex natura rei*, from the nature of the thing, and that which is just *ex condicto*, by convention. Given that the just thing is always *ad alterum*, Aquinas characterises natural right as that which is equal in relation to another person of its own nature: 'for example, when someone gives such an amount, that he receive back just such an amount'.[23] That is, in the course of this article Aquinas does not suggest that 'right' is properly anything other than 'the right thing' between free and equal persons (such freedom and equality only being possible in a civic context): natural right is nothing other than that just action which presents itself to such free and equal (i.e. political) beings out of the nature of the thing.

However, Aquinas' next article, 'Whether the right of peoples be the same as natural right', gives a different account.[24] Aquinas here alters his example of natural right in order to reduce Aristotle and the law to harmony, but thereby distorts his account of right. Here,

distinctum: sicut apparet in duobus hominibus, quorum unus non est sub altero, sed ambo sunt sub uno principe civitatis; et inter tales secundum Phil. in 5. Ethic. est simpliciter justum.'

[19] Ibid.: 'Alio modo dicitur aliquid alterum, non simpliciter, sed quasi aliquid ejus existens.'
[20] Aristotle, *Politica*, Book I, chapter II.
[21] *NE*, v, 1134b18–21, p. 103.
[22] *ST*, 2a2ae 57, a. 2: 'Utrum jus convenienter dividatur in jus naturale, et jus positivum'.
[23] Ibid., in corp.   [24] Ibid., a. 3.

he says that natural right is that which is equated to another 'according to an absolute consideration of itself: as the male of its being as such has a commensuration towards the female, so that he might produce from her; and the parent to the son, that he might nourish him'.[25] He went on to add that 'to apprehend a thing absolutely does not belong only to man, but even to the other animals; and therefore right, which is called natural ... is common to us, and to the other animals',[26] paraphrasing the famous words of Ulpian at the opening of the Digest.[27] Aquinas conceives, therefore, of a right or right action which is not right in the sense of that interpersonal equality at which the virtue of justice aims – for animals are neither persons, nor do they have virtue – but is rather right simply in the sense that it is naturally appropriate and apprehended as such by all nature. His examples of natural right are, nonetheless, all *ad alterum* in a sense: male to female, father to son. Aquinas does not lose entirely the sense of right as a due between individuals.

Aquinas' doctrine of natural right here has caused problems for his interpreters. In his philosophy, natural law is confined to rational nature. For those who see Aquinas' notion of right as intimately connected with law, it is difficult to explain his deliberate insistence here, in his most mature work, that there is natural right among animals.[28] However, the question of relation between law and right in Aquinas has provoked fierce debate, affecting as it does his status as a model for certain modern philosophies of jurisprudence. While John Finnis argues that right in Aquinas is derived from law, which is the fundamental preoccupation of jurisprudence, Michel Villey contends that the derivation of right from law is typical of subjective modes of right, wherein right is connected with such individual

---

[25] Ibid., in corp.   [26] Ibid.

[27] D. 1, 1, 1: 'Ius naturale est, quod natura omnia animalia docuit: nam ius istud non humani generis proprium, sed omnium animalium ... commune est.'

[28] E.g. Van Overbeke, 'Saint Thomas et le droit', pp. 525 and 535; M. B. Crowe, 'St Thomas and Ulpian's natural law', in *Commemorative studies*, vol. 1, 261–82. Both Van Overbeke and Crowe see an intimate connection in Aquinas between right and law. For Van Overbeke, right derives from law as its foundation. Crowe, by contrast but to the same effect, implicitly holds that Aquinas uses the terms *ius* and *lex* interchangeably to mean 'law'; thus he assumes that the discussion in the present article of the *Summa theologiae* is about law (e.g. at p. 277), and is therefore incompatible with the teaching of the treaty on laws in the 1a2ae. For the view that Aquinas uses *ius* and *lex* interchangeably at points, see G. Kalinowski in his two articles, 'Fondement', and 'Sur l'emploi métonymique du terme "ius" par Thomas d'Aquin', *Archives de philosophie du droit* 18 (1973), 331–9, who argues that the metonymy of terms in Aquinas rests on the fact that for him, the concepts of *ius* and *lex* are connected to each other in a relation of mutual causation.

actions as are governed by law, rather than being the just portion due between individuals. For him, Aquinas is the last great representative of the pure classical tradition and of a jurisprudence unsullied by the centrality of law as the command of actions.[29] The sole statement we have from Aquinas himself is at *ST*, 2a2ae 57, 1 ad 2, where he differentiates between *lex* and *ius*, but asserts that law is 'a rationale, of a kind, of right': 'lex non est ipsum jus, sed aliqualis ratio juris'.

For Aquinas, law is fundamentally and primarily connected with reason, *ratio*.[30] The original and supreme reason is that of God, and it governs the activity of all created nature: 'the eternal law is nothing other than the *ratio* of divine wisdom, in its aspect as directing all actions and all motions'.[31] All creatures are inescapably subject in all their actions to the eternal law, in one of two ways. 'We should say, that there is a double mode by which a thing is subject to the eternal law ... one mode, in which the eternal law is participated by means of cognition; another mode, which is by means of action, and passion, inasmuch as it is participated by means of an interior principle of motion.'[32] Irrationals are subject in the second way alone, in that they have an innate inclination to their proper acts and

---

[29] Villey sees the isolation of an objective 'droit' as the great achievement of classical jurisprudence; archaic civilisations, Judaism and the East knew only 'loi'. He views the attempt to relate the two as the degeneration of jurisprudence, beginning with the nominalist Ockham and continuing with his intellectual heirs Hobbes and Locke. Villey's position depends of course on an understanding of the essence of law as a moral imperative that Finnis, along with Germain Grisez and other proponents of the 'new classical theory' of natural law, would reject. See the debate between Villey and Finnis in *Archives de la philosophie du droit* 17 (1972): by Villey, the articles 'Théorie générale' (pp. 427–31) and 'Sur les essais d'application de la logique déontologique au droit' (pp. 407–12); by Finnis, 'Un ouvrage récent sur Bentham' (423–7); more generally, J. Finnis (ed.), *Natural law* (Aldershot, Hants. 1991), vol. 1, pp. 206–10.

[30] This sense is set out in the opening article of the opening question in the treatise of laws, 'Utrum lex sit aliquid rationis': *ST*, 1a2ae 90, a. 1. As for all aspects of Thomist scholarship, there is a vast literature on the topic. For Aquinas' attribution of law to reason rather than will see the general discussion in Crowe, *Changing profile of natural law* (The Hague 1977), chapter 7; more specifically W. Farrell O. P., *The natural moral law according to St Thomas and Suárez* (Ditchling 1930). For a discussion of Aquinas' doctrine of the laws in the intellectual context of the thirteenth century, see along with Crowe, *Changing profile of natural law*, chapter 6, O. Lottin, *Psychologie et morale au XIIe et XIIIe siècles*, vol. 11, *Problèmes de morale* (Louvain 1948), part 1, chapters 1–3. Aquinas' notion of natural law, again in intellectual context, is discussed in Martin Grabmann, 'Das Naturrecht der Scholastik von Gratian bis Thomas von Aquin', in Grabmann, *Mittelalterliches Geistesleben*, vol. 1 (Munich 1926), 65–103; see also Crowe, 'Thomas and Ulpian'.

[31] *ST*, 1a2ae 93, a. 1 in corp.: 'lex aeterna nihil aliud est, quam ratio divinae sapientiae, secundum quod est directiva omnium actionum, et motionum'.

[32] Ibid., a. 6 in corp.

end; but rationals are subject in both ways, in that they both have a notion of the eternal law, and have an inclination towards their end implanted in them: 'for we are born to have the virtues, as is said in "Ethics" II'.[33]

For Aquinas, it is the first mode of subjection in man, subjection in the sense of having a notion or cognitive awareness of the eternal law, that constitutes the natural law. Natural law is characterised as the 'light of natural reason, by which we discern what is good, and what is bad':[34] that is, not an inclination to a certain act, but a part of the cognitive equipment of a rational. 'Because the rational creature participates in [the eternal law] rationally and intellectually, therefore the participation of the eternal law in the rational creature is properly called law: for law pertains to reason ... but in the irrational creature [the eternal law] is not participated rationally; whence it cannot be called a law except by similitude.'[35] Aquinas allows that man has an innate series of natural inclinations, just as do all other creatures, but not that these inclinations are law; rather, that to these natural inclinations correspond, in man alone, a series of precepts which constitute the natural law.[36] One inclination man shares with all beings, viz. the appetite to conserve himself in being, and in accordance with this natural inclination the first precepts of natural law concern those things by which being is preserved. Secondly, he has a natural inclination to those things which are common to all animals, procreation, education of the young, and the like; and accordingly these activities too are commanded by the natural law. Thirdly, man has a natural inclination to the good which is proper to himself, knowledge of God and life in society; and the third set of precepts of the natural law commands the behaviour necessary for this end.[37] Aquinas never suggests that those precepts of the natural law which concern inclinations common to man and other creatures can be called laws for those other creatures. Natural inclination has the role of natural law in irrationals; man has natural

---

[33] Ibid.   [34] Ibid., Q. 91 a. 2 in corp.   [35] Ibid., ad 3.

[36] I am using the term 'series' here to suggest order without suggesting 'hierarchy' or 'ranking', accepting, with John Finnis, that we do not find this sense in Aquinas' text. As for Aristotle, for Aquinas the rational soul is unitary and comprehends within it the vegetative and sensitive souls. Thus those things to which irrational natures incline and which constitute their goods are equally goods to which rational natures incline, and not in any sense lesser or subordinate goods. See Finnis, *Natural law*, vol. I, p. 94; J. Finnis and G. Grisez, 'The basic principles of natural law: A reply to Ralph McInerny', *American Journal of Jurisprudence* 26 (1981), 21–31 (reprinted in Finnis, *Natural law*, vol. I, 341–51), p. 29.

[37] *ST*, 1a2ae 94, a. 2 in corp.

inclination *and* natural law. Aquinas is not prepared to call natural inclination, even in humans, a law, 'except by similitude'.[38]

If, then, natural right is, in one sense, the action apprehended by the non-reflexive cognition of animals, it appears that right cannot be in any way 'derived' from law in the sense that each species of law is correlated with its own particular species of right: for then natural right would have to have the sense of a moral (that is, rational and free) action. But that does not mean that right and law in Aquinas are entirely independent. Aquinas himself says that the law is *aliqualis ratio juris*.[39] In the treatise on the laws he associates *ratio* with *regula*, from which we can infer that for Aquinas, the natural law in human beings is the rule in the sense of the measure of natural right. If the law provides the rationale or measure of the right for those capable of reasoning – men – then right is connected with law without necessarily being simply a function of the law.[40] In so understanding law as giving the rationale of right, Aquinas was able – just – to tie a notion of objective right into the general framework of his theory of human moral action.

OBJECTIVE RIGHT OUTSIDE THE THOMIST TRADITION

While Aquinas was concerned to bring Aristotelian right into his own system of moral theology, the non-Thomist tradition of commentary on the *NE* is concerned far more to relate right as the object of justice to the terminology of *dominium*. The key figure in the development of this tradition was Gerald Odo or Guiral Ot, the Franciscan

[38] Thus in discussing 'Whether there be any law of lust (*lex fomitis*)', *ST*, 1a2ae 91 a. 6 in corp., Aquinas is careful to talk of the diverse inclinations of diverse creatures as laws only *quodammodo*. It is true that the language in a. 2 in corp. suggests that Aquinas conceives both of the natural inclination to virtue, and the natural awareness of human reason of the eternal law, as constituting the natural law. However, I take the distinctions at Q. 93, a. 6 in corp. to be a clarification of this point, decisively rejecting the idea that the natural inclination to virtue, which is on the same level as all creatures' inclination to their good, is natural law. For a sensitive handling of this question with a rather different conclusion, see Farrell, *Natural moral law*, pp. 82–103. The importance of the 'doctrine of natural inclinations' in Aquinas' account of natural law is also emphasised by D. J. O'Connor, *Aquinas and natural law* (London 1967), pp. 60–2. However, I cannot agree with his conclusion that *synderesis* – 'the capacity to recognise basic moral principles' – 'must be regarded as an essential *inclinatio naturalis* of a human being' (p. 61). *Synderesis* is a habit of the intellect (Q. 94, a. 1 ad 2) rather than an innate inclination to man's proper end (virtue).

[39] See above, p. 95.

[40] For this point, see the sympathetic and perceptive discussion in Aubert, *Droit romain*, pp. 103–5.

who succeeded the deposed Michael of Cesena as general of the Order in 1329. His analysis differs, however, as much from the early Franciscan tradition as from Aquinas, in bringing into relation with one another all the elements of the discourse of the juridical: law, right, due, command, just action.

Odo begins his discussion of *ius* with the objection, against the thesis of the text, that justice is (logically) prior to right.[41] For the resolution of the difficulty he makes a fundamental distinction between four 'parts' of right. Aquinas had argued that *iustum*, in the Aristotelian sense, is the primary meaning of right, but suggested that other significations had been afterwards derived from it: so that *ius* had in addition come to mean jurisprudence, the courtroom and the decision of a justiciary.[42] In the same place, he had further acknowledged that *ius* was used, but improperly, to signify law. Odo, in contrast, adopts a much stronger thesis to the effect that *ius* involves four component parts: 'The first is the command of the legislator. The second is the thing due from the subject. The third is a written text, be it written in letters in a book, or mentally in the soul, indicating both the commands and the thing due. The fourth is the work enjoined and due.'[43]

In the following paragraphs it becomes clearer what Odo has in mind by these four 'parts'. The element of command is the imperative laid down by the legislator, 'i.e. God in the case of divine *ius*, or nature in the case of natural *ius*, or man in the case of all human *iura* whatever they may be'.[44] The *ius* which is the thing due, however, is the part specifically labelled as the *iustum*. This thing can either be an action or an object, and it is due from someone to another, as in Aquinas. It is this element which corresponds strictly to the *obiectum iustitiae* of the Aristotelian text. As with Aquinas, what is important about the right thing is that it is due from the subject; it has nothing to do with personal power of action. The third element of *ius*, the text or *scriptura*, receives the characterisation of the 'dictate of reason', the *rationis dictamen*. As we saw in the last chapter, in

[41] Geraldus Odo, *Sententia et expositio cum questionibus ... super libros ethicorum Aristotelis cum textu eiusdem.* [?Venice ?1500], Book v, Q. 2, fol. 93v.

[42] *ST*, 2a2ae 57, a. 1, ad 1.

[43] Odo, *Sententia et expositio cum questionibus*: 'Prima est preceptum legislatoris. Secunda est debitum subditi. Tertia est scriptura litteralis in libro vel mentalis in anima ostendens et precepta et debitum. Quarta est opus iniunctum et debitum.'

[44] Ibid.: 'puta vel deum sicut ius divinum: vel naturam sicut ius naturale: vel hominem sicut omnia humana iura quaecunque sint illa'.

contemporary Franciscan discourse the *rationis dictamen* coincides with *lex*, law, and we may fairly assume that Odo has law in mind here. The fourth element, the work itself, is termed the *iustificatio*: the actual doing of the right thing.

What is striking about this passage in comparison with Aquinas' treatment is the emphasis laid on the legislator in any attempt at defining right. He is essential, for '*ius* necessarily presupposes a legislator'.[45] There can be no right without a legislator to command: 'for the command is prior to the due, as cause to caused ... for I cannot obey or owe [anything] before a command be given me'.[46] Right similarly presupposes 'a subject upon whom *ius* is imposed'.[47] For Odo, then, right in all its parts is primarily to do with the structure of command and obedience, rather than directly with a notion of equality and proportion between persons. In this structure, law takes on a subordinate position. Law, for Odo, has a purely ostensive rôle: the determinative rôle is assumed by the element of command, *preceptum*, which presupposes a legislator. The right thing, the *iustum*, is not independent but a function of the command of this legislator, who may be God, nature or man.

The treatment John Buridan gives the subject deepens Odo's analysis.[48] Buridan begins in the manner of Aquinas, querying the validity of the Aristotelian definition of justice. The resolution of the question demands the elucidation of the term *iustum*: 'Let us declare summarily that *ius*, *iustum*, *lex*, *iustitia* and *iustificatio* are different. *Ius* is the command or ordination of the *dominus* concerning his subjects and those things which can fall under the power of the subjects.'[49] Whereas Odo had, rather confusedly, associated the term *legislator* with *preceptum* (rather than with *lex*), Buridan drops it in favour of *dominus*. As for Odo, 'that *dominus* can be either god ... or nature ... or man'; but he goes on, 'for an equal imposes no right on an equal: but if a king should be in anything obliged to his subjects this is by

---

45 Ibid.: 'Ius enim necessario presupponit legislatorem.'
46 Ibid.: 'Preceptum enim est prius debito, ut causa causato ... nec obedire possum vel debere ante quam datum sit mihi preceptum.'
47 Ibid.: 'Item presupponit subditum cui imponitur ius.'
48 For the demonstration that it is Buridan who is borrowing from Odo, and not vice versa, see James J. Walsh, 'Some relationships between Gerald Odo's and John Buridan's commentaries on Aristotle's "Ethics"', *Franciscan Studies* N.S. 35 (1975), 237–75.
49 Johannes Buridanus [John Buridan], *Questiones super decem libros ethicorum Aristotelis ad Nicomachum* (Paris 1513), Book v, Q. 2, fol. 91 (89) r: 'dicamus igitur summarie duntaxat quod ius iustum lex iustitia iustificatio distinguuntur est enim ius preceptum domini vel ordinatio circa subditos circa ea quae possunt cadere sub potestate subditorum'.

the command or ordination of a superior *dominus*, viz. god or nature'.[50] Buridan, like Odo, distinguishes between *ius* (as precept or ordination) and law, save that for Buridan this sense of 'command or ordination' is the only proper sense of *ius*. What Buridan intends by this *ius* is suggested by his language. Firstly, right as command belongs intrinsically to a superior – who will also be a *dominus*. As we saw in chapter 1, the expression *superior dominus* had feudal overtones, referring to the lord who has *dominium directum* or overriding *dominium* in the vassal's fief.[51] Secondly, Buridan has substituted the phrase 'par in parem nullum ius instituit' for the well-known legal dictum, 'par in parem non habet imperium'.[52] For Buridan, then, *ius* or right conveys the notion of empire or ultimate jurisdictional authority. It is associated with *dominium*, and 'presupposes a subject upon whom right is imposed'. This links Buridan with the tradition which ultimately led to Mazzolini, who, as we saw, equated *ius* with *dominium* in the sense of *superioritas*. As for Odo, it is *ius* in the sense of *preceptum*, rather than *lex*, which determines human moral and legal activity.

Buridan's commentary differs from Odo's in discussing, as one of the parts of *ius*, the virtue of justice. Justice itself is said to be, uncontroversially, a habit of the will. But the difference in position of *dominus* and *subditus* entails, for Buridan, that justice is twofold: one justice of the *dominus*, which directs him towards ordaining the good for his subjects, and one justice of those subjects, which directs them towards obeying the ordinance of the *dominus*.[53] The justice of the *dominus* is prior to right and the right thing, whereas the justice of the subject is posterior. If the *dominus* is just, then the right thing which is accordance with his *ius* or right will be to the good of his subjects: the right thing is therefore integrated in the teleological order towards the good.

[50] Ibid.: 'dominus autem ille potest esse vel deus ... vel natura ... vel homo ... par enim in parem nullum ius instituit. sed si rex in aliquo. subditis obligetur hoc est ex precepto vel ordinatione domini superioris. scilicet vel dei vel nature'.
[51] See above, p. 21 and n. 37.
[52] The phrase 'par in parem imperium non habet' is the Accursian gloss on the word *imperium* at D. 30, 1, 13, 4: 'Et est dicendum, praetorem quidem in praetorem, vel consulem in consulem nullum imperium habere.' Buridan's phrasing indicates that he probably knew the text as well as the gloss.
[53] Buridan, Quaestiones, Book v, Q. 2, fol. 91 (89) r: 'Justitia autem est duplex quedam pertinens ad dominum. Alia pertinens ad subiectum. Justitia pertinens ad dominum est virtus qua dominus ordinatur ad precipiendum et ordinandum circa ea que prodesse possunt vel obesse in bonum ipsorum. Justitia vero pertinens ad subditum est virtus qua subditus inclinatur ad preceptum seu ordinationem domini observandam.'

This right thing, or *iustum*, is 'that which is conceded to each according to *ius*. For example if the *dominus* commanded or ordained certain things to be in common: the just thing is that they be in common.'[54] The just thing here appears as something which belongs to a subject: *his* right. But this just thing which is conceded to each is also something to which subjects are *obliged*: 'by right, that is, by the precept of the *dominus*, the subjects are obliged to the just thing'.[55] It might therefore seem that Buridan is making the same point as Aquinas and Odo: what is given to one by right (*iure*), another is obliged to. But later Buridan, defining the act of doing the right thing (*iustificatio*), asserts that 'not every right thing is an act of doing the right thing: because that act is an operation: but not every right thing is an operation ... however, every act of doing the right thing can be called a right thing, because it is conceded, *or rather commanded or urged*, according to the ordination of the *dominus*'.[56] The concession and the injunction do not fall on different subjects: rather, what is conceded is better said to be enjoined. The *iustum* is universally the obligation of the subject.

In making this point Buridan more emphatically than Odo takes away the notion that the *iustum* is necessarily directly *ad alterum* – the *iustum* being merely what is imposed by the *ius* of the *dominus*. Nevertheless, he still has in common with Aquinas and Odo the notion that the right of the subject has no connotation of latitude or personal choice. The connection of the extensive concept of 'right' with the good, and the political function of ordering towards the good, ensures that the language of right and its cognates justice, law, the right thing and doing the right thing are bound in with necessity rather than liberty.

This does not mean, however, that all actions committed by citizens must be directed. In explaining the Aristotelian distinction between the *ius politicum* and the other types of *ius*, Buridan asserts that

it is to be noted, that *ius politicum* is the right of preserving the due order between citizens. They are citizens, who, existing under the same

---

[54] Ibid.: 'iustum autem est quod unicuique secundum ius id est secundum domini preceptum vel ordinationem concessum. v.g. si dominus precepit vel ordinavit aliqua esse communia. iustum est illa esse communia'.

[55] Ibid.: 'ex iure hoc est ex precepto domini. subditi obligantur ad iustum'.

[56] Ibid. (italics added): 'non omne iustum est iustificatio: quia iustificatio est operatio iustum autem non omne est operatio ... sed omnis iustificatio potest dici iustum. quoniam secundum domini ordinationem unicuique concessa est. imo precepta vel persuasa'.

principate, are free and equal in living, acquiring and possessing: and I do not mean equal in the sense that one man acquires or possesses the same amount as the other, but they are free and equal in this sense, that it is licit for each equally to acquire for himself as much as he can, and to possess the things he has acquired, and to use them as it pleases him – on the condition that he does so without harming the community or his fellow citizens.[57]

A more exact or more precocious summary of the principles of libertarianism it would be hard to find. The point that needs to be made is that for Buridan, this area of free activity has nothing to do with the vocabulary of right and the right thing. Right is not part of the individual and his possibilities of action. When Buridan mentioned 'the things which can fall under the power of subjects', he was not talking about a sphere of personal right. 'Power' in this phrase means pure, i.e. non-jurisdictional, ability.

The tradition of objective right in Odo and Buridan reinforces the Thomist analysis of right as the obligation rather than the licence of the subject. Crucially, however, it undermines the nature of Aristotelian political right as independent of the legislative structure and as existing *ad alterum*. Odo and Buridan set political right precisely within what was for them a political structure – a structure of command and obedience – abandoning the Aristotelian sense of the political as the relation between free individuals within the city. In consequence, right loses its sense as an impersonal mean between persons, being seen rather as belonging to a person. To that extent, it is, as Villey would argue, 'subjectivised'. As we shall see, this tendency to relocate Aristotelian right within a legislative structure, and the parallel incipient subjectivisation of the concept, can be traced in the development of the Thomist tradition as well.

OBJECTIVE RIGHT IN LATE MEDIAEVAL THOMISM

We have almost no evidence for the nature of specifically Dominican moral theology in the fourteenth century. Although the *Summa theologiae* was undoubtedly being taught at the convents of the Dominican Order throughout the fourteenth century, there is a

---

[57] Book v, Q. 18: 'Notandum quod ius politicum est ius servandi debitum ordinem inter cives. Sunt autem cives qui sub eodem principatu commorantes sunt in vivendo. acquirendo et possidendo liberi et equales. et non dico equales sic quod quantum unus acquirit vel possidet tantum alter. sed sic sunt liberi et equales. quod licet unicuique tantum sibi acquirere quantum potest et acquisita possidere et uti eis sicut placet absque tamen communitatis et concivium lesione.'

complete lack of textual evidence for commentary on the *Summa theologiae* in this period. This is probably due to the fact that while it was unofficially being adopted as the textbook of theology in their own schools, it was to be two centuries before it was officially taught at universities, and indeed the Dominican Order itself made repeated efforts to ensure that their schools complied with the universities in using the *Sentences* as the basic textbook.[58] As we saw, Aquinas did not use the *Sentences* to discuss restitution (and therefore interpersonal morality), ensuring that his followers did not do so either. Evidence for later Thomist moral theology begins again only in the fifteenth century, and somewhat sporadically, even then.

The problem of reconstructing the history of right in Thomist circles is aggravated by the general obscurity of the course of scholasticism in the fifteenth century.[59] The reputation of fifteenth-century scholasticism has suffered at the hands of intellectual historians of all schools, emerging characterised almost universally as a period of theological decadence and logical over-subtlety: the degeneration of 'late nominalism'. In the last twenty or thirty years, two major currents in intellectual history have combined to change the picture for the better: firstly the renewed interest in the conciliar tradition with the work of Tierney, Oakley, Black and Burns, to mention only the most important names; secondly, the work of Oberman and his school in reassessing late mediaeval nominalism. In addition, more work has been done on the structure of teaching at fifteenth-century universities, and on the movement of scholars between them – particularly between Paris and the newly founded universities of Germany. Virtually no one would now uphold a picture of a nominalist stranglehold on fifteenth-century universities.

Nevertheless, if work has been done which suggests universities between 1400 and 1500 were not uniformly nominalist in orientation (Cologne, in fact, has always been acknowledged as a centre of realism), it is still the case that there has been relatively little research into what might have been the substance of alternative *viae*. The history of fifteenth-century Thomism in terms of doctrinal content

---

[58] For the history of Thomist teaching within the Dominican Order and at the universities of Europe, see R. G. Villoslada, *La universidad de Paris durante los estudios de Francisco de Vitoria (1507–1522)* (Rome 1938), chapter 11.

[59] This point and the following are made more extensively by one of the few scholars to have devoted the greater part of his attention to later scholasticism, J. H. Burns, in his most recent work, *Lordship, kingship and empire: The idea of monarchy, 1400–1525* (Oxford 1992), pp. 7–12.

remains in large measure obscure: and this is particularly true of any fifteenth-century development in (rather than simply the existence of) Thomist moral theology. The scarcity of sources makes the reconstruction of Thomist teaching on right in the fifteenth century extremely difficult, but a certain movement can be charted leading to the major Thomists of the early sixteenth century, Cajetan and Köllin.

The early fourteenth century: 'Albertising' Thomism at the University of Cologne

At the opening of the fifteenth century, the major centre of a renascent Thomism was the University of Cologne. Since its inception, Cologne had been a centre of realist intellectual activity. Albert the Great had taught there in the middle of the thirteenth century, and his two most famous students, Thomas Aquinas and Ulrich of Strasburg, had close connections with the place. Having in 1425 successfully resisted an attempt by the Electors of the Empire to force the university to return to the nominalist *via* (worried by the association of realist teaching with the ultra-realism of the Hussites and the consequent social unrest evidenced in Bohemia), the realist camp was in fact becoming increasingly divided between those who followed the doctrines of Albert and those who followed his pupil Aquinas.[60]

The leading figure among the Thomists at this time was Henry of Gorkum, who attempted (albeit unsuccessfully) to steer a conciliatory path between the extremists of both persuasions.[61] His writings bear out this stance. He wrote the first major commentary on all parts of the *Summa theologiae*, suggesting that he was a devoted Thomist; but his more marginal writings have a distinctly Albertising tinge.[62] The same combination marks the other major intellectual figure with

---

[60] For details of these events in Cologne, see A. G. Weiler, *Heinrich von Gorkum (+ 1431). Seine Stellung in der Philosophie und der Theologie des Spätmittelalters* (Zurich and Cologne 1962), 56–83.

[61] The only complete study of Henry of Gorkum is that of Weiler, but he also finds a mention in Martin Grabmann, 'Einzelgestalten aus der mittelalterlichen Dominikaner- und Thomistenschule. 6: Die Stellung des Kardinals Cajetan in der Geschichte des Thomismus und der Thomistenschule', in Grabmann, *Mittelalterliches Geistesleben*, vol. II (Munich 1936), 602–13. This article is in general useful for a brief survey of the pattern of Thomism in the fifteenth century.

[62] See for example his 'Tractatus de temerario iudicio Huyssitarum contra potestatem pape', in the volume Henricus de Gorinchem [Henry of Gorkum], *Tractatus consultatorii* (Cologne 1503).

whom we are concerned within the sphere of influence of Cologne, the Carthusian Denis Rijkel (Dionysius Carthusianus, Denys le Chartreux).[63] Denis had received a Thomist training in theology at the University of Cologne, and his early works are markedly Thomist: but his later writings show an increasing influence of Albert and Pseudo-Denys.

Both of these authors wrote practical and politically engaged tracts: Gorkum against the Hussites, and Denis on aspects of ecclesiastical and secular government. Their respective oeuvres thus bear striking resemblances to that of Jean Gerson (whose work has been shown to be particularly popular in the libraries of the Charterhouses)[64] in terms both of intellectual tradition and of the orientation of their work. All have in common the combination of Aquinas and Albert, and the interest in contemporary ecclesiological Questions. What they lack, however, is any trace of the Ockhamist tradition of handling these issues; and it is this which accounts for the major feature of their discourse relevant to our account: that when they talk about right, they do not take up the Gersonian definition from the *DVSA* and the *DPE*.

As we saw in the last chapter, Gerson combined the Ockhamist analysis of right with Scotist, Albertist and Thomist elements to produce a notion of agency under the law enabled by immediate powers known as rights. The Aristotelian analysis of the possibility of agency was inserted into a fundamentally neoplatonic universe of a series of orders governed by a hierarchy of laws. The immediate powers, which account for the possibility of agency within the Aristotelian system, consequently coincide with the varying 'nobilities' or 'goodnesses' with which creatures of differing rank within the neoplatonic hierarchy are endowed. Rights are a function of status and define a creature's scope of action in so far as it exists within its due position in law. Gerson had no use for the doctrine of right as the object of justice, divorced as it was in Aquinas from the subjective analysis of action.

For the Thomist–Albertists of early fourteenth-century Cologne, in contrast, right is the *ius* of Aquinas' Question 57, 'On right'. It is

---

[63] For details of the life and writings of Denis Rijkel, see M. Beer, *Dionysius des Kartäusers Lehre vom desiderium naturale des Menschen nach der Gotteschau* (Munich 1963), and N. Maginot, *Der actus humanus moralis unter dem Einfluss des heiligen Geistes nach Dionysius Carthusianus* (Munich 1968).

[64] See V. Gerz-von Büren, *La tradition de l'oeuvre de Jean Gerson chez les Chartreux. La Chartreuse de Bâle* (Paris 1973), pp. 6–9.

this right that they imbue with overtones of the Dionysian hierarchy. Thus in his *Summa de vitiis et virtutibus*, Denis defines justice as 'a constant and perpetual habit of the will, or a constant and perpetual virtue of the will, giving to each his right or due'. But this right or due is also a *dignitas*: 'Moreover justice is said to give to each his dignity, because it attributes him with what it is worthy [dignum] that he be attributed, or what is due to him.'[65] These dignities which are due to individuals hint at a passage of Ps.-Denys, quoted by Johannes Capreolus, the fifteenth-century southern French *princeps Thomistarum* who commented the *Sentences* according to St Thomas, in discussing the distributive justice of God: 'the order of the universe ... manifests the justice of God, whence Dionysius says in the eighth chapter of his "On the divine names", "We should see in this that the justice of God is true, that he gives to all according to the proper dignity of each existent, and preserves the nature of each in its proper order and virtue."'[66] Justice is the rendering to each his dignity or due, which is his right: but that right is not further characterised as a power in any sense.

Conversely, where Denis comes very close to the Gersonian language of power that we find in the *DVSA*, the term *ius* is conspicuously absent. In the early and heavily Thomist *Creaturarum in ordine ad Deum consideratio theologica*, written probably while Denis was still at the University of Cologne, Denis discusses the divine goodness (*bonitas*) as the ultimate end of all things, 'because in this consists the highest perfection of any being whatsoever, according to Dionysius, that it conform to the divine goodness according to its possibility, i.e. acquiring some kind of participation in it'.[67] The terms 'goodness', 'possibility' and 'participation' indicate that Denis is writing within a complex of vocabulary very close to the web of language into which

---

[65] Dionysius Carthusianus [Denis Rijkel], *Summa de vitiis et virtutibus*, vol. XXXIX, *Opera omnia* (Montreuil 1896–1913), pp. 13ff.; Book II, a. 33 (pp. 214 ff.): 'Porro justitia dicitur unicuique suam tribuere dignitatem, quia impendit cuilibet quod dignum est ei impendi, seu quod ei debetur.'

[66] Johannes Capreolus, *Defensiones theologiae divi Thomae Aquinatis*, ed. by C. Paban and T. Pègues, vol. II (Tours 1900; reprinted Frankfurt a. M. 1967), Book I, Dist. 45, Q. I, a. I, pp. 568–9: 'ordo universi ... demonstrat Dei justitiam. Unde dicit Dionysius, 8 cap. de Divinis Nominibus: Oportet videre in hoc veram esse Dei justitiam, quod omnibus tribuit secundum propriam uniuscujusque exsistentium dignitatem, et uniuscujusque naturam in proprio salvat ordine et virtute.'

[67] *Creaturarum in ordine ad Deum considerato theologica*, vol. XXXIV, *Opera omnia*, p. 98, a. 8: 'quia in hoc consistit cujuslibet entis summa perfectio, secundum Dionysium, ut divinae bonitati secundum possibilitatem suam conformetur, aliquam scilicet participationem ejus acquirens'.

in Gerson the term *ius* is woven. But Denis refrains from connecting the language of subjective possibility for the good with that of right. This feature is common to his university counterpart Henry of Gorkum. Although Henry recognises and uses a category of subjective power equivalent to a *ius* in Gersonian terms – for example, in the tract *De iusto bello* he speaks of a *facultas recuperandi concessa de iure naturali*[68] – he will not call it a right. Right for him is a due and *ad alterum*, as he elucidates in his commentary on St Thomas (2a2ae 57) where he follows Aquinas to the letter.[69]

The Summa *of Antoninus: a mid-fifteenth-century Dominican understanding of the* Summa theologiae *and the casuistic*

With the work of the Florentine archbishop Antonino Pierozzi (Antoninus Florentinus), we move back, to some extent, into the area of practical casuistic which we discussed in chapter 1. Antonino was a member of the Dominican Order and his activity, both literary and pastoral, belongs to the long tradition of Dominican and Franciscan engagement in the political and social life of the Italian city-states.[70] His great work, the *Summa* (the so-called *Antonina*, signalled as 'On vices and virtues'), belongs in one respect to the genre of *Summae confessorum*, as a work which is intended for the practical solution of cases of conscience.[71] On the other hand, the *Summa* is notable for covering the material of both the *prima secundae* and the *secunda secundae* of Aquinas: that is, both 'speculative' and 'practical' aspects

---

[68] *Tractatus De iusto bello*, in *Tractatus consultatorii*, fol. 50v.
[69] Henricus de Gorinchem [Henry of Gorkum], *Questiones in Sanctum Thomam* (Esslingen n.d.), In secundam secunde, Q. 7.
[70] For Antoninus' life and activity, and for an account of his economic thought, see R. de Roover, *San Bernardino of Siena and Sant'Antonino of Florence: The two great economic thinkers of the middle ages* (Boston, Mass. 1967). De Roover's claims for the originality of both are challenged in A. Spicciani, 'Sant'Antonino, San Bernardino e Pier di Giovanni Olivi nel pensiero economico medievale', in O. Capitani (ed.), *Una economia politica nel medioevo* (Bologna 1987), 93–120, who argues that the most important theses are already present in Olivi's *Tractatus* (found in Todeschini, *Un trattato di economia politica francescana*; see above, p. 24, n. 46).
[71] Antoninus Florentinus, *Summa* (Basel 1518), Part I, Prologus: 'Illas igitur sublimas theorias in librariis comprehensas magistris et scientia perfectis dimisi. Que autem iudicavi apta ad materias predicationum et audientiam confessionum ... accepi a doctoribus pluribus in theologia vel iureperitis: non intendens indoctus et omnis scientiae ignarus poemata condere sed recollectionem facere more fratrum pro me et mei similibus qui mecum erant: quibus nec ingenium ad altiora: nec librorum semper copia datur: et occupationes facultatem subtrahunt discurrendi per libros.'

of moral theology; and for refusing to accept any equivalence of *ius* and *dominium*.

The *Summa* is divided into four parts. The first contains *quedam generalia*, 'viz. concerning the soul and its potencies, which are held to be their [the vices' and virtues'] subjects. On the passions ... On sins in general and their effects. On the multiple laws by which vices are prohibited and virtues commanded'. The second part concerns the vices in particular. The third has as its subject 'the various estates, as much of laymen as of the clergy'. The fourth covers the virtues in particular.

As can be seen from its description, the *pars prima* of the *Antonina* coincides in subject matter almost exactly with the *prima secundae* of Aquinas' *Summa theologiae*, and Antoninus in fact uses Aquinas' material throughout.[72] However, while Antoninus' treatment is for the most part a faithful exposition of Aquinas, he makes a significant innovation in the course of the two titles 'On canon law' and 'On civil law', discussing that part of law which for Aquinas is human law. With the observation that 'human law is called positive written *ius*', and that 'law is a species of right according to Isidore', Antoninus introduces a discussion of *ius* in general, moving the discussion of right at *ST*, 2a2ae 57, 1 into the discussion of human law at *ST*, 1a2ae 95 and 96. Although Antoninus' discussion of *ius* here is in substantive terms no different from that of Aquinas – *ius* is the *obiectum iustitiae*, the *opus iustum* – his insertion of Aquinas' phrase *lex est aliqualis ratio iuris* into the consideration of law rather than of right suggests that for Antoninus, right cannot be discussed independently of law.

It is part III of the *Summa*, 'De statibus' or 'On estates', which holds the greatest interest for our enquiry. In it, Antoninus elevates to a major part of moral theology the *materia statuum* which Aquinas had treated in one brief Question towards the end of the 2a2ae. For Aquinas, *status* principally has a spiritual sense, the discussion of *status* in general being a necessary preliminary to the discussion of the *status perfectionis*, the religious estate. However, for Antoninus this is simply the strict sense of the term, and one which he explains briefly in the

---

[72] Antoninus' inclusion, against precedent, of this speculative material in what is in intention a practical handbook is perhaps to be attributed to two factors: firstly, the growing predominance of teaching of the *Summa theologiae* itself within the schools of the Dominican Order; secondly, an increasing self-consciousness and professionalism about moral theology itself, as witness Antoninus' recognition of such a field as *moralis sapientia*. As a science, this would require its foundations in an analysis of the nature of human action.

Prologue. The rest of the *Pars tertia* is taken up with an examination of the diverse material estates, both lay, clerical and religious, among which is the *status domini*. Antoninus uses the Title 'On temporal *domini*' to introduce a discussion of *dominium* which is the major source for that of Summenhart (and consequently of Mazzolini), although the latter arrive at a quite different conclusion.[73]

In considering *dominium* as part of a discussion of *status*, Antoninus reflects the original mendicant discussions in which *dominium* was precisely a question of *status* – what sort of estate it was relative to the *status perfectionis*, which was poverty. This suggests that Antoninus will view *dominium* not as a power of action, but as a position within a hierarchy relative to others. This is borne out when Antoninus contrasts the opinion of *aliqui doctores* that *dominium* and *ius* are substantively the same, 'because a person has just so much *dominium* in a thing as he has right', with that of other doctors who say that they are not the same. For these latter,

the whole reason is this: that according to the Philosopher and Simplicius in the 'Categories', the relation of *dominium* is a relation of subordination: and therefore no one is said to have *dominium* in anyone unless that person be subordinate to him: but a person cannot have a right in someone to whom he is not subordinate: on the contrary: just as a son has a right in his father, and similarly a slave in his master ... because he is obliged to them with respect to nourishment.[74]

Right is different from *dominium*, for '*dominium* seems to add to itself over and above right a certain superiority and authority'.[75] Antoninus concludes that 'according to these people' – with whom he clearly agrees – '*dominium* is described thus. *Dominium* is the right of having, possessing and using a certain thing, either simply according

---

[73] I use the term 'introduce' advisedly, in that Antoninus consistently attributes his material to others. In the discussion of *dominium*, these are anonymous *doctores*. In the case of the discussion of *ius*, the source is said to be 'quidam magnus magister in libello contra fraticellos: cuius nomen adhuc non inveni'. I regret that I too have failed to discover any text corresponding to Antoninus' discussion; its location would be of some significance, since it is the source discussion for the whole of the later tradition of contract-literature, although I have no doubt that Summenhart and Mazzolini come upon it via Antoninus.

[74] *Summa*, part III, tit. 3, cap. iii, para. 4: 'Et tota ratio est: quia secundum Philosophum et Simplicium in Predicamentis relatio dominii est relatio suppositionis: et ideo nullus dicitur habere dominium in aliquo nisi sit sibi suppositus: sed aliquis non potest habere ius in aliquo cui non est suppositus: imo econtra: sicut filiusfamilias habet ius in patre: similiter servus in domino quia tenetur eis ad alimentationem.'

[75] Ibid.: 'Dominium enim videtur sibi addere supra ius quandam superioritatem et auctoritatem.'

to the pleasure of the will: or according to some predetermined mode: out of a certain superiority and authority.'[76]

Antoninus' favoured thesis begins with the classic determining feature of *dominium* within Christian theology and philosophy: it is in the category of relation, and it is the relation of superior over subordinate. Thus the *doctores* in question who distinguish *dominium* from *ius* do so on the grounds of the association of the former with a relationship towards persons; to be a *dominus* is to have someone subordinate to oneself, to have a certain superiority or authority over them. But they appear to end with an Ockham-influenced definition of *dominium* which is not a relation but a power of acting in a certain way – having, possessing and using – with regard to things. However, this power is said to operate 'out of' a 'certain superiority or authority'. The suggestion is that *dominium* is a combination of a relationship of superiority and a right which is a power of acting.

This sense becomes clearer as Antoninus goes on to define right itself. To begin with he defines right from his definition of *dominium*: '*dominium* over and above right adds only superiority and authority: therefore right can be described with the same formula as *dominium* minus the condition: "with a certain superiority"'.[77] A right can have just as wide a scope as *dominium*, but it does not operate out of superiority or authority. 'Or we can describe it like this: that a right is a power of exercising a certain action with regard to a thing. So that if I can licitly sell a book I have a right in the sale of that book ... as a general conclusion, I have as much right with regard to a thing as I have licit power with regard to it.'[78] A right is a power of acting, rather than a relationship of superiority: a *potestas*, not a *relatio*.

Antoninus therefore distinguishes between *dominium* and *ius* in terms of authority: the power of acting is the same in the case of the *dominus* and the right-holder, but the *dominus* acts on his own, rather than on any external, authority. Thus for Antoninus a right still

---

[76] Ibid.: 'Et ideo secundum istos doctores dominium describitur sic. Dominium est ius habendi possidendi et utendi aliqua re simpliciter pro libito voluntatis: vel secundum aliquam determinatum modum ex quadam superioritate et auctoritate.'

[77] Ibid., para. 5: 'dominium addit solum supra ius superioritatem et auctoritatem: ideo potest describi ius eadem ratione sicut dominium dempta illa conditione: cum quadam superioritate'.

[78] Ibid.: 'Vel possumus sic describere: quod ius est potestas exercendi aliquem actum circa rem. Unde si licite possum vendere librum habeo ius in venditione libri ... sic generaliter concludendo quantum habeo de potestate licita circa rem: tantum habeo de iure circa eam.'

operates within a framework laid down objectively; and his reintro-
duction of the term 'licit' into the Gersonian tradition of *ius* appears
to keep its original sense of moral rectitude, rather than connoting
moral indifference. Subsequent Thomists would differ on the sense
of *licitum* and its association with the language of the just. But as a
whole they follow Antoninus in their increasing tendency to treat of
iustum together with law, and in their consciousness that the spread of
Questions treated in Aquinas' tract *De iustitia et iure* demanded the
elucidation of more than one concept of right.

Early sixteenth-century neo-Thomism

So far we have seen a Thomism flourishing and, most importantly,
developing during the course of the fifteenth century, beyond the
walls of the Dominican convents where it had been widespread from
the start. I have hesitated, however, to call this strengthening of the
Thomist *via* a renaissance or revival because it lacks the pugnacious
and self-conscious quality associated with these words. The beginning of the sixteenth century, in contrast, saw a movement which,
although having its roots in the fifteenth-century development, can
be called neo-Thomism for its evangelistic self-awareness as such.
Two Dominicans stand out from the very early stages of the
sixteenth-century movement: Thomas de Vio, Cardinal Cajetan,
whose early years were spent teaching the Thomist *via* at Padua, and
Konrad Köllin, professor of theology at the University of Cologne.[79]

Cardinal Cajetan, best known for his role in the Catholic indict-
ment of Luther, was the seminal figure in the growth of neo-
Thomism in the sixteenth century.[80] Between 1507 and 1520 he
published a commentary on the entire *Summa theologiae*, distinguished
by the critical distance it maintains from the text, a far more
sophisticated approach than that of Henry of Gorkum. It is ad-

---

[79] For Köllin, see N. Paulus, *Die deutschen Dominikaner im Kampfe gegen Luther* (Freiburg 1903), pp. 111–34; Villoslada, *Universidad*, pp. 298–9. Köllin, initially somewhat unwilling to join in the polemics with Luther, was later a far more enthusiastic participant, publishing in 1527 his *Eversio Lutherani Epithalamii*. That Köllin and Cajetan were in close contact with each other in the doctrinal response to nascent Protestantism is evident from Cajetan's quodlibetal questions against the Lutherans, which contain several responses to questions posed by Köllin in correspondence: see Thomas de Vio Cajetanus, *Quaestiones quodlibetales, cum aliquot assertionibus contra Lutheranos* (Paris 1530).

[80] The role of Cajetan in the proceedings against Luther is too well known to need discussion here. For Cajetan's position within the Thomist tradition see Grabmann, 'Stellung des Kardinals Cajetan'.

dressed to the reader, whose Questions it anticipates and whose attention it draws to the more significant passages. Cajetan's commentary on the *Secunda secundae* was finished in 1517.[81] In the course of commenting on Questions 57–79, on justice and right, he shows his penetration in raising the problem which has preoccupied interpreters ever since, Aquinas' doctrine of natural right.

As we have seen, the primary characteristic of right in the Aristotelian tradition – right as the object of justice – is that it is *ad alterum*, towards another. Right is social: that is, it occurs between equal members of a civil or political society, who alone can properly be called 'others'. Anything due between unequal members of other groupings, for example the household, is not properly right, because there is no proper 'other'. As we have also seen, however, Aquinas had jeopardised his own elucidation of this sense by his pronouncements on natural right. Cajetan shows himself to be well aware of the problem: 'In articles 3 and 4 together a doubt arises, How is it that paternal right is said to be right only through a defection from right *simpliciter*, as is said in art. 4 ... and yet between father and son there is natural right, as is said in art. 3?'[82] He responds that 'natural right is to be distinguished into natural right *simpliciter*, and *secundum quid*. For to eat and to drink, and to conserve oneself in being is not of natural right *simpliciter*, but *secundum quid*: because right is not properly of one same person towards himself, since [right] is properly towards another.'[83] Cajetan stresses that the distinction made in a. 4 between the two senses of right has to be moved back into a. 3. Father and son are not properly 'other', and thus natural right in its proper sense does not obtain between them; the implication is that natural right in its proper sense is natural right as set out in a. 2.

Cajetan's response is interesting in that *comedere*, *bibere* and *conservare seipsum* are not mentioned at this point in Aquinas' text. The phrase *se conservare in esse* is of course purely Thomist; as we have seen, for Aquinas it constitutes the natural inclination of all entities *qua* entities, and the first substantive precept of the natural law for man.

[81] Villoslada, *Universidad*, p. 43.

[82] *Secunda secundae summae theologiae cum commentariis Thomae de Vio Caietani O. P.* (Venice 1593), Q. 57, in a. 3 and 4 (fols. 131v–132r): 'In a. 3 et 4 simul dubium occurrit, Quomodo ius paternum dicitur iustum per defectum a iusto simpliciter, ut in a. 4 ... dicitur: et tamen inter patrem et filium est ius naturale, ut in a. 3 dicitur?'

[83] Ibid., fol. 132r: 'ius naturale distinguendum est in ius naturale simpliciter, et secundum quid. Comedere nam et bibere, et conservare seipsum naturalis iuris est non simpliciter, sed secundum quid: quia eiusdem ad seipsum non est proprie ius, quoniam ad alterum proprie est.'

However, neither natural law nor natural inclination, in the *Summa theologiae*, have natural right – in any sense – as their corollary. Cajetan's example of self-conservation as natural right *secundum quid* suggests that he does see natural right as the corollary of natural inclination or natural law, only stressing that conserving oneself is not properly natural right, because it is not *ad alterum*. As we noticed, Aquinas' examples of natural right as between male and female, father and son, appeared to be an attempt to preserve the principle that right is of its nature between members of a community. There is no hint in the *Summa theologiae* that he would have considered self-conservation, eating and drinking as natural right in any sense, even *secundum quid*. Rather, an offence against the natural inclination to conserve oneself in being – suicide – is (in so far as the individual is considered in himself and not as part of a community) for Aquinas a sin because it opposes charity, not because it opposes justice.[84]

The same wavering within the Thomist tradition over natural law and natural right in the question of self-conservation is evident in the work of Konrad Köllin, who belongs to the tradition of Thomist teaching at Cologne that we examined earlier in the chapter.[85] In 1512 he published a commentary on the *Prima secundae*, far more ambitious in scope than that of his predecessor Henry of Gorkum. But from our point of view most interesting are his *Quodlibeta* in dialogue, published in 1523.[86] This latter work shows interesting signs of the times; most noticeably, in the dialogue format, made use of 'in that this mode of explaining seems more agreeable, in these times'. Secondly, it displays the emphasis on moral questions that characterises the scholastic of the sixteenth century. Ulrich, Köllin's brother and the person clearly responsible for the publication of the work, explains in his prefatory letter to the printer that in the course of his conversations with his brother on scholastic topics, they had concluded that 'setting aside the honour necessarily due to the speculative part of theology, the moral part – both for the establishment of a right way of living, and furthermore for the solution of the difficulties which are wont to occur concerning cases of conscience –

---

[84] *ST*, 2a2ae 64, a. 5 in corp. and ad 1.
[85] Cf. Paulus, *Deutschen Dominikaner*, pp. 111–22.
[86] Conradus Koellin [Konrad Köllin], *Quodlibeta* (Cologne 1523). The genre of quodlibetal questions appears to undergo a brief renaissance around the turn of the sixteenth century, with Cajetan and Hadrian VI both writing their own versions; these works are exclusively devoted to practical moral theology, the speculative Quodlibet seemingly now a thing of the past.

seemed to us in this age of ours vastly more useful'. The consciousness of scholastic moral theology – now firmly recognised and named
as such – as a resource capable of rivalling humanist projects for the
good life and, in addition, fulfilling its traditional function in an
epoch where cases of conscience were increasingly complicated,
marks a new vocation for scholastic authors.

In the fourth Quodlibet, 'Ulricus' attempts to deter 'Conradus'
from discussing the Roman law principle of *Vim vi repellere licet*, for he
is sure he can add *nihil novi* to the reams of literature on the subject.
Conradus replies by asking a question: 'Since, in the course of your
reading, you have gained a perspective on everything to do with the
subject, perhaps you could reveal the solution to this mystery: What
is the reason why it says "one is allowed", and not rather "one
should"?'[87] Conradus' question is founded on a distinction he makes
between things which are of natural right, which 'appear not merely
to be permitted, but truly to be commanded [praecepta]', and those
things which are 'licit', which 'seem to be those which are not
prohibited, by law, or those which are not punished, whereby many
things, of themselves repugnant to reason, are said to be licit'.[88] This
distinction coincides with that between things absolutely good in
themselves, which are due (*debita*) and commanded (*praecepta*), and
things conditionally good, which are called licit. Applying the
distinction to the case of killing another in the attempt to preserve
one's own life, Conradus concludes that 'To intend to conserve one's
own life ... is naturally just [iustum est naturaliter]'; ' conservation is
naturally just, and due, but the killing of another, is naturally licit'.[89]

Köllin thus associates the language of right with that of due
against the language of *licitum*. But in speaking of self-conservation as
a naturally just thing, Köllin makes the same assumption as Cajetan,
that self-conservation is in question in the discussion of natural right.
This assumption is not unconnected with his use of the language of
praeceptum. The natural *debitum* is *debitum* because it is *praeceptum*, not
simply *ex natura rei*. As with Aquinas, rather than Odo and Buridan,
this *praeceptum* is part of the law. But by characterising the just thing
as *praeceptum*, Köllin's right, as with Odo and Buridan, has, firstly,

---

[87] Ibid., ɪᴠ, fol. 27v: 'Quando omnia, et cuncta illic conspexisti, pandas velim id mysterii.
Quid cause sit, ut dicatur licere, vim ire repulsum, et non potius oportere.'

[88] Ibid.: 'Enimvero de iure extantia nature, non modo permitti, verum et precepta esse
videntur, licita vero videntur que non prohibita, per legem, vel que non punita, quo pacto
an multa, de se refragantia rationi, licita dicuntur.'

[89] Ibid., fol. 29 (28) r.

become a function of the legislative structure; secondly, it has thereby similarly lost the necessity of being *ad alterum*. It is this that allows self-conservation to be a just thing.

Köllin is aware of the difficulties with the traditional Thomist doctrine of objective right, and continues the discussion in the next question. Quodlibet v concerns the maxim 'Do to another what you would have done to you, and what you would not have done to you, do not to another.' Conradus explains that this is a command of natural law, whereupon Ulricus asks why it is not a question of 'legal due', *legale debitum*. Conradus responds with a question: 'Have you ever anywhere read that justice properly speaking (of which kind is legal justice) operates with regard to oneself? – Justice is always with regard to another separate from the subject.'[90] He goes on to explain that the 'legal due' is equivalent to 'the just thing objectively', which is 'the good of another' to which the will is not naturally inclined. There is, however, also a 'moral due', to which we are naturally inclined as if to our own good. 'Whence just as I ought to will that whereby I am justly done by, so equally [I ought to will] that you are. But this is to will the just thing ... as a matter of moral due. However to will to give you this object, which is legally due to you, falls under the precept of justice, not under the common [precept] of the natural law.'[91] The general precept of the natural law, which corresponds to our own natural inclinations, is here seen to have as its corollary a moral right which is not necessarily *ad alterum*.

Together, the texts of Cajetan and Köllin bear witness to a change in the understanding of right within the Thomist tradition. Aquinas himself had attempted to use the authentic Aristotelian category of the *iustum* as the just action which is due from the individual to cover both the demands of casuistry and the Roman jurists' notion of natural right as belonging to all nature. He preserved the idea that *ius* was an action and *ad alterum* despite the fact that he had compromised its nature as political by admitting it of animals. Cajetan and Köllin avoid the problem that the jurists' sense of natural right cannot be part of Aristotle's political right, because they are beginning to understand right *per se* as a function of law. With

---

[90] Ibid., v, fol. 51r: 'Nunquid circa seipsum, proprie dictam iustitiam (cuiusmodi legalis est) uspiam legisti versari? que utique ad alterum est supposito separatum.'

[91] Ibid., fol. 51v: 'Unde sicut velle debeo, quo iuste mecum fiat, sic pariter et tecum. Sed hoc est velle fieri iustum ... debiti moralis. Verumtamen velle tibi hanc dare rem, tibi legaliter debitum, sub iustitie cadit precepto, non sub communi legis naturalis.'

their strong concept of a natural law, derived from Aquinas himself, natural right can for them be just what is commanded by natural law. In this way they preserve the Thomist sense that right is an action and positively due from an individual, rather than just licit.

However, by tying *ius* to action under the law in response to the problem over natural right, they firstly make it even more difficult for the notion to be convincingly stretched to cover the demands of the science of casuistry. Although Cajetan adheres to Aquinas' text in making no suggestion that the category of analysis has changed or even is under pressure in the consideration of restitution and theft, Köllin makes it explicit that the category of right used in the analysis of nature and natural action, connected with natural law, is different from that of the legal justice which operates between men. Köllin suggests that in this field, the authentic Aristotelian political *iustum* is the relevant category, but we shall later see the Spanish neo-Thomists Vitoria and Soto depart even further from Aquinas by turning this category into a fully elaborated notion of *dominium*. All concur with Antoninus in associating Q. 57 with the treatise on law in the 1a2ae rather than with the casuistic material of the 2a2ae.

Secondly, by understanding the *ius* that is an action as a function of law, they lose the sense that this just action must necessarily be *ad alterum* or *inter homines*. In consequence, although the *iustum* of Cajetan and Köllin is still 'objective' in the sense that it is not a quality of the subject, but rather the right thing for that subject, still it is 'subjective' in the sense that it is, precisely, for a subject rather than between subjects. In this they appear to resemble Odo and Buridan. But whereas the latter were concerned to assimilate *ius* to a structure of *domini* or *superiores*, and *subditi* or *inferiores*, the two Thomists remain faithful to Aquinas in their overriding concern with law. The natural right of Köllin and Cajetan which is derived from the natural has affinities instead with the tradition of Ockham, Gerson and their successors.

JACQUES ALMAIN AND THE CONTINUATION OF THE GERSONIAN TRADITION

The dates of Cajetan's and Köllin's discussions of right and especially natural right are respectively 1517 and 1523 at the latest. In their preoccupation with the place of self-conservation within the Thomist theory of right, they bear witness to the influence of a language of political philosophy dependent precisely on a natural right of self-conservation, a language which was the subject of intense debate at Paris and undoubtedly at other universities too in the early years of the sixteenth century. Its author was Jacques Almain, pupil of the Scottish master John Mair at the Collège de Montaigu at the University of Paris. His work is evidence of the mutual assimilability of the neo-Thomist and the Gersonian traditions of right.

Within Anglo-Saxon circles, Jacques Almain is chiefly known for his contribution, together with his master John Mair, to the 'silver age' of conciliarism in the early sixteenth century.[92] His ecclesiological positions are derived explicitly from Ockham and Gerson, and his notion of right owes a similar debt to his two predecessors. His language of right is found both in his conciliarist tracts, the *Quaestio resumptiva agitata in vesperiis*, and the *Libellus de auctoritate ecclesiae*, and – a vitally important but often neglected source – an exposition of Scotus' commentary on *Sentences* IV, Dist. 14 and following, all four of which were published posthumously at Paris in 1518.[93]

Almain wrote his *Libellus [Tractatus] de auctoritate ecclesiae*[94] at the behest of the theology faculty of the University of Paris in response to the *De comparatione auctoritatis papae et concilii* of Cardinal Cajetan.[95] Its purpose is to defend, against the arguments of Cajetan, the power of the general council of the church to judge and if necessary to depose the pope. Almain's argument concerning the power of the general council rests on two analogies: between man and the civil society, and between the civil society and the ecclesiastical society. The first analogy is derived explicitly from Thomas Aquinas, but follows a long tradition of organic metaphors for the city. The second analogy depends on an argument to the effect that the ecclesiastical society

---

[92] See, especially, the essays of Francis Oakley on Almain and Mair. The more important of these are collected in F. Oakley, *Natural law, conciliarism and consent in the later middle ages* (London 1984).

[93] For a summary of Almain's career and a list of his works, see Villoslada, *Universidad*, pp. 165–8. The importance of Almain's work on the *Sentences* has now been brought to general attention by J. Burns, 'Jacques Almain on *Dominium*: A neglected text', in A. E. Bakos (ed.), *Politics, ideology and law in early modern Europe: Essays in honor of J. H. M. Salmon* (Rochester, N. Y. 1994), 149–58.

[94] Edited in Ellies du Pin, *Joannis Gersonis opera omnia* (Antwerp 1706), vol. II, cols. 976–1012. For Almain and Cajetan, see Q. Skinner, *Foundations of modern political thought*, vol. II, *The age of reformation*, pp. 42–7; J. H. Burns, '*Jus gladii* and *jurisdictio*: Jacques Almain and John Locke', *Historical Journal* 26, 2 (1983), 369–74.

[95] For a description of Cajetan's arguments and the circumstances surrounding the debate, see F. Oakley, 'Almain and Major: Conciliar theory on the eve of the reformation', in Oakley, *Natural law*, chapter 10.

cannot be denied to be a perfect society; but this perfection is analogous to that of the civil society. What Almain seeks to demonstrate is that just as man has a natural right of self-preservation which he cannot renounce, so the community has such a right, which even if it should transfer to an authority in exercise, it always holds in reserve, and can exercise directly should it need to defend itself against its chosen authority. Thus the body of the church, represented by a general council, retains the power to defend itself against the pope if need be.

The opening words of the opening chapter, 'In which is treated of the origin of civil jurisdiction, in order that by comparison with it ecclesiastical jurisdiction might become known: and thus by natural law, the authority of the church over the pope might be demonstrated', establish Almain's basic theme:

Just as God, the author of nature, created man with the natural right, or power [potestate], of consuming those things which are necessary to his sustenance and conservation, and further of repelling those things which are harmful (on which right is founded the power of killing him, who attacks unjustly ...) ... similarly every community of persons mutually conserving each other by civil means ... has the natural power of conserving itself not only in being, but in peaceful being, to which [power] it pertains to cut off, even by death, those whose life disturbs the community.[96]

As an authority for these assertions, Almain refers to Thomas Aquinas. The du Pin edition cites *ST*, 2a2ae 65, 1, 'Whether there be any case in which it might be licit to amputate a person's limb'. But the version printed in the 1518 edition of Almain's works, the *Aurea opuscula*, refers instead to *ST*, 2a2ae 64, 2.[97] Here Aquinas discusses whether it might be licit to kill malefactors, arguing that just as it is licit to cut off the putrid limb of an individual for the sake of the health of the whole body, so it is licit to cut off the putrid limb of a community – i.e. a malefactor – for the same purpose.[98]

---

[96] *Tractatus de auctoritate ecclesiae*, col. 977: 'Quemadmodum Deus, naturae author, hominem condidit cum naturali jure, seu potestate, ea quae sustentationi ac conservationi necessaria sunt sumendi, necnon et ea quae nociva sunt repellendi (super quo jure fundatur potestas eum, qui iniuste aggreditur, interimendi ...) ... similiter et communitas quaelibet aliquorum adinvicem civiliter conservantium ... naturalem habet potestatem, se non solum in esse, verum etiam in esse pacifico conservandi, ad quam spectat eos quorum vita est in perturbationem communitatis, etiam per mortem praescindere.'

[97] Jacques Almain, *Aurea opuscula* (Paris 1518), fols. 46r–61v. I am grateful to Professor Burns for alerting me to this point. The original printing of 1512 also carries the Q. 64 citation, although I have not been able to see a copy.

[98] Ibid., Q. 64, a. 2 in corp.

As we can see, Almain wants this analogy between community and individual. But Q. 64, a. 2 does not give him the terminology of *potestas*, power.[99] This Almain grafts in from the Gersonian tradition, to create an analogy between the power of the community and the power of the individual. By further associating Aquinas' language of *salus* in these passages with the equally Thomist language of self-conservation, Almain can assimilate Aquinas on the subject of self-conservation to the natural rights discourse of Ockham and Gerson, which we examined in the last chapter. The legitimate *potestas* of Aquinas' discussion of the position of the community with regard to an unhealthy member is assimilated to the Gersonian right, the 'potestas seu facultas conveniens alicui secundum dictamen rectae rationis'.

Almain's reply to Cajetan is thus framed in terms of right and power. The *Quaestio resumptiva agitata in vesperiis* is formally rather a discussion of *dominium* – natural, civic and ecclesiastical.[100] However, both in this *Quaestio* and in the commentary on Scotus, IV, 15, Almain equates *dominium* with *ius*. Like Conrad Summenhart thirty years earlier, who as we saw in the first chapter does the same, Almain attributes the notion of the coincidence of *dominium* and *ius* to Gerson. But Almain's interpretation of Gerson forms an interesting contrast with that of Summenhart. Summenhart had read Gerson as equating *ius* and *dominium*, and in explaining the manner of the equivalence, had drawn the notion of 'power' (*potestas*) into the category of relation and therefore into the same category as *dominium*. On his understanding, right is appropriated to *dominium* as a relation of control. Almain too reads Gerson as equating right with *dominium*: but his reasoning is entirely different. '*Dominium* of every kind is nothing other than the right of using a certain thing according to right reason' – Ockham's style of *dominium*-definition and, post-Ockham, Fitzralph's and Gerson's. 'And right (as Gerson says) is nothing other than a proximate power or faculty pertaining to someone according to the dictate of right reason. And *dominium* is

[99] It may well be for this reason that the later edition gives the reference to Q. 65, a. 1, which argues that it is licit for the public power to cut off a person's limb for the good of the community.

[100] Edited in du Pin, *Joannis Gersonis opera omnia*, vol. II, cols. 961–76. A translation by A. S. McGrade of this text is forthcoming in J. Kraye (ed.), *Cambridge translations of renaissance philosophical texts: Moral and political philosophy* (New York and Cambridge, forthcoming); I am grateful to Steve McGrade for allowing me an advance look at his translation and introductory notes.

that pertinent right: and right is that faculty ... Whoever therefore
has a right of using a certain thing according to a right dictate, has a
proximate power pertaining to him according to right reason: and
such a one is said to have right and *dominium* in that thing.'[101] Almain
does the opposite of Summenhart: he assimilates *dominium* to right.
There is no mention, as in Summenhart, of a correlative obligation
or a correlatively obliged thing. Rather, this is the Gersonian power
of acting which is consequent upon a preceding law.

This connection with law is vital to Almain's notion of a right. For
Almain, a right or *dominium* is consequent on and operates according
to a binding precept of a law. Thus 'natural *dominium* is a proximate
faculty or power of assuming inferior beings to one's own sustenance,
according to the dictate of the natural law. For by natural law
whosoever is bound to conserve himself in being: out of which
obligation there arises in whomsoever a power of assuming inferior
beings to one's own conservation.'[102] Almain asserts repeatedly that
one has a natural right to or *dominium* in only that which one is
obliged to do by natural law: in positing a definition of natural right
or *dominium*, 'it is presupposed that of natural law whosoever is
obliged to conserve his body and himself in being, in so far as it is
possible for him; and this is natural to all things'.[103] It is *because* a
person is obliged that he has right or *dominium*: 'if he is obliged to
consume, therefore there is in him a faculty of using that thing,
according to the rules of natural right ... to this he is bound by
natural *dominium*, and no one can renounce such *dominium* simply and
absolutely for all eventualities'.[104] Natural right is a function of

---

[101] Jacobus Almain, *Clarissimi doctoris ... Iacobi Almain ... a decimaquarta distinctione questiones Scoti
profitentis, perutilis admodum lectura* (Paris 1526; henceforth *In IV Sent.*), Dist. 15, Q. 2, fol. 48r:
'Dominium in toto genere nihil aliud est quam ius utendi aliqua re secundum rectam
rationem. Et ius (ut dicit Gerson) nihil aliud est quam potestas vel facultas propinqua
competens alicui secundum dictamen rectae rationis. et dominium est illud ius competens:
et ius est ipsa facultas ... Quicunque ergo habet ius utendi aliqua re secundum dictamen
rectum, habet potestatem propinquam ei convenientem secundum rectam rationem: et
talis dicitur habere ius et dominium in illa re.'
[102] *Quaestio resumptiva agitata in vesperiis*, conc. 1a, col. 961: 'dominium naturale est facultas, seu
potestas propinqua assumendi res inferiores ad sui sustentationem, secundum dictamen
legis naturalis. Lege enim naturali quilibet tenetur se conservare in esse: ex qua
obligatione, in quolibet oritur potestas res inferiores sumendi in usum, ad sui conserva-
tionem.' See McGrade's introduction to his translation of the *Quaestio*, for this point.
[103] *In IV Sent.*, Dist. 15, Q. 2, fol. 48v.
[104] Ibid., fols. 49v–50r, discussing the standard topic of whether a Carthusian monk must
break his vow not to eat meat in the case of extreme necessity: 'si obligatur sumere, ergo
est in ipso facultas utendi illo secundum regulas iuris naturalis ... ad hoc tenetur dominio
naturali, et nullus potest abrenunciare simpliciter et absolute tali dominio in omne

natural law, and bears accordingly the same burden of obligation. Right is a faculty only to do, not also to forbear; and man must do what he has a natural right to do, because he cannot be exempt from natural law.

Although the languages of the *Quaestio resumptiva agitata in vesperiis* and of the exposition of Scotus on IV, 15 coincide in equating *ius* and *dominium* in the sense of *potestas*, there is an important difference between the political theories consequent upon the definition of right or *dominium* in each case. The *Quaestio* shares with the *Tractatus de auctoritate ecclesiae* the thesis that there is a natural community analogous to the natural man with a natural right of self-conservation. This power is transferred to an authority which may be one or several, while remaining in essence with the community. The exposition of Scotus, however, does not talk in terms of such an organic natural community, but rather in terms of a simple collectivity of fallen men: 'albeit the proposition, there should be superiority [superioritas] among men during the state of fallen nature, in order to coerce the evil and reward the good, be of the law of nature: nevertheless that such superiority reside in this man, or in that, is not of the law of nature, but merely of human law'.[105]

These differences are principally to be explained by the fact that Almain is doing two different things in two different places. In the latter doctrine he is following Scotus very closely, as befitted an expositor. In the former, he takes his cue from the traditional conciliarist discourse of Ockham and Gerson in regarding the church as a body. The divergence of these two traditions will be important in understanding the work of Francisco de Vitoria, which we shall examine in the next chapter. All this notwithstanding, however, in Almain the doctrine of right and *dominium* shows every sign of systematisation between the two types of writing, indicating that Almain moved his own analysis of *dominium* as right from the tractates into Scotus' far briefer consideration. The main point to make concerning this analysis is how distant it is from that of the school

---

eventum.' It should be noted, however, that the duty to self-preservation is not unconditional – the Carthusian should starve if it would cause a scandal for him to eat meat.

[105] Ibid., fols. 47v–48r: 'Item, licet illa propositio: Debet esse superioritas inter homines pro statu nature lapse ad coercendum malos, et premiendum bonos, sit de lege nature: tamen quod talis superioritas resideat in isto, vel in illo, non est de lege nature, sed solum de lege positiva.' The source of this is Ockham, III *Dial.* I. 2. 17. Again I am grateful to Steve McGrade for this reference.

which equates *dominium* and *ius* in the sense of *dominium*, or a relation of control. While Almain uses both the equivalence between *dominium* and *ius*, and the term *superioritas*, he never equates the two, because his *ius-dominium* is not a *status* or relation of control. Thus although Almain and Mair are traditionally paired in histories of political thought, the former's language of right must be firmly distinguished from that of the latter, whose commentary on iv, 15 uses the language of the equivalence of *dominium* and right in the sense traditional to teaching on restitution.

Almain belongs instead squarely within the Gersonian tradition, unadulterated by Summenhart, which fuses Ockhamist right with Scotist law to produce a sense of right as a faculty conditioned by an externally given law, not a law unto itself. Almain's direct use of the Thomist notion of self-conservation as the first imperative of the natural law, and the many references, particularly in the commentary on Scotus, to the *Secunda secundae* of the *Summa theologiae* confirm that Almain cannot be subsumed under any sweeping category of 'nominalist-voluntarist'.[106] Almain's sense of right shares with that of Cajetan and Köllin the connection with that which is commanded, and hence with the obligatory, the morally necessary. It is a long way from any sense of that which falls within the liberty or *dominium* (in its sense as associated with liberty) of the agent, or even of that which is licit or permitted.

Although Almain died prematurely young, his lectures and writings had enormous influence, constituting as they did by far the freshest voice in moral theology at the University of Paris at the beginning of the sixteenth century, the milieu in which the neo-Thomist members of the Spanish School of Salamanca received their intellectual formation.[107] We turn now to consider their reception of late mediaeval subjective rights discourse, in the work of the two most prominent figures of the School, Francisco de Vitoria and Domingo de Soto.

---

[106] This was recognised by Venancio Carro in his prejudiced but still useful study of the School of Salamanca and its antecedents, *La Teología y los teólogos-juristas españoles ante de la conquista de América* (Madrid 1944), chapter 4. Almain is not among those voluntarist theologians guilty of 'olvido de lo natural'.

[107] For further details of the Parisian milieu, see Villoslada, *Universidad*, and A. Renaudet, *Préréforme et humanisme à Paris pendant les guerres d'Italie (1494–1517)*, 2nd edn (Paris 1953).

4

Liberty and nature: subjective right and Thomism in sixteenth-century Spain

In the sixteenth century, Thomism flourished most vigorously in Italy and in Spain. In the former, despite the political engagement of Cajetan, the Thomist tradition was characterised by its development of the theoretical aspect of Thomist philosophy, to a degree where it could engage fully in debates within contemporary secular Aristotelian philosophy.[1] It is in Spain that the Dominicans continued the development of Thomist moral and political philosophy in the movement known as the School of Salamanca or the 'second scholastic'. Its 'founder', Francisco de Vitoria, was educated at the University of Paris and returned to Spain in 1523 to transmit his learning in moral theology to a range of brilliant pupils. Their writings in turn became the standard reference works in ethics and politics for the later sixteenth and early seventeenth centuries, appropriated and developed by the Jesuits into a highly sophisticated science of the moral order.

As suggested in the introduction, the major debate with regard to Vitoria and his successors, particularly Domingo de Soto, is over whether they can be said to have a 'theory' of objective or of subjective right – that is, whether the School of Salamanca represented a return to the true Aristotelian conceptions of Aquinas,[2] or whether the School perpetuated the nominalist-voluntaristic subjectivism characterising a whole range of *moderni* from

---

[1] See P. O. Kristeller, *Le thomisme et la pensée italienne de la renaissance* (Montreal 1967), pp. 59–61 for the role of Thomism in the development of Pomponazzi's theory of the soul, and the engagement of the Dominican Crisostomo Javelli in the debate.

[2] Tuck, *Natural rights theories*, p. 47; P. André-Vincent, *Droit des indiens et développement en Amérique latine* (Paris 1971), p. 55. For criticism of the former, see Daniel Deckers, *Gerechtigkeit und Recht. Eine historisch-kritische Untersuchung der Gerechtigkeitslehre des Francisco de Vitoria (1483–1546)* (Freiburg 1992), p. 160, n. 264; for objections to the latter, see the review of André-Vincent, *Droit des indiens*, by Guy Augé, in *Archives de philosophie du droit* 18 (1973), 438–43, and B. Tierney, 'Aristotle and the American Indians – again: Two critical discussions', *Cristianesimo nella storia* 12 (1991), 295–322.

Olivi to Almain.[3] Both of these positions depend on the opposition between objective right and a single notion of subjective right as a liberty of the person, associated with nominalist and voluntarist ethics. We have by now, however, sufficiently distinguished within the category of subjective right between a right taken as equivalent to *dominium* understood as a relation of control over another thing or person, related originally to liberty, and a right taken as a power of action under a law, related to obligation or necessity. In the course of the last chapter we have also established that objective right in later mediaeval scholasticism cannot be seen as a direct 'opposite' of subjective right. All of these senses of right were available to Vitoria and his successors in the writings of Mair, Almain and Cajetan. The contention of this chapter will be that not only the doctrines of right, but also the achievements within political theory in general of the School of Salamanca, cannot be fully understood without an appreciation of the complexity of the late mediaeval heritage of *ius*.

LIBERTY AND RIGHT IN FRANCISCO DE VITORIA

Francisco de Vitoria was born around the year 1485. Having entered the Dominican Order in Burgos possibly at the age of eleven, he was sent to Paris in 1510–11 to study at the Dominican Collège de Saint-Jacques. Shortly afterwards (1512–13) Vitoria began to study theology under the Belgian theologian Pierre Crockaert. Crockaert had begun as a student of John Mair, but had afterwards joined the Dominican Order at the Collège de Saint-Jacques, where he lectured on the *Summa theologiae*. Vitoria was his assistant in preparing an edition of the *Secunda secundae* in 1512.

We saw in chapter 1 how precisely the question of right and *dominium* formed the theme of commentary on *Sentences* IV, 15 as it was handled in non-Thomist hands, and we have seen how Almain was drawn to expand upon the most famous commentary on the locus, Scotus', in further pursuit of his Gersonian ideas.[4] The fourth book of the *Sentences* – which treats of moral theology – appealed in part because it offered an opportunity to write on the pressing issue of

---

[3]   Villey, 'Promotion de la loi', p. 64; Grossi, 'Proprietà', p. 124.
[4]   Almain in fact characterised Scotus' second Question on IV, 15, the Question 'On restitution', which defines *dominium*, as 'the most excellent Question among all the rest of Scotus' Questions' – for obvious reasons given his purposes.

dominium; and it is highly probable that it is this appeal of *Sentences* IV which is responsible for the evident renewed interest in the *Secunda secundae* of Aquinas, not only in Dominican circles. Historians have been wont to speak of a Thomist revival of the early sixteenth century characterised by a move to commentary on the *Summa theologiae* rather than the *Sentences*.[5] However, it has been amply demonstrated that within the schools of the Dominican Order, the *Summa theologiae* had for a long time been gradually replacing the *Sentences* as the basic textbook of theology,[6] and we have seen how in the Thomist university of Cologne, at least, the *Summa theologiae* had been commented on by academic staff. Rather, what was new and fertile at the Collège de Saint-Jacques under Crockaert was the exploitation of the *Secunda pars* and in particular the *Secunda secundae*. For those, particularly Dominicans, who were committed to the *via Thomae*, the *Secunda secundae* formed the equivalent of *Sentences* IV. With its Questions 57–79 'On justice and right' and its Question 62 'On restitution', it too offered its commentators an opportunity to engage with the political side of moral theology. Vitoria had attended Almain's lecture 'On natural, civil and ecclesiastical *dominium*' and was doubtless familiar with his exposition on Scotus. Between his return to Spain in 1523 and his death in 1546, he produced what can be seen as a Dominican answer to Almain's moral-theological *oeuvre*: a commentary on the *Secunda pars* of the *ST*, the main weight of which lies on Questions 90–108 of the *Prima secundae* and 57–79 of the *Secunda secundae*, together with a series of engaged *relectiones* on issues of political morality.

Vitoria begins his commentary on these Questions 57–79 by following Aquinas closely, understanding *ius* as the *iustum* and the *obiectum iustitiae*, and asserting that *ius* coincides with *debitum* and is *ad alterum*: definitions which of themselves substantiate the position of those historians who wish to mark him as a theorist of 'objective right'. In the question of the divisions of right, too – into natural and positive, and then into natural, of peoples, and civil – Vitoria again essentially follows Aquinas. Beginning by characterising the *ius naturale* as that which is necessary, in the sense of that to which we cannot but assent, he extends it to all animals: 'Cicero … says that natural right is that which … a certain innate force implanted. And … the jurisconsult says, that natural right is what nature has taught

---

[5] E.g. Skinner, *Foundations*, vol. II, p. 135.   [6] See above, chapter 3, p. 103 and n. 58.

all animals ... it is clear that nothing is of natural right unless it can be recognised by natural illumination.'[7] However, we saw that Aquinas, even in extending natural right to animals, had been careful to stress that this right is between animals, and is in a certain sense apprehended, thus preserving the character of the Aristotelian *iustum* as *ad alterum*. Vitoria's consequent dicta lose this sense entirely. For him, natural right has the sense of what any nature naturally does – its specific activity: 'there are many things which are of natural right which do not extend to all animals. This is clear, because it is natural right that fire ascend and burn; but this is not common to all animals, because not to a stone.'[8] If a stone can have natural right, it is clearly nothing that depends on cognition, even the primitive perceptions of animals. Nor is it even *ad alterum*. It is that activity which is naturally congruent to a certain nature.[9]

But the definitions of Question 57 are not the end of the story. As we saw, Question 62 of the 2a2ae concerns the ever-controversial subject of restitution; and it is here that Vitoria begins his redefinition of the nature of right in a subjective sense.[10] Vitoria makes a point of referring his audience to the practice of the *moderni* in using *Sentences* IV, 15 as a locus to discuss restitution. Remarking that the Lombard himself and the *antiqui* did not exploit the text in this way, he goes on to say that 'the *moderni* began to extend the subject matter [they included] on these words of the Master, because they could not find in the Master any other place wherein they might more

---

[7] Francisco de Vitoria, *Comentarios a la secunda secundae de Santo Tomás*, ed. by V. Beltrán de Heredia (Salamanca 1934), III, Q. 57, a. 2, n. 5. (Henceforth, using the notation introduced by Deckers, *Gerechtigkeit*, I shall refer to this work as *Comm ST* (V), followed by the specification of the Question, article and number: the present locus is thus *Comm ST* (V) 57, 2, 5.) The reference is to Cicero, *De inventione*, Book II.

[8] *Comm ST* (V) 57, 3, 2. Aristotle had of course used the example of fire in his discussion of the natural and the conventional just thing at *NE*, 1134b18, but it was in illustration of 'immutable and everywhere the same' rather than of the just thing: 'And it seems to some that all [just things] are of this kind, that that which is by nature is immutable and has the same force everywhere, as fire burns both here and in Persia.'

[9] The introduction of Cicero here is possibly not without significance for Vitoria's interpretation of Aquinas' notion of natural right. The *quaedam innata vis inseruit* of the definition of natural right at *De inventione*, II involves no sense of apprehension which the *docuit* of Ulpian's definition still bears.

[10] Vitoria's treatment of the material of restitution is discussed authoritatively and exhaustively in Deckers, *Gerechtigkeit*, pp. 154ff. Deckers' work is an essential corrective to those interpretations of Vitoria which view him as a theorist of objective right without thereby falling into an over-simplistic characterisation of Vitoria's notion of subjective right. Many of his conclusions are in agreement with my own, obviating the need for extensive reconsideration here, although I believe his claims for the 'modernity' of the commentary on 2a2ae 62, 1 to be overstated.

conveniently treat of this subject ... Mair raises fifty Questions. Hadrian too discusses it at length, and Saint Thomas, as you see, here [at 2a2ae 62] discusses everything at great length.'[11] Vitoria does not here distinguish between those who treat of restitution on any ground other than that of simple length of treatment. Thus he includes Scotus among the *antiqui* who wrote little, even though he must have been aware that it is Scotus' commentary which forms the basis for most of the later extended treatments which differ profoundly from Aquinas' handling of the subject.

It is hard to see what Vitoria might have been doing in classing Aquinas together with Mair as both concerned with restitution. If he had hoped to suggest that Aquinas' treatment was essentially in line with nominalist and Scotist commentary on IV, 15, he would not have deceived his audience for a minute. His own words acknowledge that the relation of Q. 62 to IV, 15 is a matter of burning interest for them, and the opening words of his substantive treatment would have given him away: 'But before we approach the subject matter of restitution, we must speak of *dominium*.'[12] Aquinas had defined *dominium* in discussing theft: it is the tradition springing from Scotus' commentary on IV, 15 which insists that *dominium* be defined prior to considering restitution. Vitoria's audience would have known immediately that Vitoria considered the 2a2ae deficient in this respect, and that what they were listening to was a revision – however respectful – of Aquinas, rather than an elucidation. However, instead of merely arguing that another category of right – *dominium* – was demanded for the treatment of restitution, Vitoria argues instead that Aquinas' 'just thing' *is* in fact *dominium*.

Vitoria's commentary on a. 1 of Q. 62 demonstrates his use of the multiple strands of late mediaeval rights discourse to slide from Aquinas' understanding of right to that embedded in the casuistic of restitution. One of his guides in this process appears to be the *Antonina*, which he had edited in 1520–1.[13] Ostensibly repeating the definition of right given by Aquinas, what he in fact does is to focus

---

[11] *Comm ST* (V) 62, 1, 3: 'moderni incoeperunt dilatare materiam super ista verba Magistri, quia non invenerunt in Magistro alium locum ubi commodius tractarent materiam hanc ... Majoris facit quinquaginta quaestiones. Hadrianus etiam hoc late disputat, et Sanctus Thomas, ut videtis, hic latissime disputat omnia.'

[12] Ibid., n. 4: 'Sed antequam materiam de restitutione aggrediamur, loquendum est de dominio.'

[13] *Francisco de Vitoria: Political writings*, ed. by A. Pagden and J. Lawrance (Cambridge 1991), p. xxx.

like Sant'Antonino on the phrase of Aquinas' at Q. 57, a. 1, 'lex est
quodammodo ratio iuris', and to expand it as if it formed the main
theme of Aquinas' doctrine of right. He also uses Antonino's
language of the licit: he interprets 'lex est quodammodo ratio iuris'
as signifying that right is *quod lege licet*,[14] thereby detaching the *iustum*
from the sense of 'due' which it had held in Köllin. As we shall see,
however, this does not mean for him that right could be 'repugnant
to reason', which was Köllin's sense of 'licit'.

Vitoria goes on to argue further that this objective sense of right as
a function of law is a nominal definition only, and that in substance,
right is what Conrad Summenhart says it to be: 'it should be noted
that Conrad, who is the author of that noble tract "On contracts",
posits in Q. 1 a definition of that term "right" ... He says that right is
a power or faculty pertaining to a person according to the laws.'[15]
True to his source, Vitoria next considers the question of whether
dominium is equivalent to *ius*. *Dominium*, he says, is defined in three
ways. Firstly, 'strictly and peculiarly, so that it signifies a certain
eminence and superiority, the same way that princes are called
domini'.[16] When *dominium* is understood in this way, it is not the same
as right, because right is a broader category, for the wife has a right
in her husband, but not *dominium*, because she is not called the *domina*
of her husband. This is Summenhart's point concerning the relation
between his strict and his general sense of *dominium*, derived from
Antonino (although for Antonino superiority was the only definition
of *dominium*).

Secondly, *dominium* is defined in a legal sense as property, in which
sense it is, again, not equivalent to right.[17] This was the definition
which Aquinas used in order to treat of restitution. But for Vitoria,
this sense is not appropriate for the purpose. Restitution is due not
only in the case of goods taken from a *dominus*, but in the case of
anyone with any kind of right over an object, and the correct way to

---

[14] *Comm ST* (V) 62, 1, 5: 'Jus ergo ... nihil aliud est nisi illud quod licet por leges. Patet hoc ex
Sancto Thoma supra, Q. 57, a. 1 ad 2, ubi dicit quod lex non est proprie jus, sed est ratio
juris, id est, est illud ratione cujus aliquid est licitum.'

[15] Ibid.: 'Et ideo de diffinitione quid rei notandum est quod Conradus, qui fecit tractatum
illum nobilem De contractibus, q. 1 ponit late diffinitionem illius nominis "jus" ... Dicit
ergo quod jus est facultas vel potestas conveniens alicui secundum leges.'

[16] Ibid., n. 6: 'Uno modo, stricte et peculiariter, ut dicit eminentiam quandam et superioritatem, eo modo quo principes vocantur domini.'

[17] Ibid., n. 7: 'Secundo modo dominium capitur, latius quidem, sed proprius, ut capitur in
Corpus juris civilis et apud jurisconsultos prout tantum valet sicut proprietas, id est
secundum quod distinguitur ab usu et usufructu et possessione.'

handle restitution is to find a means of equating all injury with theft. Vitoria therefore joins the casuistic of restitution in positing a third sense of *dominium*, in which it is equivalent to right: 'because if someone were to take something from a person with use, usufruct or possession, he would be called a thief, and would be bound to restore it to them ... because it would be a case of *contrectatio rei alienae* against the will of the *dominus*, but not of the proprietor'.[18]

Vitoria thus appears to adopt from Summenhart the weak sense of *dominium* in which its peculiar senses of eminence or superiority, and of property, are lost in its equivalence with right. However, as Q. 62 proceeds it becomes clear that Vitoria does not think of his concept of *dominium-ius* as simply juridical hold on other objects or persons. He imbues it with the same senses of freedom and authority which it has in traditional mendicant theology and in Aquinas' tract *De perfectione spiritualis vitae*. Thus he does not accept that it can be predicated of irrationals: to do so, as does his source Summenhart, is 'wholly improper'.[19] *Dominium*-right is for Vitoria that whereby man is made in the image of his *dominus*, God, who 'communicated [his *dominium*] to no irrational creature. And thus St Thomas says ... that only a rational creature has *dominium* of its act ... and that even man is not *dominus* in respect of natural actions and the sensitive appetite.'[20] This is the reasoning which we encountered in chapter 1: only that has *dominium* which is not determined by its object, and thus is free – that is, the spiritual powers of intellect and will. Vitoria in equating this *dominium* with right, against his earlier Thomist position that there is a *naturale iustum* which belongs to all nature, excludes the activity of all irrational nature from the universe of the juridical.

It is important to stress that what Vitoria inserts into Aquinas' Q. 62 is a doctrine of *dominium* rather than of right, because of the recent assertion that what Vitoria proposes in the course of his discussion is a contract-theory of the political unit based on a notion of man as the bearer of natural subjective rights.[21] As we have seen, although Vitoria speaks of *dominium* as right, right for him has the sense of

---

[18] Ibid., n. 8: 'quia si aliquis subriperet rem ab usurario vel usufructuario vel possessionario, diceretur fur, et teneretur illis restituere ... qui diceretur contractatio rei alienae invito domino, et tamen non invito proprietario.'

[19] Ibid., n. 10.

[20] Ibid., n. 11: 'Hoc dominium ... nulli creaturae irrationali communicavit. Et ita Sanctus Thomas ... dicit quod sola creatura rationalis habet dominium sui actus ... quod homo etiam non est dominus respectu actionum naturalium et respectu appetitus sensitivi.'

[21] Deckers, *Gerechtigkeit*, pp. 282–3.

control or decisional authority which belongs properly to *dominium*. It is *de iure naturali* – of natural right in the sense of natural law – that man conserve himself in being:[22] but man is not said to have the 'natural right' of conserving himself in being. Rather, what he has is a consequent *dominium* over all the creatures of the earth: 'whatsoever man was then *dominus* of all things in the law of nature, because whosoever could use any object he liked and even abuse it according to his pleasure, as long as he did not harm other men or himself'.[23]

This *dominium* had by all men over all things is never called 'natural *dominium*'. This is instructive if we compare Vitoria's commentary with that of Almain on Scotus, IV, 15, who had throughout talked of *dominium naturale*, connecting it intimately, as we saw, with the *content* of the natural law and giving it the sense of being for, and obliging to, the realisation of that content. For Vitoria, natural law has the sense of obligation, but the *dominium* which is consequent upon it is not specifically said to be 'natural' nor ordained specifically to the natural act of self-conservation. Vitoria does not posit the plurality of specific *dominia* invoked in both the Gersonian and the Summenhartian rights traditions to explain the powers of different species of creature. Instead, Vitoria puts forward the traditional distinction between the spiritual and the natural, where *dominium* belongs only to spiritual beings and is connected with liberty. *Dominium* is singular and unitary, although it can be over different things. To speak of man in Vitoria as 'Träger natürlicher subjektiver Rechte'[24] is to use seventeenth-century natural rights language which does not fit the text: Vitoria's *dominium* is not '*ein* natürliches subjektives Recht',[25] it is *the* (unqualified) subjective right, or better, subjective right *simpliciter*. It belongs to everyone, rather than its being one among a set of rights belonging separately to each individual. Vitoria's notion of the common *dominium*-right consequent on the law of nature is not a mark of his 'modernity',[26] but on the contrary of his traditionalism, his adherence to the Augustinian

---

[22] *Comm ST* (V) 62, 1, 13: 'de jure naturali est quod homo conservet se in esse'.

[23] Ibid., n. 16: 'quilibet homo erat dominus omnium tunc in lege naturali, quia quicunque posset uti qualibet re et etiam abuti pro libito suo, dummodo non noceret aliis hominibus vel sibi'.

[24] Deckers, *Gerechtigkeit*, p. 191.   [25] Ibid., p. 220.

[26] Cf. ibid., p. 193: 'Insofern Vitoria bei der Behandlung zahlreiche Gerechtigkeitsfragen ... nicht nur die Normen des *jus naturale* zugrundegelegt, sondern auch die Annahme, daß der Mensch Träger natürlicher subjektiver Rechte ist, trägt seine Gerechtigkeitslehre frühneuzeitliche Züge'; p. 215: 'Vergleicht man Vitorias Eigentumslehre jedoch mit der des Thomas von Aquino, dann tritt ihre "Modernität" zutage: Der spezifisch neuzeitlichen

dualism of spirit and nature and the high scholastic understanding of the words of Genesis.

However, this *dominium* of man is indeed the ground for a theory of political power founded on consent, as Vitoria goes on to consider the origin of distinct *dominia* as opposed to the unbounded natural *dominium*.[27] As we saw in chapter 1, Scotus had argued that the division of the originally common *dominium* could not come about by that natural law which laid down this common *dominium*. He therefore suggested that the natural law had been revoked after the Fall, yielding a period of the licence to appropriate. The divisions resulting from this appropriation were then legitimised by the law of an authority to whom the people had consented, either father or elected prince.

For his part, Vitoria is far too much of a Thomist on the question of law, at least, to suppose that the natural law could ever have been revoked. His argument instead is that the possibility of division is contained within the original *dominium* itself: 'Item, if man was *dominus* of all things by natural right, he could do whatever he wanted.'[28] For Vitoria, Scotus' licence of appropriation is not separate from but a part of original *dominium*. Again, anyone can transfer any object to the *dominium* of another: 'this is proved from the definition of *dominium*, for *dominium* is the faculty of using an object as one personally sees fit'.[29] In the same way, out of this *dominium* the people consent to the power of a prince with regard to their affairs: 'the prince is elected by the people. But the people gives him such an authority that he can dispose of the goods of citizens ... he has in himself the consent of the people given in order that he can lay down dispositions concerning the things of the republic.'[30]

Denkfigur "natürliche subjektive Rechte" kommt in der Eigentumslehre Vitorias eine zentrale Funktion zu.'

[27] This discussion, as indeed the entire course of Vitoria's analysis of restitution, is heavily indebted to Scotus' commentary on IV, 15, to which Vitoria was probably alerted by Almain's commentary. It is this debt which determines the consideration, at this point, of the authority of the prince. For Vitoria's dependence on Scotus and generally for his notion of *dominium* in its aspect as translatable by the term 'property' ('Eigentum'), see G. Otte, *Das Privatrecht bei Francisco de Vitoria* (Cologne and Graz 1964), esp. pp. 41–55.

[28] *Comm ST* (V) 62, 1, 20: 'Et item, si homo esset dominus omnium de jure naturali, poterat facere quidquid vellet.'

[29] Ibid., n. 29: 'probatur ex diffinitione dominii, quia dominium est facultas ad utendum re pro arbitrio suo'.

[30] Ibid., n. 33: 'princeps est electus a populo. Sed populus dat ei istam auctoritatem ut possit disponere de bonis civium ... princeps habet in se consensum populi datum ut possit disponere de rebus reipublicae.'

Political authority comes into being from a natural-law state where all men are equal in the sense that none is *superior* and none is *inferior.*[31] There is no political organisation given in nature.

Vitoria's concern with the sphere of personal authority and personal freedom is confirmed in his commentary on Q. 64, 'On homicide'. The first article of Question 64 treats of 'Whether it is illicit to kill any living things whatsoever'. Aquinas had used the article to argue that it is licit for men to kill animals for their use. Vitoria raises two further questions: whether it is licit to kill animals if no utility is derived therefrom; and secondly, whether it is licit to kill animals solely for the sake of pleasure. This mode of following up St Thomas allows Vitoria to intervene to discuss the burning subject of hunting.

Vitoria argues that although the king may make a law limiting capture of wild animals, lesser lords may not do so. 'So I say that they cannot appropriate wild animals to themselves unless it is by ancient custom, because it is tyrannical that they make laws concerning the appropriation of wild animals and against the people's liberty to hunt because wild animals are common to all. On the contrary, princes should rather defend this liberty.'[32] Vitoria allows that some differentiation according to status should remain, 'so that greater licence is given to those who are greater and of superior dignity'.[33] However, it still belongs only to the king to 'limit the liberty of the people'. To those who argue that it is useful to the people to be prevented from hunting, 'because there are many who waste their time, and neglect their farming, and cease the business of producing food in order to go hunting', and that the lord has a moral duty to procure the utility of his subjects, Vitoria has a ready answer:

[the private gain] is not useful to them, since [the lords] take away their liberty from them, because liberty is more useful than that private good. It is better for the farmer to have the liberty of hunting all year round, albeit he hunts nothing, than that he toils and produces food. So that since the lords do them such grave injury thereby, they have no arguments or excuse to defend themselves against the charge of sinning mortally in preventing their subjects from hunting.[34]

---

[31] Ibid., n. 21.
[32] Ibid., 64, 1, 5: 'Unde dico quod non possunt appropriare sibi feras nisi ex antiqua consuetudine, quia tyrannicum est quod faciant leges de appropriatione ferarum et contra libertatem populi ad venandum quia ferae sunt communes. Immo potius debent defendere principes hanc libertatem.'
[33] Ibid.
[34] Ibid., n. 9: 'illud non est illis utile, postquam tollunt ab eis libertatem, quia libertas est

Semantically, these passages show a coincidence of the terms 'liberty', 'licence' and 'right' (the last being implicit in the accusation of injury). Substantively, they show an emphasis on the absolute value of liberty, notwithstanding the fact that it is not necessarily directed towards the good. It is better that the subject be able to direct himself towards his perceived good than that he should be directed towards a real good by an external agency.

This sense of the value of independent authority is demonstrated in the next article, on the homicide of evil-doers, and specifically the case of killing an attacker in self-defence. Vitoria begins his treatment of this specific case of conscience with the commandment of the Decalogue, 'Non occides', and discusses the various solutions to the difficulty put forward by other theologians. 'The third way of solving it, which comes closer to the truth, is that in the commandment in question it is only prohibited to kill on private authority; thou shalt not kill on private authority, but certainly however on public authority.'[35] Vitoria's answer is significant. Ascertaining that what is meant here by divine or civil authority for an action is that that action is licit by divine or civil law, he objects that 'it follows that it is never licit for teachers to beat their pupils nor parents their children unless on public and divine authority ... who, I beg, would say that it is not licit for them to beat them on private authority? Again, in the same way it would follow that it would not be licit even to eat on private authority, since whoever eats, eats by divine or civil law.'[36] What Vitoria objects to is the transference of agency from the private individual to the law. Even though the individual in a civil society may do what the law dictates, nevertheless he does so on his own authority and thus responsibly. Vitoria's repeated critique of Mazzolini and Summenhart (otherwise much admired by him) who attribute *dominium* and right to animals is part of the same point. Man is distinguished by his control over his own actions and this is

magis utilis quam illud bonum privatum. Melius est agricolae habere libertatem venandi toto anno, licet nihil venetur, quam quod laboret y gane de comer. Unde postquam in hoc faciunt illis tam gravem injuriam, nullis certe argumentis nec excusatione possunt domini defendere quin peccent mortaliter arcendo subditos a venatione.'
[35] Ibid., 64, 2, 8: 'Tertius modus est, qui magis accedit ad veritatem, quod in illo praecepto prohibetur solum occidere privata auctoritate; non occides privata auctoritate, bene tamen publica.'
[36] Ibid.: 'Sed contra hoc sequitur jam quod nunquam licet praeceptoribus flagellare discipulos nec parentibus filios nisi auctoritate publica et divina ... quis, obsecro, diceret quod non liceat illis auctoritate privata flagellare illos? Item, eodem modo sequeretur quod nec liceret comedere auctoritate privata, quia qui comedit, lege divina vel civili comedit.'

not taken away by the fact that some of these actions may take place under the law. He *acts* in the full sense of the term, as opposed to the animals which *are acted upon*.

Over the course of commenting Aquinas' analysis of restitution and of homicide, then, Vitoria first fuses the sense of right with that of *dominium*, and then expands that sense from the narrow notion of *ad libitum* control over an object, to a broad notion of personal and self-referential authority conceded by a particular law. This authority is not to be confused with mere unpunished ability: the authority is authority with regard to an act which is good, or at least, not bad.[37] But nonetheless it evades the sense of the necessary: licit has the sense of being positively good but not therefore compulsory (as opposed to the sense it bears in Köllin, for whom the licit has the sense of the merely unpunished). *Dominium*-right is the authority to do *or not to do* a good act. It is specifically bound in with the distinction of man as a rational and free creature from the rest of nature which operates necessarily.

By contrast, the *relectio* which Vitoria gave specifically on the subject of civil power – *De potestate civili* – adopts a very different approach.[38]

---

[37] See ibid., 64, 3, 3. Here Vitoria discusses the standard Question of whether it is licit to kill an adulterous woman caught *in flagrante delicto*: 'It appears so, because the law gives a licence.' But Vitoria agrees with the common opinion of theologians in saying that the husband sins in so killing his wife. 'And if you say: therefore the law is iniquitous ... I reply ... and I say, that the civil law does not give the husband a faculty and a licence and an authority to kill a wife caught in a shameful act, but gives him only impunity. And thus the law in question only permits, but does not concede.' Compare the discussion of the important early sixteenth-century jurist Fortunius Garcia in his tract *De ultimo fine iuris canonici et civilis*, in *Tractatus illustrium iurisconsultorum* (Venice 1584–6), vol. I, fols. 106–32, n. 165: 'it is questioned whether civil laws permitting a father, or even rather giving him a faculty, so that he might kill his daughter [taken in adultery], are valid in true justice ... [the law] does not have the power, which it vainly concedes to the husband, because it is against the law of God, from whom is all power'.

[38] The *Relectio De potestate civili* is edited in T. Urdanoz, *Obras de Francisco de Vitoria* (Madrid 1960), 149–95 and translated into English from the original manuscripts in *Vitoria*, ed. by Pagden and Lawrance, 3–44. I have quoted from the Urdanoz edition as the critical edition, although recognising its shortcomings (*Vitoria*, ed. by Pagden and Lawrance, p. xxxv). The difference between the political philosophy of the *Relectio De potestate civili* and the commentary on the *Summa theologiae* is well brought out by Deckers, *Gerechtigkeit*, pp. 283ff., although his comparison is in part based upon his notion that the commentary on the *Summa theologiae* involves a concept of plural natural subjective rights. The *Relectio* has been extensively analysed elsewhere: see F. Castilla Urbano, *El pensamiento de Francisco de Vitoria. Filosofía política e indio americano* (Barcelona 1992), esp. chapter 3, and the discussion in J. A. Fernández-Santamaria, *The state, war and peace: Spanish political thought in the Renaissance, 1516–1559* (Cambridge 1977), pp. 54–87, who believes that Vitoria's different pronouncements on the origin of civil power can be ultimately reconciled. See also the summary but cogent remarks in *Vitoria*, ed. by Pagden and Lawrance, pp. xviii–xx. I shall therefore

It belongs to a series of such *relectiones* or special lectures given by Vitoria between 1528 and 1549 on politically engaged subjects and which are similar in form and in content to the special lectures which Almain gave in Paris on the subject of civil and ecclesiastical power. The political doctrine advanced in the *Relectio De potestate civili*, delivered in Salamanca in 1528, differs from that put forward in the commentary on restitution in the same way that the political doctrine of Almain's commentary on Scotus IV, 15 differs from that of the conciliarist tractates, stressing the natural necessity of civil power rather than its free constitution by the common consent of individual and autonomous human beings.

Vitoria begins his lecture by reminding his audience of the Aristotelian notion of the final cause – which he calls the first among the four causes laid down by Aristotle in his *Physics* – and of the consequent notion of hypothetical necessity: necessity given the end or the purpose. Nothing, he says, can sufficiently account for the features of creation except the hypothesis that they are necessary towards some end. The feature of creation in question is of course the civil power; and Vitoria correspondingly begins by analysing the necessity of the *civitas* of which it is the power. The *civitas* is necessary for the remedy of individual human deficiencies. Men are, firstly, inadequately equipped by themselves even for mere survival; secondly, they are inadequate singly to their need for companionship and conversation. Necessity, not liberty, is thus the key concept in considering the origin of the political community or *civitas*. The *civitas* is necessary to man's natural end of preserving himself in being and in being good; it is thus 'the most natural community and most in conformity with nature', and a 'product of nature'.

This product of nature, this natural entity, has like all natural entities the right of self-conservation. Vitoria employs Almain's argument to the effect that just as every individual man has 'the power and right of self-defence by natural law, since nothing can be more natural than to repel force by force', so the community or commonwealth has this same power, to the extent of being able to excise limbs which threaten the *salus* of the whole.[39] This power, Vitoria goes on, must then be delegated to a ruler of some description,

confine my discussion here simply to the difference in the notion of right it employs, which has gone unremarked by its interpreters.

[39] Vitoria, *Relectio De potestate civili*, in Urdanoz, *Obras*, 157: 'quilibet homo iure naturali habeat potestatem et ius defendendi se. Siquidem nihil magis naturale quam vim vi repellere.'

preferably a king. As we saw, however, Almain's argument had the deliberate consequence that the community has power against its ruler – be that the temporal community against the prince, or the spiritual community against the pope. Vitoria is therefore led to argue that the power of a king is not from the commonwealth, but from God himself: so that it is not a question of the community transferring its power, but merely its authority. The community authorises that the power be in one man or another.[40]

Vitoria does not elaborate on the sense of 'right' with which man and community are endowed. But if right and power here have their Almainian sense, then this is a faculty which is not capable of non-exercise. Its very presence is determinative of human action, is part of the obligation of natural law. It is not the personal authority to do or not to do which is the feature of the *dominium-ius* of the commentary on the *ST*. However, in this *relectio*, just as in Almain's *Quaestio resumptiva agitata in vesperiis*, the notion of individual subjective right is brought in purely by way of analogy. It plays no motive role in the formation of the *civitas*: the dynamic or the agency belongs to the impulse of living with his fellows with which God endowed man at his constitution. The doctrine of this *relectio* differs from that of the commentary on the *ST* in locating the formation of the *civitas* in the world of natural causality and necessity: of science, rather than of the history of peoples.

Vitoria's *oeuvre* as a whole is thus split between two senses of right: not between 'objective right' and 'subjective right', but between two different senses of the latter. The first a sense of subjective right which involves the notion of obligation and law: natural right in this sense, the natural right of the *Relectio De potestate civili*, is associated with a politics of nature and necessity. The second sense, wherein right is coincident with *dominium* and bears the sense of liberty and

---

[40] Ibid., pp. 161-4; *Vitoria*, ed. by Pagden and Lawrance, pp. 14-17, and see also their Introduction, p. xix. That these qualifications of Vitoria's are prompted by the consequences of Almain's analogy is suggested by the fact that both in the *De potestate civili*, and discussing the same point in commenting on *ST*, 1a2ae 90, 3 ('Can anybody legislate?'), Vitoria draws his audience's attention to the question of the power of the pope over the church: the pope is not merely the vicegerent of the church, but has his power over it or his care of it from God. Similarly, although Aquinas may have characterised the temporal prince as the *vicem gerens seu curam habens communitatis*, 'the Doctor does not understand that he has authority from the community, but that he bears the care of it' (*curam gerit*, an amalgam in the best scholastic tradition). See the above article in Vitoria, *Comentario al Tratado de la Ley (I–II, 90–108)*, ed. by V. Beltrán de Heredia (Madrid 1952).

freedom from obligation, is at the base of the politics of free consent and of independent personal authority within the *civitas* which characterises the commentary on the 2a2ae. Vitoria's work and its position within the intellectual tradition of rights discourse cannot be properly understood without an appreciation of this distinction. Nor, moreover, can that of his most important successor, his fellow Dominican, Domingo de Soto: for Soto's work, as I shall seek to show, constitutes an attempt to resolve the tension between the two notions of right without thereby sacrificing the theoretical insight peculiar to each. Soto's problem is that of reconciling the conflicting claims to right of nature and liberty.

DOMINGO DE SOTO: THE HERITAGE OF VITORIA

The work of Domingo de Soto is poorly served in comparison to that of his compatriot and teacher Vitoria. Soto tends to be regarded as less brilliant than his predecessor and less logical than a good scholastic might be: a trait displayed to the full in his analysis of natural law and natural right.[41]

The thrust of the present analysis of the *De iustitia et iure* (*DIEI*) will be to argue, against this consensus, that Soto's text does not represent a confusion over the essence of natural law and natural right. Soto does not oscillate confusedly between attributing law and right to all nature, and attributing it solely to rational nature (and thus human nature in the terrestrial context). The suggestion, instead, is that it can be read as a coherent response to what is ultimately the peculiarly Thomist problem of the analysis of (external) human activity: the basic problem of how to reconcile the traditional

---

[41] Thus Bernice Hamilton, his major interpreter in English, writes that Soto's '*De Justitia et Jure* is more scholastic than Vitoria's work, and thus closer to Suárez; yet he is less logical than either, partly because (like St Thomas himself) he wavers in his analysis of the natural law': B. Hamilton, *Political thought in sixteenth-century Spain: A study of the political ideas of Vitoria, De Soto, Suárez and Molina* (Oxford 1963), p. 8. In this she follows the conclusion of the Spanish scholar, Venancio Carro, for whom Soto fails to 'ser lógico' in his analysis of natural right: V. Carro, *Domingo de Soto y su doctrina jurídica* (Madrid 1943), pp. 166-7. Carro's detailed knowledge of the work is marred by his desire to make it conform to theological orthodoxy. Thus Carro does not want to allow that Soto definitely posits a natural right for animals; this is an 'error', as we learn from the analysis of the 'genio y penetración' of Domingo Bañez two pages further on. A more useful analysis of the themes considered here can be found in Jaime Brufau Prats, *El pensamiento político de Domingo de Soto y su concepción del poder* (Salamanca 1960); and Brufau Prats, *La escuela de Salamanca*, chapters 3-6. I regret that I have been unable to consult D. Ramos-Lissons, *Estudio sobre la ley en Domingo de Soto* (Rome 1977).

distinction between natural and free agency, embedded in the scholastic account of salvation and meritorious action, with the naturalistic ethics and politics of Aristotle. Aquinas had advanced the beginning of a solution in proposing that man is subject to the eternal law in two ways: firstly, in the same way as all other creatures, in having a natural inclination to his proper good; secondly, in the sense of having an innate recognition of its precepts. Because he did not see natural inclination as properly law, however, he encountered no problem of different levels of legitimation in the human individual; and because he did not integrate right into the subjective process of human action, the whole issue was not for him a question of right.

For his successors in the Thomist tradition, however, legitimate subjective activity was very much a question of right. The course of the Thomist tradition had drawn upon two notions of subjective right: that which equated right with *dominium* and liberty – spirituality; and that which connected right primarily with nature as that faculty justifying action which is the result of each nature's natural inclination to its own good. Vitoria, as we saw, involved the former in his commentary of the *Summa theologiae*, but adopted the latter in his *Relectio De potestate civili*. He thus avoided the issue of the relationship between these two notions of right.

The present contention is that Soto's book, specifically entitled 'On justice and right', yields on careful reading a solution to the problem, which is able to save both Christian liberty and the notion that human activity is integrated in the natural operation of the world of created nature, and to safeguard the right of agency at each level. It does so by validating and giving effect to both notions of right. Instead of adopting one or the other or hesitating between the two, like his mentor Vitoria, Soto separates out two levels of right and justification: one that characterises all nature including man, and another that applies only to rationals and therefore to man alone upon earth. His response to both traditions of scholastic rights discourse is to legitimate and to justify by natural law and natural right both the conscious, end-directed activity of man alone among terrestrials, and in addition the activity born of the natural inclinations of all creatures, including man.[42]

---

[42] This perspective is also suggested, in a different context, by J. Brufau Prats: 'La aportación de Domingo de Soto a la doctrina de los derechos del hombre y las posiciones de Bartolomé de las Casas' (*La escuela de Salamanca*, chapter 6, p. 114).

Domingo de Soto was born Francisco de Soto in 1494–5 in Segovia of a family of limited means.[43] He studied first at the nominalistically orientated University of Alcalá, where he gained his degree of Master of Arts in 1516. Subsequently pursuing his studies in theology at Paris, he began by attaching himself to the school of John Mair, but probably after his first year switched allegiances to the teaching of Francisco de Vitoria at the Collège de Saint-Jacques. Soto returned to Alcalá in 1519–20, where he obtained the chair of arts, leaving in 1524 to join the Dominican Order and change his name to Domingo. Later that year he was transferred, on account of his academic qualifications, to the famous convent of San Estebán in Salamanca, which was by then home to Vitoria. At Salamanca Soto pursued an active academic career, interrupted for a period of seven years by official duties at the Council of Trent and as confessor to the emperor Charles V. In 1550 and 1551 he was a member of the Juntas appointed to decide the case of Sepúlveda against Las Casas.[44] In 1552 he rejoined the University of Salamanca, obtaining the prestigious Cátedra de Prima, which he held until 1559. He died late in 1560.

Soto's works fall into three main categories. A first is constituted by commentaries on Aristotelian logic and natural science.[45] The second comprises works of theology written in an academic context, of which the most famous are the *De iustitia et iure libri decem*, first published at Salamanca in 1553–4 and reedited by Soto in 1556–7, which latter edition was reprinted twenty-seven times in the course of the sixteenth century; and *In quartum sententiarum commentarii*, first published at Salamanca in 1557–8 and reprinted, again in the course

---

[43] For details of Soto's biography, see the fundamental series of articles by V. Beltrán de Heredia in *Ciencia tomista* 43 (1931), 357–573 and 44 (1931), 28–51: 'El maestro Domingo (Francisco) de Soto en la Universidad de Alcalá'; 45 (1932), 35–49: 'El maestro Domingo de Soto en la controversia de Las Casas con Sepúlveda'; 57 (1938), 38–67 and 281–302: 'El maestro Domingo de Soto, Catedrático de Vísperas en la Universidad de Salamanca (1532–1549)'. See also the 'Introducción biográfica' in Carro, *Soto*, 13–60.

[44] For details of Soto's role in the famous debate, see Beltrán de Heredia, 'Domingo de Soto en la controversia de Las Casas', and Carro, *Soto*, pp. 45–58. For a more recent treatment, see J. Brufau Prats, 'La revisión de la primera generación de la escuela', in *La ética en la conquista de América: Francisco de Vitoria y la Escuela de Salamanca* (Madrid 1984), 383–412, and in general the series of articles, ibid., part III: 'Respuesta universitaria a la duda indiana'; and Pagden, *Fall of natural man*, chapter 5.

[45] In order of composition, these are the *Summulae*; *In dialecticam Aristotelis, Isagogae Porphyrii, Aristotelis categoriae et De demonstratione*; *Super octo libros Physicorum commentaria*; *Super octo libros Physicorum quaestiones*, all of which were printed and reprinted.

of the sixteenth century, at least thirty-two times.[46] The exhaustive volume of these two works and their massive distribution throughout Europe make Soto the major figure of the mid-century School of Salamanca. In addition to his academic output, however, he also produced a series of works engaging in the polemic against the Protestant reformation, of which the most important are the *De natura et gratia*, dedicated to the Council of Trent and first published in 1547 together with the *Apologia contra Catarinum*, and the *Commentarius in epistolam ad Romanos*, written in 1548–50.

For the purposes of this enquiry, it is with the *Ten books on justice and right* that we are principally concerned. The work constitutes essentially a commentary on Questions 57–79 of the 2a2ae, the same set of Questions upon which Vitoria commented in such detail. However, Soto's is very far from being merely a more extensive version of the work of his predecessor in the Prima chair. Soto has felt free not only to introduce extraneous material where relevant, but also to change the order of the Questions and to create new ones. Moreover, and more importantly, Soto's conclusions diverge substantially in places from those of Vitoria. The divergence is explained partly by the intellectual context in which Soto was writing. While Vitoria had spent fourteen years learning and teaching theology at Paris, and had thus formulated his basic positions in response to a Parisian discussion dominated by Mair and especially Almain, Soto was there for only two to three years as a student of theology, before returning to teach first arts at Alcalá, and only then theology at Salamanca. He therefore formulated his positions on moral theology far in time and place from the Parisian circles with which Vitoria had been concerned, and in an intellectual environment where a Thomist orientation was a given. The tradition of Scotist commentary on *Sentences* IV, 15, with its account of the division of *dominia* and the origin of political right in precisely this division, is no longer an issue. Soto is positively disdainful of those authors who write 'a tractate on restitution' at IV, 15.[47] This does not mean Soto is unconcerned with *dominium*: on the contrary, he devotes a whole book to the subject (Book IV). But his approach to the question of *dominium* and *ius* is not dictated by the literature on restitution.

---

[46] The figures are Carro's, *Soto*, p. 59; see ibid. for details of his minor works of academic theology.

[47] See chapter 1, n. 45.

In general terms, Soto's priority in treating of right and *dominium* appears to be the desirability of integrating nature firmly into the sphere of the juridical. The origin of this preoccupation with the problem of natural activity is probably to be sought in his background in arts teaching. During his four-year professorship of arts at Alcalá (1520–4), Soto was obliged to cover the material of the entire arts course, from the *Summulae* of Peter of Spain to Aristotle's *Metaphysics*.[48] While holding the Cátedra de Vísperas in Salamanca, he lectured on the theological texts of Aquinas and Peter Lombard, but his literary activity centred around the editing and publishing of his philosophical notes.[49] Thus the final crystallising of his ideas on logic and physics – especially the latter – coincided with the formation of his interpretation of Aquinas. The language of the *Questions on the Physics* has left its mark on the commentary on justice and right, particularly in the many arguments and illustrations from natural science which mark the text, and it is not unreasonable to suppose that the concern with Aristotelian nature and agency which marks the *Questions* may lie at the root of Soto's manner of treating the moral theological notion of rightful agency. For Soto, right is a function of nature as much as it is of liberty.

Soto opens his work with a consideration of law, on the grounds that it is impossible to investigate the virtue of justice without first investigating the rules according to which it operates.[50] Right presupposes law.[51] Again, therefore, we see the explicit neo-Thomist move to link Aquinas' tractate on the laws with his treatment of justice and right: Book 1 of the *De iustitia et iure* constitutes a commentary on 1a2ae 90–108. Like Aquinas, Soto's consideration of the specific laws begins with the eternal law, the overall *ratio* of creation which exists causally in God. 'God ... out of eternity

---

[48] Carro, *Soto*, p. 17.

[49] Thus in 1539 we find him publishing a revised edition of his *Summulae*; in 1543 he published his *Dialectica*. From the spring of 1544 he worked simultaneously on his commentary on the *Physics* and on his *Questions* on the same text. This work was, however, cut short by his summons to the Council of Trent, and, while an unfinished edition went to press in Salamanca in 1545, a full version did not appear until after Soto's return to Salamanca in 1551 when he was able to complete the work: Carro, *Soto*, pp. 20–1.

[50] Domingo de Soto, *De iustitia et iure libri decem* (Madrid 1967; facsimile of Salamanca 1556), vol. 1, Proem. Although there exists a first edition of Salamanca 1553–4, the edition of 1556 is the author's own emended version, and succeeds the first as the *editio princeps*. See Carro, *Soto*, Prólogo to vol. 1, p. x.

[51] See Carro, *Soto*, pp. 65–7.

conceived in his mind the order and dispensation and rule of the universe of things, in the likeness of which conception all laws are to be constituted: that ordainment and commandment therefore is called the eternal law in accordance with its nature.'[52]

Eternal law is distinct from natural law. Like Aquinas, he argues that the natural law is connected with natural reason and therefore applicable to human activity alone. Thus,

because ... God is author of nature, he ingrafted in individual things each their own instincts and stimuli by which they might be driven towards their ends: but on man particularly he impressed a natural norm into his mind which would govern him according to reason which is natural to him: and this is the natural law: viz. of those principles which without discursive reasoning are *per se* apparent by natural illumination.[53]

God impresses in irrationals instincts and stimuli, 'for example, in the bee, to make honey: in the swallow, to build a nest: and in the earth, to bring forth crops', by which they *are moved* to their ends; but in angels and rationals he impresses a rule, by which they *move themselves* to their ends.[54] This is what makes rational creatures free and irrationals unfree. Man himself numbers among the irrationals which are moved with respect to 'natural actions: for example, feeding, growing and the like'.[55] Because irrationals are not possessed of reason, 'the instincts impressed upon them do not have the proper nature of law, like the natural law in us'.[56]

Soto further appears to concur with Aquinas in positing the distinction between the two modes in which man is subject to the eternal law: through the mode of cognition, and through inclination, only the former being properly law.[57] Besides man's innate cognition of the ends of his actions, he has an inclination or impulse for his own proper (i.e. rational) good, virtue: 'just as with all other things to their ends, so even more is there implanted in man by nature (which

---

[52] *DIEI*, I, Q. 3, a. 1 in corp.: 'Deus ... ab aeterno universarum ordinem et dispensationem et regimen mente concepit: cuius conceptionis instar leges omnes constituendae sunt: illa ergo ordinatio et praeceptio lex aeterna secundum naturam suam nuncupatur.'

[53] Ibid.: 'Mox quia idem Deus author est naturae singulis rebus suos indidit instinctos et stimulos quibus in suos fines agerentur: sed homini praecipue naturalem normam mente impressit quae se secundum rationem quae illi naturalis est gubernaret: atque haec est lex naturalis: eorum scilicet principiorum quae absque discursu lumine naturali per se nota sunt.'

[54] Ibid., a. 4, conc. secunda; cf. *ST*, 1a2ae 93 a. 5 in corp., 'irrational creatures do not act upon themselves, but are acted upon by others'.

[55] *DIEI*, I, Q. 3, a. 4.   [56] Ibid., ad 3.

[57] Ibid., conc. 3a: 'ex utraque autem parte, sc. tam cognitionis quam appulsus, substernuntur [humanae actiones] aeterni legi.'

is the work of God) an inclination and force towards that by which he conforms to the eternal law. For we are born to the virtues (as in Book II of the Ethics of Aristotle).'[58] Therefore 'as much according to his cognition, as according to his propensity for the good – both necessary for free motion – human actions are subject to the eternal law'.[59]

However, in the second article of his Question on natural law, which asks 'Whether the natural law contain several precepts', the distinction between inclination and law appears to be under pressure. As we have seen, in answering this Question Aquinas had posited a series of inclinations corresponding to a series of ends, and had argued that the precepts of the natural law corresponded, in man alone, to these inclinations. Man or human nature has several inclinations on different levels. Soto, however, insists that the nature of man in itself 'consists of several partial [natures]: for he is a being ... and a living thing, then ... an animal, and finally a man, and therefore in accordance with all these grades of nature he has particular first principles'.[60] These 'first and *per se* known principles' are 'those which nature impressed upon us' and are the 'proper precepts of the natural law'.[61] Thus 'in so far as he is a being, this is his most general precept of all: the good is to be sought out and pursued, the bad rejected and avoided'.[62] But for Soto, 'this precept is common to all the *res* of the world':[63] all natures have this precept of natural law impressed upon them. The term 'precept' is therefore not limited to rationals alone: in its synonymity with 'principle', it appears to be approaching the sense of 'inclination' itself. In this vein Soto continues that 'since the first of all natural goods is to be, there immediately follows another more particular principle which is, Each must preserve its proper being. For all things desire to conserve themselves.'[64] Again, in so far as he is an animal man has another

---

[58] Ibid., conc. tertia: 'sicuti caeteris rebus ad suos fines, sic homini, imo praestantius indita est a natura, quae opus Dei est, inclinatio quaedam et pondus ad id quo legi aeterni consonat. Sumus enim (ut II Ethic. Ar.) ad virtutes nati.'

[59] Ibid.

[60] Ibid., I, Q. 4, a. 2 in corp.: 'natura autem hominis ex pluribus partialibus constat. Est enim ens, quae utique natura communis illi est cum universis rebus. Mox est cum viventibus vivens, deinde inter animalia animal, ac demum homo, ergo secundum omnes hos naturae gradus peculiaria habet prima praecepta.'

[61] Ibid.

[62] Ibid.: 'quatenus est ens, hoc est generalissimum ei omnium praeceptorum: Bonum est expetendum et prosequendum, malum autem respuendum et fugiendum.'

[63] Ibid.: 'Hoc enim praeceptum cunctis rebus mundi commune est.'

[64] Ibid.: 'Mox quia primum naturalium bonorum est esse, inde statim cadit particularius aliud

principle of natural law and precept, 'which pertains to the mingling of male and female. For this is in animals the peculiar mode of conserving the species.'[65] This suggests by analogy that all animals have the natural law precept of *commixtio masculi ac foeminae*. In addition to the precepts of animal nature, however, humans have peculiar principles or inclinations 'for the cognition of God, and the good of virtue ... for society and civility'.[66]

Soto therefore appears to be drawing animals into the universe governed by natural law by adopting a sense of natural law as inclination or at least principle of inclination. That animal inclination is seen as natural law is confirmed in the course of Soto's discussion of the 'law of lust', the *lex fomitis*. Aquinas had said that the sensual inclinations of various creatures are 'in a certain way' laws.[67] But Soto drops Aquinas' repeated qualifications. 'For an inclination is said to be a law in two ways. In one way, inasmuch as a legislator directly promotes his subjects to an honest end; and in another, inasmuch as he deprives them as a punishment and permits them to be carried by the impetus of nature. So that that drive of sensuality towards its objects, which for brute beasts would be natural law, that is, consonant with their nature, for men is a curving and a deflexion of his nature in so far as he is rational.'[68] Animal inclination towards animal good is natural law.

Soto here and in the course of answering the question as to whether the natural law contains more than one precept is particularly concerned to avoid the suggestion that since inclinations have the nature of precepts or law, man's indiscriminate desire for objects of sense should be a law to him. For Soto, the problem with man's appetite for the objects of sense is that it can be contrary to the good of reason.[69] Therefore he clarifies that even though 'all inclinations, even of the sensitive appetite, belong to the natural law', they do so 'on a differing rationale: for as far as they are considered, not as obeying reason, but tending in their sensual objects, they are called natural precepts on the same rationale as in brute animals; but as far

principium quod est, Esse proprium cuique conservandum est. Omnia enim appetunt se conservare.'

[65] Ibid.   [66] Ibid.   [67] See above, n. 19.

[68] Ibid., Q. 3, a. 3, in corp.: 'Bifariam nam inclinatio aliqua dicitur lex. Uno modo inquantum per ipsam directe legifer promovet subditos in finem honestum, atque altero modo inquantum in poenam eos destituit permittitque naturae impetu ferri. Unde illa sensualitatis insultus in sua obiecta, quae brutis animantibus esset naturalis lex, nempe suae naturae consonans, hominibus est obliquitas ac deflexio naturae suae quatenus est rationalis.'

[69] Ibid., in corp.

as they are governed by reason, they are the peculiar precepts of man'.[70] For Soto as opposed to Aquinas, therefore, there is something peculiar about the inclinations of man *qua* 'of man', that they are tempered or moderated by reason. It is these rationally governed inclinations which form the natural law for man.

Natural law for Soto is thus a series of inclinations, principles or precepts, just as nature itself is serial. Man as an *ens* and a *vivens* has the basic inclinations of conservation, nutrition and growth, and as *ens* and *vivens*, these are his natural law. As an *animale* he has the inclination of sense towards the objects of sense, and this is his natural law in so far as it is regulated by reason. As a *rationale* his natural law is his inclination towards the good of reason, that is, God and virtue. This last inclination cannot be other than governed by reason, because it is the inclination of reason itself.

In sum, although Soto has destroyed the distinction between inclination and law, he has not therefore fallen into feeble-minded oscillation on the question of whether natural law is the peculiar preserve of human beings or whether it is also common to animals.[71] Soto both saves Aquinas' insights into the peculiar nature of human activity, that it is consciously regulated, while holding that there is no absolute break in the mode of legitimation between irrational and rational creatures. Although Soto has broken the intrinsic connection between *lex* and *libertas*, his distinction between *instinctus* and *libertas* has not been overridden, but corresponds to that between unconscious and conscious inclination.

Soto's position on natural law thus diverges from that of the *Summa theologiae*. However, some of the language of this discussion – the language of plural *naturae* and of *inclinatio* – is very close to that of a passage in Aquinas' commentary on the *NE*.[72] Discussing the

---

[70] Ibid., Q. 4, a. 1, ad 2: 'conceditur, inclinationes omnes, etiam appetitus sensitivi ad legem naturae pertinere, ratione tamen diversa: nam quatenus considerantur, non ut rationi obedientes, sed tendentes in sua sensualia obiecta, dicuntur praecepta naturalia ea ratione qua in brutis: sed quatenus ratione gubernantur, sunt peculiaria praecepta hominis.'

[71] So Hamilton, *Political thought*, pp. 14–16 and 22–3. According to her, Soto is simply confused about natural law, hesitating between conceiving it as reason or as instinct, as peculiar to man or as common to men and animals. Carro does not acknowledge any sense of law as inclination; but this gives rise to a difficulty in his understanding of Soto's doctrine of right: see below, p. 148, n. 79.

[72] *Sententia libri ethicorum*, Book v, Lectio 12, 1134 b 19ff. (tex. 1019). For considerations concerning the date and circumstances of composition of the commentary – fundamentally, that is, whether it is 'early' or 'late' Aquinas – see V. J. Bourke, 'The *Nicomachean Ethics* and Thomas Aquinas', in Maurer, *Commemorative studies*, vol. I, 239–59, whose arguments for an earlier date, c. 1264, seem to me to be convincing.

subject of natural right, Aquinas argues that 'the natural *iustum* is that to which nature inclines man. However, there is in man a double nature. One nature, inasmuch as he is an animal ... But another nature which is specifically of man, which is proper to him inasmuch as he is a man.'[73] Each of these natures, Aquinas continues, has its proper inclination, and consequent upon that inclination is the peculiar natural right of that nature: 'The jurists call that alone natural right, which is consequent upon the inclination of the nature which is common to both man and the other animals, such as the union of male and female, the education of children and other things of this kind. But that right which is consequent on the inclination proper to human nature, i.e. inasmuch as man is a rational animal, the jurists call the right of peoples.'[74] Aquinas' point is that both *iusta* are natural *iusta*; but the latter is peculiar to specifically human nature.

If this text is indeed in the background to Soto's interpretation of natural law, then our sense of the sort of connections Soto makes between inclination, law and right is increased. We have already seen that for Soto, right presupposes law and that therefore the treatment of law must precede that of right. Secondly, we have seen that Soto regards natural law as inclination. Now this text of Aquinas suggests a line of Thomist thought in which the naturally right thing is a consequence of natural inclination – and thus, for Soto, of

---

[73]　Ibid.: 'Est autem considerandum, quod iustum naturale est ad quod hominem natura inclinat. Attenditur autem in homine duplex natura: una quidem secundum quod est animal, quae est sibi aliisque animalibus communis; alia autem est natura hominis quae est propria sibi in quantum est homo, prout sc. secundum rationem discernit turpe et honestum.'

[74]　Ibid.: 'Iuristae autem illud tantum dicunt ius naturale quod consequitur inclinationem naturae communis homini et aliis animalibus, sicut coniunctio maris et feminae, educatio natorum et alia huiusmodi; illud autem ius quod consequitur propriam inclinationem naturae humanae, in quantum sc. homo est rationale animal, vocant ius gentium, quia eo omnes gentes utuntur, sicut quod pacta sint servanda, quod legati etiam apud hostes sint tuti, et alia huiusmodi.' Kalinowski argues that this passage illustrates Aquinas' metonymy between *ius* and *lex*: 'lorsqu'il explique dans la *Sententia libri Ethicorum* les termes "ius", "iusta", "ius naturalia", "iusta legalia", "iusta gentium" etc., il pense constamment à la loi ou aux lois ... Ainsi, en illustrant par des exemples les *iusta naturalia*, Saint Thomas énumère-t-il des principes de la loi naturelle' ('Emploi métonymique', pp. 335–6). This view is also put forward by H. V. Jaffa, *Thomism and Aristotelianism: A study of the commentary by Thomas Aquinas on the 'Nicomachean Ethics'* (Chicago 1952), pp. 174–7. While I accept that the sense of *iustum* and *ius* in the passage does change from 'the right thing' to 'law' ('quod pacta sint servanda' appears to be more an example of a law than of a right thing), it still seems to me that the *ius naturale* which is said to be common to man and to animals has the sense of 'the naturally right thing', rather than any sense of precept.

natural law. If we now turn to look at Soto's doctrine of right, we find that it fits precisely into this framework.

The topic of right forms the subject of Book III. Soto begins with a Question 'On right', the order of which corresponds to that of Aquinas' Question of the same title.[75] In the opening article, 'Whether right be the object of justice', Soto follows Aquinas' Aristotelian response very closely, although characteristically reinforcing his point with an argument from natural science.[76] Thus right is the 'equality of things', the object at which the virtue of justice aims: 'justice creates equality between one who owes and another to whom he owes something'; and therefore seemingly is only applicable between rational creatures in society.

However, as with Vitoria and Aquinas himself, Soto's next two articles – 'Whether the division of right into natural right and positive right be appropriate to the genus', and 'Whether the right of peoples be the same as natural right' (which correspond to Aquinas' articles) – undermine the Aristotelian premisses from which he begins. Soto's discussion is fundamentally that of Vitoria, although it is more extensive and recognises explicitly that there are two definitions of 'natural right' in play: a definition by formal cause, which he attributes to Aristotle, and which is the sense of 'everywhere the same' or necessary; and a definition by efficient cause, notably evident in the texts of Cicero and the jurists, which is the sense of 'implanted by nature'.[77] But he goes on to use 'natural right' in the same sense as Vitoria, as the proper activity of any nature: 'every right of nature is necessary *simpliciter* ... But the necessity of any thing is to be considered according to its nature. For if the nature of a thing is immutable, then its right also will be immutable: for example, because the sky is an immutable thing, its motion is also immutable.'[78] With

---

[75] *ST*, 2a2ae 57.

[76] *DIEI*, III, Q. 1, a. 1 in corp.: ' lest anyone should accuse us of perversion of order, in that we should rather speak of justice before right, let him know that the teaching is Aristotle's in Book II of the "De anima" ... that he who is about to treat of potency or habit, should take his starting point from the object ... For the eye is not properly defined by this, that it is in this or that way composed; but [by this], that it is the sense of perceiving colours.'

[77] *DIEI*, III, Q. 1, a. 2 in corp.

[78] Ibid., ad 1: 'concesso, ius omne naturae esse simpliciter necessarium natura sua ... At vero id quod natura sua est necessarium, potest mutatis rebus mutari. Necessitas quippe uniuscuiusque rei secundum eius naturam perpendenda est. Si enim natura rei immutabilis est, tunc et ius eius erit simpliciter immutabile: ut, quia coelum res est immutabilis, eius motus est immutabile.'

Vitoria, Soto goes far beyond Aquinas in his understanding of natural right. Aquinas had enlarged the sense of Aristotelian natural right to accommodate the juristic perception of naturally right behaviour even among animals; the two neo-Thomists see natural right in the activity of all natures.[79] This latter perception is of course the product of a profoundly Thomistic concept of a legitimated universe.

Vitoria and Soto thus concur in positing an objective natural right or 'just thing' for all creatures, and in these passages Soto's conclusions are likely as much dictated by Vitoria's lectures as by his own understanding of natural law as inclination. Where the two pursue divergent paths is over the question of *dominium*, and it is in his discussion of this subject that Soto's peculiar understanding of natural inclination and natural right come into play.

Soto, like Vitoria, sets his treatment of *dominium* in relation to restitution. Book IV of the *DIEI* is entitled 'On commutative justice', which for Soto as for Vitoria is to do with *dominium* and its restitution:

it is worth our while, as we enter the subject of commutative justice, to talk beforehand in this book ... firstly about the *dominium* of things, and then about their restitution. For *dominium* ... is the basis and foundation of all [those things] ... which are done through commutative justice. And moreover all those vices which are opposed to this virtue, are violations and corruptions of *dominia* ... Which type of injury ... must be redeemed by benefit of restitution.[80]

Like Vitoria, then, Soto feels it necessary to insert a discussion of *dominium* before considering restitution. However, he immediately distances himself from his predecessor. His first Question, 'On *dominium* in general', begins with the query 'Whether *dominium* be the same as the right and faculty of things', and Soto proceeds to take issue with the entire tradition of the equation of *dominium* and right upon which Vitoria's commentary is based.[81]

---

[79] Carro argues that these passages on natural right in Soto are not meant to suggest that there is a natural right which is common to men and animals, for right and law correspond, and law is limited to rationals. Carro sees in the mentions of a natural right of animals only a lapse of perfect logic on Soto's part, which does not however affect his stance that animals are incapable of right.

[80] *DIEI*, IV, Proem: 'de justitia commutativa sermonem nobis euntibus operae pretium prius est ... primum de rerum dominio, mox de earum restitutiones hoc quarto libro disserere. Enimvero dominium ... basis fundamentumque est omnium ... quae per justitiam commutativam celebrantur. Ac perinde cuncta quae huic virtuti adversantur vitia, violationes quaedam sunt et corruptelae dominiorum ... Quae subinde iniuriarum genera ... restitutionis beneficio repensari debent.'

[81] Soto's account of *dominium* in the *DIEI* represents a development of themes he had elaborated earlier in his *Relectio De dominio* of 1534–5: see Brufau Prats, *Escuela de Salamanca*, chapter 5.

As we saw in the last chapter, Vitoria had taken advantage of Q. 62 (on restitution) of his commentary on the 2a2ae to slide from an objective to a subjective notion of right. Affirming that the definition of right as the 'just thing', the object of justice, was a purely nominal definition, he had argued firstly, that the real definition of right was a power or faculty pertaining to the individual under the law; secondly, that this licit or legal power was the same as *dominium*. In that *dominium* can pertain only to those made with will and reason in the image of God, right in this sense belongs to man alone among terrestrial creatures. He thereby reintroduced the split in the analysis of human and animal action threatened by his – and Aquinas' – concessions to the jurists, and his own Thomist assumption that all natural activity constitutes the just thing for each individual nature.

Soto follows Vitoria to some extent, in positing a sense of right as 'faculty' or 'power'. Although Soto makes no such point as Vitoria concerning 'nominal' and 'real' definitions of right, it is nonetheless clear that the sense of 'right' switches in Book iv to synonymity with 'faculty' in the sense of a subjective power. It is using 'right' in this sense, however, that he goes on to argue, against Vitoria, that *dominium* and right are not the same.

Soto is as eager as Vitoria to situate his discussion with regard to the issue of commentary on *Sentences* iv, 15. However, his attitude to that tradition is unrelentingly hostile. 'But really, with regard to the definition of the term [*dominium*] the latest writers [*iuniores*] make heavier weather than is necessary: for example Gerson ... Conrad ... and several others on iv, 15.'[82] According to Soto, they say 'first of all ... that "right" is understood in two ways. Firstly, for "law" ... Secondly, for a legitimate power ... Finally they say that *dominium* is the same thing as right taken in the second sense.'[83] Answering their case, it first appears as if Soto disagrees both with their second sense of right, and with its assimilation to *dominium*. 'For right is the same as the just thing. For it is the object of justice: viz. the equity which justice constitutes among men: but *dominium* is the faculty of a master in his slaves or in those things which he uses at his own will, and for his own convenience.'[84] However, this is the last time that right is

---

[82] *DIEI*, iv, Q. 1, a. 1 in corp.

[83] Ibid.: 'Primum enim omnium, aiunt isti, ius bifariam accipi. Primo pro lege: quo significatu dicimus, Ius Civile, et Canonicum. Secundo pro legitima potestate, qua quis fungitur in personam aliquam vel rem. Deinde aiunt dominium idem prorsus esse quod ius secundo modo acceptum.'

[84] Ibid.: 'Ius nam idem est quod iustum. Est enim obiectum iustitiae: puta aequitas quam

defined as the object of justice. Thereafter, Soto's point is that 'Dominium does not signify any right and power whatsoever, but only that which is in a thing which we can use at our own pleasure for our own profit.'[85] Right is used throughout the rest of the work in the sense of 'licit subjective power', of which *dominium* is a species. *Dominium* itself is finally defined as 'the proper faculty and right of a person in any thing, which he can usurp in his own profit in any use whatsoever permitted by law'.[86] 'Faculty' is defined as deriving from 'facility', in opposition to Gerson's derivation of the term from *fas*, and is said to be a species of the genus 'power' (*potestas*): power can mean any ability, licit or illicit, but faculty is restricted to licit ability.

The contrast Soto wishes to draw is between the kind of power that a master has over a slave, and that which a father has over his sons or a prelate over his subjects, which can only be used to their good, rather than at the pleasure of the right-holder. Against Antoninus and (explicitly) Summenhart, Soto insists that superiority does not imply *dominium*: for there are some superiors (fathers, husbands, prelates) who have no *dominium*. That is, for Soto there is a *ius in personam* which is not *dominium*. He goes on to destroy another founding argument of the restitution tradition (and of Vitoria's account): the possibility of theft does not imply *dominium*, 'for it is enough for there to be a case of theft, that it happen either against the will of the *dominus*, or against him to whom the object belongs, even if he be not the *dominus*, but the possessor by another right'.[87] Thus not every *ius in re*, either, is *dominium*.

Having separated *dominium* from other rights, Soto takes up the Question of 'Whether the *dominia* of things pertain only to God, and intellectual and rational creatures'.[88] Here Soto again attacks the *neoterici*, who, 'following the lead of Gerson, dream up many things scarcely consonant with reason. For he, an otherwise serious author, multiplied ... the species of *dominia* into many. Among which he attributed many *dominia* to brute beasts, and furthermore many to creatures devoid even of sense.'[89] In reply, Soto uses the entire

iustitia inter homines constituit: dominium autem facultas est domini in servos vel in res quibus suo arbitratu, ob suumque commodum utitur.' The passage is quoted by Tuck, *Natural rights theories*, p. 47, in support of his thesis that Soto along with the rest of the School of Salamanca espoused an 'objective' theory of right. However, this thesis does not appear to be able to accommodate the usage of the terms 'power' and 'faculty' in connection with 'right' which immediately follows.

[85] *DIEI*, IV, Q. I, a. I in corp.   [86] Ibid.   [87] Ibid.   [88] Ibid., Q. I, a. 2
[89] Ibid. The accusation is unfair, as we saw in chapter 3.

familiar battery of arguments from the ancient Christian tradition to prove that *dominium* can only belong to rationals, and therefore to man alone among the creatures of the earth. Thus a '*dominus* ... is he alone in whose faculty it is placed, to use a thing in this way or that way for his own profit: but this belongs to no creature unless through the intellect and the will: and therefore man alone upon earth stands out by reason of *dominium*'; '*dominium* of exterior things belongs to no creature unless by this reason, that it be *dominus* of its own actions: for the *dominium* that each has in his own actions is the cause and root of that which he has in other things: but man alone is *dominus* of his own actions'.[90] *Dominium* is for the sake of use: but use is only possible for those things which can recognise an end for that use, and only rationals can be conscious of an end as an end. Again, the controlled and directed action which is use is possible only for those who have *dominium* of their own actions: and thus it is this which grounds *dominium* of externals. No irrational or insensate, therefore, can have *dominium* of another thing.

In addition to these tenets of the Christian tradition of man as the image of God, however, Soto has another, more legal, argument. 'Whoever has *dominium* of a thing, is affected by injury when it is taken from him. But brute animals are capable of neither justice, nor injury ... The reason for this is that since they are not free, they are not of their own right [sui iuris], but whatever they are, they are of man, for the sake of whom the world was created.'[91] If animals are not capable of injury, then neither are they capable of *dominium*. Here, injury (*iniuria*) is opposed not to right (*ius*) *per se*, but to *dominium*, which is associated with being *sui iuris*, under one's *own* right. That is, injury is associated with the possibility of the possession of oneself and other things, the right to be *dominus* or the right to be in the relation of *dominium* over something. Similarly, Soto concludes from the fact that animals are incapable of injury that 'whoever takes food or life from a cow or a slave does it no injury, but only its *dominus* ...

---

[90] Ibid.: 'Dominus ... ille solus est in cuius facultate est situm, re sic, aut aliter in suum commodum uti: hoc autem nisi per intellectum et voluntatem nemini congruit: solus ergo homo in terris dominii ratione fulget; Dominium externarum rerum nemini nisi hac ratione convenit, quod sit ipse suarum actionum dominus: dominium enim quod quisque habet in suos actus causa est et radix eius quod habet in alias res: est autem solus homo suarum actionum dominus.'

[91] Ibid.: 'Quicunque dominium habet cuiuslibet rei, iniuria afficitur dum illi auferetur. Bruta autem animalia neque iustitiae capaces sunt, neque iniuriae ... Cuius ratio est, quod cum non sint libera, non sunt sui iuris; sed quicquid sunt, hominis sunt, propter quem orbis conditus est.'

and thus the grazing herds have no *dominium*, or right, in the grasses: but only natural appetite, and even power'.[92] The arguments which deny *dominium* to beasts also deny any *ius in re*, any right that is *in* anything else. And so we see that Soto, who was so anxious to deny the equivalence between *dominium* and other sorts of *iura, in personam* and *in re*, in the end acknowledges the common quality of all these rights (including *dominium*): that they are all faculties relating to other things. Animals cannot have any such faculties on the same grounds that they cannot have *dominium*. But that this is an impossibility for brute beasts or insensates does not necessarily foreclose the possibility that they might have a right in another sense: a right of acting in a certain way – that is, a right which is not over something else but which is simply for their natural activity.

The desirability of this interpretation lies in its ability to account for three small but important phrases in Questions 2 and 4 of Book IV. Discussing, firstly, whether a man can be *dominus* of another man, Soto asserts that 'even if men were created by God free: nevertheless so innate in all animals is the desire and right of preserving life, that the wretched men can for its sake drive themselves into slavery';[93] again, arguing that in the case of the extreme necessity of both a creditor and his debitor, the debitor is not bound to return the goods he owes, he holds that 'so innate in man is that most general desire, and so right of all things of preserving itself, that at that point he owes nothing to anybody more than to himself'.[94] Thirdly, in the course of describing the genesis of the *civitas* or commonwealth and of political authority, Soto declares that 'God through man gave to individual things [*rebus*, not, as he could easily have said, *hominibus*] the faculty of conserving themselves, and resisting their contraries.'[95] We saw above how Soto limits the term 'faculty' – as opposed to 'power' – to right.

---

[92]　Ibid.: 'Et ideo qui iumento et atmento vel pabulum sustulerit, vel vitam, nullam ei irrogavit iniuriam, sed domino ... nullum ergo pecudes habent dominium neque ius in herbas, sed tantum appetitum naturalem: atque etiam potestatem.'

[93]　Ibid., Q. 2, a. 2 in corp.: 'Nam etiamsi homines facti sunt a Deo liberi: tamen tam innatum est animantibus cunctis desiderium ac ius servandi vitam, ut possint se eius gratia miseri in servitutem adigere.'

[94]　Ibid., Q. 7, a. 1 in corp.: 'Enimvero tam intime innatum est homini generalissimum illud rerum omnium desiderium, ac subinde ius servandi sese, ut nulli quicquam tunc plus debeat quam sibiipsi.'

[95]　Ibid., Q. 4, a. 1 in corp.: 'Deus per naturam dedit rebus singulis facultatem se conservandi, suisque resistendi contrariis.'

Soto's attribution, in these two passages, of a right of self-preservation to all animals is consonant with a passage in the discussion in Book III of the relationship between the right of nature and the right of peoples. Here, Soto is considering a passage of Florentinus in the Roman law, to the effect that 'beating off injuries' is of the right of peoples. The objection to it is that 'beating off injuries, is a conclusion of that principle, Every thing desires to conserve itself; therefore the right of peoples is the same as natural right'.[96] As we saw, the principle of self-conservation is of the natural law of all things; its conclusion is that for all things, it is of natural right to repel force with force, or to 'resist their contraries', the corollary of *se conservare in esse*.

In the language of Book III, then, the act of self-conservation is a natural right, that is, a natural just thing, that which is naturally equated to a nature: for we argued that for Soto in Book III, a thing's natural activity constituted its (natural) right. But in Book IV, right as 'faculty' is of the genus of 'power' or potency to act – not of the act itself. However, a text of Soto's pupil Miguel de Palacios suggests the sense in which both are 'right'. Palacios insists that right as the just thing is properly a work, an *opus*, which obliges to its performance. He acknowledges, however, that 'it has pleased others that right be a faculty to act'; and his solution is as follows. Since 'every faculty is a just power, and a just power is [i.e. has its nature as such] from the doing of a just thing, which it is its power to do; and the doing of the just thing – the just action – is right itself: therefore this faculty is called a right from the doing itself, and therefore is secondarily, not primarily, a right'.[97] The model is exactly that of the Aristotelian potency: the power is defined by the act, and is of the same essence but ontologically secondary.

Palacios' elucidation here of a sense of right as a power for action appears to correspond to the usage we find in Soto. A right *per se* (i.e.

---

[96] *DIEI*, III, Q. I, a. 3 in corp.

[97] Miguel de Palacios, *Praxis theologica de contractibus et restitutionibus* (Salamanca 1585), Chapter II: 'Quid sit ius, et quae partes eius: Aliis placuit ius esse facultatem ad recte agendum, id quod fuit Gersonis opinio ... Caeterum quia omnis facultas est iusta quaedam potestas, et iusta potestas est ex iusti actione, quam operari potest et actio iusti seu iusta actio est ipsum ius, ideo facultas haec aliunde dicitur ius, ex ipsa videlicet operatione, propterea, secundario dicitur ius, non primario.' For brief details of Palacios, see L. Pereña Vicente, *La universidad de Salamanca, forja del pensamiento político español en el siglo XVI* (Salamanca 1954), pp. 51–2; Brufau Prats, 'Revisión'. It is noticeable that Palacios, who explains the Gersonian right in the sense of faculty as a power towards a just act, does not number Gerson among those who equated right and *dominium*.

not *in re* or *in personam*) is a legitimate ability or power, faculty, for an action dictated by the natural law in its sense as inclination, and which thus constitutes objective natural right. The natural law in its sense as inclination dictates first and foremost the conservation by all natures of their nature, and thus the primary natural right is the right of self-conservation. All natures, including man, possess this right of their essence as such.

The ultimate effect of Soto's discussion in Book IV is thus to split right into two levels. He reserves a sense of right – that right of which all *dominia* are species – to creatures possessed of reason and will and thereby safeguards the traditional Christian theology of man as made in the image of God and set apart from and over the rest of creation. This sense of right belongs to humans in that they can act consciously towards an end, and are therefore capable of using other creatures and things. *Dominium* of action, the result of the operation of the intellect and the will, is itself the primary *dominium*, and upon it follows *dominium* of externals. However, Soto also preserves a sense in which the natural potentials and activity of all creatures – including man – have the nature of right through being the result of the desire for its particular good innate in all creatures, which constitutes their natural inclination and hence their natural law. Unlike liberty and *dominium*, right is a faculty which is determined to one action which is commanded by law. In this sense of right, natural activity of man is susceptible of the same juridical analysis as is that of all created natures.

It is this latter notion of right which Soto exploits when he comes to translate into his own language the Aristotelian account of the genesis of the *respublica* or *civitas* through the nature of man, and thereby to legitimate the civic commonwealth and the civil power. Soto, heavily involved in the political stand of the entire School of Salamanca – against the enslavement of the American Indians and against the Lutheran heresy[98] – insists that the city or political commonwealth be of nature. Like Vitoria in his commentary on the 2a2ae, Soto in his own gives his account of the genesis of cities in the course of discussing *dominium* (answering the Question 'Whether any one man be *dominus* of the whole earth').[99] Unlike Vitoria, however, he makes no reference to the *dominium* of man, depending entirely on the deployment of the notion of right:

---

[98] See the references in the introduction, n. 2.   [99] *DIEI*, IV, Q. 4, a. 1.

God through nature gave to individual things the faculty of conserving themselves and resisting their contraries: not only with regard to the safekeeping of their temporal well-being, but also through his grace with regard to the prosperity of their spiritual well-being. But since in their scattered state they were not able to exercise this faculty commodiously, he added to them the instinct of living communally, so that united they might be sufficient each to each other. However, the commonwealth thus congregated could in no way govern itself, drive off enemies and check the temerity of malefactors, unless it selected magistrates, to whom it granted its faculty: for otherwise the collectivity, without order or head, would not represent one body, nor could it provide for those things that were expedient.[100]

The primary determinant of the political community is the faculty – which, on the evidence of the passages cited above, we may call the right – of each man of conserving himself in being, and not merely in being but in human being. According to the natural law as inclination, it is right that men do these things, and therefore they have the right of so doing. It is this, not any *dominium*, which legitimates the *respublica*: *dominium* cannot generate the legitimate entity which is the civic commonwealth.

However, it is apparent that Soto wants to go still further in his emphasis that the commonwealth is the product of natural inclination and right rather than of *dominium*. According to him, human beings were unable to exercise their right of being human on their own, and therefore God added, not the *libertas*, but the *instinctus* of living communally. As we saw, *instinctus* is the opposite of Soto's first *lex naturae* which is connected with liberty, and its reappearance here serves to push the desire to live communally out of the conscious natural law of man and into the unconscious natural law of animals and all *entia*. This move, in the context of elucidating an Aristotelian natural politics, suggests that Soto the natural scientist – despite his resolution of the relationship between the natural and the human in his second Question on natural law – still believes that a truly natural explanation must be in terms of blind motive forces; and that in his

[100] Ibid., in corp.: 'Deus per naturam dedit rebus singulis facultatem se conservandi, suisque resistendi contrariis: non modo quantum ad incolumitatem temporalis salutis, verum et per eius gratiam quantum ad prosperitatem spiritualis. Hanc autem facultatem cum exequi commode dispersi nequirent, adiecit eis instinctum gregatim vivendi, ut adunati alii aliis sufficerent: congregata vero respublica neutiquam se poterat gubernare, hostesque propulsare, malefactorumque audaciam cohibere, nisi magistratus deligeret, quibus suam tribueret facultatem: nam alias congregatio sine ordine et capite, neque unum corpus repraesentaret, neque ea providere posset quae expedirent.'

aspect as conscious, man is outside the realm of natural causality. The result is that, for Soto, man like any animal is under the natural necessity of exercising his determinate right to self-conservation by congregating with his fellows.

This does not mean, however, that for Soto the natural commonwealth is only for the realisation of nature in the sense of physical nature, the nature man shares with the animals. The city is not only *ad incolumitatem temporalis salutis*, but also *ad prosperitatem spiritualis*:[101] 'Aristotle most excellently said that the city is constituted for the sake of being, but exists for the sake of living well ... For by that reason whereby man is born to felicity, by the same reason he is a civil animal.'[102] The city enables the realisation of moral virtue, 'which alone perfects the good man'.[103] Men living in cities are governed by laws which 'are all to be instituted for the good of the soul, in which our felicity consists ... For the citizens cannot preserve a seemly state of the commonwealth in their external actions, unless they are strengthened with the internal habits of the virtues.'[104] Moreover, men in civil society are in a position through teaching and example to help each other towards realising the human good.[105] As a Christian Aristotelian, Soto's human good is of course ultimately eternal beatitude; but this does not make the city and the moral virtues purely instrumental.

However, Soto's account of the genesis of the city lapses into confusion over the question of transferring the faculty for realising the good from individuals to prince. Soto's text wavers between the characterisation of the original community as a *per accidens* combination of individual substances, or as an organism in the full Aristotelian

---

[101] It is interesting that when this passage is taken up by the prominent contemporary jurist Diego de Covarruvias, the latter phrase is omitted: 'At cum Deus ipse per naturam dederit rebus singulis facultatem se conservandi suisque resistendi contrariis, quantum ad incolumitatem salutis, nec homines facultatem hanc exequi dispersi potuissent ... [etc.]' Although *incolumitas salutis* might be held to be ambiguous between temporal and spiritual meanings, Covarruvias underlines his concentration on the physical advantages of the city by inserting after 'adunati aliis sufficerent', 'victumque facilius complures quam singuli compararent, tutiusque ab incursu ferarum et hostium degerent.' For the jurist, the city is for living, not living well. See Diego de Covarruvias y Leyva, *Practicarum quaestionum liber unus*, Chapter I, n. 2, in *Opera omnia* (Frankfurt 1592), vol. II.

[102] *DIEI*, I, Q. 2, a. 1, discussing whether the effect of the laws be to make men good.

[103] Ibid.: 'bonum autem virum sola perficit moralis virtus'.

[104] Ibid.: '[leges civiles] omnes ad bonum animae, quo nostra foelicitas agitur, instituendae sunt ... Haud quippe externis actionibus decorum possunt cives servare reipublicae statum, nisi internis virtutum habitibus vigeant.'

[105] Ibid.

sense of a *per se* unity.[106] On the former account, the original community is a mere collection of individual beings, not functionally united and having no form of its own: 'without order or head', and not representing one body. On this account, however, 'it' ought not to have any 'faculty' of doing anything, for, as it has no unity or nature as one being, so it can have no specific activity. But it is clear that Soto *does* see the original congregation as having such a faculty of self-government and self-protection, and, moreover, as being able to act as a unity in granting it to magistrates. Thus 'the power of governing itself, and therefore the power of instituting laws ... was necessary to the civil [commonwealth] by reason of its end ... this [power] descends through natural law, by which every commonwealth has the authority of administering itself, which it could transfer to kings'.[107] 'For [secular kings and monarchs] are not created proximately, and, as they say, immediately, by God ... but as is held in the "l. quod placuit, ff. de const. princ.", kings and princes are created by the people, in whom it has transferred its empire and power.'[108]

In the background of Soto's hesitation between the two accounts of the original congregation is the pervasive presence of Almain and his analogy between the individual and his right of self-conservation, and the body politic and its right of government. According to Almain, the right of government in the commonwealth is the same faculty which naturally characterises the individual human being. This naturalistic account of political power was taken up, as we saw, by Vitoria in the *Relectio De potestate civili*, and combined with a Christian–Aristotelian theory of the human drive towards life in society: a combination to which Soto's account is heavily indebted. But Soto encountered the same problem as Vitoria: Almain had used the analogy precisely because it yielded a power naturally inherent in the community, which connection with nature, Almain was able to argue, precluded its ever being irrevocably alienated to a ruler of any

---

[106] For this Aristotelian contrast, see Sarah Waterlow, *Nature, change and agency in Aristotle's 'Physics': A philosophical study* (Oxford 1982), pp. 88–9, and chapters 1 and 2.

[107] *DIEI*, 1, Q. 6, a. 4 in corp., discussing whether the civil law obliges in conscience: 'civili [respublicae] necessaria fuit ratione finis potestas seipsum gubernandi, atque adeo leges ... instituendi ... haec autem per legem naturalem descendit, qua quaelibet respublica seipsum administrandi authoritatem habet, quam et regibus conferre potuit.'

[108] Ibid., Q. 1, a. 3 in corp., discussing whose reason has the nature of law: 'Saeculares autem reges et monarchae secus habent. Haud enim a Deo proxime et, ut aiunt, immediate creati sunt ... sed ut habetur l. quod placuit ff. de const. princ. reges et principes a populo creati sunt, in quod suum transtulit imperium et potestatem.'

kind. Exercise of the political power is thus dependent on the consent of the community. Soto's response is to combine the emphasis of certain Roman law texts on the complete cession of power by the community to a ruler, with the (incoherent) suggestion that the community without a ruler is somehow an imperfect body.

In sum, the political community, once formed in the sense of being governed by an official (or officials) holding the faculty or right of conserving and protecting it, is a body, unified functionally. This community is yet another natural body under the natural law in the sense of inclination towards the natural good: the fundamental natural good being, as we have seen, self-conservation. Correspondingly, like all natural bodies, it has the natural right of conserving itself and defending itself: of repelling enemies (the external source of destruction) and suppressing malefactors (the internal source). All citizens are parts of that body, and the prince's right is the right of the commonwealth or *respublica* – the public right, *ius publicum* – to use the other citizens as the head uses the other members of the body in the preservation and defence of that body. To the extent that the being of each member is involved in the being of the whole, each member is under the direction of the head rather than under its own. Thus Soto asserts categorically at the very beginning of the *DIEI*, in arguing that the law must always be ordered towards the common good, that 'Every part is, in the order of nature, directed towards its whole, as the imperfect to the perfect: but all the citizens are parts of the *civitas*, therefore the law laid upon them ought to form them towards the common good of the whole *civitas*: like the parts of a unitary body which are ordered towards the service of the whole.'[109]

This is not, however, the whole of the story. Man is not only a part, and for the sake of the whole, but also – as Soto stressed in describing man's aptitude for *dominium* – perfect, made in the image of God, and thus for the sake of himself, *propter seipsum*. His activity cannot therefore be wholly susceptible of analysis in terms of the functioning of the political community and the domain of public

---

[109] Ibid., Q. 1, a. 2 in corp.: 'Pars omnis ad suum totum naturali ordine dirigitur sicuti imperfectum ad perfectum: quicunque autem civium partes sunt civitatis, lex ergo illis praescripta in bonum commune totius civitatis debet eos instituere: veluti partes unius corporis quae ad servitium totius ordinem habent.' Soto stresses that the 'common good' in this argument is the natural felicity obtainable in this lifetime, which coincides with 'the quiet, and the tranquil and peaceable state of the commonwealth'. The existence of this secular 'common good' is not overridden by, but is referred to, the supernatural 'common good' which is eternal felicity in God.

right. In some aspect, man must also be under his own direction, *free*, if he is to have the distinctive characteristic of man at all. For Soto, this is the whole problem of the political. Man must live in a community in order to live and to live well, and that community must be a political community – that is, a community governed by a ruler who holds the power of the community – if it is to fulfil its function of providing for life and the good life. It is each individual man's determinate natural right, necessarily exercised, of living such a life which justifies (makes to be a right) the power of the community in him as one of its members. But that public right must extend only so far as each individual plays a necessary part in the survival of the whole community, i.e. is a member rather than a separate individual. Beyond that, man must not only have his own rights as an individual, but he must also have their exercise within his own control: in other words, he must be *sui iuris*, have *dominium* of himself or his liberty.

The extent to which man is distinct from the community of which he is a member is brought out by Soto in the first two Questions of Book v, which discuss the respective powers of community and individual with respect to the person and limbs of that same individual.[110] The first article of the first Question reiterates the inferiority of the right of beasts to that of man, with the result that man may kill animals to his use: 'even if life be common to us and to the rest of the animals: it is nevertheless not so on an equal right: but their [life] is for the sake of ours. And therefore neither he who kills his own beast does it any injury, nor does he who kills another's, do any [injury] to the beast, but only to its possessor.'[111] Although Soto's point is to underline the subordination of the rest of animate creation to man, it is noticeable again that Soto does not deny right to beasts, but only insists that their right is not equal to man's.

Soto goes on to consider the Question 'Whether it be licit to kill malefactors'. His first point is that just as the imperfect is for the sake of the more perfect – the same reasoning that justifies the killing of brute beasts – 'by the same right, since every part is made by nature

---

[110] *DIEI*, v (which as a book takes as its themes those injuries which occur in incidents which take place wholly against the will of the person in question, i.e. 'whenever harm is done someone against right ... either in his person, or in a related person, or in his goods'), Q. 1 'On homicide' and Q. 2, 'On the mutilation of limbs', corresponding to *ST*, 2a2ae 64 and 65.

[111] Ibid., Q. 1, a. 1 ad 1: 'etsi vita nobis cum caeteris animantibus communis sit: non tamen aequo iure: sed sua est propter nostram. Et ideo neque qui suam occidit pecudem ulli facit iniuriam neque qui occidit alienam, ullam irrogat pecudi, sed possessori.'

for the sake of the whole body ... the consequence is that where the
safety of the commonwealth demands, that same commonwealth has
the right of putting a citizen to death, lest it infect the whole':[112] just
as one may cut off a poisoned limb lest it destroy the whole body.
Thus justifying the killing of the malefactor is on the one hand the
right of the commonwealth or the public right to conserve itself in
being. But on the other is the loss of right on the part of the
malefactor: 'when man falls from [his proper dignity], then he
degenerates into the lowliness and servitude of brute animals:
according to the Psalm, Man when he was in honour, did not
understand, he has become like unto the herds, etc. And thus it is
licit to kill him just as it is to kill a beast. For he is corrupt
humanity.'[113] The proper dignity of man is 'to live according to
reason: for through this he is free and existing for the sake of
himself';[114] as we have seen, to be free and for the sake of oneself is
to be *sui iuris*, to have *dominium* over oneself and thus the supreme
right in oneself. When man sins he betrays his own rationality and
loses his freedom and thereby his proper right; the commonwealth
may therefore kill him for the sake of its own purposes without injury
to him.[115]

The loss of right in himself is the crucial factor in justifying the
action of the commonwealth in killing a malefactor. The utility of the
commonwealth is not enough, for then it would be licit for the
commonwealth to kill an innocent in its own defence. But as Soto
stresses in article 7 of the same Question, 'Whether it be licit in any
case to kill an innocent', this can never be the case, because it offends
the right possessed by each individual of his essence as a being
distinct from the whole: 'a member does not have a being [esse]
distinct from the being [esse] of the whole: nor in any way is it for the
sake of itself: nor is it of itself capable of right or injury. But a man,

---

[112] Ibid., a. 2 in corp.: 'Pari ergo iure cum omnis pars a natura facta sit propter totum corpus
    ... consequens fit ut ubi incolumitati republicae expediverit, ius eadem ipsa habeat civem
    morte resecandi, ne totam inficiat.'

[113] Ibid., ad 3: 'quando autem [a dignitate sua] decidit, tunc in vilitatem et servilitatem
    brutorum animalium degenerat: secundum illud Psalmi, Homo cum in honore esset non
    intellexit, comparatus est iumentis etc. Ob idque perinde atque brutum licet eum occidere.
    Est enim corruptus homo.'

[114] Ibid.

[115] It may not, however, kill him simply because he has committed a crime. 'For the nature
    even of the most iniquitous sinner is to be cherished in so far as it is a remote image (or
    creation) of God: and therefore the sinner is only killed for the cause of the common good'
    (*DIEI*, v, Q. 1, a. 7 in corp.). The commonwealth does not take vengeance in any sense,
    but merely gains the right to use the sinner to its own good, viz. by killing him.

although he be a part of the commonwealth, is nevertheless also an individual existing [existens] for the sake of himself, and thereby *per se* capable of injury, which the commonwealth cannot visit upon him.'[116] Thus the commonwealth cannot, for example, sacrifice an innocent citizen to the demands of a besieging tyrant, although it may expose a citizen to danger of death in the cause of defending the commonwealth. The latter action is licit because the commonwealth has the right of using its members in any way necessary to the defence of itself as a whole. But in the former case, the citizen in question is not integrated into a necessary defence offered by the whole, but is being demanded, out of the malice of the attacker, in his capacity as an individual. The commonwealth has consequently no right in his person: 'there is in an innocent no [reason] why there should accrue to the commonwealth any right of killing him'.[117]

The commonwealth has a right in the life of an innocent to the extent that such a person cannot kill himself without doing injury to the commonwealth – although not to himself.[118] But the commonwealth has no right to force a person to preserve his life at the cost of great suffering to that person, for example by undergoing amputation. Discussing the question whether a person may cut off one of his own limbs, to which the reply is not unless it is necessary for his overall health, Soto stresses that in this latter case 'it is not the office of the commonwealth to force him to do so'.[119] If a person should so opt to cut off a limb for the sake of his health, he will certainly do it

---

[116] *DIEI*, v, Q. 1, a. 7, in corp.: 'membrum non habet esse distinctum ab esse totius: neque ullo modo est propter se, sed propter totum: neque per se est capax iuris vel iniuriae. Homo autem quamvis sit pars reipublicae, est nihilominus et suppositum propter se existens, atque adeo per se capax iniuriae, quam respublica non potest illi irrogare.' Both this passage and that cited in n. 109 are discussed by Hamilton, *Political thought*, pp. 30–1. As she rightly points out, Soto's stress on an existence of the individual distinct from that of the community is to do with the Christian foundations of his politics. But it is perhaps too simple merely to say that 'Soto ... while stressing the common good, always returns to the ultimate good of the individual, as any Christian political theory is perhaps bound to do.' It is not simply a case of the paramountcy of individual salvation: human beings are capable of salvation because they are creatures of reason and will, made in the image of God; this characteristic is *dominium in seipsum* or liberty, a right in themselves, and it is this right which cannot be overridden by the community and its right, which exists only at the level of natural law as inclination to the good. Soto stresses the proper existence of the individual as a matter of *right* – the book is after all called 'On justice and right' – something which Hamilton does not discuss.

[117] *DIEI*, v, Q. 1, a. 7 in corp.

[118] Ibid., a. 6: 'he who contrives death to himself, does not act contrary to justice with respect to himself, but contrary to charity: with respect to the commonwealth and to god, however, he acts contrary to justice'.

[119] *DIEI*, v, Q. 2, a. 1, 'Utrum quempiam suo mutilare membro sit licitum'.

by right: 'This is proved. For each has the right of preserving his
proper life'; but the commonwealth cannot force him, nor can any
other moral or spiritual authority, 'for he is not bound to preserve
his life at the cost of such torture. Nor is he to be judged his own
killer.'[120] The way in which an individual preserves his life is his own
responsibility. 'And the reason is: because each individual is the
guardian of his own life: the commonwealth, of the common good.'
More strongly still, Soto insists that 'the commonwealth has in this
no right at all'.[121] In the matter of preserving his own life, the
individual is not a member of the commonwealth, and therefore the
commonwealth has no right; more, each man has as an individual
not only the right of self-conservation, but also the liberty – he is *not
bound* – not to do so if it will involve excessive pain.

This brief article demonstrates in this way both Soto's separation
of the rights of the individual from the right of the community, and
also the fact that for him, an individual human being, if he has rights
of his own, inevitably – of his nature as human – has liberty with
regard to those rights. These two points are further brought out in
Soto's treatment of the subject of homicide in self-defence. In the
eighth article of his Question on homicide, 'Whether each have the
proper right to kill his attacker in defence' ('Utrum ius sit unicuique
proprium invasorem sui defensum occidere'), Soto argues that every
individual has 'the natural right proper to each' ('ius naturale
unicuique proprium') of defending himself, and that if he kills in this
cause that killing will be licit, that is, will not constitute an injury to
the aggressor.[122] But granted it may be justified to kill in self-

---

120 Ibid., in corp.: 'Probatur. Nam unusquisque ius habet propriam servandi vitam ... At vero
quod ingentissimum dolorem in amputatione membri aut corporis incisione ferat, profecto
nemo cogi potest: quia non tenetur tanto cruciatu vitam servare. Neque est censendus sui
homicida. Imo vera est illa Romana vox dum crus illa aperiretur, Non est tanto dolore
digna salus.'
121 Ibid.: 'Et ratio est: quia unusquisque est suae vitae custos: respublica vero boni communis
... Sed nunquid non potest respublica ... subditum cogere, ut dum ad salutem fuerit
necessarium, membrum sibi permittat abscindi? Respondetur quod respublica in hoc
nullum habet ius.'
122 Although Soto here, like Cajetan in his commentary on the locus (2a2ae 64, a. 7), treats
homicide in these circumstances as an accident of defence, arguing that it is not licit on
private authority to kill with the intention of so doing, he had shortly before asserted more
controversially that 'to kill an attacker in blameless defence, is in no way prohibited by
that commandment ["Thou shalt not kill"] ... It is not a legitimate response, that the
attacked does not intend to kill another, but to defend himself. For even if the ultimate end
be defence, nonetheless to kill the attacker is taken as the means: for a person defending
himself can with right intention go for the throat': *DIEI*, v, Q. 1, a. 1 in corp.

defence: is a person then bound to do so? Vitoria had argued that he was not:

Cajetan holds the opposite, and it is the common opinion which I consider true ... that a person is not bound *qua* a private person, i.e. on his own account to kill another who attacks unjustly ... someone who has bread vital for the conservation of his life, may give it to his father or friend, and patiently embrace death ... Thus even for an enemy – albeit more for a friend – [I can lay down my life], because the fact that he may be my enemy does not take from me the liberty, that I might not kill him.[123]

Soto appears to make substantively the same point: 'it is licit to lay down one's life for one's friend. And therefore it clearly follows that the attacked may permit himself to be killed, in order that he might not kill ... [except in extraordinary circumstances] it is both the case that the attacked has the right of defending himself: and that nevertheless, it is free for him to renounce such a right out of charity.'[124] But the final sentence makes clear the difference between the two. For Vitoria, a person both defends himself and forbears to do so out of his liberty, which is the same as his *dominium* and also his right. For Soto, a person who defends himself will do so by right, because like all creatures he has the natural right of self-conservation. But, unlike the rest of terrestrial nature, each individual man has that right as his own: it falls within his *dominium* and his liberty, and therefore *it is free for him* to renounce it if he will. A person renounces his natural right not by the exercise of (yet another) natural right, but by the exercise of liberty or self-*dominium*. Unlike animals or other creatures who have natural rights, man is alone in being aware of having natural rights and being able to make a conscious decision to exercise them or to renounce them.

---

[123] *Comm ST* (V) 2a2ae, Q. 64, a. 7, n. 4: 'Oppositum tenet Cajetanum, et est communis opinio quam puto vera ... quod non tenetur quis pro privata persona, sc. pro se occidere alium invadentem injuste ... qui habet panem necessarium ad conservandam vitam suam, potest dare patri vel amico et patienter amplecti mortem ... sic etiam pro patre possum ponere vitam et pro amico. Ergo etiam pro inimico, licet plus pro amico, quia quod sit inimicus meus non tollit a me libertatem, quin possum non occidere illum.'

[124] *DIEI*, v, Q. 1, a. 8 ad argumentum: 'demonstratum, licitum esse vitam ponere pro amico. Unde palam consequitur posse invasum permittere se occidi, ne occidat ... et ius habet invasus quisque defendendi se: et nihilominus ei liberum est propter charitatem iuri eiusmodi renuntiare.' The extraordinary circumstances are cases involving kings, dukes 'or any other person who might be very useful to the commonwealth'. Such a person when attacked is not free to renounce his right of self-defence, but is bound to exercise his right to kill in self-defence for the sake of the common good. Conversely, a 'lowly person, whose life has no importance with regard to the common good', is bound not to exercise his right when attacked by an important public person. Soto does, however, say only that he is bound "by charity", not that he is bound by right.

Soto's treatment of homicide and mutilation of the person in Book v is the culmination of his system of right. It can be read as a critique of that of Vitoria in his commentary on the *Summa theologiae*, and a development of the notions sketched in the *Relectio De potestate civili*. Distancing himself from Vitoria on the *Summa theologiae*, Soto separates a sense of right from that of liberty, and is thus enabled to justify the natural action of all creation including man. It is likely that Soto, the natural scientist, could not accept the kind of total separation of the account of human activity from that of the rest of the natural world that Vitoria had posited. But a further underlying determinant of his move may well have been the question of the city or political community. Without some justification for the natural as opposed to the spiritual actions of man, a city which is the result of natural activity has no justification – no right. Thus the city in Vitoria's commentary on the *Summa theologiae* is justified but is founded not on natural action but on free consent. Soto instead legitimates and justifies the natural inclinations for political life described but not adequately developed at the beginning of the *Relectio De potestate civili*. However, he did not thereby sacrifice the right of liberty upon which Vitoria insisted to such effect in the commentary on the *Summa theologiae*. Soto's great achievement was to defend simultaneously the right of the city and the right of the individual man within it. It is this which enables him to be at once the perpetrator of fundamental error, and 'the most learned theologian of our time', to the jurist Fernando Vázquez, whose own solution to the problem of political right is the subject of the next chapter.

5

The language of natural liberty:
Fernando Vázquez de Menchaca

Fernando Vázquez is a figure of some obscurity in the history of political thought today, despite his having been notorious among contemporaries, a major influence on Grotius and cited consistently throughout the second half of the sixteenth century and the first half of the seventeenth.[1] Partly this is because his work has been appropriated to the history of international law, in a century – unlike the sixteenth and seventeenth – wherein the external relations of states are treated largely separately from their internal structures.[2] Partly also it is due to his having been a humanist jurist and therefore escaping the categories of enquiry into the scholastic political thought of sixteenth-century Spain and of the counter-reformation in general. Latterly he has been resurrected, if at all, only as a theorist of the voluntarist tradition of subjective right.[3]

---

[1] Among them, Hugo Grotius, writing sixty years after the publication of Vázquez's work: 'Scholasticam subtilitatem cum legum et canonum cognitione coniunxerunt, ita ut a controversiis etiam populorum ac regum non abstinerent, Hispani duo Covarruvia et Vasquius: hic magna libertate, modestius alter, nec sine exacto quodam iudicio': Hugo Grotius, *De iure belli ac pacis libri tres* (Paris 1625), Prolegomena, sig. i iv v. See also Grotius, *De iure praedae commentarius*, trans. by G. L. Williams (Oxford 1950), Chapter xii (published as the pamphlet *Mare liberum* in 1609), p. 249: 'As a matter of fact, this entire question has been quite thoroughly discussed by Vázquez, the pride of Spain, a jurist who in no instance leaves anything to be desired in the keenness of his investigation of law nor in the candour with which he expounds it.' For Grotius' use of Vázquez and of the School of Salamanca in general, see P. Borschberg, *Hugo Grotius' 'Commentarius in Theses XI': An early treatise on sovereignty, the just war, and the legitimacy of the Dutch Revolt* (Bern 1994), 73–101.

[2] For an account of Vázquez as a theorist of international law, see Camilo Barcia Trelles, 'Fernando Vázquez de Menchaca. L'école espagnole du droit international du XVIe siècle', *Recueil des Cours* 1 (1939), 433–533; A. Miaja de la Muela, *Internacionalistas españoles del siglo XVI. Fernando Vázquez de Menchaca, 1512–1569* (Valladolid 1932). A more detailed but unreliable study with particular reference to the doctrine of the freedom of the seas is E. Reibstein, *Die Anfänge des neueren Natur- und Völkerrechts* (Bern 1949).

[3] E.g. Tuck, *Natural rights theories*, p. 51, remarks that Vázquez's work 'includes a definition of *dominium* in terms of liberty which could have come straight out of Gerson'. Cf. Seelmann, *Vázquez*, p. 162, who, although laying emphasis on the purely juristic origins of Vázquez's thought, includes the Franciscan notion of *dominium*-right as a contributory

In this chapter I want to insist on both the significance of Vázquez's work for the history of political thought, and his relation to the School of Salamanca. He represents a major step in the development of a radical legal tradition the analysis of right of which is based on a preoccupation with *fact*, or what escapes juridical determination. In parallel, I want to suggest that he should be read neither in isolation from, nor as a continuation of,[4] the work of the Spanish Dominicans, but rather as a positive response to its achievements, and particularly to that of Soto. As we saw, in order to cope with the indeterminate aspect of agency which is peculiar to man, Soto had acknowledged a second sense of right over and above that with which he had characterised all nature: *dominium in seipsum* or liberty, constituting the foundation of all *dominia* over external objects. But in the analysis of natural agency of whatever kind – determinate or indeterminate – he had never left the universe of right; to have done so would have been impossible within a philosophical and theological framework which connects agency, as actualisation of form, with the good and hence the naturally legitimate, and understands right as a derivative of law.

The effect of Soto's synthesis was to safeguard both the right of the city and that of the individual within it. Vázquez is not unappreciative of his defence of the latter, but as a lawyer he is not heir to the theology of the image of God upon which it is based. However, what he grasps to the full is the import of Soto's founding of the city upon the determinate natural right of human beings to conserve themselves in being: the consequent necessity of political subjection. With materials alien to Soto, a synthesis of Ciceronian humanism and the Roman law, Vázquez combats Soto's conclusions at their root, which is the notion of a natural right of any entity of conserving itself in

---

factor: 'Die theoretische Konstruktion der "Symbiose von Eigentum und Freiheit" jedoch gewinnt Vázquez aus vielfältigen Diskussionen des Mittelalters, nicht etwa nur aus dem "Voluntarismus" der franziskanischen Tradition oder den sozialen Stömungen [sic] seiner Zeit.'

4   The view of Vázquez as, wholly or in part, a rights theorist of the 'voluntarist tradition' leads to his being seen in both of these perspectives: in the former, where the historian believes that the School of Salamanca has no doctrine of subjective rights (so Tuck, *Natural rights theories*, p. 51, who describes Vázquez as an 'intersticial figure' amidst the prevailing 'Vitorian Thomism'); in the latter, where the historian accepts the Grossi–Villey thesis of the School as a hotbed of Franciscan theory (cf. the concluding remarks by Seelmann, *Vázquez*, pp. 161–2, who, although he stresses the legal sources of Vázquez's thought, does not see it as in any way opposed to the account given by Grossi of the second scholastic).

being. Vázquez would replace this universal natural right with a universal natural liberty.

Little is known of Vázquez's life.[5] Born at Valladolid in 1512, the son of a member of the royal council of Castile, he studied both civil and canon law at Valladolid and Salamanca, obtaining the licenciate at Salamanca in 1549. Thereafter he pursued a career in public office, while writing a tripartite treatise on law entitled *De successionum creatione, progressu et resolutione* which was first published, probably in its entirety, at Salamanca in 1559.[6] In 1561 he was invited by Philip II to join the group of jurists and theologians accompanying the king to the final session of the Council of Trent. It was here that he found the opportunity to write, or at least to prepare for publication, his most famous work, the *Controversiarum illustrium usuque frequentium libri tres*, first published at Venice in 1564.[7]

These two works share certain features. In style, they are both works of humanist jurisprudence in that they are written in classicizing Latin, in an ironic mode with frequent claims to novelty and elegance of argument, and incorporate extensive quotation from the Roman poets. Moreover, they share the same philosophical basis in viewing the world of right as in constant flux, with rights having genesis, life and death – creation, progression and resolution – just like entities of the natural world. The latter, shorter and more flamboyant work, which handles predominantly questions of common law and public law, refers the reader frequently to the earlier for the details. But it is evident that by the time of the *Controversies*, Vázquez's thought on political issues had become more radically original, and his emphasis on the natural liberty of men more marked. In the course of this chapter I shall therefore concentrate on exposing the language and structure of the *Controversies*, referring back to the *De successionibus* as Vázquez does.

Vázquez opens the *Controversies* with a substantial Preface. Beginning with a rhetorical denunciation of those enemies of justice who

---

[5] For the most recent account, see Seelmann, *Vázquez*, pp. 25–30.

[6] See ibid., pp. 33–5, for details of this work and its publication history. Later editions bear the overall title of *De successionibus et ultimis voluntatibus*.

[7] See ibid., pp. 30–3, for the publication history of this work. It is now generally accepted that Venice 1564 constitutes the first edition of the *Controversiarum illustrium*. As I have not been able to see a complete copy of this edition, I have used the second, that of Frankfurt 1572. In so far as I have been able to check, however, the differences between the two editions are very slight and are mainly a matter of spelling and punctuation.

hide behind her cloak and whose machinations have inspired him to write in her defence, he goes on to narrate an incident which took place at the Council in February 1563, in which he himself played a major part. At issue was the question of precedence between the representatives of the king of France and those of the king of Spain. An arrangement that the French party should speak first after the papal representative in a debate over marriage law provoked the intervention of Vázquez on behalf of the Spaniards. Vázquez reproduces in his Preface the two letters he then wrote, which are to the effect that the church, particularly, must heed the claims of justice; and he goes on to give the arguments he used verbally to support his petition.[8]

The eighteen arguments given fall under two master arguments for the justice of the precedence of the king of Spain. The first is bipartite: the contention that 'to the greatest belongs the most honour', together with the idea that political greatness is a thing of the moment, and must be understood only for the time of the argument. The king of Spain is indubitably the greatest at the moment; and therefore his representatives should have the honour of precedence. The second concerns the service of the ruler to his people: to him who does the greatest good to mankind belongs the greatest reward. The king of Spain rules over the greatest portion of mankind, and in so doing serves them and effects their good: therefore he should have the reward of honorary precedence. These two basic arguments foreshadow the two themes which will dominate the whole work: the idea of the mutability of civil right, and that of the ordination of the prince to the convenience of the people. Just as the Preface moves smoothly from the fragility of civil right to an exposition of the limited nature of princely power, the main body of the work moves with equal ease from the elaboration of the latter theme to demonstrating that civil right is merely the constantly evaporating surface of the great ocean of *de facto* occurrence.

Vázquez needed a decisive argument for why the Spanish king should have precedence. He understands this as a need to demonstrate the 'prelacy' (*praelatio*) of the Spanish king over the French king

---

[8] He adds, however, that 'it should not be supposed that I then voiced every argument here appended, but merely those which most commended and fostered the justice of our cause. I have added the others for the sake of ornament, as is usual': *Controversies*, Preface, n. 17. The rivalry between the French and the Spanish at Trent is described in Hubert Jedin, *A history of the Council of Trent*, trans. by E. Graf, 2 vols. (London 1957–61).

and over anyone else, prelacy being understood as a position of superior right. In order to forestall the claims of any other monarch to such prelacy, Vázquez links the possession of prelacy to power: 'to the greater and the more powerful a more eminent position is owed';[9] and power to wealth: 'Riches and wealth suppose power, power dignity and just prelacy ... he who has greater riches, revenues, supplies and wealth, is understood as being more powerful, nor is there any doubt that in virtue of this he is held to be more worthy and more noble.'[10]

For this power which accrues to an individual through force of riches, Vázquez uses the word *potentia* rather than *potestas*. As we shall see, Vázquez reserves *potestas* for that power conceded by the citizens to the prince, which is specifically a power, limited by law, to look after their good. *Potentia* signals that purely *de facto* power which has nothing to do with law or right, and everything to do with sheer might. Power in the sense of *potentia* puts a person in possession of prelacy: but possession belongs to the world of fact rather than right and is subject to all the instability and mutability of that sphere:

Nor is it to the point, that some other King or Prince may have said that he is or was in possession of prelacy, for since that is a thing of fact, it is not to be believed unless proved ... And anyway, even if that state of affairs had once obtained, or we conceded freely that it had obtained, still it would not constitute an objection, because right in things of this sort every day arises, and every day comes to an end.[11]

In a thing such as prelacy, which has 'no duration and successive extension', the right of possession – 'if it be proper to name it a right, for we should more justly and more usefully call it a shadow' – ends with the first and present occasion. The conclusion follows:

We should understand him to be the most powerful, who is most powerful at the time when the controversy is being aired ... but if we look at the present time, it cannot fail to be certain, sure and undoubted to anyone who knows anything of the world ... that our Lord, the most puissant King of Spain, is more powerful than all the princes of all the world, and

9 *Controversies*, Preface, n. 25: 'maioribus et potentioribus eminentior sedes debeatur'.
10 *Controversies*, Preface, nn. 77–9: 'Divitiae et opes ponunt potentiam, potentia autem dignitatem et iustam praelationem ... qui maiores divitias, redditus, et proventus, ac opes habet, is potentior intelligatur, nec dubium est, quin per hoc dignior et nobilior habeatur.'
11 *Controversies*, Preface, n. 25: 'Nec ad rem quoque pertinet, quod alius forte Rex aut Princeps dixerit, se esse aut fuisse in quadam possessione praelationis, nam ea res facti cum sit, credenda non esset, nisi probaretur ... Quinimo etiam si id aut unquam fuisset, aut fuisse gratis concederemus, adhuc obesset nihil, nam ius in rebus huiusmodi quotidie oritur, et quotidie finitur.'

therefore to be accorded the prelacy over the rest. Nor is it relevant that in older times other Princes may have been more powerful, for nothing is more frequent or more habitual, than that kingdoms, empires, principates, potentates and monarchies should every day change, ebb and flow, increase, diminish, be extinguished, be born and born again, and vanish, so that those which have vanished, are now as fable and shadow.[12]

The force of this argument is that it will defeat both an opponent who argues from abstract philosophical principles (by locating the criterion in the empirical field of history) and an opponent who claims an ancient historical right (by denying that the issue has anything to do with right). Vázquez's whole thesis is that the attempt to justify power – to prove that it is a matter of right – is misplaced. But he makes his argument sustainable with the idea that a position of power can be *res facti*, a thing of fact, and still command the respect of men. Vázquez treats as morally significant the fact that people generally consider the more affluent to be of higher dignity than others, because 'vox populi vox dei est', and because 'according to Cicero, "Tusculans" III, "maxime magister populus"'.[13] If the people, on grounds of wealth, says that a certain person is greater, more worthy and more excellent, then so he is. 'So that Iohannes Boemus is no fool when he says in his book "On the customs of the peoples", that in many cases the despicable and the good are distinguished not so much by nature as by the customs and opinions of men.'[14] Vázquez's regard for the common opinion of men is part

---

[12] *Controversies*, Preface, nn. 33–4: 'Potentiorem autem accipere debemus eum, qui potentior est eo tempore quo controversia vertitur ... sed inspecto tempore praesenti nulli omnino, qui non sit rerum inexpertus, desinit esse certum, fixum et indubitatum ... quin potentissimus Hispaniarum Rex et Dominus noster sit omnibus totius orbis principibus potentior, ergo reliquis omnibus praeferendus. Nec ad rem pertinet, quod priscis forte temporibus alii Principes fuissent potentiores, nam nihil frequentius aut usitatius, quam regna, imperia, principatus, potentatus, monarchias quotidie mutuari, fluctuare, augeri, deminui, extingui, nasci, renasci, evanescere, ut quae evanuerint, semel tam pro fabula et umbra sint.' For Vázquez's argument within the context of the Spanish debate about empire, see A. Pagden, *Lords of all the world: Ideologies of empire in Spain, Britain and France, c. 1500–c. 1800* (New Haven and London 1995), pp. 40–62.

[13] *Controversies*, Preface, nn. 85–6. As authority for this usage of the phrase 'vox populi, vox dei' Vázquez refers us to Soto, *DIEI*, v, i, vi and ix. At *DIEI*, v, i, vi, however, what Soto says is not 'vox populi, vox dei' but 'vox populi, vox naturae': not the voice of the creator God, but the voice of God's creation, nature, speaking through the people. I have not been able to find the reference at v, i, ix.

[14] Ibid.: 'Unde Ioann. Boemus non inscite in lib. de moribus gentium ait, Multis in rebus turpe et honestum non tam natura, quam hominum distingui moribus et sententiis.' The *Omnium gentium mores, leges et ritus* of the German scholar Johann Boemus was written in 1520 and widely read and imitated throughout the sixteenth century (see N. Broc, *La géographie de la renaissance, 1420–1560* (Paris 1986), pp. 82–9, for remarks on the work and its fortunes). It is essentially a work of comparative ethnology, opening with a description of the original

and parcel of his general concern with plain fact rather than the intricacies of claims to right.

After introducing the theme of the mutability of right, Vázquez goes on to his second major argument. This claims that the service the prince does the community renders him worthy of reward. For these ideas he draws on the Augustinian themes of mediaeval political literature. The principal theme is the traditional idea that 'the kingdom is not for the sake of the king, but the king for the sake of the kingdom, or for the sake of the utility of the kingdom or the citizens', and that kings came into being to impose justice on malefactors.[15] 'Empire and kingdom are nothing but jurisdiction ... And so in that book of the Old Testament which is called the book of Judges, the talk is preponderantly of kings, and yet it is called "of Judges", as if Judges, and Kings, are taken as the same thing.'[16] All rulers

state of man, and going on to consider in three books the inhabitants and customs of Africa, Asia and Europe. Although I have been unable to find the particular quotation which Vázquez here reproduces in any of the editions which might have been available to him, Boemus' description of the original state of nature from which different peoples diverged in the course of time is very close to that of Vázquez, and is almost undoubtedly one of his sources. In drawing on a work like Boemus', the presuppositions of which are essentially historical and relativist, Vázquez allies himself firmly with the growing sixteenth-century interest in custom and culture as the source of explanation for the newly encountered diversity of human behaviour. Whereas for his theologian contemporaries, however, this interest was fuelled by the demands of consistency in philosophy and theology (see Pagden, *Fall of natural man* for an account of the pressures on the Aristotelian worldview imposed by the discovery of America), for sixteenth-century jurists the stimulus came from the increasing historicity of the study of jurisprudence and the parallel dethronement of the *Corpus iuris civilis* as the universal authority in questions of law.

15 *Controversies*, Preface, nn. 104–5. Vázquez gives his sources for his particular understanding of the coming into being of the principate as Baldus' commentary on the law *Ex hoc iure* under the title *De iustitia et iure* in the Digest (D. 1, 1, 5), and Chapter 54 of Alphonso Guerrero's *Thesaurus christianae religionis* (the relevant chapter is in fact chapter 53, *De Regibus, et principibus, et de authoritate regia*.) Vázquez may not have read Baldus for himself, since Guerrero refers to the same passage of Baldus in giving his account of the origin of kings: 'Baldus in l. ex hoc iure tit. de iustitia et iure, said, that it was through wars that there came into being the division of peoples, and through force of necessity, because the lesser was being oppressed by the greater and the poor man by the rich, and the strong oppressed the weak, and therefore kindly nature granting solace to human misery, established Kings or rulers; thus Kings were created of necessity, because all things need a head, and men are quick to disagree, and so they need kings, and Baldus says ... that Kings derive their origin from the right of peoples ... But I say, that Kings are given by God to wreak vengeance on malefactors, and to the praise of good men': Alphonsus Guerrero, *Thesaurus christianae religionis* (Venice 1559), Chapter LIII, n. 1. Guerrero is concerned with the mediaeval figure of the king as *minister dei*, derived from Augustine's commentary on Romans 13; Vázquez is far more concerned with the idea that he is directly the minister of the people.

16 *Controversies*, Preface, n. 107: 'Imperium enim et regnum nihil aliud est quam iurisdictio ... Et ideo in vet. Test. lib. ille qui Iudicum inscribitur, magna ex parte circa reges versatur, et tamen Iudicum inscribitur, quasi Iudices, et Reges, pro eodem accipiantur.' The idea of the king as the people's appointed officer of justice is reinforced by Vázquez's extensive use of

are understood as created, chosen or given not for their own sake or that of
their own utility, but for the sake of the citizens and the utility of the
citizens, in the likeness and image of the guardianship of minors, which is a
force and a power [potestas] over free individuals to protect those, who
otherwise could not protect themselves ... so the kingdom was invented and
given to protect those who whether because of youth, or senility, or bodily
or mental illness, or sex, or weakness, cannot protect themselves against the
more powerful [potentiores], and thus [it was invented] at the urging of
human necessity.[17]

The weak are in danger because human beings, who naturally live in
society, nevertheless do not naturally live at peace:

Finally, as Cicero says ... we seem to be born in such a way, that there
should be some kind of society between us ... But there is no doubt that this
very society and familiarity or communion is wont to beget discord ... For
the human mind is prone to disagreement ... And since it is naturally the
case, that everyone wants better for himself than for anyone else ... it was
necessary that there should be, and be in authority, someone who would
quell this sort of quarrel and suit, lest the citizens should continually be
rushing and raging for weapons and bloodshed. Thus, both human
necessity, and the natural appetite for society (for according to the
Philosopher, man is naturally a sociable animal), gave birth to the social
and political life of man, society gave birth to discord and dissent, discord
to the principate and the civil juridical power [potestatem].[18]

the *Tractatus de syndicatu omnium officialium* of the fifteenth-century Neapolitan jurist Paris de
Puteo (c. 1413–93), published in vol. II of the series *Tractatus universi iuris* (Lyons 1549) and
also a source for Guerrero. This work of Paris is continually cited by Vázquez throughout
the Preface and Book I in support of his restriction of the Prince to the service of the
people. The subject of the tract is *syndicatus*, that process by which the actions of officials in
the republican communes of Northern Italy were subject to scrutiny at the end of their
term of office. Paris extends the point that magistrates, servants of the people, should be
judged as to whether they have exceeded the terms of their mandate, to emperors, kings
and feudal lords, beginning his tract with three chapters on the *excessus* of emperors, kings
and barons. For the themes of liberty and tyranny in Paris, see Diana Perry, 'Paridis de
Puteo: A fifteenth-century civilian's concept of papal sovereignty', in D. Wood (ed.), *The
church and sovereignty, c. 590–1918: Essays in honour of Michael Wilks* (Oxford 1991), 369–92. As
we shall see, Vázquez adopts the argument of this kind of text, but sets it within a wider
notion of natural tyranny and natural liberty, which enables him to transcend the
mediaeval and bring his philosophy into the context of Renaissance thought.

[17] *Controversies*, Preface, n. 119: 'non propter se aut suam utilitatem, sed propter cives
civiumve utilitatem creati, delecti aut dati intelliguntur, ad similitudinem et imaginem
tutelae minorum, quae est vis ac potestas in capitibus liberis ad tuendos eos, qui aliter se
tueri commode nequirent ... ita et regnum ad tuendos eos, qui vel per aetatem, vel
senium, vel morbum corporum, vel animarum, vel sexum, vel imbecillitatem sese adversus
potentiores tueri non possunt, inventum datumque fuit, sicque humanis necessitatibus id
exigentibus.'

[18] *Controversies*, Preface, nn. 121–2: 'Denique, ut Cic. ... testatur [*Laelius de Amicitia*, v. 19], sic
nos nati videmur, ut inter nos esset societas quaedam ... Nec dubium est, quin haec
societas ac communio sive familiaritas soleat parere discordias ... Est enim ingenium

This account diverges sharply from that of Vázquez's Salamancan contemporary Soto. The critical difference is that, for Vázquez, there is a stage between the natural congregation of men and the establishment of political power. Whereas, on the Dominican synthesis, the establishment of political power is part of the same natural movement which led men to congregate, for Vázquez there is one motive which leads him to congregate, and another to set up political power. For Soto, men are either the subjects (*subditi*) of a political power, preferably a king, or they are less than men, living in a state where they cannot preserve themselves. For Vázquez, men are fully men in civil society, without being subject to any power.

This society of citizens which opts freely for political power as a solution to its inherent difficulties plays a key role in Vázquez's political thought. His whole political point is that the prince is the creature of the citizens, and that his existence, contingent upon their will, can never override their fundamental characteristic of being free citizens rather then subjects. But in these same passages the paradoxical relationship of Vázquez to Cicero is evident. Ciceronian society necessarily involves the citizens' feeling mutually obliged: only thus can the free commonwealth function. Ciceronian liberty is the opposite of unbridled licence. What Vázquez takes from Cicero is the idea that liberty should be the peculiar quality or characteristic of the citizen. But by setting the prince in the sphere of regulation and right, he moves the citizen into a sphere of liberty which consequently cannot be the self-regulating liberty of the civic humanist tradition.[19] The freedom with which he characterises his citizens is such that the Ciceronian society cannot exist.

In the course of this second argument for the king of Spain, Vázquez has developed further his opposition between *potentia* and *potestas*. In the passages quoted, *potestas* designates a power which is directed to a particular end (of protecting minors, of pronouncing justice) and has been established for this purpose. By contrast, *potentia*

humanum proclivum ad dissentiendum ... Cumque natura ita comparatum sit, ut omnis sibi melius quam alteri esse malit ... necessum fuit esse et praeesse, qui huiuscemodi discordias ac lites componeret, ne ad arma necesque passim cives prosilirent ac furerent. Ergo et humana necessitas, et naturalis appetitus societatis (est enim homo secundum Philosophum animal sociabile) peperit hominum vitam socialem et politicam, societas discordiam, dissensum, discordia principatum iuridicamque potestatem.'

[19] For liberty in Cicero and the republican tradition as the peculiar quality of the citizen (the equivalence of *civitas* and *libertas*), and as inherently involving the notion of restraint or law, see Ch. Wirszubski, *Libertas as a political idea at Rome during the late republic and early principate* (Cambridge 1960), esp. pp. 3–4, 7–9, and 30.

is undirected might. *Potestas*, as the creation of the people, stands in opposition to *potentia*, which is that quality possessed in different degrees by the 'free individuals', who naturally use that freedom and that power to oppress whomsoever they can. Here again, then, we see foreshadowed the opposition between the political and the natural, the created and the *de facto*; but there is also introduced the coincidental distinction between the directed and the indirected, that subject to regulation and that free from it. Vázquez thereby adopts a philosophical language which lies in explicit contradiction to that of Soto, for whom the natural, the *de iure*, the political and the regulated all coincide in a philosophy of politics based on a subjective natural right which is dictated by the law of nature, in the Thomist sense of law as directive of actions. For Vázquez, by contrast, the natural as the undirected stands in opposition to the political as the regulated. The political ruler is not possessed of that natural *potentia* and *libertas* which the subjects enjoy: if he appropriates them to himself, he becomes a tyrant.

Kings, princes and rulers of all descriptions are, for Vázquez, particularly prone to turn to tyranny; sometimes openly, sometimes in the guise of officers of justice. This is his motive for writing the *Controversies*, 'in the hope that I might be able to offer some relief to the unrestrictedness [laxitati] which should characterise the human race, but is now under pressure from the intervention and device of the powerful [potentiorum] or of illustrious Princes, or their flatterers'.[20] Here, tyranny coupled with the *servitus* of the people is opposed to justice coupled with the *laxitas* of the people. This is the traditional mediaeval contrast between king and tyrant, just rule and domination. What is revolutionary in Vázquez is that he brings out the implicit paradox that the people need a king or agent of justice precisely because their *laxitas* consists of mutual unregulated *potentia*, enslavement and tyranny. Natural liberty[21] is, precisely, tyranny – whether of ruler or ruled: but the liberty of the subjects is licit tyranny, while that of the prince (should he usurp it) is illicit tyranny.

---

[20] *Controversies*, Preface, nn. 11–12: 'si forte huic humani generis laxitati, potentiorum Principumve illustrissimorum, adulatorum plerunque interventu et opera, fatigatae, opem ferre aliquantulum possemus.' The paradigm example of the flatterer aiding the tyrant is Aristotle and his doctrine of natural (i.e. just) slavery, 'with which unhappy pronouncement he conspired not merely to defend, but even to commend, the funereal tyranny of Alexander the Great'.

[21] Although not here, Vázquez constantly associates *libertas* and *laxitas* in the hendiadys *laxitas libertasque*; e.g. at *Controversies*, Book I, Chapter XXIX, n. 17: 'naturalis libertas, ac laxitas'.

While contemporary civic humanist literature bewails the growth of emulation (*aemulatio*) and avarice (*avaritia*) as opening the door to tyranny, Vázquez's point is that *aemulatio, avaritia* and tyranny constitute precisely that liberty of which the humanist tradition is so beloved.

Throughout the Preface, then, Vázquez is mapping out oppositions on which he will elaborate in the two books which follow. The two sets of arguments use two different literatures as source material: the first draws on a specifically sixteenth-century humanist literature of custom; the second draws on the late mediaeval and early renaissance language of liberty and citizenship which was developed in the republican communes of Northern Italy, and on the Augustinian strand of political thinking, which has affinities with the republican vocabulary in the idea that political power is a judiciary power and the *officium* of its holder. Such source material is alien to the Aristotelian tradition which forms the basis of contemporary Dominican political philosophy. However, in considering the next two books we shall see that Vázquez's work is not simply a humanist island cut off from the main scholastic intellectual environment, but a deliberate reply to his Spanish contemporaries. Vázquez uses humanist materials to construct his own account of the progress of man from natural to political life, which pivots on the notion of a civic society between the loss of Arcadia and the establishment of a political regime. It is in this civic society that he fuses the two languages of his source materials, where the *de facto* activity of the custom literature meets the freedom of the republican literature. But Vázquez imposes continuity between the two vocabularies at the expense of the regulated liberty, contrasted with unregulated licence, of the civic republican tradition to which he owes his conception of civic society as opposed to political subjection. For Vázquez, Arcadia has vanished, and the Ciceronian self-regulating liberty of citizens is a dream consigned to the optative mode. Not content with dominating nature, man at liberty continually attempts to dominate his fellow man: and this demands that each man's *dominium* be reduced to a sphere wherein he cannot damage his fellow citizen overmuch, guarded by the sword of justice.

Books I and II examine these two dominations respectively, treating first of princes and secondly of prescription. By thinking of both books in terms of natural liberty and its decline, we shall not miss the continuity between two books which are, on the surface, an

Italian republican tract 'De principe', and a renaissance 'legal
humanist' tract 'De praescriptione'. There is no doubt that they
function as, and are intended to be, contributions to these genres:
but the work read as a whole is a contribution to the Spanish genre
of *De iustitia et iure* and an answer to that question of natural agency
to which the Dominicans and especially Soto found such a successful
response.

BOOK I: 'OF PRINCES'

Vázquez begins with a division of the qualities of princes (understood
as any rulers) into three categories: 'pure, simple and legitimate'
('meri et simplices atque legitimi'); 'legitimate, but not simple or
pure' ('legitimi, sed non simplices aut meri'); 'neither pure nor
legitimate' ('nec meri nec legitimi').[22] A 'pure' and legitimate prince
is one who is the pure creation of the people, for the sake of ruling
them to their own utility: 'Those princes are pure and legitimate,
who are chosen by a free people to rule the people; there can be no
principate more just nor less obnoxious than this, and this principate
has in view the pure utility of the citizens, not that of the rulers.'[23]
The legitimate but not 'pure' princes are feudal lords, those
possessed of the *ius vassalitii* (the right of holding others in a relationship of vassalage). The *ius* of these latter princes has in view their
own private utility, rather than that of their subjects, and 'is
constituted in that which is my own' (*in meo*) rather than 'that which
belongs to another' (*in alieno*).[24] A right's being to one's own private
utility is thus connected to its being over one's own. Finally, 'those
princes are said to be illegitimate, who have conquered the people
with force, and violence, and arms, and their power is *de iure* null:
because legitimate and juridical power is not to the bad'.[25]

---

[22] *Controversies*, Book I, Chapter I, n. I.

[23] Ibid., n. 2: 'Meri et legitimi sunt, qui a populo libero eliguntur ad regendum populum, quo
principatu alius iustior esse nequit, nec gratior, isque spectat ad meram civium non etiam
ad regentium utilitatem.'

[24] Ibid., n. 3. See José Maria Serrano Serrano, 'Las ideas políticas de Fernando Vázquez de
Menchaca', *Revista de estudios políticos* 206–7 (1976), 249–302 for the distinction between
jurisdiction and property in Vázquez. Serrano does not, however, draw out the full
linguistic implications of this distinction.

[25] Ibid., nn. 4–5: 'Illegitimi vero Principes dicuntur, qui vi, et violentia et armis populum
debellarunt, et istorum potestas de iure nulla est: quia iuridica et legitima potestas non est
ad malum.' The language of the Preface suggested that *potestas* was *only* used to denote a
legitimate and juridical authority, in opposition to *potentia* which signified *de facto* might.
Here, however, we find *potestas* being used as if there could be a *de facto potestas* which was

The term *merus*, pure, is familiar from the phrase *merum imperium*, normally used to designate absolute or unlimited authority. At the beginning of Chapter IV, Vázquez is forced to stress his own understanding of *merus*: '*imperium* is called *merum*, not for that reason, that it is free, but for this reason, that it is pure and without any admixture, and thus without any admixture of tyranny, and consequently pertaining solely to the matter of exercising jurisdiction among the citizens, and not to undermining what is useful to them'.[26] Vázquez's difficulty is that the term *merus* belongs, in contemporary legal discourse, to a complex of terms associated with unfettered liberty. Vázquez (as we shall see) is dependent on this vocabulary, which gives him a sense of liberty independent of both the theological and the Ciceronian notions, for his characterisation of the citizen; hence it is vital for him to make clear that it can never apply to the prince in the same sense. I shall try to lay out this vocabulary as it figured for the sixteenth century by using a text of the famous early sixteenth-century Bartolist jurist, Jason Maynus (Giason del Maino).[27]

The text of Maynus in question is his commentary on the law 'Si sic legatum', under the title 'De legatis' in the Digest.[28] The law is to the effect that a legacy cannot be given over to the arbitrary and unrestrained disposal of an heir: 'A legacy can be placed in the

not necessarily to the good (*in bonum*). However, this is a unique use of language on Vázquez's part; everywhere else in the work, Vázquez is insistent that a *potestas* cannot be *in malum*: 'no *potestas* is to the bad, but rather to the good ... for all *potestas* consists in jurisdiction, and is nothing other than jurisdiction ... and all *potestas* has in view one object and aim, namely, justice'; '*potestas* to the bad is called not so much a *potestas* but a *tempestas* ... we have the power to do only that, which we have the power to do honestly and without injury to anyone': *Controversies*, Book II, Chapter LI, n. 55 and n. 65. The opposition between *potestas* and *tempestas* originates with Baldus in his famous consilium *Rex Romanorum* (consilium 316), and in his consilium 345.

[26] *Controversies*, Book I, Chapter IV: 'sic imperium merum dicitur, non quidem ea ratione, quia liberum sit, sed ea ratione, quia purum est, sine cuiusdam rei mistura, et sic sine ulla tyrannidis mistura, et consequenter pertinens ad solam iurisdictionem inter cives exercendam, non ad eorum utilitates subvertendas'.

[27] In attempting to reconstruct the linguistic network in which particular words and phrases are situated for a sixteenth-century lawyer, I have proceeded with the use of a sixteenth-century lexicon of canon and civil law, the *Lexicon utriusque iuris* of Johannes Bertachinus, published at Venice in 1518–19. Under each heading Bertachinus gives not only explicit definitions proffered by sundry jurists (predominantly Bartolus and Baldus), but also examples of usage serving indirectly to define the term in question. By means of this lexicon it is possible to discover which laws concerning which issues served as *sedes materiae* for the discussion of the import of particular terms. I have chosen Jason Maynus' commentary on the Digest as one of the most widely used commentaries of the sixteenth centuries.

[28] D. 30, 75: Jason Maynus, *In primam (secundam) Infortiati partem commentaria* (Lyons 1542), fol. 115.

judgement of an heir *qua* a good man: but not in his pure will ... or
thus: A legacy is valid which is not placed in the pure power of the
legatee: but in his equitable judgement.'[29] Jason's commentary is an
extended consideration of that wording which implies restriction on
a power or faculty, and that which implies that the power is free of
any restraint. The fundamental opposition in the text is between the
will (*voluntas*) on the one hand, and the 'judgement of a good man'
(*arbitrium boni viri*) on the other. Jason gives an extensive catalogue of
words which convey the judgement of a good man, among which is
the term *potestas*: 'Similarly the word *potestas* refers to the judgement
of a good man because that is said to be in our power which we have
the power to do honestly.'[30] But, Jason continues:

> Limit all that has been said so that it applies when words like this appear on
> their own: for then they indeed imply the judgement of a good man ... It is
> different if there is added the word 'full' or 'free' or something similar: for
> then ... they imply pure and free will ... So that if a testator gives an
> executor a full or free faculty or power, he is understood to give it over to
> his pure and free will ... Ioannes ab Imola says, that those words 'let him
> have a free faculty' are understood to refer to a faculty which is not
> regulated by law.[31]

Jason then gives the two words which of themselves imply an unrestrained power or faculty; firstly, *voluerit* ('if he should will'). 'Bartolus
says ... that the force of that word *voluerit* is that someone can do
[facere] his will even unjustly ... Again, the word *voluerit* or *volo*
signifies pure fact and not judgement, according to Baldus.'[32] The
second term is *libuerit* ('if he should so please'), 'which similarly
implies pure and free will'. 'For according to Bartolus it is the same
thing to say "if he should so please" [libuerit] as to say "if he should
so freely will" ["libere voluerit", implicitly etymologising] ... and

---

[29] Ibid., n. 1: 'Legatum potest conferri in arbitrium heredis tanquam boni viri: sed non in eius
     meram voluntatem. h.d. vel sic. Valet legatum quod non est positum in mera gravat[i]
     potestate: sed in sui arbitrii equitate.'
[30] Ibid., n. 19: 'Similiter verbum potestatem refertur ad arbitrium boni viri quia illud dicitur
     posse quod honeste possumus.'
[31] Ibid., nn. 21–2: 'Limita predicta omnia ut procedant quando talia verba simpliciter
     proferuntur: tunc bene important arbitrium boni viri ... secus si adiiciatur verbum plenum
     vel liberum aut simile: tunc ratione adiuncti important meram et liberam voluntatem ...
     unde si testator dat executori plenam aut liberam facultatem vel potestatem: intelligitur in
     eius meram et liberam voluntatem conferre ... Ioann. de Imola ... dicit: quod illa verba
     liberam habeat facultatem: intelliguntur de facultate non regulata a iure.'
[32] Ibid., n. 27: 'dicit Bar .... quod virtus istius verbi voluerit. est ut possit quis voluntatem
     suam facere etiam inique ... Item verbum voluerit vel volo significat merum factum et non
     arbitrium, sec. Bal.'

thus because of that adverb "freely" it is taken for pure will ... so that if it is given to someone that he do according to his pleasure, such words imply free will.'[33] Jason finishes his exposition, however, with a firm statement: 'add that every power of judgement committed to someone in something which is not his own [in re aliena] is understood to be committed with justice: whatever the wording of the commission'.[34]

In this language, 'free' means something like 'absolved from the bounds of right and reason', dissociated from justice and right, and associated with will and *factum*. It is nothing to do with the Ciceronian *libertas*, which is a responsible freedom, opposed to licence (*licentia*), which is pure unbridledness: in the language of the law, the significance of the two terms is reversed, as Jason feels obliged to point out. *Licentia* is derived from *licitum*, which is the same as *iustum*, and therefore *licentia* involves the *arbitrium boni viri*, 'although Innocent ... appears to hold the contrary – i.e. that licence should be understood as free and wholly uncaused will; and this seems to be the intention of the orators when they make a distinction between licence and liberty: because licence signifies something unbound and without reason, not so liberty; and therefore licence has a bad sense, liberty a good sense'.[35] Nor can it be anything to do with the liberty of the Franciscan tradition. As we saw, *libertas* in this tradition is the attribute of rationals alone, belonging to them as made in the image of God and as part of the sphere of right as opposed to fact. In contrast, *libertas* in the vocabulary under consideration here is associated with the will as a thing of fact as opposed to right.[36]

---

[33] Ibid., n. 34: 'nam idem est dicere libuerit quod libere voluerit sec. Bart .... et sic propter illud adverbium libere intelligitur pro mera voluntate ... unde si committitur alicui quod faciat sec. libitum suum talia verba important liberam voluntatem.'

[34] Ibid., n. 37: 'adde omne arbitrium commissum alicui in re aliena intelligitur commissum cum iustitia: quibuscunque verbis committatur'.

[35] Ibid., n. 19: 'quamvis Inno. ... videatur tenere contrariam: quod licentia intelligatur libera voluntas sine aliqua causa: et istud videntur velle oratores dum constituunt differentiam inter licentiam et libertatem: quia licentia significat quid absolutum sine ratione: secus in libertate: et ideo licentia significat in malam partem: libertas in bonum.' Cf. Bartolus, *In universum ius civile commentaria* (Basel 1562), vol. II, p. 708 (commenting on D. 34, 1, 9): 'verbum licentia, importat arbitrium boni viri, quod probo. Nam nomen licentia, descendit a verbo licet, quod tantum est dicere, quantum licitum sit. Sed non est dubium, quod ista verba, si tibi videtur iustum, vel licitum, important arbitrium boni viri.'

[36] To this vocabulary also belong the dicta of Panormitanus used by Mazzolini (borrowing from the *Angelica*) to define *Liber* and *liberum dominium*, which Mazzolini recognised as belonging to the sphere of fact (above, p. 46). Although Mazzolini cannot be said to be a direct source for Vázquez, their views on liberty share a common root.

Vázquez thus defines the power by which the prince acts –
iurisdictio, a power regulated by right – through an implicit contrast
with another power of action which is not determined by right, but
which is free, operating at will, *de facto* and belonging to a *dominus*.
With this in mind we are in a position better to appreciate Vázquez's
definition of *dominium*.[37] Vázquez outlines his idea of what it is to
have *dominium* in the midst of answering the question 'whether the
prince can impede the free use, or even abuse, of our goods'.[38]
Vázquez's response, phrased in language which is by now familiar to
us, is as follows:

> Let it be the rule, then, that everyone have the freest [liberrimum] use of
> his own thing ... The reason being, that whatever each man of sound mind
> and legal age should will [voluerit], and whatever should be his pleasure
> [libuerit] with regard to his own things, is thought to be profitable to him
> when looking at the matter from the standpoint of the law, albeit from the
> standpoint of men's common opinion it is perfectly useless to him ... In
> accordance with which we can clearly gather what the true definition of
> *dominium* is, for it is the natural faculty of [doing] that, which it pleases
> [libet] anyone to do [facere], unless it be prohibited in any way by force or
> by right ... For what else is it, I ask, to have *dominium* in things, than to have
> that freest [liberrimam] and 'at pleasure' [ad libitum] faculty with regard to
> that thing?[39]

Here Vázquez finally and explicitly defines the power of the
citizens as the opposite of princely power: a free faculty *in suo*,
operating at will and *ad libitum*. He is clearly using the other side of
the same private-law vocabulary of personal powers that he used in
order to define the power of the prince. The use of this vocabulary

---

[37] See the discussion in Seelmann, *Vázquez*, pp. 76–98. Seelmann undertakes a detailed
investigation of the wording of this definition, but he concentrates on theological sources,
associating the *facultas* component with Soto's usage of *facultas*, and looking for the origins
of the idea of liberty in Franciscan theology. Although Seelmann refers to a text of Maynus
which talks of the *dominus* as having a 'free faculty of disposing' ('liberam facultatem
disponendi'), his failure to examine the mediaeval legal concept of *facultas* causes him to end
only in speculation on possible links between theological and legal usage: 'Auf welchem
Weg Jason zur "facultas" gelangt, ist nicht ersichtlich; ob er Summenhart kennt, wird nicht
deutlich' (*Vázquez*, pp. 91–2).

[38] *Controversies*, Book 1, Chapter XVII: 'Princeps liberum rerum nostrarum usum, aut etiam
abusum, impedire, an possit.'

[39] Ibid., nn. 2–5: 'Sit ergo regula unumquemque rei suae liberrimum usum habere ... Ratio,
quia quod quisque homo sanae mentis et legitimae aetatis voluerit, quodque ei libuerit
circa res suas, id utile ei esse inspecta legis censura reputatur, quamvis inspecta communi
hominum opinione inutile ei sit ... Secundum quae plane colligetur qualis sit vera dominii
definitio, est enim naturalis facultas eius, quod facere libet, nisi quid vi aut iure prohibeatur
... dominium enim in rebus habere, quid obsecro aliud est, quam eam liberrimam et ad
libitum facultatem habere circa illam rem?'

implicitly functions to place the exercise of the prince's power in the sphere of right, and that of the citizens in the sphere of fact. But Vázquez strengthens the contrast between princely and citizen activity with his use of Florentinus' definition of liberty from the Roman law to define *dominium*.[40] This use, unprecedented in the legal literature before Vázquez,[41] brings into play the critical new term of 'natural': the power of the citizens is a natural faculty, whereas the power of the prince is characterised as 'invented' in the course of time. This suggestion, however, puts Vázquez at odds with another part of the Roman law, for which particular *dominia* of distinct things are of the *ius gentium* and not of the *ius naturae*, as far from nature as kingdoms themselves.[42]

In his own interpretation of the progress from the *ius naturae* through the *ius gentium* to the *ius civile*, Vázquez draws on a doctrine developed in the civil law literature of a twofold *ius gentium*, the *ius gentium primaevum* and *secundarium*.[43] By the renaissance, this doctrine had acquired – at least in humanist circles of jurisprudence – the colouring of the decline of human nature from original innocence to corruption and wickedness.[44] Vázquez's account fits squarely into this tradition. The simple *ius naturale* is that *ius* which is common to both men and all animals; it includes such general provisions as *coniunctio maris et foeminae* and *educatio liberorum*.[45] The *ius gentium primaevum* is that *ius* which is natural to men only, connected with their use of reason: 'the primary right of peoples which pertains to men is nothing other than the very nature of men or a certain native

---

[40] Institutes 1, 3, 1–2: 'Et libertas quidem est, ex qua etiam liberi vocantur, naturalis facultas eius quod cuique facere libet, nisi si quid aut vi aut iure prohibeatur.'

[41] Seelmann (*Vázquez*, p. 72) refers in this connection to the work of the jurist Benincasa, published in 1561, wherein the definition of *libertas* is adduced to justify the model of a definition of *dominium* qualified by *nisi*, although there is no suggestion that *dominium* may be equivalent to *libertas*.

[42] E.g. at D. 1, 1, 5: 'Ex hoc iure gentium introducta bella, discretae gentes, regna condita, dominia distincta, agris termini positi, aedificia collocata, commercium, emptiones venditiones, locationes, conductiones, obligationes institutae.'

[43] See Seelmann, *Vázquez*, pp. 106–31 for a summary of the various accounts of the *ius gentium* in mediaeval Roman and canon law as background to Vázquez's doctrine.

[44] See for example, the commentary on the title *De origine iurium* by Hieronymus Cagnolus (Girolamo Cagnolo, 1492–1551), *In constitutiones et leges primi, secundi, quinti et duodecimi Pandectarum ... aurearum enarrationum Liber primus* (Venice 1561), fol. 79. Cagnolus was a fundamentally Bartolist jurist, but wrote a humanistic commentary on the *Regulae iuris* which is frequently cited by Vázquez.

[45] E.g. at *Controversies*, Book II, Chapter LXXXIX [LXXXVIII r], n. 24: 'naturale ius dicitur quod omnibus animantibus tam brutis quam ratione utentibus commune est.'

instinct and natural reason'.[46] It includes such things as *religio erga Deum et parentes*. The *ius gentium secundarium*, in contrast, is the *ius* which is constituted by human beings out of this first state of rational nature: 'the secondary right of peoples is that, which did not come into being simultaneously with the human race, but which with the decline of the ages is found to be practised by most of those peoples which are governed by customs and laws, and do not live a life of the woods in the mode and manner of wild beasts'.[47] This *ius* in the beginning was purely the civil right of one people, 'but was afterwards, gradually or in succession accepted also by all or most of the peoples, so that this right should be understood to be in origin a civil right only, but in its sanction and reception it began to be the right of the peoples'.[48] The secondary right of peoples is thus not natural but positive law, and is mutable just as is civil law.[49] It is established to deal with circumstances arising from human necessity, and it includes all commerce and contracts.

According to Vázquez, the liberty of all men belongs to the primary right of peoples, the natural right peculiar to man: 'the primary right of peoples dictates, that all men should share a common liberty'.[50] But *dominium* does not: 'in the beginning ... all things were in common ... Nor were *dominia* of things, or possessions, yet invented or recognised.'[51] *Dominium* is rather an invention of the *ius gentium secundarium* which replaces the pure operation of human nature: 'we are taught that all kingdom, empire, and jurisdiction is of

---

[46]   Ibid., Book I, Chapter x, n. 18: 'ius gentium quod ad homines attinet nihil aliud est quam ipsa natura hominum aut instinctus quidam nativus, ratioque naturalis.'

[47]   Ibid., Book II, Chapter LXXXIX, n. 25: 'Ius autem gentium secundarium est, quod non simul cum ipso genere humano proditum fuit, sed labentibus temporibus a plerisque earum gentium, quae moribus et legibus reguntur, nec ritu aut more ferarum sylvestrem vitam agunt, receptum reperitur.'

[48]   Ibid.: 'idque ius initio, ut ius tantum civile non etiam gentium esset necessaria, et coacta ratione fatendum est, quamvis postea ab omnibus, vel plerisque gentium paulatim aut successione admissum quoque fuisset, ut sic tale ius inventione civile tantum esse intelligatur, sed approbatione et veluti hospitio gentium earum ius esse coepit.'

[49]   Ibid., n. 26: 'sicque id ius gentium secundarium non tam naturale, quam positivum dicitur esse, sicque non fixum, et immobile, sed commutabile esse dicitur, non secus quam ius civile.'

[50]   Fernando Vázquez, *De successionibus et ultimis voluntatibus* (Frankfurt 1610), vol. I, *De successionum creatione* (henceforth *De succ. creat.*), Book I, para. I, n. 44: 'ius gentium primaevum dictat, quod omnibus hominibus communis sit libertas.' Cf. *Controversies*, Preface, n. 125: 'omnia censentur permissa, quae non reperiuntur nominatim prohibita ... et haec est illa naturalis libertas a Deo optimo maximo data.'

[51]   *Controversies*, Book I, Chapter IV, n. 3: 'initio rerum ... omnia erant communia ... Nec dum erant inventa, seu cognita dominia rerum nec etiam possessiones.'

the secondary right of peoples (which we call positive ...): which is also proved by reason, for from that right all *dominium* has come forth'.[52] Vázquez wants *dominium* to be both the natural faculty of liberty and an unnatural development connected with the invention of jurisdiction. As we shall see, its paradoxical status results from the shift in the sense of 'natural' from the original life of man to the present.

Natural liberty is a free faculty, unregulated by right and by reason. But as we saw, Vázquez insists that specifically human nature is right reason: not the irrational and free will, but the *arbitrium boni viri*. The implication is that liberty understood as the freedom to do what one wants belongs to the *ius naturale* understood as common to both rationals and irrationals. That it should belong to all men, certainly, is of *ius gentium primaevum*, but man shares the quality itself with all the rest of animate nature. This is confirmed by Vázquez's choice of the term *laxitas* as a synonym for both human and animal *libertas*. This is a rare classical term, used mainly of inanimates like the air, conveying unboundedness or lack of physical restriction on movement; more pertinently to Vázquez's text, the Roman law also speaks of a *naturalis laxitas* of the wild boar which has been loosed from a net.[53] As freedom of arbitrary movement, it is the natural attribute of all animates.

The natures of man and beast differ, however, in two respects: men have natural reason, which dictates their peculiar natural right, including the tenet that all men should be at liberty; but they also have a 'natural instinct of dominating', which overrides their reason to the extent that they behave less objectively rationally than other animals.[54] It is the growth of that side of human nature which is the instinct to dominate which necessitates the principate: 'the principate ... was necessary among men, lest the weaker of them be oppressed by the stronger. It is otherwise among the rest of the animals which, because they do not prey on their own species, do not need a prince or governor of their particular species, and thus no lion is set in

---

[52] See ibid., Book I, Chapter XLI, n. 30: 'edocemur omne regnum, imperium, iurisdictionem esse de iure gentium secundario (quod nos positivum appellamus ...) id quod et probatur ratione, nam ex eo iure omne dominium processit'.

[53] D. 41, 1, 55, discussing the situation of taking or loosing a wild animal from the *laqueum* set by another: 'sin autem aprum meum ferum in naturalem laxitatem dimississes et eo facto meus esse desisset, actionem mihi in factum dari oportere.'

[54] *De succ. creat.*, Book I, para. I, n. 44.

authority over another'.[55] All jurisdiction and principate was 'invented for the suppression of the wicked'.[56]

Vázquez reinforces the distinction between natural liberty and invented principate or jurisdiction with the further opposition between natural and artificial. In the golden age of nature, any rare malefactor did not necessitate a prince, because the multitude of good men recognised their natural obligation to quell the malefactor and rescue the victim. This defence which everyone had against injury Vázquez characterises as a 'natural defence', in opposition to the 'artificial defence' which is the principate:

> That natural defence protected things as much as persons ... so that there is no doubt, that by the force of that natural obligation, by which other men were bound to rescue the victim of injury and violence, that victim was to be rescued and was in fact rescued ... which occurs today by artificial defence (which happens by means of principate and jurisdiction) after such laborious, troublesome, everlasting and expensive delays and suits that it would have been better, more advised and more useful to the victim not to have sought at all such help as is the artificial defence.[57]

Man is distinguished from the beasts by the fact that his liberty is vitiated by his natural instinct to dominate: but he is also distinguished by his ability to make – *facere* – artifacts which however inadequately will compensate for the defects of his nature. Political as opposed to civic society is the domain of this artificial remedy.

These 'artificial principates and jurisdictions'[58] are characterised as servitude (*servitus*), which lies in opposition to the perfect and complete liberty of the *ius gentium primaevum*, the *de facto* faculty of doing anything one might want.[59] But Vázquez emphasises yet again

---

[55] *Controversies*, Preface, n. 124: 'Ergo principatus ... necessarius fuit in hominibus, ne imbecilliores a fortioribus opprimentur. non sic in reliquis animantibus, quae, ut praedam in alterum animal suaemet speciei non exercent, ita et principe aut moderatore suaemet speciei non egent, sicque leo non praeest leoni.'

[56] Ibid., Book i, Chapter xli, n. 32.

[57] Ibid., n. 36: 'Denique naturalis illa defensio tam res quam personas intuebatur, sicque ... non dubium est, quin ex vi illius naturalis obligationis, qua reliqui homines ad iniuriam aut vim patienti subveniendum tenebantur, is subveniendus esset, et subveniretur ... id quod hodie ex defensione artificiali, quae per modum principatus et iurisdictionis fit post tam laboriosas, molestias, immortales, sumptuosasque moras et lites contingit, ut satius, consultius, utilius plerunque fuisset vim aut iniuriam patienti tale auxilium defensionemque artificialem non implorasse.'

[58] Ibid., n. 40: 'principatus et iurisdictiones artificiales'.

[59] Ibid., n. 37: 'nec dubium est quin principatus et iurisdictio huic omnimodae libertati aliquantulum adversetur, non secus quam quaedam servitus, quam iuri naturali adversari in comperto est'. The characterisation of jurisdiction and principate as a servitude is not original to Vázquez: Bertachinus, *Lexicon*, under the entry *Servitus* cites a comment of Baldus

that this perfect natural liberty was only lost through the fact that what man habitually wants is to dominate and tyrannise others. 'Social life makes desirable, and even imperative, empire (that is, judges or magistracies), not just because the human race is prone to dissent, but mostly because all men are so prone *as if to tyranny*, or at least to self-love, that all of them naturally want things better for themselves than for the other, as we said.'[60] Human nature is such that after the loss of the golden age, liberty is nothing other than the faculty for tyranny.[61]

This, of course, was Vázquez's point when he distanced his 'pure' prince from the prince with a *ius in suo*, which is to his own utility rather than that of others, and carries the possibility of an 'admixture' of tyranny. But the 'legitimate, but not simple or pure' prince, the feudal lord, is still not the illegitimate tyrant. So long as acting out of self-love is confined to the sphere of one's own, it is the legitimate faculty of *dominium*. *Dominium* is the vicious *libertas* of the period after the golden age restricted to the sphere of a particular *res*. To this extent it is regulated, and this regulation to particular spheres is the invention of the *ius gentium secundarium*. In this respect, *dominium* is an incorporeal right, an invention of civil right, and therefore not natural.[62] As the remnant of original liberty, however,

---

on *l. cum servum, C. De servis fugitivis* (C. 6, 1, 6): 'Servitutis species est esse sub iurisdictione alterius.'

[60] *Controversies*, Book 1, Chapter XXI, n. 23 (italics added): 'Socialis autem vita desiderat et deposcit imperium (hoc est, iudices aut magistratus) tum quod humanum genus est ad dissentiendum proclive, tum maxime quod omnes homines quasi ad tyrannidem, vel saltem ad amorem sui adeo sunt proclives, ut omnes natura sibi melius esse malint quam alteri, ut supra disseruimus.'

[61] See Boemus, *Omnium gentium mores*, fol. 3v: in the beginning, men 'did not thirst for honour or wealth', and moved about 'free and roaming' like the beasts; but with the ageing of the world (*adolescente mundo*) and the discordance of human appetites, pursuits and envies, groups of men congregated to suppress what is now the 'liberty of roaming *and doing harm*', 'congregati hominum coetus eam pervagandi nocendique libertatem communibus auxiliis prohibituri': it is the *same* faculty of liberty which has become noxious with the decline of the ages.

[62] See *Controversies*, Book 1, Chapter XVII, n. 7, following the definition of *dominium* as liberty: 'dominium nihil aliud est quam quoddam ius incorporeum'. This assertion is made to demonstrate the thesis that we have *dominium* in incorporeal rights, which suggests to Seelmann (*Vázquez*, p. 46) that Vázquez adopts the equation of *dominium* and *ius*, being developed from Bartolus through to the texts of Summenhart and Mair, and that he belongs to this same tradition of the progressive 'Subjektivisierung' of right. Seelmann takes Vázquez's association of *dominium* with *libertas* as further evidence of his affinity with this 'voluntarist' tradition of right outlined by Grossi. However, as we have tried to show, Vázquez's notion of *libertas* serves rather to distance him from the theologians. Moreover, Vázquez makes no reference at all in this context to the equation of *ius* and *dominium* by the theologians, referring rather to Gerson and Soto as those who have posited a Bartolist

it is a natural faculty. In so far as it is a constituent of human commerce and the possible object of precisely that free faculty which is itself, *dominium* is a *ius* – that is, it functions as part of the *ius gentium secundarium* and is therefore 'regulated by right'. But in its aspect as the power of action over a certain *res*, it is pure and absolute freedom, part of nature and part of *factum*. The *dominus* does not act *by right*, *iure*, although with respect to his position in human affairs it will be appropriate to say that he *has* a right. In contrast, the prince *acts* by right.

In this first book, Vázquez has been concerned primarily with liberty as a phenomenon within the civic state: that is, once the movement has occurred from the natural to the civil and artificial. In Book II, Vázquez turns to consider the topic of prescription, an area of the Roman law which he can use to examine that movement in more detail, treating as it does the transition from the *de facto* to the *de iure*. In the process he considers the question of what things can be subject to this movement, and what things must remain forever beyond the sphere of right. In so doing he is able to reinforce the more strictly political conclusions of his first book.

BOOK II: 'OF PRESCRIPTIONS'

In mediaeval and renaissance Roman law, prescription (*praescriptio*) is the process whereby long-term *de facto* occupation of a particular good can be recognised *de iure* as a case of *dominium*.[63] The doctrine of prescription had been heavily elaborated in the course of mediaeval commentary on the *Corpus iuris civilis*, but the specific tract *De*

---

definition of *dominium*. It does appear, however, that Vázquez's text retains the confusion of language we noted in Bartolus: see above, p. 22.

[63] In classical Roman law, the process is known as *usucapio*, with *praescriptio longi temporis* being the equivalent for the provinces, which were covered by a different law of ownership. Between the classical period and Justinian's codification, the distinction fell into desuetude, with a simple *praescriptio* of thirty or forty years being recognised. Justinian reintroduced the distinction in applying usucaption to mobiles, and prescription to immobiles: H. F. Jolowicz and B. Nicholas, *An historical introduction to the study of the Roman law*, 3rd edn (Cambridge 1972), pp. 151–5, 506. The conflicting accounts of usucaption and prescription in the *Corpus iuris civilis* caused detailed discussion among the commentators, particularly in the sixteenth century with the introduction of a historical study of the Roman law. Vázquez himself takes a modern stance in arguing that the term 'prescription', taken broadly, is equivalent to usucaption (*usucapio*), as against those who limit usucaption to mobile objects and prescription to immobile objects. Secondly, he argues that the possible objects of this process extend beyond corporeal things (*res corporales*) to rights (*iura*) and court actions (*actiones*), characterised in the Roman law as *res incorporeales*.

praescriptione is a renaissance genre, its development connected to the growing historicism of the study of the law, and the interest in customary and local law which marks legal literature in the sixteenth century.[64] In explaining how *dominia* and servitudes come into being, it offers Vázquez an ideal opportunity to expand on his themes of the natural and the free. Through mapping Roman poetry on to Roman law, Vázquez creates a moral dynamic of human history which can serve both to legitimate and to lament the practice of his own day.

As we have seen, Vázquez thinks in terms of a decline of mankind from innocence and freedom to wickedness and tyranny. At the beginning of the second book, Vázquez reiterates his theme of the original, non-dominative life of man, quoting from Virgil's *Georgics*: 'Before Jove no farmers ploughed the fields / Nor was it licit to mark or divide the open earth / With a boundary-line: they looked to their needs in common.'[65] In connection, Vázquez renews the theme of

---

[64] The language for the renaissance analysis of the Roman law concept of prescription (the acquisition of *dominium* over a *res* by possession for a certain defined period of time) was to a large extent determined by mediaeval treatments of the topic in the course of standard commentary. Particularly important was Bartolus' *repetitio* on the *l. Quominus* under the title *De fluminibus* (D. 43, 12, 2), which was elaborated by Jason Maynus commenting on the same locus. The tract on prescription, however, appears to be connected as much with the *mos gallicus* as with the *mos italicus*. The first of its kind, which forms the background to most later treatments (including Vázquez's), was written in the early years of the sixteenth century by the Bartolist Johannes Franciscus Balbus (Giovanni Francesco Balbo, b. c. 1480), who had however been a pupil of the French humanist Claude de Seyssel. The subject of prescription is closely allied with that of custom (*consuetudo*), interpreted as the mode by which long-term *de facto* practice is recognised as *de iure*. The widely read *Tractatus de antiquitate temporis* of Aymon de Cravetta (Aimone Cravetta, 1504–69) devotes most of the fourth part to a consideration of the differences and similarities between prescription and custom. The subject was taken up and elaborated with poetic and philosophical reference by the French humanist lawyer André Tiraqueau. These three treatments of prescription constitute Vázquez's principal points of reference for the doctrines of Book II, Tiraqueau in particular being important for Vázquez as a literary model. For Tiraqueau and the historical school of law in the sixteenth century, see the fundamental study of Donald Kelley, *Foundations of modern historical scholarship: Language, law and history in the French renaissance* (New York and London, 1970).

[65] *Controversies*, Book II, Chapter LI, n. 11: 'Et Virgilius lib. 2. Georgicarum: Ante Iovem nulli subigebant arva coloni: / Nec signare quidem aut partiri limite campum / Fas erat: in medio quaerebant.' The reference is in fact to *Georgics*, Book I, lines 125–8, in *P. Vergili Maronis Opera*, ed. by R. A. B. Mynors (Oxford, 1969), p. 33 (line 128 should read 'in medium quaerebant'). The verb *subigere* literally means 'to turn up, to plough'; but its frequent figurative use means 'to drive into submission, to subject', and that Virgil is deliberately using this undertone of the word appears confirmed in lines 128–9: 'quaerebant, ipsaque tellus / omnia liberius nullo poscente ferebat.' The animate earth gave its fruits *freely*, without being *demanded*. The verb *poscere* carries the sense of insistent demand and sometimes implicitly of demand for money, and is therefore used of tyrants, e.g. by Cicero of Antony at *Philippics* 5, 24: 'superbum, semper poscentem, semper rapientem, semper ebrium'. See the *Oxford Latin dictionary* (Oxford 1968).

the rest of nature serving as a sign of what man was and should be; the conclusion of the poets is that 'as the birds or the airborne race in the sky and the air, and as the scaly swarms in the oceans and seas, have nothing proper but simply common use: so too the human race upon the land would have common use, no differently from other land animals'.[66] Birds, fish and land animals apart from man live *in* their respective environments, without attempting to restrict it with bounds, and *with* their fellows of their own species, not vying with them for proper possession. The attempt to dominate the earth, and that to dominate fellow man – the twin tyrannies of man – go hand in hand.

According to Vázquez, it is immoveable objects which are 'especially' naturally in common. 'For *dominium* in moveable objects – such as we have in the wild animals we may catch, the pictures someone might paint, or in the clothes someone might make, and so on – owes its origin to the primeval right of nature itself.'[67] As the passage makes clear, *dominium* in moveables is secured by the proper labour or artifice of the individual, for 'the maker is accustomed to have control of his own object'.[68] But it is equally clear that for Vázquez, such *dominium* in moveables in the age of innocence did not prejudice the non-dominative character of that age: it is not the exercise of tyrannical liberty.[69]

Vázquez uses the notion of prescription to explain the temporal process of the coming-into-being of *dominia distincta* in immoveables:

Since, therefore, as much with regard to natural law as to the primaeval law of peoples ... all things were in common, and especially all fields, open tracts, estates and other immoveable things, it follows, that he who adduces that a certain immoveable thing is his own, must prove it, because he has

---

[66] *Controversies*, Book II, Chapter LI, n. 12: 'ut volucres seu aëreum genus in caelo vel aëre, utque squamea turba in aequore vel ponto nihil proprium habent praeter usum communem: ita et humanum genus in terris communem usum non secus quam reliqua animantia terrestria haberet.'

[67] Ibid., Chapter LIII, n. 7: 'nam ab ipso iure naturali primaevo descendit ... dominium in rebus mobilibus, quale est in feris quas coepissemus, aut in tabulis quas quis depinxisset, aut in vestibus quas fabricasset, et similibus'. For the idea that a person of the primary right of peoples has *dominium* in the products of his own labour, Vázquez refers to the fifteenth-century jurist Paulus da Castro, 'and other doctors', on the *l. ex hoc iure* (D. 1, 5).

[68] *Controversies*, Preface, n. 109, demonstrating the rationale of God's original immediate government of Adam and Eve.

[69] This holds even for the capture of beasts, for, as we saw in examining Book I, to prey on members of diverse species is *fas* for all animals, and does not affect the harmony of nature.

against him the presumption of the law ... but that proof, if we took away the practice of prescription, would be almost impossible.[70]

The process of prescription explains why some things have come under the particular *dominium* of particular individuals. But, importantly, it also explains why some things have not. At the end of the second book, Vázquez discusses which *res* can be prescribed and which cannot, in particular the question of why the land is subject to prescription while the sea is not.[71] According to Vázquez, by the *ius naturae* and the *ius gentium primaevum* both sea and land were in common, but under the *ius gentium secundarium* the land alone became subject to *dominium* or private property. 'The reason for the difference between sea on the one hand, and the land, and rivers, on the other is that in the former case ... the primaeval right has stayed intact, and was never partitioned off from the common use of men, and applied to any particular individual or individuals.'[72] No one can acquire by prescription a particular right over the sea, because there are not and can never be any particular rights over the sea: 'in the oceans and the open waters there neither is, nor can be, any right for the human race, apart from with respect to common use'.[73]

As we saw,[74] Vázquez holds that *dominium* can be equally over concrete things (*res, res corporeales*), and legal abstracts (*res incorporeales*) such as obligations, actions and servitudes. The process of prescription thus covers both these kinds of object: once acquired, obliga-

---

[70] *Controversies*, Book II, Chapter LI, nn. 14–16: 'Quum ergo tam inspecto iure naturali quam iure gentium primaevo ... omnia essent communia praesertim omnes agri, campi, praedia, et reliqua immobilia, superest, ut qui aliquid immobile suum esse duxerit, illud probare debeat, quia contra se habet praesumptionem iuris ... sed ... ea probatio, si removerimus usum praescriptionum, esset paene impossibilis.'

[71] Whether the sea can be prescribed is a discussion common to all authors writing on prescription; the terms of that discussion are set by the mediaeval jurists and in particular by Bartolus' commentary on the *l. Quominus* (see above, n. 64); see Johannes Franciscus Balbus, *Tractatus de praescriptionibus* (Cologne 1573), Part V, Q. 6: 'Whether those things which belong by right of peoples can be prescribed, Bartolus raises this question in his commentary on the *l. Quominus*.' The particular issue is whether the Venetians and the Genoans can prohibit others from sailing in their respective gulfs, which is interpreted as a question of whether they have prescribed these gulfs. The question is always answered in the affirmative, although the reasoning differs slightly from author to author. Vázquez raises the issue as a matter of course in his tract on prescriptions, but controversially asserts that the sea cannot be prescribed.

[72] *Controversies*, Book II, Chapter LI, n. 39: 'Ratio differentiae inter mare ex una parte, et terram, vel flumina, ex altera, quia illo casu ... mansit integrum ius primaevum, neque unquam fuit a communione hominum separatum, et alicui, vel aliquibus applicatum.'

[73] Ibid., n. 34: 'in aequoribus et aquis nullum ius est, aut esse potest humano generi, praeterquam quoad usum communem'.

[74] Above, n. 62.

tions, actions and servitudes, like distinct *res*, lie in opposition to natural liberty and belong to the *ius gentium secundarium*. A servitude in late mediaeval jurisprudence is a special kind of right which is held by a *persona* or a *res* in another *persona* or *res*: the latter is then said to owe a servitude, and 'is forced to suffer and cannot act'.[75] It is the standard doctrine of the tractate literature and commentary on prescription that no *res* is presumed to be subservient to another in this way unless it be proven (just as in the case of *dominium*). Hence Vázquez, discussing prescription of the *servitus aquae ducendae*, asserts that 'here the presumption of the law was against the prescriptor, because every *res* is presumed to be free'.[76] The sense of 'free' (*liber*) here is 'free from servitude', and this is the sense of *liber* throughout the prescription literature. It is the natural condition of all *res* before the inventions of the *ius gentium secundarium*. If a *res* was never under servitude, always free, no servitude can be prescribed. For Vázquez's follower Grotius, the sea is free – *mare liberum* – in the sense that no servitude over it can ever be prescribed.[77]

Prescription is thus the mode by which things lose their freedom to human masters. But the reason why they must do so is to be found in the criminal audacity which characterises the human race alone amongst all other creatures. With the decline of the ages, man begins to use his artifice not only to make items like pictures and clothes, but in order to use the earth in ways not contained within the system of nature, ways which are not compatible with the common use of all. This is the beginning of tyranny and domination, and artifice takes on pejorative overtones as the instrument of human *audacia*.[78] It is *qua* put to use by man in this way that natural objects are given a jural characterisation under the secondary *ius gentium* and become subject to obligation:

but as to why the secondary right of peoples created [fecit] that separation [from common use] with regard to tracts of land and rivers, but forbore to do so [facere] with respect to the sea, reply thus, that in the former case it was expedient that it should so happen, but in the latter not. For it is

[75] Bertachinus, *Lexicon*, under the entry *Servitus*: 'Servitutem debens cogitur pati et non potest agere. l. quoties. i. para. servitutem. et ibi bar. ff. de servi' [D. 8. 1. 15].
[76] *Controversies*, Book II, Chapter LXXVIII, n. 1: 'hic autem erat iuris praesumptio contra praescribentem, quia quaeque res praesumitur libera'.
[77] Grotius, *De iure praedae*, Chapter XII.
[78] See Vázquez's discussion of empire (*Controversies*, Book I, Chapter XX) which he argues depends upon the crossing of the seas. Vázquez draws on the poetry of Horace and Claudian to urge that the seas are there as natural barriers, which man with his *audacia* has used artifice to overcome. This is *vetitum nephas*, forbidden and unholy crime.

agreed, that if many hunt, or fish on a piece of land, or in a river, the wood is easily rendered void of game, and the river of fish – which is not the case with the sea. Again, the navigability of rivers is easily damaged, and hindered by buildings [aedificia], which in the sea is not the case ... And again, a river is easily emptied by water being led off it, not so in the sea, therefore the rationale is not the same in both cases.[79]

Because man exploits, therefore (apart from the natural activities of preying on other species) man begins to make (*facere*: for example, *aedificia*), and therefore he is forced to make more things, this time separate rights to protect individual exploitations. All servitude – like jurisdiction, as we saw in Book I – is unnatural or artificial and has an artificial origin. 'Nulla servitus habet causam naturalem', 'no servitude has a natural cause'.[80]

For Vázquez, all these artificial entities nevertheless share the characteristic of natural entities, that they have a fixed span of life, after which they perish. They do not escape the flux of the world, for 'every *res* is naturally dissolved through the same causes, through which it is born'.[81] Prescription is that mechanism which allows such a creature to be pronounced dead, and brings a new one into life. Those creatures of civil right which are actions and obligations are born mortal and therefore dissolve, 'just as man is dissolved at the advent of death, and this simile is very apt. For Seneca says that death is nothing other than the terminus of life, and so he says that after death there is nothing, and death itself is nothing ... whence Ausonius said: "Should we wonder that men perish, great monuments crumble: / And death comes even to rocks and names." '[82] Vázquez emphasises (against his source and literary model, André

---

[79] *Controversies*, Book II, Chapter LXXXIX, n. 39: 'sed quare ius gentium secundarium, ut eam separationem, quoad terras et flumina fecit, eandem quoad mare facere desiit, responde, quia illo casu expediebat ita fieri, hoc autem casu non expediebat, constat enim, quod si multi venentur, aut piscentur in terris, vel flumine, facile nemus feris, et flumen piscibus evacuatum redditur, id quod in mari non est ita. Item fluminum navigatio facile deterior fit, et impeditur per aedificia, quod in mari non est ... Item per aquae ductus facile evacuatur flumen, non ita in mari, ergo in utroque non est par ratio.'

[80] Ibid. Vázquez follows Baldus (on Decretals, I, 2, 6) arguing that 'nulla servitus habet causam naturalem sed aut impositiciam aut prescriptam.'

[81] Ibid., Chapter LIII, n. 7: 'omnis enim res naturaliter per quascunque causas nascitur, per easdem dissolvitur'. The reference is to the *regula iuris* D. 50, 17, 35.

[82] Ibid., Book II, Chapter LV, nn. 6–8: 'non aliter atque homo mortis adventu resolveretur, accommodatissimaque est haec similitudo. nam teste Seneca mors nihil aliud est, quam terminus vitae, sic ipse ait post mortem nihil est, ipsaque mors nihil ... Unde Ausonius cecinit: Miremur periisse homines, monumenta fatiscunt. / Mors etenim saxis nominibusque venit': Ausonius, *Opuscula* (London 1919), VI, 32.

Tiraqueau)[83] that it is not time alone which is responsible for the flux of rights and obligations, for time is nothing, and out of nothing nothing comes into being, nor into it is anything dissolved. Such mortality is as much the characteristic of creatures of the law, as of all creatures.

Vázquez's detailed examination of prescription bears out the general attitude of the Preface: that rights are not permanent fixtures, tending as they do to dissolution and to the liberation of what was previously under servitude. But Vázquez brings Book II back round to the specifically political themes of the Preface and Book I with a consideration of 'what things can or cannot be prescribed'.[84] Most things are capable of being brought under servitude by the provisions of the *ius gentium secundarium*; but some things must remain forever free or *extra commercium nostrum*,[85] eluding the practices of the *ius gentium secundarium*. These are things which are not *in bonis nostris*, not capable of being possessed or used and thereby appropriated or brought under servitude. Such objects cannot enter into the sphere of civil right which regulates human transactions.

Within the prescription literature in general, prominent among these *imprescriptibilia* is *facultas*, where by a *facultas* is understood a power of free choice of doing something or not, at will. 'Prescription even of the most venerable, of whose commencement there is no memory to the contrary, does not proceed in those things which are purely voluntary or are matters of faculty.'[86] An example is the *facultas eundi per viam publicam*, 'the faculty of walking down a public way'. If I have such a faculty, which I never exercise, still not after thirty years nor one thousand years can another person prescribe that faculty, i.e. acquire for themselves my faculty of walking down the public road, with the result that they can prohibit me from doing so. A faculty is, in this connection, expressly contrasted with a right

---

[83] André Tiraqueau, *Tractatus de praescriptionibus*, Glos. IV (Dix ans), in *Opera omnia*, vol. VI (Frankfurt 1616), 52–80. For the life and works of Tiraqueau, see J. Bréjon, *André Tiraqueau (1488–1558)* (Paris 1937), esp. pp. 217–22 for the *Tractatus de praescriptionibus*, and pp. 340–52 for his philosophical interest in the history, customs and culture of diverse peoples as the true source of law.

[84] From Chapter LXXXII: 'Quinta pars quae res illas intuetur, quae praescribi possunt vel non possunt.'

[85] See Book II, Chapter LXXXII, n. 13: 'homo extra commercium esse videri deberet, non aliter quam res sacra aut religiosa'; Chapter LXXXIX, n. 48: 'quae sunt imprescriptibilia ex legis dispositione, ut via publica, homo liber, res sacra, nec per annos mille praescribitur'.

[86] Cravetta, *Tract. de antiq. temp.*, part IV, n. 214: 'non procedit praescriptio etiam antiquissima cuius memoria non est in contrariam, in his quae sunt mere voluntaria aut facultatis'.

(*ius*): if I have a *ius* of doing something, which I do not exercise, then after thirty years another person may claim to have prescribed that *ius*, to the extent that I no longer have it. But a faculty, which lies within my own free will, can never enter the sphere of civil law. 'The faculty of going along a public road is not subject to prescription, because that possibility of going is not a right, but a faculty.'[87]

In spite of this, however, 'not only can a faculty be prescribed when conjoined to it there is a court action, but also even when from the exercise of such a faculty there arises a right which may be alleged in court';[88] correspondingly, 'where there is such a faculty from the exercise of which in an act, no right, no court action nor exception can be acquired, but all there is is its exercise, which lies in the free *arbitrium* of him who exercises it – like going to church, or down a public road – and in that case such freedom of *arbitrium* can never be prescribed'.[89] If this total lack of contact with the sphere of the court, the sphere of right, does not obtain, 'then that power is not of pure faculty, but it is a right and not a faculty'.[90] Hence the associated tag, *facultas est quid facti*, 'a faculty is a thing of fact'; 'a faculty which is a thing of fact is not subject to prescription'.[91]

Vázquez himself, within Book II, does not discuss the issue whether a *facultas* can be prescribed, referring the reader to his earlier work, the *De successionum creatione*.[92] Here we find that Vázquez emphasises that aspect of the doctrine of *facultas* which stresses that if its exercise has any contact with the sphere of right, then it can be prescribed. 'Again, I ask in general, Whether the rights of faculty can be subject to usucaption? ... reply, that if the faculty belongs to me with respect to an object, which is possessed by no one, then that faculty cannot be prescribed: [according to] the law *viam publicam* ... But if that faculty belongs to me with regard to an object, which is

---

[87] Balbus, *Tract. de praescr.*, Part V, p. 433., n. 1: 'nunquam praescribitur facultati eundi per viam publicam, quia istud posse ire non est ius, sed quaedam facultas.'

[88] Cravetta, *Tract. de antiq. temp.*, Part IV, n. 254: 'non solum facultati praescribitur quando cum ea coniuncta est actio, sed etiam quando ex usu talis facultatis nascitur ius deducibile in iudicium'.

[89] Balbus, *Tract. de praesc.*, Part V, n. 4: 'ubi est talis facultas ex qua per explicationem actus nullum ius, nulla actio, nulla exceptio quaeri potest, sed solum insurgit explicatio eius quod in libero explicantis arbitrio consistit, sicut est ire ad ecclesiam, vel per viam publicam, et tunc illi libertati arbitrii nunquam praescribitur.'

[90] Andrea Barbazza, *Consilia* (N.p. 1517), Consilium 51, *Scripsit sapientiae fons*, fol. 125, n. 11: 'tunc illa potentia non est merae facultatis sed est ius et non facultas'.

[91] Balbus, *Tract. de praesc.*, Part V, n. 3: 'facultati autem quae facti est non praescribitur'.

[92] The reference is at *Controversies*, Book II, Chapter LXXXIX, n. 47: 'Praescribi an possit ius facultatis, para. 22. n. 26 [de succ. creat.].'

possessed by another, then it can certainly be prescribed.'[93] Thus, in
the case of an heir about to come into an inheritance, 'although the
will of acquiring the inheritance cannot be taken from the heir,
through prescription or otherwise, because it consists in fact and in
the mind; nevertheless the faculty, and power can be prescribed,
because it consists in right'.[94] A faculty with regard to another's *res* is
located within the sphere of right. But a faculty with regard to that
which does not belong to another is implicitly free, imprescriptible
and operating *de facto*. In the same vein on the same topic, Matthew
Wesembeck, the influential Dutch jurist of the early *usus modernus*,
argues that

what is said, that those things which are a matter of pure faculty, can never
be prescribed, should be understood with regard to those things which are
absolutely such, not relatively. For servitudes, and similar things owed by
others, although they be a matter of pure faculty, nevertheless are subject to
prescription through lack of use. But those things which are a matter of
absolute faculty, and belong to a person by right of *dominium*, and are not
owed by others, but are part of proper *dominia*: these are never prescribed,
but together with *dominium* they are possessed by the mind of the *dominus*,
and his will: and thus the rationale of usucaption does not extend that far:
because they belong to the absolute right, and faculty of each: in such a way
as although they be never prescribed, still the *dominia* of things are not
rendered uncertain thereby, but rather are strengthened.[95]

For Wesembeck as for Vázquez, *dominium* is *absoluta facultas* because it
operates arbitrarily and at will. Anything which has its existence in

---

[93] Vázquez, *De succ. creat.*, Book I, para. 22, Limitatio XII, n. 26: 'Denique generaliter quaero,
An iura facultatis possint usucapi? . . . dic, quod si facultas competit mihi respectu rei, quae
a nullo possidetur, tunc ea facultas praescribi non potest: l. viam publicam. ff. de via publ.
. . . Quod si ea facultas competat mihi respectu rei, quae ab alio possidetur, tunc bene
praescribitur.' The reference is to D. 43, II, 12.

[94] Ibid.: 'Ergo licet voluntas acquirendi hereditatem heredi tolli per praescriptionem, vel alias,
non possit; quia in facto, et animo consistit: tamen facultas, et potestas praescribi poterit,
quia in iure consistit.'

[95] Matthaeus Wesembecius, *Paratitla in Pandectas iuris civilis* (Basel 1568), pp. 252–3, n. 2: 'Porro
quod dicitur. ea quae merae sunt facultatis, nunquam praescribi: de his quae sunt absolute
talia, non relative est accipiendum. Nam servitutes, et similia ab aliis debita, quamvis
merae sunt facultatis, tamen per non usum praescribuntur. At quae absolutae sunt
facultatis, et iure dominii competunt, nec ab alio debentur, sed insunt propriis dominiis:
haec non praescribuntur, sed una cum dominio possidentur ab animo domini, et voluntate:
eoque nec eo trahitur usucapionum ratio: quia posita sunt in cuiusque iure absoluto, et
facultate: ut quamvis nunquam praescribantur, tamen non reddantur propterea incerta
dominia rerum, sed magis confirmentur.' For details of Wesembeck and his influence on
the seventeenth-century *usus modernus*, see Alfred Söllner, 'Die Literatur zum gemeinen und
partikularen Recht in Deutschland, Österreich, den Niederlanden und der Schweiz', in
H. Coing (ed.), *Handbuch der Quellen und Literatur der neueren europäischen Privatrechtsgeschichte*, II/
I (Munich 1977) 501–614, pp. 507, 512–13.

the mind and will of man cannot be prescribed, because these are beyond right. It is therefore protected against all encroachments from specious claims of right, particularly from princes, such as Vázquez laid out in the Preface to his work. Significantly, however, while for Vázquez *dominium* is *liberrima facultas*, and also in some sense a *ius*, Wesembeck is prepared to merge the two notions in the concept of *ius absolutum*: a power that is rightful, but also free.

Correspondingly, the man who is free, *homo liber*, is also *extra commercium nostrum*, recalcitrant to *dominium* and servitude. A man is free (from servitude) who is *sui iuris*, under his own right and not anyone else's. This is the natural condition of man as of all *res*: but the necessities which demanded the introduction of the *ius gentium secundarium* also dictated that man should be subject to servitude: 'man was not born to be subject to another man ... and servitude is against nature ... but because those captured in war used to be massacred, therefore servitude ... was permitted ... even though man should otherwise be seen as *extra commercium nostrum*, not otherwise than a sacred or holy thing'.[96]

Vázquez makes an important distinction between servitudes. On the one hand individuals can be under servitude due to captivity in war or by birth (*captivitas*, *nativitas*); on the other, they can be under servitude because they made such a contract. The former modes Vázquez characterises as *praeter voluntatem suam*, without their will, and the result is that if such individuals manage to escape, they are automatically free and *sui iuris* again:

the laws ... concerning the case of a captured wild animal, which becomes free [*libera*] again as soon as it escapes our hands, are most rightfully applied to slaves [i.e. those captured in war], so that as soon as they escape from the hands of their captors, they become *sui iuris* [under their own right]; nor do they appear to commit a mortal, or even a venial sin thereby, any more than does the wild animal, which after it had been captured, ran away – escaped – took flight.[97]

---

[96] Vázquez, *Controversies*, Book II, Chapter LXXXII.

[97] Ibid., Chapter IX, nn. 20–1: 'leges ... loquentes in fera capta, quae cum primum evaserit a manibus nostris libera fit, rectissime etiam ad servos ... aptantur, ut cum primum a manibus capientis evaserint, sui iuris fiant, nec peccare mortaliter aut venialiter videntur, non magis quam ipsa fera, quae capta cum esset, aufugit, evasit, evolavit.' According to the School of Salamanca and to the generality of lawyers, the captive justly enslaved (enslaved in a just war) is rightfully (*de iure*) a slave and therefore acts wrongly – he commits a sin – in denying that servitude by trying to escape. For Vázquez, on the other hand, any enslaved captive just happens to be a slave, *de facto*, and if he happens to escape, he is restored to his freedom (which, as we have seen, is purely *de facto*).

The case is different for those who sold themselves into servitude: having exchanged their liberty at will and for a price, they have abdicated their right in themselves permanently.[98]

Vázquez uses the model of the individual slave to consider a final case of a *res libera*, the *populus liber*. As with all *res*, the *populus* was originally *populus liber*, free from servitude. As we saw, in Book I, human wickedness forces the people to put itself in servitude to a prince. This gives rise to the question of whether the people can acquire 'liberty and the relaxation of subjection' (*libertatem ac ditionis laxitatem*) from the prince.[99] Vázquez's answer is that 'whether by force or on their own initiative they began to be subject, there is no doubt that they can repair to their own freedom from restriction (*laxitatem suam*) and vindicate themselves therein':[100]

Even if of their own initiative they subjected themselves to another's authority and power, it is fair that they are free to renounce it and secede from it, since the initial deed was done [factum] for the convenience of the subjects themselves; and so they can repair themselves to, and seize, their own *laxitas* either openly, or secretly, with fraud, with force, with arms ... for nothing is so natural, than that each thing should be dissolved in the same way as it was put together ... and every *res* easily reverts to its nature or origin ... and no one can impose such a law upon his own will and *arbitrium*, from which it is not licit for him to withdraw.[101]

Vázquez's justification depends both on his philosophico-legal theory of the flux of all things, and yet again on the notion of liberty drawn from the Roman law of legation or last wills: the last sentence in the passage is derived from the oft-quoted legal dictum, 'nemo enim eam sibi potest legem dicere, ut a priore ei recedere non liceat',[102] which

<hr/>

[98] Cf. ibid., Book II, Chapter LXXXII, n. 16: 'homo liber qui se vendiderit non poterit unquam invito domino se a servitute eripere ... itaque licet non abnegemus, quin fera, quae serva erat (sive captivitate, quia eam caepimus, sive nativitate ...) cum primum a nobis evaserit, sui iuris aut laxitatis fiat ... Idemque et in servis ... arguendo de servitute ferarum ad servitutem servorum, tamen si servi facti fuerunt non captivitate, non quoque nativitate, et sic praeter voluntatem aut factum suum servi sint facti, et sponte sua, et non gratis, sed pretio cessat ratio illorum iurium.'

[99] Ibid., Book II, Chapter LXXXII.

[100] Ibid., n. 3: 'sive vi sive sponte sua subditi esse coepissent, non dubium est quin possent in suam laxitatem sese recipere ac vindicare'.

[101] Ibid., nn. 3–4: 'sive etiam sponte sua se subiecerint alienae ditioni ac potestati, cum id ob ipsorum subditorum utilitate initio factum fuerit, ei renunciare atque ab ea recedere eis liberum esse par est, sicque ab ea subiectione poterunt se in suam laxitatem recipere, ac eripere, vel palam, vel clam, vel dolo, vel vi, aut armis ... nihil enim tam naturale est, quam unumquodque eo modo dissolvi quo colligatum fuit ... et quaeque res de facili revertitur ad suam naturam seu originem ... neque enim quisque voluntati et arbitrio suo eam legem imponere potest, a qua sibi recedere non liceat.'

[102] D. 32, 22.

defends the radical liberty of the will-maker even from the bonds of his own previous wills. *Voluntas* and *arbitrium suum* are such things as cannot be subject: they cannot be brought into the sphere of right. This might be taken to imply, as Vázquez realises, that subjects can free themselves from their prince without the lapse of any period of time. However, this is not so, 'for in the case of kingdoms or principates which for a thousand years or more have been passed on by succession, not election, and where it is not clear by what right the men or peoples were first subjected ... there is no reason why we should not believe that they were subdued and subjected by the best of rights'.[103] What Vázquez stresses is that in all cases, the principle holds that 'unumquodque eo modo dissolvitur, quo colligatum fuit': the hypothetical prince

> justified his empire and jurisdiction either by force, or by consent, or by time ... but if they were subjected by force, then by that same force they could return themselves to their natural laxity ... and if they were made bound, and subject by consent, then that consent is of its nature revocable, since they are seen to have subjected themselves for their own utility, not that of their prince. Whence it should be free for them to alter their will ... for those things which come into being by consent, are dissolved even while the parties are still alive by a contrary will.[104]

Vázquez adds that the consent of previous generations can certainly not bind future citizens[105] (although, as in the case of the individual slave, he is clear that all these *rationes* fail if the people surrendered their liberty for a price).

Vázquez's understanding of the fragility of *imperium* or political society in the *Controversies* marks a profound change from his more conservative earlier work. In the Preface to the *De successionum progressu*, Vázquez had not acknowledged any possibility of civil society without *imperium*. Vázquez combines Cicero with Roman law to argue for the *necessity* of subjection to a properly political power:

---

[103] *Controversies*, Book II, Chapter LXXXII, n. 6: 'nam in regnis seu principatibus qui iam diu ab hinc annos mille, vel etiam plures successione non electione deferuntur, neque apparet quo iure primum ... homines vel populi fuissent subacti, non est cur non credamus optimo iure subactos subditosque fuisse.'

[104] Ibid.: 'nam princeps ille suum imperium ac ditionem iustificabat, aut vi, aut consensu, aut tempore ... at si vi fuerunt subacti, vi quoque sese poterunt in suam laxitatem recipere ... quod si consensu fuerunt facti obnoxii, et subditi, is consensus sui natura revocabilis est, quasi ad suam non ad sui principis utilitatem se subdidisse videantur. unde voluntatem mutare liberum esse debet ... nam et quae consensu fiunt, etiam inter vivos contraria voluntate dissolvuntur.'

[105] Ibid., n. 9: 'consensus maiorum non nocet civibus postea natis qui non consenserunt'.

The individual who wished to live a political life in a common society, and not a life of the woods, in the manner of beasts, also both wished and conceded that he should obey his fatherland, or whoever represents the fatherland, so that the brawls ... of the citizens would be reduced to peace, and from that tacit, or express consent he is seen to have obliged himself naturally to obey and respect his fatherland or the representative thereof, nor is anything so properly natural and peculiarly innate in the human race from its inception, than to stand by conventions, and to be obliged by reason of consent ... And this is that 'common undertaking of the commonwealth', which each one of the citizens is seen to promise his fatherland, and by which he is bound to it.[106]

Vázquez goes on to argue that since human society is impossible without obedience to a common authority, 'it is piously to be believed' that the political structure has been in existence since the very beginning of the human race.[107]

On this account, membership by consent of a political society carries with it an obligation in conscience to obey the laws of its legislator. Vázquez argues that the law, as the *communis Reipublicae sponsio*, has the same nature as a contract between particular private individuals, and obliges in the same way: 'just as private individuals, by reason of their contracts and pacts, are mutually constrained by necessity and bound: because obligation is the bond of right, by which we are constrained by necessity ... so all the citizens are constrained by the law ... and just as the law of a contract constrains and binds those who make the contract, by reason of their consent ... so a general law binds the citizens by reason of their consent'.[108] Such law binds even those who dissent, because 'even those who struggle against it are seen to have given their consent to this matter from the beginning, at the time when they subjected themselves to

---

[106] *De succ. creat.*, vol. II, *Tractatus de successionum progressu*, Preface, ad Lib. I, nn. 5–7: 'Denique qui in communi societate vitam polyticam agere, et non sylvestrem, more ferarum voluit, is sane aut patriae, aut qui [*sic*] patriae vices gerit, obedire quoque et voluit et concessit, ut civium rixae ... sedarentur, et ex isto consensu tacito, vel expresso sese naturaliter ad patriae aut eius vicem agenti obediendum obtemperandumque obligasse videtur, nec quicquam tam humano generi a sui primordio proprium naturale ac peculiare innatum, quam conventiones servare, et ex consensu obligari ... Et haec est illa communis Reipublicae sponsio, quam quisque civium patriae suae polliceri, quaque ei restringi videtur.' The reference is to D. 3, 1: 'Lex est commune praeceptum, virorum prudentium consultum, delictorum quae sponte vel ignorantia contrahuntur coercitio, communis rei publicae sponsio.'

[107] *De succ. creat.*, nn. 9–10.

[108] Ibid., n. 58: 'ut privati inter sese ex suis contractibus, et pactionibus astringuntur necessitate, et ligantur: quia obligatio est iuris vinculum, quo necessitate astringimur ... ita et lege omnes cives astringuntur ... et ut lex contractus ipsos contrahentes ex suo consensu obstringit, et ligat ... ita et lex generalis ex civium consensu eos ligat'.

the prince, or to their Commonwealth; and even those who were silent can lead a social and political life, and are understood to have chosen it, only on this mental condition: according to the law *ius pluribus*, and the doctors in the said *loci*: and thus it is not licit for any one or other to depart afterwards from this consent'.[109] The citizens are therefore bound principally among themselves, rather than to the legislator: it is the fact that they have mutually bound themselves, by their consent, to obey the law, which gives rise to a natural obligation, which is an obligation in conscience.[110]

Everything has changed by the time of the *Controversies*. Not only has Vázquez lost his enthusiasm for principate and jurisdiction, as we have seen, but he has removed its support in the obligation of the citizens. He still holds that civil law is contract, on the same argumentation as in the *De successionum progressu*;[111] but he no longer thinks that it obliges in conscience. The principal reason for his change of heart appears to lie in his growing sense that principate or jurisdiction is inescapably noxious to some extent, and therefore to be limited as far as possible only to the good of the citizens: 'and no one halfway sane will deny, that it would be the most pernicious thing in the world for those citizens, if the laws and precepts of the prince to whom they themselves had given jurisdiction, were to be directed towards their eternal death'.[112] The prince has no power to oblige beyond the power given him by the citizens; nor, in fact, do princes generally wish to oblige in conscience: 'it appears to have been enacted, as much by the citizens or populace, as by the legislators themselves, that either the citizens obey the law, or that they undergo the statutory punishment: not that they are obliged to both'.[113]

Vázquez backs up these arguments with a new account of contract. In the former work, Vázquez had argued that all contracts are of the

---

[109] Ibid., n. 59: 'Et sane huic rei consensum ab initio etiam ipsimet reluctantes, quo tempore se principi, aut suae Reipublicae subdiderunt dedisse videntur, et etiam taciti sub hac conditione mentali socialem, et politicam ... vitam agere possunt, et eligere intelliguntur: d. l. ius pluribus [D. 1, 1, 11], et Docto. in dictis locis: sicque postea ab hoc consensu discedere, uni, aut alteri non licet.'

[110] Ibid., nn. 86–8.   [111] Cf. *Controversies*, Book I, Chapter XXIII.

[112] Ibid., Chapter XXIX, n. 1: 'nec ullus modo sanus abnegabit, quin ipsis civibus perniciosissimum esset, si ad mortem aeternam leges illae aut praecepta principi [s?] quibus [cui?] ipsimet iurisdictionem dederunt converterentur'.

[113] Ibid., n. 4: 'tam ab ipsis civibus seu popularibus, quam ab ipsis legislatoribus id actum videtur, ut vel cives legi pareant, vel poenam statutam subeant, non ut ad utrunque teneantur'.

ius gentium secundarii, because all contracts are a result of necessity, which did not exist at the beginning of the human race, but came into being later.[114] However, although contracts are an invention of the *ius gentium secundarium*, the keeping of them belongs to the *ius gentium primaevum*, that *ius* which is natural to humans alone, for 'nothing is so congruent with natural reason, and with human trust, as to observe what one has been pleased to do, and to keep faith'.[115] It follows that all contracts from the beginning gave rise to two obligations: 'the first natural, that is, due to the instinct of reason and nature peculiar to man: the other from the contract itself ... And albeit the first was ineffective, still the second was effective, because it was brought into effect by the hand of the king ... Thus the first obligation is still in force today; the second has gone, to be replaced by civil obligation ... which is not brought into effect by the hand of the king, as before, but by means of [legal] actions.'[116] To contract is therefore to lay upon oneself a double bond: the obligation which binds one by rational instinct to keep one's word, and the civil obligation which is enforced with the possibility of a court action.

By the time of the *Controversies*, however, Vázquez has changed his mind. He now argues that contract does not specifically oblige in any way: 'the person who by contract promised that he would do something, or would not do something: if he does not do it, or on the contrary does do it, he is obliged and suffers damages to the extent of his adversary's interest; but he is not understood to be categorically obliged to the original action, either naturally or civilly'.[117] For Vázquez in the *Controversies*, the only source of obligation is natural law – the instinct of reason – and divine law.[118] No arrangement of the *ius gentium secundarium* has any hold on individuals at all; and just as the person who contracts is liable to damages, but not strictly obliged in any way, 'similarly, he who transgresses the precept of a law ... is not categorically obliged to it either naturally or civilly, but

---

[114] Ibid., n. 34.   [115] Ibid.
[116] Ibid.: 'altera naturalis. i.e. ex instinctu rationis, et naturae hominibus peculiaris: altera ex ipso contractu ... Et licet prima esset inefficax, tamen secunda erat efficax, quia per manum regiam ad effectum producebatur ... Prima ergo obligatio et hodie viget, secunda vero recessit, et eius loco successit obligatio civilis ... quae non per manum regiam, ut antea, sed per actiones ad effectum producebatur.'
[117] Ibid., n. 7: 'qui ex contractu promisit se aliquid facturum, vel non facturum, si id non fecerit vel adversus id fecerit, tenetur et damnabitur in eo, quod interest adversarii, neque ad principale factum praecise obligatus intelligitur civiliter aut naturaliter'.
[118] See ibid., n. 17.

only to undergoing the punishment if he acts in violation ... And this appears to be the opinion of all unlettered men the world over, to whom we must give our assent, because the voice of the people, is the voice of God.'[119]

The citizens, then, are not morally bound to the city and to the keeping of its laws. This has two consequences: firstly, the contingency of any one individual's membership of a city; secondly, the contingency of the city itself. In the pre-political, but still social, state man is a free agent. His one moral obligation is not to commit suicide:[120] otherwise, he may watch out for his conveniences (*utilitates*) or not, as he wishes. Man is not obliged to act prudentially. Under the laws of the city, it is presumed that each individual citizen entered the political environment in order to further his proper utility: 'that each individual entered into that society entirely for the sake of his own convenience, both appears to be the case from the interpretation of the law, and accords with natural reason and right, since well-ordered charity should begin with oneself'.[121] This means, for example, that no citizen can be obliged to offer his life for the others, and that no citizen can be obliged to inform on a possible danger to the city or offer help to another:[122] not that such acts are not wholly praiseworthy, but that they exceed the virtue of the common man. It is for the convenience even of such unprepossessing specimens of humanity – petty tyrants riddled with self-interest and living in perpetual fear of losing their things – that the city has existence, and it cannot rightly force them to be any better than they are, since they invented it to protect them in their habits of greed and cowardice. Furthermore, if any citizen feels that his utility is not being sufficiently cared for by a particular city, it is open to him to seek it elsewhere: 'any citizen is allowed to change his home and to migrate from city to city, or from region to region ... any citizen is allowed to look out for his own safety, albeit the whole people may perish, as Aeneas did when there was no more hope of saving Troy,

---

[119] Ibid., n. 7: 'ita, et qui praeceptum legis ... transgreditur, non tenetur ad id praecise, naturaliter aut civiliter, sed tantum ad poenam subeundum si contrafecerit ... et ita videntur sentire omnes homines illiterati quotquot sunt in mundo, quibus assentiendum et consentiendum est, quia vox populi, vox Dei'.

[120] Ibid., Book I, Chapter XI, nn. 1–6.

[121] Ibid., Chapter XIII, nn. 2–3: 'unusquisque in eam societatem ivisse ob suam potissimum utilitatem, et videtur ex legis interpretatione, et congruit naturali rationi et iuri, cum charitas bene ordinata debet incipere a se ipso'.

[122] See ibid., Chapter XVI, esp. n. 12.

and as happens every day, and such is the opinion and the voice of the people'.[123]

Vázquez acknowledges Soto's achievement in recognising that 'individual citizens are not in the same relation with respect to others as are foot or hand with respect to the whole body'.[124] But he deplores the fact that Soto still distinguishes between the whole, the *respublica*, and the private citizen; for Vázquez, the society of private citizens is all there is: 'among the citizens there is nothing but a kind of society of good faith contracted ... to this end, that each might thereby the better lead his life in safety, and with every convenience'.[125] Soto had insisted that men must of the necessity of their nature be parts of the whole which is the *respublica*. Vázquez admits (as we saw in his Preface) a certain necessity in the princely power as the only means of quelling civil strife; but 'since that right, be it of nature or of the peoples [the right under which the citizens in the social state, before the establishment of principate, are living], does not induce a categorical necessity, but only a causative necessity, that is, so that it would be possible to lead a more commodious life, it follows that no people can be forced to live under *imperium*'.[126] Albeit the Vázquezian anti-hero found himself unable to protect his interests sufficiently without contracting with others to make an artificial protector, and putting himself under servitude to him, the Cicero-

---

[123] Ibid., Chapter xiii, n. 16: 'cuicunque civium licere domicilium mutare migrareque de urbe in urbem vel de regione in regionem ... cuique civium licebit saluti suae consulere, licet totus populus pereat, sed ut fecit Aeneas cum iam salus Troiae desperata esset, et ita fit quotidie, et talis est opinio et vox populi, quem vocem naturae et Dei probavimus'.

[124] Ibid., Chapter xiii, n. 2: 'non enim singuli cives respectu aliorum se habent ut pes aut manus respectu totius corporis'. Vázquez refers to Soto, *DIEI*, v, 1, 7 ('Homo autem quamvis sit pars reipublicae, est nihilominus suppositum propter se existens').

[125] *Controversies*, n. 2: 'inter cives solummodo est quaedam bonae fidei societas ... ad hunc finem contracta, ut quisque in tuto, et cum omni commoditate vitam agere possit'. Thus where Soto argues that 'the commonwealth is not bound to endanger itself defending a private citizen', Vázquez responds that it is wholly against the good faith upon which the society of private individuals is founded to leave a citizen to his fate: n. 13, citing the same locus of the *DIEI*.

[126] Ibid., Chapter xxi, n. 23: 'Caeterum cum id ius, sive naturae, sive gentium, non inducat necessitatem praecisam, sed tantum causativam, nempe, ut commodius liceat degere vitam, superest, ut nulla gens possit compelli invita et repugnans vivere sub imperio.' Cf. ibid., Preface, n. 125: 'an sub principe vivere omnibus hominibus necessum sit? ... ius gentium est commutabile, nec unquam, quo ad omnes homines induxit necessitatem praecisam ... ergo si in aliqua civitate libera cives convenirent, ne ullum haberent principatum, magistratum aut iudicem ... talis conventio et regimen proculdubio valeret. nec video quid possit huic rei impedimento esse, idque probatum est, quia omnia censentur permissa, quae non reperiuntur nominatim prohibita ... et haec est illa naturalis libertas a Deo o. m. data'.

nian hero remains a possibility and an ideal. The right created by the anti-heroes can never bind a society of heroes to a servitude it does not need.

The positions of Book II, then – the tendency of rights to dissolution, and the recalcitrance of certain *res* to servitude of any kind – underpin the more specifically political conclusions of Book I. The combined force of the languages of Book I and Book II is to set up an opposition between the artificial political unit (the city) and right on the one hand, and between nature and liberty on the other.

Vázquez's exploitation, in this manner, of the possibilities inherent in the language of the Roman law serves to distance him radically from both of the main theological rights traditions which we have so far traced. We saw how for the Dominicans, man's natural activity is *iure*, not free, and characterised as *agere* or *actus*. Man does not have the liberty of conserving himself: he is driven to form a city by his needs. His natural activity is derived from his nature or form, which is peculiar to man, and which stands in a causal relationship to the activity which constitutes his self-actualisation (form being, precisely, the formal cause). This activity is *iure* precisely because it is necessitated, that is, in the sphere of necessary causality and therefore of *ratio*; in a Thomist system, all law and right is connected with *ratio*. Within such a system, *facere* plays a very minor role and bears a pejorative sense in relation to *agere*: human *agere* is the actualisation of human form, whereas *facere* is the transference of any arbitrary form on to disposed matter.[127] In contrast, the Franciscan system, which owes its philosophical foundations more to Augustinian neoplatonism than to Aristotelianism, does not make use of the opposition between *agere* and *facere* in any way. The relevant distinction within their moral system is the legal distinction between right and fact. But for the Franciscans too, man's natural activity in so far as he is human must be *de iure*, the difference being that for them, it is always free, because human activity is distinguished from animal activity by the absence of objective determination. Animal activity coincides with the *de facto* and the necessary; humans act with right, which is the liberty by which they are made in the image of God.

Vázquez's synthesis of the languages of the Roman law stands in

---

[127] For the philosophical contrast between the natural substance as agent and the artificer, see Waterlow, *Nature, change and agency*, pp. 27–9 and 39–42; the moral contrast is laid out at *Ethics*, II, 4.

opposition to both theological traditions equally. Against the Dominicans, Vázquez cuts the causal link between specifically human activity and human form. For Vázquez, what man does in contrast to all other nature is *facere*, which is arbitrary and non-necessitated. The city is not natural and necessary, but artificial and contingent – not the locus of man's humanity, but an ambivalent product which ideally would not exist at all. Into his anti-Dominican stance Vázquez brings all the Augustinian language, common to the 'moral economy' literature, of the city as a relative good, its officers paid to secure justice as far as possible, but otherwise to leave the citizens to their liberty. But against the Franciscan notion of liberty as inseparable from will and reason, and as therefore constituting the distinction between brute and man (which is the distinction between the natural and the spiritual), Vázquez's language of liberty allows a thing to be free which has no reason. The quality of free faculty (liberty) unifies all animate beings and allows their activity to be analysed in the same terms, and in this Vázquez's construction responds to the Thomist system, wherein all nature is subject to analysis in the same terms of potential and form.

Vázquez's political construction, founded on the legal notion of an original absolute natural liberty, artificially limited by compact, stands behind a tradition of radical juristic political thought which is generally recognised as beginning with Grotius, for whom Vázquez was a major source.[128] It was largely Grotius who was responsible for turning this discourse of faculty or absolute right into one of *ius* in general: for defining his terms at the beginning of the *De iure belli ac pacis*, he wrote that 'The jurists call faculty by the name of "one's own"; but we shall hereafter call it right in the proper or strict sense of the term.'[129] The elucidation of that tradition is beyond the scope of this book: in the next chapter we can do no more than suggest how the political argument of one of the most important figures of seventeenth-century political thought, Thomas Hobbes, can be illuminated when considered as a contribution to the specific discourse of natural liberty.

---

[128] See Tuck, *Natural rights theories*, chapter 3.
[129] Hugo Grotius, *De iure belli ac pacis*, I, i, 5: 'Facultatem Iurisconsulti nomine Sui appellant: nos posthac jus proprie aut stricte dictum appellabimus.'

6

Natural liberty in the next century: the case of Thomas Hobbes

The debt of Thomas Hobbes to the radical politics of contemporary jurisprudence has long been recognised.[1] It is from Grotius and his follower Selden that Hobbes derives the notion of an original absolute natural right. As we saw, it was Grotius in the *De iure belli ac pacis* who turned Vázquezian 'faculty' into 'right' *per se*. However, Grotius had at the same time categorised liberty as only a subdivision of right in this sense, together with property and credit.[2] There is no sense, as there is in Vázquez, that *dominium*, right over other goods and persons, *is* liberty in the sense of being the remnants of the natural liberty of doing what one will; and his 'right of war and peace' is not a deduction wholly from natural liberty, but based on the twin foundations of liberty and of property, and their successive alienation. Unlike in the *De iure praedae*, therefore, the language of natural liberty is not a prominent feature.

By contrast, Hobbes throughout the three versions of his political philosophy exploits the specific language of natural liberty. The present chapter therefore considers what light may be shed by reading Hobbes within the legal tradition. I suggest that Hobbes' natural right is Vázquez's natural liberty – *liberrima facultas, ius absolutum* – but that, unlike Vázquez, he regards it as inherently vicious. His whole concern is to establish and then to fix the city against the flux of nature. His argument sets out to show the construction of the only city which will be proof against the tendency to return to nature, and which is therefore the *definition* of the city as opposed to the condition of nature. The instrument of this construction is the submission of the will and the judgement of each individual to the will and judgement of a sovereign.[3] This chapter will suggest

---

[1]   See Tuck, *Natural rights theories*, chapters 5 and 6 for the account of this.
[2]   *De iure belli ac pacis*, i, i, 5.
[3]   *Leviathan* (henceforth *Lev.*), ed. by R. Tuck (Cambridge 1991), p. 120.

that that strand of Hobbes' argument which concerns the submission of the will, or *obligation*, is in essence a legal argument relying on the kind of vocabulary we have been examining in the last chapter.[4]

At least one contemporary reading sees Hobbes' argument in precisely this way. In 1660 Roger Coke – grandson of Sir Edward – published a work entitled *Justice vindicated from the False Fucus put upon it, by T. White Gent., Mr. T. Hobbs, and H. Grotius*. Appended to this critique of a certain branch of contemporary political philosophy was his *Elements of Power and Subjection: Or the causes of all Humane, Christian, and Legal Society*. Throughout his critique of the *De cive* (he does not consider *Leviathan*), it is clear that he sees what Hobbes has to say about the will as pivotal to his political philosophy, but also as nonsensical. For Coke, Hobbes' theory depends on the untenable notion that it is possible for a person to bind his own will: 'where there is no precedent humane Law obliging, there cannot any man be obliged or bound to anything by his pact or contract; for to be bound, is in relation, and must presuppose something which does bind; but if nothing binds me but my Will, (which is a contradiction) I may unbind me when I will, for my Will is free'.[5] Hobbes, of course, accepts the impossibility of binding oneself, and even welcomes the argument for the case of the sovereign: for it is precisely this which ensures that the freedom of the sovereign is incapable of limitation.[6] Coke's point is that the illimitability of freedom bites at the very foundation of Hobbes' argument, rather than simply crowning its conclusion: '*every Man* binds himself forsooth, and therefore every

---

[4]   To imply that the submission of the will constitutes obligation is of course to anticipate the argument of this chapter. I shall argue that reading Hobbes in the light of contemporary legal vocabulary supports the contention that obligation in Hobbes is primarily a matter of giving up right; see B. Barry, 'Warrender and his critics', *Philosophy* 42 (1968) (reprinted in J. Lively and A. Reeve (eds.), *Modern political theory from Hobbes to Marx: Key debates* (London and New York 1989), pp. 40–62); and see also S. Darwall, *The British moralists and the internal ought: 1640–1740* (Cambridge 1995): I regret that this volume appeared too late for me to take full account of its findings. But I shall also hope to show how an awareness of the legal tradition enables us to fill out this notion of giving up right, through shedding more light on what, for Hobbes, right actually is. Related to this point is the question of what debt Hobbes owes to the voluntarist tradition in his formulation of right. Here I suggest that although, as Noel Malcolm ('Hobbes and voluntarist theology') argues, Hobbes' formal opposition between law and right as liberty may owe a great deal to voluntarist theology, nevertheless the voluntarist tradition is not the primary source for his substantive understanding of right as a natural faculty and as natural liberty.
[5]   Roger Coke, *Justice vindicated from the False Fucus put upon it, by T. White Gent., Mr. T. Hobbs, and H. Grotius. As also Elements of Power and Subjection* (London 1660), 'Observations on Mr. Hobbs DE CIVE', p. 27.
[6]   *Lev.*, p. 184.

man may when he will disoblige himself: for, *unumquodque dissolvi potest eo ligamine, quo ligatum est*'.[7] Hobbes is thus, to Coke, guilty of an error Vázquez did not make; but that Coke includes the Vázquezian position in his critique of this whole line of arguing is clear from his *Elements of Power and Subjection*, wherein he sets out his own account of the origins of government:

If to command and obey, as Supreme power and Subjects, had been an humane artifice or invention, then was there a time when men lived out of the offices of commanding and obeying ... But there was never any such time recorded in sacred or prophane history, or that they were invented or introduced by men: To command therefore and obey, as supreme powers and subjects, is no humane artifice or invention.

It is the silliest thing in the world for men to dream of a Golden Age, in which all things were alike and common to all men, and that men lived promiscuously in a parity or equal condition; and never tell when that time was, or who lived therein: And to say that the Dominion and Subjection now in use, Mans will brought in; and yet never tell who, any where in the world, did ever introduce it. And sure if this commanding and obeying were brought in by the wills of men, against that natural right and law wherein God hath made man, it could not possibly continue at all times and in all places of the world, but that somewhere men would return to their natural liberty.[8]

Unlike Hobbes, Vázquez had held that men could return to their natural liberty – no law being laid permanently upon their will – and had positively hoped for it. Coke, although agreeing with Vázquez that if government is the product of human will, it can be dissolved, nevertheless thinks that the fact that nowhere have people returned to their natural liberty demonstrates that there never was any such thing, and that government is not an invention of the peoples.

Coke thus read Hobbes' political theory as principally an argument (albeit false) from the Roman law. The rest of this chapter will be devoted to showing that he did not thereby mistake the sense of the text: that although coming to the opposite conclusions, Hobbes' texts find one of their crucial senses when read as turning on the same axes as those of Vázquez.

As we saw in the last chapter, Vázquez in the *Controversies* supposes an original state of men as one of *naturalis libertas laxitasque*: the natural condition of man which is both free from captivity and free from

---

[7]   Ibid., p. 29. Italics mine.
[8]   *Elements of Power and Subjection*, 'Observations on Mr. Hobbs DE CIVE', p. 29.

servitude. Nobody is in chains, because nobody has the instinct to dominate others; and nobody is under obligation, because the instinct for domination has not yet necessitated any kind of contract nor any 'artificial defence'. Although today men are often both in captivity and in servitude, they retain the possibility of escaping from both. Otherwise they have a degree of present liberty – *dominium* – which is what remains of that natural faculty given all the prohibitions of force and right imposed by the *ius gentium secundarium* and the *ius civile*. The whole construction is based on the legal definition of liberty understood as free faculty, what Wesembeck called *ius absolutum*, which has its being in the will and the soul.

We find this interpretation of liberty again in the early seventeenth century with a contemporary of Grotius', the Dutch *usus modernus* jurist Marcus Lycklama of Nijeholt (c. 1570–1626). Lycklama, from Friesland, was a jurist of some renown who was active for many years at the States-General in the Hague.[9] His *Membranarum iuris libri septem*, first published at Franeker in 1608–9, were divided into 'Eclogues', one of which was devoted to Florentinus' definition of liberty. Here he distinguished between *vis* and *ius* in terms of the distinction between body and soul: 'Free men are so-called from freedom ... which is the natural faculty of a person to do what he wants, unless he be prohibited by force (faculty of body) or right (faculty of mind [*animi*]).'[10] Freedom, the faculty of doing what one will, can be hindered by two things, by another's force or another's right: the implication is that the former, faculty of body, impedes the doing, whereas the latter, faculty of soul, impedes the will. The absolute freedom to do what one will is *naturalis libertas* or *laxitas*, and is common to animals as much as to men: 'Liberty is contained in natural right ... which is common to man and all animals; because the rest of the animals also enjoy natural liberty ... which Ulpian calls natural laxity.'[11] Men, like animals, can be captured; but again, like animals, they regain their natural liberty if they can escape: as a result of war, 'free men also are brought into slavery, who, however,

---

[9] For brief details of his life and works, see R. Dekkers, *Bibliotheca belgica juridica* (Brussels 1951), p. 105.

[10] Marcus Lycklama, *Membranarum iuris libri septem* (Leeuwarden 1644), Book IV, Ecloga xi, p. 143: 'Liberi a libertate appellantur ... quae est naturalis facultas ejus, quod cuique facere libet, nisi, si quid vi (facultas corporis) vel jure (facultas animi) prohibeatur'.

[11] Ibid.: 'Libertas jure naturali continetur ... quod homini cum omnibus animalibus commune est; quia libertate naturali gaudent et cetera animalia ... quam Ulpianus vocat naturalem laxitatem.'

if they evade the power of their enemies, regain their former liberty ... in a certain similitude of the right which is observed in other wild animals. For when we have caught these, they are understood to be ours, as long as they are restrained in our custody: but if they escape that custody and return to their natural liberty, they cease to be ours.'[12]

Libertas naturalis is therefore a condition of both body and soul. But for Lycklama, as for Vázquez, it is the *libertas animi* which is juridically significant in that it justifies the escape from physical custody into the liberty of the body as well. Lycklama insists that servitude in the sense of captivity does not damage the liberty of the soul, which he equates with nature *per se*: servitude 'is a constitution of the right of peoples, by which a person, in so far as he is a man composed of body (for indeed "body" is elsewhere taken for "man" ...), is subjected to an alien master against nature, or the liberty of the soul ... since there can be no such *dominium* or possession of nature as there is of the body, by the force of which the weaker man obeys the stronger, the cowardly the brave'.[13] 'Natural right does not require a free body, but the freedom of nature, which ... is not taken away by the right of peoples, by which the estate and condition of man is altered as regards his body.'[14] Thus 'the enormity of war drives the liberty of souls into a strait, but does not eradicate it completely'.[15]

Throughout *The Elements of Law*, *De cive* and *Leviathan* (both the English and, particularly, the Latin versions), Thomas Hobbes uses the terms 'liberty of nature' or *libertas naturae*, and 'natural liberty' or *libertas naturalis*. It is very striking, however, that these terms are never defined *per se*, despite the fact that by the time of writing *Leviathan*, Hobbes had come to define both 'liberty' and 'natural right' very

---

[12] Ibid.: 'liberi quoque homines in servitutem deducantur, qui tamen, si evaserint hostium potestatem, recipiant pristinam libertatem ... ad similitudinem quandam iuris, quae observatur in ceteris feris animalibus. Haec quidem ubi ceperimus, eo usque nostra esse intelliguntur, donec nostra custodia coerceantur: cum vero evaserint custodiam nostram et in naturalem libertatem se receperint, nostra esse desinunt.'

[13] Ibid.: '[Iure servitutis:] quae est constitutio Iurisgentium, qua quis, qua homo corporeus (siquidem corpus alibi pro homine sumitur ...) domino alieno contra naturam, seu libertatem animi, subjicitur ... cum nullum naturae vel dominium vel possessio esse possit, sicuti corporis, cujus vi homo imbecillior paret potentiori, vecors, generoso.'

[14] Ibid.: 'Ius vero naturale non requirit corpus liberum, sed naturae libertatem, quae, quatenus eam natura duce simul cum luce haustam contemplamur, Iuregentium non tollitur, quo duntaxat status hominis et conditio quoad corpus mutatur.'

[15] Ibid., p. 144: 'Libertatem igitur animorum in angustum redigit belli immanitas, non extirpat.'

sharply indeed. Hobbes can use the term 'natural liberty' or 'liberty of nature' generally for the natural condition of men;[16] he can use it specifically for the liberty of the body;[17] he can also use it as equivalent to the right of nature, *Jus Naturale*.[18] In *Leviathan*, showing its Vázquezian roots, it is something that individuals 'return' (*redire*) to or 'relapse' (*relabi*) into out of the civil state: 'those who are citizens under a monarch, can by right ... neither throw off monarchy nor slide back into the liberty of nature';[19] 'if the monarch should renounce the supreme power for himself and for his heirs, the citizens return to the absolute liberty of nature'.[20] But it is also something that it is most important to see that they *retain* in the civil state.[21]

In the course of what follows I hope to show that Hobbes' 'natural liberty' is primarily the *naturalis libertas* of the jurists. It is the natural faculty of doing what one will, the right of nature as Hobbes defines it, and it is primarily what the jurists would call a *facultas animi*. It is the possibility of formulating one's own proper will, and of using what power one has in accordance with that will, and which the use of force cannot entirely eliminate. At almost every point where Hobbes uses the phrase 'natural liberty' or 'liberty of nature', I believe it can be shown that this is the concept he has in mind: his deployment of the notion is conditioned by the part that it plays within juristic discourse. To the extent to which it is a key concept in Hobbes' argument, that argument is essentially one belonging to the

---

[16] E.g. in *The Elements of Law*, ed. by F. Tönnies, 2nd edn with Introduction by M. M. Goldsmith (London 1969) (henceforth *EL*), Chapter 14, p. 73: 'the estate of men in this natural liberty is the estate of war'.

[17] E.g. in *Leviathan* (henceforth *Lev.*), Chapter 21, p. 147: 'that naturall *liberty*, which only is properly called *liberty*'.

[18] E.g. at *Lev.*, Chapter 26, p. 185: 'the Right of Nature, that is, the naturall Liberty of men'.

[19] Hobbes, *Leviathan*, in *Opera philosophica quae latine scripsit omnia*, vol. iii, ed. by W. Molesworth (London 1841) (henceforth *Lev. latine*), p. 132: 'qui sub monarcha cives sunt, neque monarchiam rejicere neque ad libertatem naturae relabi ... jure possunt' (cf. Vázquez's contrary dictum, above, p. 196: 'ei renunciare atque ab ea recedere [subditis] liberum esse par est, sicque ab ea subjectione poterunt se in suam laxitatem recipere'). The English *Leviathan* reads 'they that are subjects to a Monarch, cannot without his leave cast off Monarchy, and return to the confusion of a disunited Multitude' (*Lev.*, p. 122); here, as in many places, the Latin work brings out the elements of Hobbes' thought that belong to the juristic tradition, which is a Latin discourse.

[20] *Lev. latine*, p. 169: 'Si monarcha summae potestati pro se et haeredibus suis renuntiet, redeunt cives ad libertatem naturae absolutam.'

[21] At *Lev.*, pp. 146–7; and see below, p. 225. For my appreciation of Hobbes' insistence on this point I am very much indebted to the recent article by Quentin Skinner, 'Thomas Hobbes on the proper signification of liberty', *Transactions of the Royal Historical Society* (1992), 121–51.

juristic tradition, and imports the juristic distinction between *libertas* and *natura* on the one hand, and *servitus* and *artificium* on the other.

However, there is another argument involved in Hobbes' text. This is an argument about 'liberty' *per se* (rather than 'natural liberty'). This is the liberty which Hobbes defines as the absence of external impediments to physical motion, and which, as Quentin Skinner has recently shown, became increasingly important to him.[22] It makes liberty a *facultas corporis* rather than a *facultas animi*. This is not a concept from the juristic tradition – nor, I shall suggest, is Hobbes quite sure how it meshes with the notion he has imported from that tradition of natural liberty. Its eventual result is to draw a distinction between the natural and the physical, on the one hand, and the artificial and the will, on the other. But this dichotomy does not coincide with that of the jurists outlined above. I shall argue that the problems with liberty in Hobbes' political theory, which are most obvious in the famous Chapter 21 of *Leviathan*, spring from the incompatibility of his two lines of argument.

The clearest basic account of Hobbes' conceptions of liberty, obligation and right is to be found in the *Elements of Law*, Hobbes' first, and, as the title suggests, most strongly juristic sketch of his political argument. Here we originally encounter the notion of liberty in connection with the account of how we determine ourselves to one action or another:

The alternate succession of appetite and fear, during all the time the action is in our power to do, or not to do, is that we call DELIBERATION; which name hath been given it for that part of the definition wherein it is said that it lasteth so long, as the action whereof we deliberate, is in our power; for so long we have liberty to do or not to do: and deliberation signifieth the taking away of our own liberty.[23]

An action is within our power to do or not to do, according to Hobbes, for as long as it is neither impossible nor done.[24] Liberty is formally defined as the liberty to do or not to do that action; and in the process of decision-making, we habitually put an end to our own liberty. This deliberation, this relieving ourselves of our liberty, is the process that results in will: 'In deliberation the last appetite, as also

22 Skinner, 'Proper signification'.
23 *EL*, p. 61. For another account of liberty (and obligation) in Hobbes which similarly privileges Hobbes' account of deliberation of the will, see W. von Leyden, *Hobbes and Locke: The politics of freedom and obligation* (London 1982).
24 *EL*, p. 61: 'till the action be either done, or some accident come between, to make it impossible'.

the last fear, is called WILL (viz.) the last appetite will to do; the last fear will not to do, or will to omit.'[25] Will is therefore defined retrospectively by the production of the action: a 'will' to which an action does not follow is not a will, but only an inclination, because – clearly – it leaves the individual concerned still at liberty to do or not to do, given that he has not done it.[26] Will is the end of deliberation and the final loss of liberty because it is by definition that which immediately produces an action, a 'doing', which cannot be compatible with the liberty to do or not to do. Thus 'it is all one ... to say will and last will: for though a man express his present inclination and appetite concerning the disposing of his good, by word or writing; yet shall it not be accounted his will, because he hath liberty still to dispose of them otherwise; but when death taketh away that liberty, then it is his will'.[27]

Thus liberty as a liberty of doing or not doing is the state of being not yet deliberated, of not yet having a will. It is striking that for this earliest formulation of his notion of the will as the last appetite in deliberating, Hobbes should have been prompted by a consideration of the liberty of the testator. As we saw in the last chapter, the development of the legal vocabulary of radical liberty had been greatly stimulated by precisely this issue, and the dictum that 'no one can lay such a law upon his own will, from which it is not licit for him to recede', originally describing the liberty of the testator, had found political application in Vázquez's theory of the dissolution of the *civitas*. It is a tradition of *arbitrary* liberty: the possibility of acting on one's own whim, *ad libitum*.

Hobbes' formulation is of course not that of the jurists, in so far as Hobbes does not think that the will has any substantive being, and therefore it cannot have freedom predicated of it, for according to Hobbes liberty is only of bodies. Thus a person's liberty, to which that same person puts an end by willing one thing rather than another, is not a liberty of the will, but of the person who has not yet willed. This liberty is *liberum arbitrium*: '*Liberum arbitrium* ... is not the liberty of the will but of the person willing.'[28] Hobbes insists that there is no sense in which the will is itself voluntary – I cannot will to will – nor the passions which are the will.[29] Consequently, there cannot be a definition of liberty which supposes that a person may

[25] Ibid.   [26] See *Lev.*, p. 45.   [27] *EL*, pp. 61–2.
[28] *Lev. latine*, p. 160: 'Liberum denique arbitrium, non voluntatis libertas sed volentis est.'
[29] *EL*, p. 63.

will one way or the other: 'When we say that someone has the *liberum arbitrium* of doing this or that, this should always be understood together with the condition, *if he will*; for it is an absurdity to say that someone has the *liberum arbitrium* of doing this or that whether he will or no.'[30] Liberty is the liberty of doing what an individual wants.[31]

Hobbes follows up his definitions of liberty and the will with a further consideration of what actions may be said to be voluntary or to 'have beginning in the will':

Voluntary such as a man doth upon appetite or fear; involuntary such as he doth by necessity of nature, as when he is pushed, or falleth, and thereby doth good or hurt to another; mixed, such as participate of both ... The example of him that throweth his goods out of a ship into the sea, to save his person, is of an act altogether voluntary: for, there is nothing involuntary, but the hardness of the choice, which is not his action, but the action of the winds; what he himself doth, is no more against his will, than to fly from danger is against the will of him that seeth no other means to preserve himself.[32]

The 'example' in question is Aristotle's;[33] but the issue of whether fear vitiates the will was a frequent topic of commentators on the Roman law. Philip Decius (Filippo Decio, 1454–1535), the author of the most influential sixteenth-century commentary on the *Regulae iuris*, argued as follows:

A will that is coerced is still called a will, when violence is not precisely brought to bear, but is conditional: for example: unless you do this, I will kill you. For in that the person chooses to do it rather than die, his will is there ... It is otherwise when a person is precisely forced to do something, because then he does not appear to consent in any way: because he is rather said to suffer, than to act.[34]

---

[30] Thomas Hobbes, *De homine*, in *Opera philosophica quae latine scripsit omnia*, vol. II, ed. by G. Molesworth (London 1839), Chapter XI, p. 95: 'Quando dicimus liberum esse alicui arbitrium hoc vel illud faciendi vel non faciendi, semper intelligendum est cum apposita conditione hac, *si voluerit*; nam ut quis liberum arbitrium habeat faciendi hoc vel illud utrum velit necne, absurde dicitur' (italics in the original).

[31] This stance on liberty and the will is one of Hobbes' most strongly and consistently held philosophical positions. It stems from Hobbes' materialist philosophical premises. However, Hobbes throughout his writings is prepared to refer to the will as if it had substantive being – as when he defines the covenant of subjection as the submission of the will and the judgement of the individual to the will and judgement of the sovereign (see above, p. 205 and below, p. 228). When he talks in this way he should be understood as referring, by 'will', to the ability of all animals to deliberate themselves, i.e. to put an end to their own liberty; and this is the sense in which I shall be using the term 'will' in elucidating Hobbes' texts.

[32] *EL*, p. 63.   [33] *NE*, 1110a.

[34] Philippus Decius, *In tit. ff. de regulis iuris* (Lyons 1553), *Reg. iur.*, iv, n. 6: 'voluntas coacta voluntas dicitur, quando violentia praecise non infertur, sed est conditionalis: puta: nisi sic

'Coacta voluntas etiam voluntas est': the phrase was a widely used legal maxim. However, Decius went on to qualify his words somewhat. A will which is coerced is, according to him, not a spontaneous will (depending on the meaning of 'spontaneous'); and hence cases of coerced will, though undoubtedly cases of will, are not the same as cases where there had been no coercion.[35] But Matthew Wesembeck in his *Paratitla* gave a far more uncompromising account, distinguishing between force (*vis*) and fear (*metus*) in a discussion which (in the marginalia) refers the reader to Aristotle's account:

Force is the onslaught of a greater object, which cannot be repelled: as when with inescapable violence a bond of surety, money etc. is snatched from someone ... For when something is extorted by violence, the source of the action comes from another quarter and extrinsically: nor can it be said to take place at the will of the sufferer any more than it is at the sailor's will that the ship is dashed against the rocks by the storm. But where something takes place by fear of impending violence or danger, for example something is given, or handed over, or conceded, then the origin of the action is within the sufferer: which proceeds from a judgement in no way hindered, and from a will choosing the lesser evil. In which case what is said is true, that a coerced will is still a will, and obliges in the strictness of the law.[36]

Wesembeck makes no distinction between *voluntas simpliciter* and *voluntas spontanea*. A will is a will, *tout court* – and it obliges.[37]

The essence of Hobbes' argument in Chapter 12 of the *Elements of Law* is thus that all actions proceeding from the activity of deliberation are voluntary. Moreover, all such actions are the actions of an individual who was free to do or not to do: for without that liberty, deliberation is unintelligible.

We next encounter the notion of liberty in Chapter 14, which

---

feceris, te interficiam. In eo enim quod elegit ita facere potius quam mori, eius voluntas est ... Secus quando quis praecise cogitur aliquid facere, quia tunc nullo modo consentire videtur: quia potius dicitur pati, quam agere.' For the use of the *regulae iuris* in the renaissance period, see P. Stein, *Regulae iuris* (Edinburgh 1966), chapter 9, for Decius, ibid., p. 162.

35 Ibid.

36 Wesembecius, *Paratitla*, p. 143 (on D. 4, 2, 'Quod metus causa gestum erit'): 'Vis est maioris rei impetus, qui repelli non potest: ut cum inevitabili violentia chirographum, pecunia etc. alicui eripitur ... Cum enim violentia quid extorquetur, principium actionis aliunde et extrinsecus venit: nec magis dici id potest voluntate patientis fieri, quam volente sit nauta, cum tempestate ad scopulum navis alliditur. At ubi impendentis violentiae periculive metu quid fit, puta datur, trahitur, conceditur, tum intus in patiente existit actionis origo: quae a iudicio nequaquam impedito, et voluntate minus malum eligente proficiscitur. Quo casu verum est quod dicitur, voluntatem coactem esse voluntatem, et iuris rigore obligare.'

37 See below, p. 216.

considers 'what estate of security this our nature hath placed us in'. Hobbes argues that 'that which is not against reason, men call RIGHT, or *jus*, or blameless liberty of using our own natural power and ability. It is therefore a *right of nature*: that every man may preserve his own life and limbs, with all the power he hath.'[38] The liberty or right to ensure this end in any way possible yields the right to all things that may appear necessary as means;[39] but this right to all things is nothing but a liberty of action with respect to all things: 'Every man by nature hath right to all things, that is to say, to do whatsoever he listeth to whom he listeth, to possess, use, and enjoy all things he can.'[40] This estate is 'natural liberty',[41] wherein every individual 'is free to do, and undo, and deliberate as long as he listeth; every member being obedient to the will of the whole man; that liberty being nothing else but his natural power, without which he is no better than an inanimate creature, not able to help himself'.[42] Natural liberty is thus the liberty we encountered in Chapter 12, the state of being not yet deliberated as to the way in which one will use one's forces. It is 'the liberty that nature hath given [a man], of governing himself by his own will and power'.[43]

Throughout Hobbes' account of liberty, the accent is on the individual's own will, the fact that he himself is the source of his deliberation. Common (implicitly) to all animates – *commune omnibus animantibus* – it is the *libertas naturalis* or *naturalis laxitas* of the jurists. Its contrary is the state of being deliberated, or having a will. However, unlike the legal tradition we have been looking at, Hobbes does not envisage the estate of natural liberty as one of innocence and therefore peace, a Golden Age. For Hobbes, the estate of natural liberty is an estate of war, because the liberty of each individual conflicts with that of others. If I am my own arbitrary deliberator, what I will is very likely incompatible with what you will, leading to strife among individuals.[44] Hence the way out of the

---

[38] *EL*, p. 70.   [39] Ibid., p. 71.   [40] Ibid.
[41] Ibid., p. 72: 'the estate of men in this natural liberty is the estate of war'.
[42] Ibid., p. 116.   [43] Ibid., p. 79.
[44] I have no space here to discuss the various interpretations of what makes for conflict in the Hobbesian state of nature. Suffice it here to point to Hobbes' signalling of the desire for dominion as one such cause, e.g. at *Lev.*, Chapter 17, p. 117: 'The finall Cause, End, or Designe of men, (*who naturally love Liberty, and Dominion over others,*) in the introduction of that restraint upon themselves, (in which we see them live in Commonwealths,) is the foresight of their own preservation ... that is to say, of getting themselves out from that miserable condition of Warre, which is necessarily consequent ... to the naturall Passions of men' (my italics). The 'miserable condition' is an estate not unlike the state that Vázquez envisages

natural state of war must consist in some measure of deliberation designed so as to harmonise otherwise conflicting wills. In other words, individuals in a condition of arbitrary liberty naturally and primarily respond to the conflict of wills by attempting damage to others: specifically, to the *body* of others; and in turn recognise the threat to their own bodily well-being from the similar responses of others. Hobbes' whole political theory rests on the idea that individuals will be so concerned to keep others off their body that they are prepared to allow them access to their will instead. This determination of the will constitutes Hobbes' account of obligation.[45]

For Hobbes in *The Elements of Law*, an individual can be obliged both by laws and by covenants of his own making. Both of these – as we should expect from the contraries of natural liberty – affect the individual's will: but they do so in different ways. A covenant is a specific type of contract whereby an individual agrees to give up a part of his radical liberty, or right to all things, in exchange for some benefit to himself. Whether an individual simply relinquishes that right, or whether he transfers it to another specific individual who accepts it, what he does thereby is to *declare his will*: either 'no more to do that action, which of right he might have done before', or 'not to resist, or hinder [the specific other], according to that right he had thereto before he transferred it'.[46] A covenant, like a final act of deliberation, is a *willing* to act in one way rather than another, and thus is similarly an end to natural liberty with regard to that action. Hobbes is clear that although contracts are generally phrased in terms of the exchange of rights, it is important to keep in mind that what is being affected is the natural liberty of each individual to do or not to do: 'For seeing that by nature every man hath right to every thing, it is impossible for a man to transfer unto another any right that he had not before. And therefore all that a man doth in transferring of right, is no more but a declaring of the will, to suffer him, to whom he hath transferred his right, to make benefit of the same, without molestation.'[47]

For Hobbes, as for Wesembeck, the declaration of will generates

developing with the decline of the ages, wherein men are possessed of the same *libertas* and *laxitas* as before, but use it to attempt to dominate others, thus generating war.

[45] Obligation, therefore, is always and by definition only for the sake of bodily life and liberty; where bodily life and liberty are menaced, there can be no obligation. See also Malcolm, 'Hobbes and voluntarist theology', pp. 160–4, for whom the 'moral' obligation of covenant is grounded in the prudential precept of self-preservation.

[46] *EL*, pp. 75–6.   [47] Ibid., p. 76.

*Therefore, that we do
suggests, that we do
not give up all of our will*

obligation. To have an obligation is to have a will. Discussing covenants in the same chapter, Hobbes argues that:

In all contracts where there is trust, the promise of him that is trusted, is called a COVENANT. And this, though it be a promise, and of the time to come, yet doth it transfer the right, when that time cometh, no less than an actual donation. For it is a manifest sign, that he which did perform, understood it was the will of him that was trusted, to perform also. Promises therefore, upon consideration of reciprocal benefit, are covenants and signs of the will, or last act of deliberation, whereby the liberty of performing, or not performing, is taken away, and consequently are obligatory. For where liberty ceaseth, there beginneth obligation.[48]

When I covenant, I make a sign to another of my will to perform a certain action at a future time. The covenant is a declaration of my will: but it is the having of the will itself which constitutes my obligation, not the fact that I have covenanted. The covenant is simply the sign of my deliberation.[49] Hence in a covenant I oblige myself, just as in coming to any decision I oblige myself. Moreover, just like Wesembeck, Hobbes discounts fear as voiding a covenant: 'it is not therefore void, because extorted by fear. For there appeareth no reason, why that which we do upon fear, should be less firm than that which we do for covetousness. For both the one and the other maketh the action voluntary.'[50]

Hobbes differentiates contract of any kind from *free gift*. Contract represents a transference of right in return for some reciprocal benefit, whereas in cases of free gift, right is transferred *gratis*, in return for nothing. In the latter, verbal declarations of intent – promises – do not amount to declarations of will: 'he that promiseth to give, without any consideration but his own affection, so long as he hath not given, deliberateth still, according as the causes of his affection continue or diminish; and he that deliberateth hath not yet willed, because the will is the last act of his deliberation'.[51] On one level, it is difficult to understand why the consideration of reciprocal benefit should make such a difference to the declaration of action: may an individual not equally will whether or not he stands to gain by it? But the point becomes clear if we bear in mind the purpose of contract. In contract – the way out of the state of nature – an

---

[48] Ibid., p. 78.
[49] Grotius, *De iure belli ac pacis*, ii, xi, 4, 2–3, speaks of the formal act of contract as the *signum deliberati animi*. Unlike Hobbes, however, he gives no account of what might be this *libertas animi* which is ended with the act of will.
[50] *EL*, p. 79.   [51] Ibid., p. 77.

individual attempts to acquire access to the only thing which he cannot gain control of in the state of nature: another's will, that is his liberty. For in the state of nature, no matter what the individual may rightly do to the goods another possesses and even to his person, he cannot deprive him of his natural liberty, his right which is his liberty to do as he will. Free gift is like free action in that it does not have as its goal any alteration of another person's natural liberty or right. Hence until a person actually gives, all his promises that he will are merely expressions of his continued desire so to do, which does not, of course, affect his liberty in any way. A contract is different, for in this case the individual in question intends to access another's will, his liberty, which he can only do by allowing that other to access his own. Hence declaration of intent to another person in such circumstances stands as a declaration of will, a sign that a person has deliberated and is therefore obliged. This also explains why Hobbes thinks that 'all obligations are determinable at the will of the obliger'.[52] It is not just that the individual has deliberated, ended his liberty, as he would in deciding on any free action. It is that he has given another access to his liberty, to end it or not as he will. The difference between a covenant and a decision to act is that in the former the individual concerned does not simply oblige himself to act in a particular way: he obliges himself *to another person*, the covenantee.

Hobbes famously insists that there is no security for the performance of covenants of mutual trust between individuals in the estate of universal war, and that therefore such covenants are void. Thus attempts by individuals in that condition to acquire access to other individuals' natural liberty will fail, and they will remain open to attack and the possible 'destruction of their nature'. Hence an overarching union, 'which is defined ... to be the involving or including the wills of many in the will of one man ... or of one COUNCIL',[53] between a mass of individuals is necessary if their survival is to be realised. 'The making of union consisteth in this, that every man by covenant oblige himself to some one and the same man, or to some one and the same council ... to do those actions, which the said man or council shall command them to do; and to do no action which he or they shall forbid, or command them not to do.'[54] Union among men is thus effected by means of obligation and is unnatural – 'concord amongst men is artificial, and by way of covenant'[55] – just as

[52] Ibid., p. 79.   [53] Ibid., p. 103.   [54] Ibid.   [55] Ibid., pp. 102–3.

for the jurists of the last chapter, 'nulla servitus habet causam naturalem'. The universal covenant which each individual must make has a paradoxical nature: it is a declaration of the will to have the will declared by another. The obligation that is the acceptance of the will of another is law; but that obligation is only an obligation because of a previous covenant – i.e. a declaration of one's *own* will – to accept the will of another: 'whatsoever is a law to a man, respecteth the will of another, and the declaration thereof. But a covenant is the declaration of a man's own will. And therefore a law and a covenant differ; and though they be both obligatory, and a law obligeth no otherwise than by virtue of some covenant made by him who is subject thereunto, yet they oblige by several sorts of promises.'[56] This understanding that all obligations are taken upon oneself is, as Michael Oakeshott said, 'Hobbes's deepest conviction about moral duties'.[57]

It has been objected to Hobbes' theory that it entails that one is free to keep the law if one has the will to.[58] But in fact this is not the case. Hobbes defines the will as the last appetite before action. A free action is one which is the immediate result of an act of will; and this is not true of acting in keeping with the law, for the relevant act of will was the original covenant to 'respect the will of another', and hence to take it as law. This relationship between liberty and the law was commonly discussed by lawyers in commenting on the *regula iuris*: 'Velle non creditur, qui obsequitur imperio patris vel domini' ('he is not believed to will, who obeys the command of a father or master'). Here sixteenth-century commentators discussed the case of someone who obeys because bound or obliged to do so. Hence Decius writes,

Note that a person is not thought to will, who does an action on the order of a father or master: for albeit he may not be precisely compelled to obey, since even when the master gives an order a slave can refuse to perform it ... Nevertheless in obeying that act is not called voluntary ... because properly and truly he is not said to will: nor does the act seem to be voluntary ... because that is said to take place out of will, which proceeds from a free judgement of the mind.[59]

<hr>

[56] Ibid., p. 185.
[57] M. Oakeshott, 'The moral life in the writings of Thomas Hobbes', reprinted in M. Oakeshott, *Hobbes on civil association* (Oxford 1975), 75–131, p. 112.
[58] See M. M. Goldsmith, 'Hobbes on liberty', *Hobbes Studies* 2 (1989), 23–39, p. 29.
[59] Decius, *In tit. ff. de regulis iuris*, Reg. iv, n. 1: 'Nota quod non reputatur velle ille qui actum facit ex iussu patris vel domini: licet enim praecise non cogatur obedire, quia etiam iubente domino servus potest nolle adire ... Tamen obtemperando actus ille non dicitur voluntarius

Cagnolus concurs:

more generally, Decius understands that that is properly said to take place voluntarily which proceeds from a free judgement of the mind ... [However] it is not believed, that the son or the slave who obeys the command of a father or master wills: because they are not free to will because of the obedience to which they are constrained ... for that which takes place with a command forcing it cannot be said to take place spontaneously.[60]

This is precisely the Hobbesian position on obligation: the will is fixed, and therefore the *libertas* of the mind towards a range of options is ended. Thus Hobbes is not open to the objection that his theory makes a person free to obey the law but not to disobey. Hobbesian subjects are not free to obey law, as they are already deliberated.

The political construction of the *Elements of Law* is therefore a construction of the will by means of obligation, and is as artificial as liberty is natural. The roots of the theory lie in orthodox contemporary jurisprudence. The problem for Hobbes lies not in accounting for obligation, but in accounting for the violation of such obligations. Hobbes recognises that in the natural condition of mankind, there is every likelihood that someone who makes a covenant will renege upon it – will withdraw himself from his obligation, will take on a different will and do something else. This violation dissolves the covenant.[61] Nevertheless, according to Hobbes' account the individual is supposed to have divested himself of the liberty of so doing. Hobbes is therefore led to liken reneging on covenants – which is the substance of injury or rightlessness – to a contradiction in terms, and absurdity: 'For as he, that is driven to contradict an assertion by him before maintained, is said to be reduced to an absurdity; so he that through passion doth, or omitteth that which before by covenant he promised not to do, or not to omit, is said to commit injustice ... he that violateth a covenant, willeth the doing, and the not doing of the same thing, at the same time; which is a plain contradiction.'[62] Thus

---

... quia proprie et vere non dicitur velle: nec actus voluntarius videtur ... quia ex voluntate fieri dicitur, quod ex libero mentis arbitrio proficiscitur.'

[60] Hieronymus Cagnolus, *Omnium legum tituli ff. de regulis iuris copiosa interpretatio* (Lyons 1546), fol. 32: 'Dec. intelligit generalius quod voluntarie fieri proprie illud dicitur quod ex libero mentis arbitrio proficiscitur ... non [autem] creditur, velle filius vel servus qui patris dominicaque obsequuntur imperio: quia liberum non habent velle propter obedientiam cui astricti sunt ... quod enim cogente imperio fit not potest dici sponte fieri.'

[61] *EL*, p. 79.   [62] Ibid., p. 82.

'injury is an absurdity of conversation, as absurdity is a kind of injustice in disputation'.[63] But injustice or absurdity of conversation is a fact, and a fact which dissolves all obligation and returns a person to natural liberty: to put it more correctly, a fact that *is* that dissolving.

Conversation or society has to take place in the face of a majority of non- or minimally self-consistent people, who constantly dissolve themselves from their obligations. It is here that fear has its role. The covenant of union necessarily involves a covenant of non-resistance to the sovereign, which establishes a 'power of coercion' over all subjects.[64] Fear of this is what will drive the majority to keep the covenant of union and obey the laws: 'there is an *oderunt peccare* in the unjust, as well as in the just, but from different causes; for the unjust man who abstaineth from injuries for fear of punishment, declareth plainly that the justice of his actions dependeth on the civil constitution, from whence punishments proceed; which would otherwise in the estate of nature be unjust, according to the fountain from whence they spring'.[65] Without coercive power, the covenant that establishes the commonwealth is void, and its laws 'leave men still in the estate of nature and hostility. For seeing the wills of most men are governed only by fear, and where there is no power of coercion, there is no fear; the wills of most men will follow their passions of covetousness, lust, anger and the like, to the breaking of those covenants, whereby the rest also, who would otherwise keep them, are set at liberty, and have no law but themselves.'[66] Hobbes writes as if the individual who obeys the law out of fear has nevertheless left the estate of nature. But we remember that Hobbes had been at pains to emphasise that fear does not affect liberty, that liberty which is *libertas naturalis* or *libertas animi*, the *liberum arbitrium* of all animates. The implication is that a person who contracts, and keeps to it only through fear, is a person still in possession of *libertas naturalis*: because his action in keeping faith is the result of an immediate will induced by fear. Hobbes' political theory is primarily about the institution of such a fear as will cause men to hold to their obligations. But fear does not, on his own principles, alter the state of nature. By the time of *Leviathan*, Hobbes has recognised that no amount of terror will ever fix civil society against the return to nature – because action caused by fear *is* nature.[67]

---

[63] Ibid.

[64] Ibid., p. 111. In *EL*, Hobbes is not yet clear that the covenant of union *is* the covenant of non-resistance.

[65] Ibid., p. 83.   [66] Ibid.   [67] *Lev.*, p. 232.

The usage of the terms *libertas naturalis* and *ius naturale* in the *De cive* seemingly follows the pattern set in the *Elements of Law*. Natural right is 'the liberty, which everyone has of using his natural faculties according to right reason'.[68] Hobbes' Latin phraseology shows clearly the origins of his concept in the jurists' *libertas naturalis*: it is *ius primaevum*,[69] the right by which 'in the purely natural state, or before men had mutually bound themselves by any pacts, it was licit for each to do whatsoever and to whomsoever he pleased'.[70] As Hobbes says, in Chapter 14 considering laws and pacts, 'right is natural liberty, not constituted but left over by laws'.[71]

In this latter chapter, Hobbes conceives an original natural liberty progressively restricted by a series of laws. 'Take away laws, and liberty is complete; first of all it is restricted by natural law, and divine law; civil laws further restrict what remains; and what is left over by the civil law, can again be restricted by the constitutions of particular towns and societies. So there is a great divide between law, and right; for law is a bond, and right is liberty, and they differ as contraries.'[72] So what liberty citizens have is the remains of natural liberty, their natural ability to deliberate themselves rather than being deliberated by laws. Natural liberty is ended, just as in the *Elements of Law*, by pact and by law: but the latter, again, only obliges in virtue of a precedent pact to obey.[73] Thus obligation is still, as in the *Elements of Law*, primarily a matter of the individual's voluntary agreement to restrain his liberty.

However, it is in *De cive* that Hobbes first starts to confuse his juristic language with another argument about liberty. We saw how, in *The Elements of Law*, Hobbes had wanted to say that a person is at liberty to do or not do *x* if *x* is the immediate result of deliberation and thus voluntary. A person is by nature, naturally, at liberty: this is his natural right as an animate rather than an inanimate. Obligation

---

[68] *De cive*, ed. by H. Warrender (Oxford 1983), p. 94.

[69] Ibid., p. 130: 'quamdiu cautio ab invasione aliorum non habetur, cavendi sibi quibus-cunque modis voluerit & potuerit, unicuique manere *Ius* primaevum'.

[70] Ibid., p. 95: 'in statu merè naturali, sive antequam homines ullis pactis sese invicem obstrinxissent, unicuique licebat facere quaecunque & in quoscunque libebat'; cf. the jurists' definition of liberty as 'naturalis facultas quod cuique facere libet'.

[71] Ibid., p. 207: 'Est autem *ius*, *libertas naturalis*, à legibus non constituta, sed relicta.'

[72] Ibid.: 'Remotis enim *legibus*, *libertas* integra est; hanc primo restringit *naturalis lex*, & *divina*; residuam restringunt *leges civiles*; & quae lege civili superest, restringi rursus potest, à *constitutionibus* particularium urbium & societatum. Multum ergo interest inter *legem*, & *ius*; *lex* enim *vinculum*, *ius libertas* est, differuntque ut contraria.'

[73] Ibid., p. 206.

is contrary to liberty and is consequently artificial. Although Hobbes there speaks of physical chains as 'natural bonds',[74] implying that he might conceive obligations or bonds of trust as artificial bonds, it is important that all he can mean is that those bonds are artificial: they are not bonds on an artificial liberty, but on natural liberty. In parallel, Hobbes in the _Elements of Law_ never uses the phrase 'natural liberty' as the contrary of 'natural bonds': their contrary is plain 'liberty', which is not defined as such.

In Chapter 9 of _De cive_ Hobbes introduces his argument concerning liberty _per se_. The motive for his doing so seems clear from his introduction of the subject: 'Commonly, to do everything at our own whim, with impunity, is held to be liberty; not to be able to do that, servitude: which cannot happen in civic society and with the peace of the human race; because there is no civic society without the power of command and the right of coercion.'[75] That is, if the mass of people persist in a certain belief about what liberty is, they will always complain that they do not have it. Hence liberty requires redefinition as 'nothing else than the absence of impediments to movement; so that water contained in a vessel is therefore not free, because the vessel is an impediment to its flowing out, but when the vessel is broken it is freed. And every thing has more or less liberty, according as it has more or less space in which it moves; so that someone kept in a large cell has more freedom than one who is kept in a narrow one.'[76] Liberty, on this definition, is a purely corporeal state which can be predicated of anything that has body, and, Hobbes points out, 'in this sense all slaves and subjects are free, who are not in chains or incarcerated'.

As a liberty which can be predicated of anything that has body, corporeal liberty is clearly not equivalent to natural liberty or the right of nature. And yet there are signs that Hobbes was beginning to lose his hold on the juristic notion of natural liberty as he sought to introduce the new element in the interests of political theory. Discussing the difference between the bound and the unbound slave

---

[74] _EL_, p. 128.

[75] _De cive_, p. 167: 'Vulgo omnia nostro arbitratu facere, atque id impunè, _libertas_; id non posse, _servitus_ iudicatur; quod in civitate, & cum pace humani generis fieri non potest; quia civitas sine imperio & iure coërcendi nulla est.'

[76] Ibid.: 'nihil aliud est quam _absentia impedimentorum motûs_; ut aqua vase conclusa, ideò non est _libera_, quia vas impedimento est ne effluat, quae fracto vase _liberatur_. Et est cuique _libertas_ maior vel minor, prout plus vel minus spatij est in quo versatur; ut maiorem habeat _libertatem_ qui in amplo carcere, quam qui in angusto custoditur.'

– the equivalent passage to that in the *Elements of Law* where he had talked of 'natural bonds' and of 'liberty' – Hobbes in Chapter 8 of *De cive* appears to equate 'corporeal liberty' with 'natural liberty'. 'Not everyone captured in war, whose life is spared, is understood to make a pact with his master: because not everyone is trusted so far as to be left so much of his natural liberty, that he could run away, or default on his duties, or plot some harm or loss to his master if he wanted. And such people do indeed serve, but inside workhouses, or bound with chains.'[77] By contrast, a captive who makes a pact to serve has the confidence of his master, 'by which the master leaves him in corporeal liberty, to the extent that unless there had intervened an obligation and the bonds of pact, he could not only run away, but even kill his master'.[78] In these neighbouring passages, the phrases 'natural liberty' and 'corporeal liberty' are being used in the same way: 'natural liberty' is being understood as that liberty which is natural, where 'natural' is equivalent to 'corporeal'.

Returning to the definition of liberty in Chapter 9, Hobbes here goes on to hold that motion can be hindered by impediments other than 'the external and absolute', namely 'arbitrary' impediments which only count as such because of the operation of our choice: nothing impedes our jumping off the side of a ship except that we cannot possibly wish to do so.[79] More or less absence of these is also more or less liberty: but a liberty implicitly only predicable of things possessing *arbitrium*. 'And in this consists civil liberty. For no one, be he subject, or son, or slave, is so impeded by penalties proposed by the city, father, or master, however severe, that he cannot do ... all the things which are necessary for safeguarding his life and health.'[80]

Civil liberty here is therefore that sphere in which people can act at will, without fear of punishment; and Hobbes' point, in reply to those who complain about the absence of such liberty, is that in whatsoever dominion, there is always enough to allow the subject to

[77] Ibid., pp. 160–1: 'Non omnis bello captus, cuius vitæ parcitum est, pacisci cum domino intelligitur, quia non omni ita creditur, ut relinquatur ei tantum libertatis naturalis, ut vel aufugere, vel ministerium detrectare, vel machinari *domino* malum aut damnum aliquod, si cupiat, possit. Et serviunt quidem hi, sed intra ergastula, vel compedibus vincti.'
[78] Ibid., p. 161: '[fiducia] qua *Dominus* eum in libertate corporali relinquit, ita ut nisi intervenissent obligatio, & vincula pactitia, non modo aufugere, sed etiam *Dominum* ... vitâ spoliare possit'.
[79] Ibid., p. 167.
[80] Ibid.: 'Atque in hoc consistit *libertas* civilis; nemo enim sive *subditus*, sive *filius* familias, sive *servus*, ita *civitatis* vel *patris* vel *Domini* sui, utcunque severi, poenis propositis impeditur, quin omnia facere ... possit, quae ad vitam et sanitatem suam tuendam sunt necessaria.'

live a human life. This liberty is not corporeal liberty; but neither is it the remnants of natural liberty in the jurists' sense. For as we saw above, it is one of Hobbes' cardinal tenets that factors which affect our deliberation, i.e. which cause us to will one way rather than the other (here, penalties attached to certain actions), do not limit natural liberty in the sense of that liberty which is ended by deliberation.

The discussion of liberty in *De cive* thus serves to confuse the clear juridical understanding of natural liberty in two ways. On the one hand, although Hobbes in this work never explicitly calls corporeal liberty 'natural liberty', there are signs that he is indeed capable of thinking of corporeal liberty as 'natural' liberty. There is some hesitation, that is, over whether natural liberty is corporeal liberty or the liberty of doing what one will. On the other hand, Hobbes further introduces into the notion of doing what one will the additional element of being free from the threat of punishment. This is equally foreign to the juristic tradition and to his own account of acting at will, which stems from that tradition. In *Leviathan*, as we shall see, Hobbes drops freedom from punishment as an element of liberty, in any signification. But *Leviathan* inherits from *De cive* the confusion over the relation between natural and corporeal liberty.

It is *Leviathan* which contains Hobbes' most explicit statements of the concept of liberty. Quentin Skinner has recently argued persuasively that the course of events in England caused Hobbes to sharpen the anti-classical definition of liberty already apparent in *De cive* in order to intervene decisively in the debate over the legitimacy of the government of the Rump.[81] Hobbes whittled down the 'proper signification of liberty' to the absence of external impediments in order to suggest that the objection to the Rump, that it had reduced England to the slavery it had experienced under the king, was misplaced. Slavery, the absence of liberty, was the state of being physically chained up, or dragged about by force. Manifestly, the Rump had not effected this state of the population of England.

If *Leviathan* is that work of Hobbes which is most concerned with and explicit about liberty, however, it is also the work which has caused most confusion as to what Hobbes understands by the term. Fundamentally, the problem is that although Hobbes appears to

---

[81] Skinner, 'Proper signification'.

define liberty purely in terms of body – as the absence of impediments to corporeal motion, as in *De cive* – he nevertheless appears to
allow impediments to liberty which are not physical: specifically, laws
and covenants.[82]

Hobbes in *Leviathan* gives the same account of deliberation as we
find in the *Elements of Law* and in *De homine*: that is, we have from the
beginning a definition of liberty as the precedent state of one whose
act is immediately voluntary. However, we first encounter a definition of 'liberty' in Chapter 14, '*Of the first and second* NATURALL LAWES,
and of CONTRACTS', where it is juxtaposed with a definition of natural
right:

> The RIGHT OF NATURE, which Writers commonly call *Jus Naturale*, is the
> Liberty each man hath, to use his own power, as he will himselfe, for the
> preservation of his own Nature; that is to say, of his own Life; and
> consequently of doing anything, which in his own Judgement, and Reason,
> hee shall conceive to be the aptest means thereunto.

> By LIBERTY, is understood, according to the proper signification of the
> word, the absence of externall Impediments; which Impediments, may oft
> take away part of a mans power to do what hee would; but cannot hinder
> him from using the power left him, according as his judgement, and reason
> shall dictate to him.[83]

This passage initially appears to suggest that natural right is liberty
in the proper signification. A closer look, however, suggests that the
two concepts do not coincide, and are not meant to do so. The right
of nature is the liberty to use one's power – i.e. to act or do – as one
wills. Liberty, properly, is the absence of external impediments,
impediments which (implicitly) are such because they diminish
power. But, Hobbes goes on, the presence of such impediments is no
hindrance on 'using the power left him, according as his judgement,
and reason shall dictate to him' – the liberty of which is, precisely,
the right of nature. So it appears that the liberty which is the right of
nature is not intrinsically damaged by physical impediments. Thus a
person in the state of nature who is, for example, tied up by another,
does not lose that liberty which is his natural right, to struggle and to

---

[82]   See, for example, the analysis by J. Roland Pennock, 'Hobbes' confusing "clarity" – the
case of "liberty"', in K. C. Brown (ed.), *Hobbes studies* (Oxford 1965), 101–16. A. G.
Wernham in the same volume, 'Liberty and obligation in Hobbes', 117–39, argues for a
differentiation between senses of 'liberty' in Hobbes, as does D. D. Raphael, 'Hobbes', in
Z. Pelczynski and J. Gray (eds.), *Conceptions of liberty in political philosophy* (London 1984),
27–38.

[83]   *Lev.*, p. 91.

escape if he can. He can still use what power is left him *as he wills* – the right of nature, *libertas naturalis*, as we have encountered it in the *Elements of Law* and *De cive*, and as we encounter it in Chapter 26 of *Leviathan*: 'the Right of Nature, that is, the naturall Liberty of man'.[84] It is the faculty of self-deliberation, and it does not cede to force. In the condition of nature, 'every man has a Right to everything; even to one anothers body':[85] but *not* 'even to one anothers will'. As Lycklama put it, 'libertatem animorum in angustum redigit belli immanitas, non extirpat'. No amount of physical violence will ever bring men out of the condition of nature: for the condition of nature is precisely that estate in which force is our only recourse.

Having established this, Hobbes goes on to describe the way out of the state of nature in the same way as in the *Elements of Law* and in *De cive*: not by restraining the body, but by deliberation through covenant, and specifically the overarching covenant that establishes the sovereign and the commonwealth. His accounts of the establishment of commonwealths bear out the distinction between corporeal liberty and natural liberty or natural right. In the case of the '*Common-wealth* by *Acquisition*', that is, 'where the Soveraign Power is acquired by Force', men singly or together submit themselves to 'that Man, or Assembly, that hath their lives and liberty in his Power', for fear.[86] Here it is not 'the Victory, that giveth the right of Dominion over the Vanquished, but his own Covenant. Nor is he obliged because he is conquered, but because he commeth in, and Submitteth to the Victor.'[87] The obligation is due to the self-deliberation of the conquered, the act of will that alters the liberty of willing, not to any act of force committed by the conqueror on the body of the conquered. The conquered covenants to obey – he obliges himself to be obliged – in return for 'his life, and the liberty of his body'.[88] That is, he agrees to the restriction of his will in exchange for the security and liberty of his body, which at the time of conquest lie as much in the conqueror's power as the liberty of his will does not. If the conqueror does not allow the conquered the security and liberty of his body, then those who are conquered 'have no obligation at all; but may break their bonds, or the prison; and kill, or carry away captive their Master, justly'.[89] All this is nothing more than what

---

[84] Ibid., p. 185.   [85] Ibid., p. 91.
[86] Ibid., Chapter 20, '*Of Dominion* PATERNALL, *and* DESPOTICALL', p. 139.
[87] Ibid., p. 141.   [88] Ibid.   [89] Ibid.

Vázquez and Lycklama had to say on the subject, and it turns on the distinction between natural liberty and corporeal liberty.

The 'Common-wealth by *Institution*' displays the same dependency on the self-deliberation to end self-deliberation of the multitude concerned:

A *Common-wealth* is said to be *Instituted*, when a *Multitude* of men do Agree, and *Covenant, every one, with every one*, that to whatsoever *Man*, or *Assembly of Men*, shall be given by the major part, the *Right* to *Present* the Person of them all ... every one ... shall *Authorise* all the Actions and Judgements, of that Man, or Assembly of men, in the same manner, as if they were his own, to the end, to live peaceably amongst themselves, and be protected against other men.[90]

In so doing they 'submit their Wills, every one to his Will, and their Judgements, to his Judgment ... as if every man should say to every man, *I Authorise and give up my Right of Governing my selfe, to this Man, or to this Assembly of men, on this condition, that thou give up thy Right to him, and Authorise all his Actions in like manner*'.[91] An individual who covenants with his fellows to establish a sovereign gives up his natural liberty or right to use his own power as he himself will – his right of governing himself – to a certain end, his own protection: just as, in considering the doctrine of the *Elements of Law*, we saw that all contract or covenant – restraint of will – is to the end to protect and enhance the life of the body.

Subjects in general are, therefore, those who have given up their 'natural liberty' or 'liberty of nature'. This is confirmed by the fact that Hobbes speaks of those who lose their subjection as returning to the 'liberty of nature'.[92] But Hobbes returns to the topic of liberty to devote a specific chapter, Chapter 21, '*Of the* LIBERTY *of Subjects*', to explaining precisely what liberty subjects can be said to have. Here his purpose is to draw a contrast between 'Liberty in the proper sense', and 'the *Liberty of Subjects*'. The general thrust will be that subjection to a common power does not diminish liberty in the proper sense.

Hobbes begins by asserting that

LIBERTY, or FREEDOME, signifieth (properly) the absence of Opposition; (by Opposition, I mean externall Impediments of motion;) and may be applyed no lesse to Irrationall, and Inanimate creatures, than to Rationall. For

---

[90] *Lev.*, p. 121. I have no space here to consider in full Hobbes' doctrine of personation and authorisation.
[91] Ibid., p. 120; italics in the original.   [92] See above, p. 210 and n. 19.

whatsoever is so tyed, or environed, as it cannot move, but within a certain space, which space is determined by the opposition of some externall body, we say it hath not liberty to go further ... But when the impediment of motion is the constitution of the thing itself, we use not to say, it wants the Liberty; but the Power to move; as when a stone lyeth still, or a man is fastned to his bed by sicknesse.[93]

He goes on to say that 'according to this proper, and generally received meaning of the word, *A* FREE-MAN, *is he, that in those things, which by his strength and wit he is able to do, is not hindred to doe what he has a will to*'.[94] Although commentators have worried about this encompassing of the liberty of unwilled and willed motion in one analysis, I cannot see that there is a problem so far. Hobbes is arguing that a thing is unfree if there exists a corporeal impediment to a course of action it would otherwise have taken. In the case of an inanimate, it would have been unable to help itself taking that course of action; in the case of an animate, that action would have been the result of an act of will. But this does not seem to affect the notion of liberty involved; and indeed Hobbes is obviously keen to stress that it does not.

What should be remarked, however, is that Hobbes in positing this single notion of liberty for both inanimates and animates presupposes that the animates are in the state of nature – specifically, that man is in the state of nature (since other animals never leave it, being incapable of contract). Formulating his definition of human freedom the way he does, man – and presumably any animate, for Hobbes insists that beasts have wills as much as men[95] – is comparable to water or stones in freedom or unfreedom only if the action externally hindered or unhindered is the result of will or deliberation: the condition of which is natural liberty. But this is not a *corporeal* condition. Hobbes is picturing liberty in the proper signification – corporeal liberty – as supervenient (or not, as the case may be) on the internal state of natural liberty and thus the faculty of deliberation or will-formation.

Natural liberty – the faculty of immediate volition – is blocked by covenant and law; corporeal liberty – liberty in the proper signification – is blocked by external physical impediments to the motion of a body in the condition of nature, which, in the case of animates, is *willed* motion. The distinction is clear: but we can see how confusion

---

[93] *Lev.*, pp. 145–6.   [94] Ibid.; italics in the original throughout.
[95] Ibid., p. 44.

could arise between them in the case of animates, for natural liberty as much as corporeal liberty constitutes the condition of their free (in the proper signification) action. An animate's being free in the proper signification involves its having its natural liberty. And Hobbes goes on, shortly afterwards, to speak of that liberty 'which only is properly called liberty' – i.e. liberty in the proper signification, corporeal liberty – as 'natural liberty': a term which everywhere else in *Leviathan* he uses for *libertas animi*, that which is lost on entering civil society. Hobbes in this chapter, having stepped out of the confines of his juristic argument, has fallen prey to a confusion over the sense of 'natural' with regard to the phrase 'natural liberty'. It is this which explains the puzzling paragraph following his definition of the free man, in which he talks of that freedom as being restrained by law and covenant: 'And therefore, when 'tis said (for example) The way is Free, no Liberty of the way is signified, but of those that walk in it without stop. And when we say a Guift is Free, there is not meant any Liberty of the Guift, but of the Giver, that was not bound by any law, or Covenant to give it. So when we *speak Freely*, it is not the liberty of the voice, or pronunciation, but of the man, whom no law hath obliged to speak otherwise than he did'[96] – even though his declared enterprise is to demonstrate that freedom is a purely corporeal condition.

Hobbes goes on to repeat his point about the relation of fear and liberty: that they are consistent (that fear does not block liberty):

Feare, and Liberty are consistent; as when a man throweth his goods into the Sea for *feare* the ship should sink, he doth it nevertheless very willingly, and may refuse to do it if he will: It is therefore the action, of one that was *free*: so a man sometimes pays his debt, only for *feare* of Imprisonment, which because no body hindred him from detaining, was the action of a man at *liberty*. And generally all actions which men doe in Common-wealths, for *feare* of the law, are actions, which the doers had *liberty* to omit.[97]

As we saw, in the *Elements of Law* this point was made in relation to natural liberty: fear, as a constituent of deliberation, does not diminish the faculty of deliberation in any way. Someone who acts through fear must have been in possession of natural liberty or

---

[96] Ibid., p. 146. I would argue that these are all examples of liberty being blocked by law, even the first, given that the discussion of *viae liberae* in the legal literature is (as we saw in the last chapter) always in relation to *libera facultas* or *naturalis libertas*, which is *facultas animi*. However, even if the relevant 'stop' is intended as corporeal, this still upholds the point with regard to Hobbes' confusion here.

[97] Ibid.

natural right, and cannot argue that he was not. Here in Chapter 21 of *Leviathan*, Hobbes makes the point refer to corporeal liberty: my fear of imprisonment or of the law does not make me any less free, because it does not constitute a corporeal and external impediment. He uses it as part of an argument designed to show that people are still at liberty – in the proper signification – even when they are subject to a commonwealth and have therefore given up natural liberty or natural right. But as his first illustration of his point shows, the fact that a person directly wills an action dictated by fear is still part of his explanation for why fear does not diminish liberty: 'he doth it nevertheless very willingly'. He thus again undermines his own argument with the suggestion that the subject of the commonwealth who obeys the law out of fear is still in possession of natural liberty or natural right – not merely of an exclusively corporeal liberty.

Hobbes follows his exposition of 'corporeal' liberty with an account of the '*Liberty* of *Subjects*'.[98] Whereas corporeal liberty is restrained only by bonds which are corporeal in nature – external impediments to motion – the liberty of subjects is restrained by 'Artificiall Chains, called *Civill Lawes*, which they themselves, by mutuall covenants, have fastned at one end, to the lips of that Man, or Assembly, to whom they have given the Soveraigne Power; and at the other end to their own Ears'.[99] Hence the liberty of subjects 'lyeth ... only in those things, which in regulating their actions, the Soveraign hath praetermitted'.[100] This formulation echoes that of *De cive*, where Hobbes talks of the progressive restriction of original liberty by natural, divine, and civil law: liberty here being the jurists' natural liberty, *libertas animi*, which is restricted by law and covenant. It also looks forward to the words of Chapter 26 of *Leviathan*, '*Of* CIVILL LAWES': 'the Right of Nature, that is, the naturall Liberty of man, may by the Civill Law be abridged, and restrained: nay, the end of making Lawes, is no other, but such Restraint; without the which there cannot be any Peace'.[101] Hence civil law, the constraint on the will, restrains natural liberty in the sense of the liberty of deliberation. The constraint is artificial; but the remaining liberty is not artificial, but natural. A solid core of this natural liberty is always retained by a subject with regard to those actions, even if they be commanded by the sovereign, which directly threaten their corporeal

---

[98] Ibid., p. 147.   [99] Ibid.   [100] Ibid., p. 148.   [101] Ibid., p. 185.

security or liberty: for the sake of safeguarding which they made the original covenant – gave access to their will – in the first place.[102] Otherwise, the amount of natural liberty remaining is at the discretion of the sovereign.

The overall intention of Chapter 21 is clear. Hobbes wants to argue that subjects are possessed entirely of their corporeal liberty, and retain their natural liberty – the right of governing themselves, of using their power as *they* see fit – over a range of actions about which the law is silent. That is, he wants to argue that subjects retain their corporeal liberty to act (which they value) even when they have lost their natural liberty to do so. But his argument is confused because this is something his own definition of liberty in the proper signification will not allow. For the argument to work, he would have had to have kept to the definition of liberty (*per se*) in the *De cive*, where it signifies the pure absence of physical impediments to any kind of motion – immediately willed or not. But that definition lacks the rhetorical appeal of the definition in *Leviathan*. Hobbes wants to show both that liberty in the proper signification is something subjects do not lose in civil society *and* that it is something that they value and recognise as being liberty (Hobbes stresses that he is referring to 'the proper, and generally received meaning of the word'); and ordinary people would not necessarily be persuaded by the argument that they have a fair degree of a freedom they value and recognise as such if they are in a large prison. Hobbes' own words suggest that the ordinary people he was concerned with would have defined liberty as something which lets a person do what he will, and is valuable as such. Hobbes is therefore led to cloud his argument for liberty in the proper signification with the inclusion of the mention of the will. It is this which allows him to slide into using the term 'natural liberty' for his 'liberty in the proper signification', and to transfer the very powerful argument concerning fear from being a point about the liberty of deliberation to being one about liberty in the proper signification or 'corporeal' liberty.

However, Hobbes' failure completely to separate out corporeal liberty from natural liberty entails that the account of political obligation in *Leviathan* encounters the same difficulties as the original account in the *Elements of Law*. Hobbes is sure, in *Leviathan*, that although subjects are obliged by the law or 'artificial bonds', the

---

[102] Ibid., pp. 150–2.

majority will only obey out of fear: 'These Bonds in their own nature but weak, may neverthelesse be made to hold, by the danger, though not by the difficulty of breaking them.'[103] If there is no apparent danger, there is every likelihood of 'potent men' 'breaking through the Cob-web Lawes of their Country':[104] that is, using their power as they themselves will, or governing themselves. According to the overt arguments of Chapter 21, the explanation for this is that although they are not possessed of natural liberty, they nevertheless retain corporeal liberty. But if they had really given up natural liberty, they would already be deliberated on obeying the law. Hobbesian subjects who obey the law only out of fear, or who break through it, are still in possession of their natural liberty because they still have the liberty of deliberating themselves. If the force of civil laws comes only from fear of punishment, then, despite Hobbes' language, laws are not bonds in any sense whatsoever (not even 'weak' bonds): they are not corporeal bonds, which is the point he wants to make in Chapter 21; but neither do they constitute obligations. If Hobbes' commonwealth functions only on fear, it is a state of natural liberty.

In fact, Hobbes insists that no commonwealth can ever be fixed against the return to nature if force is the only thing driving people to keep the laws. The grounds of the sovereign's rights

have the rather need to be diligently, and truly taught; because they cannot be maintained by any Civill Law, or terrour of legall punishment. For a Civill Law, that shall forbid Rebellion ... is not (as a Civill Law) any obligation, but by vertue onely of the Law of Nature, that forbiddeth the violation of Faith; which naturall obligation if men know not, they cannot know the Right of any Law the Soveraign maketh. And for the Punishment, they take it but for an act of Hostility; which when they think they have strength enough, they will endeavour by acts of Hostility, to avoyd.[105]

Subjects have to be brought to realise that they have lost their natural liberty through their agreement to the conditions of civil society. There are consequently certain matters – those set out in the laws of the commonwealth – about which they must realise that they are already deliberated as subjects of that commonwealth. It is that recognition alone which will take them out of the state of nature. Terrorised subjects who look upon the power of the commonwealth as an enemy to be confounded have slipped back into natural liberty ('relabi in libertatem naturalem') and are deliberating as in the state of nature.

[103] Ibid., p. 147.   [104] Ibid., p. 204.   [105] Ibid., p. 232.

Thus, in the end, the emphasis on fear as the means of maintaining a commonwealth turns out, on Hobbes' own admission, to be misplaced. Instead, the people must be taught the content of the law of nature, that is, justice. Discussing the difference between the just and the unjust man, Hobbes argues that

> a Righteous man, does not lose that Title, by one, or a few unjust Actions, that proceed from sudden Passion, or mistake of Things, or Persons: nor does an Unrighteous man, lose his character, for such actions as he does, or forbeares to do, for feare: because his Will is not framed by the Justice, but by the apparent benefit of what he is to do. That which gives to humane Actions the relish of Justice, is a certain Noblenesse or Gallantnesse of courage, (rarely found), by which a man scorns to be beholding for the contentment of his life, to fraud, or breach of promise.[106]

The unjust man 'does, or forbeares to do', for fear: the formula of doing or forbearing belongs to the definition of natural right or natural liberty.[107] The will in question is the act of will which immediately precedes action, and such an act of will implies that the unjust man is in possession of natural liberty. For Hobbes in *Leviathan*, there can only be a commonwealth secure against this nature if subjects can be brought to recognise that they are obliged by covenants, and on those grounds to keep them: that is, to admit themselves a restraint of their natural liberty, and thus to act justly. But this is *virtue*, which if the subjects possess or come to possess, the rationale for the Hobbesian sovereign is gone.[108] At this point a Vázquez would hail the return of the golden age of civic heroes, and an end to the purely contingent necessity of political subjection.

For all their differences, Vázquez and Hobbes both belong to the same tradition of subjective right. This right is primarily the natural

---

[106] Ibid., p. 104. These undeniably 'deontological' aspects of Hobbes' thought were brought out by A. E. Taylor in his classic article, 'The ethical doctrine of Hobbes' (*Philosophy* 13 (1938), 406–24), even if the sense of what he said has been distorted by the not altogether appropriate association of his thesis with that of Howard Warrender. But that there is a 'deontological' aspect to Hobbes' moral theory does not mean that there is a 'Kantian' aspect: for as we have seen, Hobbes has been very careful to tie the notion of obligation to the process of deliberation through appetite, and therefore to the human animal's desire for self-preservation. See the remarks in David Boonin-Vail, *Thomas Hobbes and the science of moral virtue* (Cambridge 1994), pp. 92–114.

[107] *Lev.*, p. 91.

[108] See R. E. Ewin, *Virtues and rights: The moral philosophy of Thomas Hobbes* (Boulder, Colo. and Oxford 1991), who argues that Hobbes is essentially a virtues theorist, and, in the conclusion, that if people have enough of the Hobbesian virtues, they do not need the Hobbesian sovereign.

liberty of a person to do what he will: a liberty which is restricted but not entirely eliminated by the invention of the commonwealth or political power. For both authors, this right is of the essence of animate as opposed to inanimate nature. As such, Vázquez refuses to call the liberty of the state of nature a right at all: it is rather a fact. His account of the rise of principate and jurisdiction shows how among men alone the fact of liberty has become the limited right of *dominium*. But its essential character as fact is reflected in the fact that its exercise is free, not regulated by right; and it stands in opposition to the power of principate, which is artificial and restrictive of nature. Hobbes' natural liberty is similarly this *ius absolutum*, the free faculty of will. Like Vázquez's natural liberty, it is in part surrendered to a commonwealth which is an 'Artificiall Man' offering an artificial order. Both theories display the distinctive mark of this type of natural rights theory, its characteristic divorce of the political structure from the nature of man. It is this which sets it apart from the natural rights theory of the later Aristotelian tradition, wherein rights are integrated in the teleology of human life, of which the city is also a part. The right of the city absorbs its citizens' right to the extent that citizenship by itself fulfils human nature. To the extent that it does not, the city must leave the citizen his own proper right and his proper liberty. But that liberty is never threatened by the true political commonwealth, because it is part of human nature which the polity by nature promotes. By contrast, citizenship of a commonwealth does not realise but restricts the nature of Hobbesian man, that is, his right or natural liberty.

The conclusion of this survey, then, is that by the middle of the sixteenth century two very different natural rights idioms were already in place. They were to have varied fortunes. The Vázquezian tradition faltered after Hobbes and has always provoked mixed reactions among political theorists of a broadly liberal cast; but its distinctive appeal has never been entirely overlooked. By contrast, the later Aristotelian tradition continued to be developed in the seventeenth century through the work of Francisco Suárez and others, but has been rejected by modern political Aristotelians who remain opposed to the language of rights and the primacy of justice. Perhaps the time has come for a corresponding reawakening of interest in the Aristotelian politics of such thinkers as Soto, for whom the issue of the relations between individuals and commonwealth cannot but be a question 'of justice and right'.

Bibliography of works cited

PRIMARY SOURCES

Almain, Jacques, *Aurea opuscula*. Paris 1518.
Clarissimi doctoris ... Iacobi Almain ... a decimaquarta distinctione questiones Scoti profitentis, perutilis admodum lectura. Paris 1526 [*In IV Sent.*].
Quaestio resumptiva agitata in vesperiis ... de dominio naturali, civili et ecclesiastico, in Ellies du Pin (ed.), *Joannis Gersonis opera omnia*. Vol. II, cols. 961–76. Antwerp 1706.
Tractatus de auctoritate ecclesiae et conciliorum generalium adversus Thomam de Vio, in Ellies du Pin (ed.), *Joannis Gersonis opera omnia*. Vol. II, cols. 976–1012. Antwerp 1706.
Angelus de Clavasio, *Summa angelica*. Nuremberg 1488.
Antoninus Florentinus, *Summa [Antonina]*. Basel 1518.
Aquinas, Thomas, *De perfectione spiritualis vitae*, ed. in *Sancti Thomae de Aquino. Opera omnia iussu Leonis XIII P. M. edita, cura et studio Fratrum Praedicatorum*. Vol. XLI, parts B–C, 67–111. Rome 1969.
Sententia libri ethicorum, in *Sancti Thomae de Aquino. Opera omnia iussu Leonis XIII P. M. edita, cura et studio Fratrum Praedicatorum*. Vol. XLVII. Rome 1969.
Summa theologiae, Editio altera romana (Leonina). Rome 1894 [*ST*].
Aristotle, *Categoriae et liber de Interpretatione*, ed. by L. Minuo-Paluello. Oxford 1949.
Ethica Nicomachea, ed. by I. Bywater. Oxford 1894 [*NE*].
Politica, ed. by W. D. Ross. Oxford 1957.
Astesanus de Asti, *Summa de casibus conscientiae*. Nuremberg 1482.
St Augustine, *De trinitate libri XV*, ed. by W. J. Mountain. Vol. I, Books I–XII. Turnholt 1968.
Aureol, Peter. 'Le Quolibet de Nicholas a Lyre, OFM', ed. by E. Longpré (falsely attributed to Nicholas of Lyra), *Archivum Franciscanum Historicum* 23 (1930), 42–56.
Balbus, Johannes Franciscus, *Tractatus de praescriptionibus*. Cologne 1573.
Barbazza, Andrea, *Consilia*. N.p. 1517.
Bartolus of Sassoferrato, *In universum ius civile commentaria*. Vol. II. Basel 1562.
Bertachinus, Johannes, *Lexicon utriusque iuris*. Venice 1518–19.

Boemus, Johann, *Omnium gentium mores, leges et ritus*. Paris 1538.
Bonagratia de Bergamo, *Tractatus de paupertate Christi et apostolorum*, ed. by L. Oliger, *Archivum Franciscanum Historicum* 22 (1929), 292–335 and 487–511.
St Bonaventure, *Apologia pauperum*, in *Opera omnia edita cura et studio pp. collegii a S. Bonaventura*. Vol. viii, Opusculum xi. Quaracchi 1897.
In secundum sententiarum commentarius, in *Opera omnia edita cura et studio pp. collegii a S. Bonaventura*. Vol. ii. Quaracchi 1882.
Buridan, John, *Questiones super decem libros ethicorum Aristotelis ad Nicomachum*. Paris 1513.
Cagnolus, Hieronymus, *In constitutiones et leges primi, secundi, quinti et duodecimi Pandectarum . . . aurearum enarrationum Liber primus*. Venice 1561.
Omnium legum tituli ff. de regulis iuris copiosa interpretatio. Lyons 1546.
Cajetanus, Thomas de Vio, *Quaestiones quodlibetales cum aliquot assertionibus contra Lutheranos*. Paris 1530.
Secunda secundae summae theologiae cum commentariis Thomae de Vio Caietani O. P. Venice 1593.
Capreolus, Johannes, *Defensiones theologiae divi Thomae Aquinatis*, ed. by C. Paban and T. Pègues. Vol. ii. Tours 1900. Reprinted Frankfurt a. M. 1967.
Coke, Roger, *Justice vindicated from the False Fucus put upon it, by T. White Gent., Mr. T. Hobbs, and H. Grotius. As also Elements of power and subjection*. London 1660.
Covarruvias (y Leyva), Diego de, *De Regula possessoria malae fidei*, in *Opera omnia*. Vol. i. Frankfurt 1592.
Practicarum quaestionum liber unus, in *Opera omnia*. Vol. ii. Frankfurt 1592.
Cravetta, Aymon de, *Tractatus de antiquitate temporis*. Venice 1549.
Decius, Philippus, *In tit. ff. de regulis iuris*. Lyons 1553.
Durandus a Sancto Porciano, *In quattuor sententiarum libros questiones*. Paris 1508.
Fitzralph, Richard, *De pauperie salvatoris I–IV*, ed. by R. Lane Poole as Appendix to Wyclif, *De dominio divino*.
St Francis of Assisi, *Regula II Fratrum minorum (Regula bullata)*, in *Opuscula sancti patris Francisci Assisiensis. Edita cura et studio P.P. collegii St. Bonaventurae*, 63–74. Quaracchi 1904.
Gallensis, Johannes, *Communiloquium sive summa collationum*. Wakefield 1964. Original edn, Jordanns de Quedlinburg, Strasburg 1489.
Garcia, Fortunius, *De ultimo fine iuris canonici et civilis*, ed. in *Tractatus illustrium iurisconsultorum*. Vol. i, fols. 105r–132v. Venice 1584–6.
Gerson, Jean, *De passionibus animae*, in *Jean Gerson. Oeuvres complètes*, ed. by P. Glorieux. Vol. ix, 1–25. Paris 1973.
De potestate ecclesiastica, in *Jean Gerson. Oeuvres complètes*, ed. by P. Glorieux. Vol. vi, 210–50. Paris 1965 [*DPE*].
De vita spirituali animae, in *Jean Gerson. Oeuvres complètes*, ed. by P. Glorieux. Vol. iii, 113–202. Paris 1965 [*DVSA*].

Definitiones terminorum theologiae moralis, in *Jean Gerson. Oeuvres complètes*, ed. by P. Glorieux. Vol. IX, 133–42. Paris 1973.

Godfrey of Fontaines, *Quodlibet V*, ed. in M. de Wulf and J. Hoffmans, *Les quodlibets cinq, six et sept de Godefroid de Fontaines*. Louvain 1914.

Grotius, Hugo, *De iure belli ac pacis libri tres*. Paris 1625.

    De iure praedae commentarius, trans. by G. L. Williams. Oxford 1950.

Guerrero, Alphonsus, *Thesaurus christianae religionis*. Venice 1559.

Henry of Gorkum, *Questiones in Sanctum Thomam*. Esslingen n.d.

    Tractatus consultatorii. Cologne 1503.

Henry Totting of Oyta, *Tractatus de contractibus*. Paris 1506.

Hobbes, Thomas, *De cive*, ed. by H. Warrender. Oxford 1983.

    De homine, in *Opera philosophica quae latine scripsit omnia*, ed. by W. Molesworth. Vol. II. London 1839.

    The Elements of Law, ed. by F. Tönnies, 2nd edn with introduction by M. M. Goldsmith. London 1969 [*EL*].

    Leviathan, in *Opera philosophica quae latine scripsit omnia*, ed. by W. Molesworth. Vol. III. London 1841 [*Lev. latine*].

    Leviathan, ed. by R. Tuck. Cambridge 1991 [*Lev.*].

Isidore of Seville, *Etymologiarum libri*. 2 vols. Vol. I, *I–X*, ed. by W. M. Lindsay. Oxford 1911.

Jandun, John of, *Super libros Aristotelis de anima*. Venice 1561.

Javellus, Chrysostomus, *Opera philosophica*. Lyons 1580.

Köllin, Konrad, *Quodlibeta*. Cologne 1523.

Ledesma, Martin, *Secunda quartae*. Coimbra 1560.

Liber de causis, ed. by A. Pattin, *Tijdschrift voor Filosofie* 28 (1966), 90–203.

Lycklama, Marcus, *Membranarum iuris libri septem*. Leuwaarden 1644.

Mair, John, *In quartum Sententiarum*. Paris 1519.

Marino da Caramanico, Proem to the *Liber constitutionum* of Frederick II, ed. as Appendix to F. Calasso, *I glossatori e la teoria della sovranità*. 3rd edn, Milan 1957.

Marsilius of Padua, *Defensor pacis*, ed. by R. Scholz. Hanover 1932.

Maynus, Jason, *In primam (secundam) Infortiati partem commentaria*. Lyons 1542.

Mazzolini da Prierio, Sylvester, *Summa summarum quae sylvestrina nuncupatur*. Strasburg 1518.

Nédellec, Hervé de, *De paupertate Christi et apostolorum*, ed. by J. G. Sikes, *Archives d'histoire doctrinale et littéraire du moyen âge* 11 (1937–8), 209–97.

Ockham, William of, *Opus nonaginta dierum*, in J. G. Sikes and H. S. Offler (eds.), *Guillelmi de Ockham. Opera politica*. Vols. I–II. 2nd edn, Manchester 1963 [*OND*].

    Quaestiones in II librum Sententiarum I–XX, in *Opera philosophica et theologica: Opera theologica V*. St Bonaventure, N. Y. 1981.

    Quaestiones in librum tertium Sententiarum (Reportatio), in *Opera philosophica et theologica: Opera theologica VI*. St Bonaventure, N. Y. 1982.

    Quodlibeta septem, in *Opera philosophica et theologica: Opera theologica IX*. St Bonaventure, N. Y. 1980.

Odo, Geraldus, *Sententia et expositio cum questionibus ... super libros ethicorum Aristotelis cum textu eiusdem.* ?Venice ?1500.

Olivi, Peter John, *Quaestio quid ponat ius vel dominium,* ed. by F. Delorme, in 'Question de P. J. Olivi, *Quid ponat ius vel dominium* ou encore *De signis voluntariis', Antonianum* 20 (1945), 309–30.

Palacios, Miguel de, *Praxis theologica de contractibus et restitutionibus.* Salamanca 1585.

Paris de Puteo, *Tractatus de syndicatu omnium officialium,* in *Tractatus universi iuris.* Vol. II, fols. 335–445. Lyons 1549.

Pecham, John, *Tractatus pauperis,* ed. by A. G. Little, in C. L. Kingsford, A. G. Little, F. Tocco (eds.), *Pecham de paupertate,* 13–90. Aberdeen 1910.

Raymund of Peñafort, *Summa de poenitentia et matrimonio cum glossis Ioannis de Friburgo.* Farnborough, Hants., 1967. Facsimile of Rome 1603 edn.

Rijkel, Denis (Carthusianus), *Creaturarum in ordine ad Deum consideratio theologica,* in *Opera omnia.* Vol. XXXIV, 99–221. Montreuil 1896–1913.

Summa de vitiis et virtutibus, in *Opera omnia.* Vol. XXXIX, 7–242. Montreuil 1896–1913.

Scotus, Johannes Duns, *Opera omnia editio nova. Juxta editionem Waddingi ... a patribus franciscanis de observantia accurate recognita.* Vols. X, XII and XVIII. Paris 1893–4.

Quaestiones super libris Aristotelis de anima, ed. by H. Cavellus. Lyons 1625.

Soto, Domingo de, *De iustitia et iure libri decem.* Madrid 1967. Facsimile of Salamanca 1556.

In quartum sententiarum librum commentarii. Salamanca 1566–79.

Summenhart, Conrad, *Septipertitum opus de contractibus pro foro conscientie atque theologico.* Hagenau 1515.

Tiraqueau, André, *Tractatus de praescriptionibus,* in *Opera omnia.* Vol. VI, 52–80. Frankfurt 1616.

Tudeschis, Nicolaus de, *Super tertio decretalium.* Lyons 1534.

Vázquez de Menchaca, Fernando, *Controversiarum illiustrium usuque frequentium libri tres.* Frankfurt 1572.

De successionibus et ultimis voluntatibus. Frankfurt 1610.

Virgil, *Georgics,* in *P. Vergili Maronis Opera,* ed. by R. A. B. Mynors. Oxford 1969.

Vitoria, Francisco de, *Comentario al Tratado de la Ley (I–II, 90–108),* ed. by V. Beltrán de Heredia. Madrid 1952.

Comentarios a la secunda secundae de Santo Tomás, ed. by V. Beltrán de Heredia. Salamanca 1934 [*Comm ST* (V)].

Francisco de Vitoria: Political writings, ed. by A. Pagden and J. Lawrance. Cambridge 1991.

Relectio De potestate civili, ed. in T. Urdanoz, *Obras de Francisco de Vitoria,* 149–95. Madrid 1960.

Wesembecius, Matthaeus, *Paratitla in Pandectas iuris civilis.* Basel 1568.

Wyclif, John, *De civili dominio,* ed. by R. Lane Poole. London 1885.

De dominio divino libri tres, ed. by R. Lane Poole. London 1890.

Zanardus, Michael, O. P., *Commentaria cum quaestionibus in tres libros Aristotelis de anima*. Venice 1616.

SECONDARY SOURCES

André-Vincent, P., *Droit des indiens et développement en Amérique latine*. Paris 1971.

Aubert, J.-M., *Le droit romain dans l'oeuvre de saint Thomas*. Paris 1955.

Augé, G., 'Compte rendu de P. André-Vincent, "Droit des indiens et développement en Amérique latine"', *Archives de la philosophie du droit* 18 (1973), 438–43.

Barcia Trelles, C., 'Fernando Vázquez de Menchaca. L'école espagnole du droit international du XVIe siècle', *Recueil des Cours* 1 (1939), 433–533.

Barry, B., 'Warrender and his critics', in J. Lively and A. Reeve (eds.), *Modern political theory from Hobbes to Marx: Key debates*, 40–62. London and New York 1982. Originally published in *Philosophy* 42 (1968).

Bastit, M., *La naissance de la loi moderne. La pensée de la loi de saint Thomas à Suárez*. Paris 1990.

Beer, M., *Dionysius des Kartäusers Lehre vom desiderium naturale des Menschen nach der Gottesschau*. Munich 1963.

Beltrán de Heredia, V., 'El maestro Domingo de Soto, Catedrático de Vísperas en la Universidad de Salamanca', *Ciencia tomista* 57 (1938), 38–67, 281–302.

'El maestro Domingo de Soto en la controversia de Las Casas con Sepúlveda', *Ciencia tomista* 45 (1932), 35–49.

'El maestro Domingo (Francisco) de Soto en la Universidad de Alcalá', *Ciencia tomista* 43 (1931), 357–573; 44 (1931), 28–51.

Bergfeld, C., 'Katholische Moraltheologie und Naturrechtslehre', in H. Coing (ed.), *Handbuch der Quellen und Literatur der neueren europäischen Privatrechtsgeschichte*. Vol. II/1, 999–1033. Munich 1977.

Bierbaum, M., *Bettelorden und Weltgeistlichkeit an der Universität Paris. Texte und Untersuchungen zum literarischen Armuts- und Exemtionsstreit des 13. Jahrhunderts (1255–1272)*. Münster i. W. 1920.

Black, A., *Guilds and civil society in European political thought from the twelfth century to the present*. London 1984.

'The individual and society', in J. H. Burns (ed.), *The Cambridge history of medieval political thought, c. 350–c. 1450*, 588–606. Cambridge 1988.

Boonin-Vail, D., *Thomas Hobbes and the science of moral virtue*. Cambridge 1994.

Borschberg, P., *Hugo Grotius' 'Commentarius in Theses XI': An early treatise on sovereignty, the just war, and the legitimacy of the Dutch Revolt*. Bern 1994.

Bösl, K., 'Potens und pauper. Begriffsgeschichtliche Studien zur gesellschaftlichen Differenzierung im frühen Mittelalter und zum "Pauperismus" des Hochmittelalters', in *Alteuropa und die moderne Gesellschaft. Festschrift für Otto Brünner*, 60–87. Göttingen 1963.

Bourke, V. J., 'The *Nicomachean Ethics* and Thomas Aquinas', in A. A. Maurer (ed.-in-chief), *St Thomas Aquinas, 1274–1974: Commemorative studies*, 2 vols., vol. I, 239–59. Toronto 1974.

Boyle, L. E., 'The *Summa confessorum* of John of Freiburg and the popularization of the moral teaching of St Thomas Aquinas and some of his contemporaries', in A. A. Maurer (ed.-in-chief), *St Thomas Aquinas, 1274–1974: Commemorative studies*, 2 vols., vol. II, 245–68. Toronto 1974.

'Summae confessorum', in *Les genres littéraires dans les sources théologiques et philosophiques médiévales. Actes du Colloque international de Louvain-la-Neuve, 25–7 mai 1981*, 227–37. Louvain-la-Neuve 1982.

Bréjon, J., *André Tiraqueau (1488–1558)*. Paris 1937.

Broc, N., *La géographie de la renaissance, 1420–1560*. Paris 1986.

Brown, D. C., *Pastor and laity in the theology of Jean Gerson*. Cambridge 1987.

Brufau Prats, J., *La escuela de Salamanca ante el descubrimiento del nuevo mundo*. Salamanca 1989.

'La noción analógica del *dominium* en Santo Tomás, Francisco de Vitoria y Domingo de Soto', *Salmanticensis* 4 (1957), 96–136. Now reprinted in Brufau Prats, *La escuela de Salamanca*, 11–47.

El pensamiento político de Domingo de Soto y su concepción de poder. Salamanca 1960.

'La revisión de la primera generación de la escuela', in *La ética en la conquista de América: Francisco de Vitoria y la Escuela de Salamanca*, 383–412. Madrid 1984.

Burger, C., *Aedificatio, fructus, utilitas: Johannes Gerson als Professor und Kanzler der Universität Paris*. Tübingen 1986.

Burns, J. H., 'Jacques Almain on *Dominium*: A neglected text', in A. E. Bakos (ed.), *Politics, ideology and law in early modern Europe: Essays in honor of J. H. M. Salmon*, 149–58. Rochester, N. Y. 1994.

'*Jus gladii* and *jurisdictio*: Jacques Almain and John Locke', *Historical Journal* 26, 2 (1983), 369–74.

Lordship, kingship and empire: The idea of monarchy, 1400–1525. Oxford 1992.

'Scholasticism: Survival and revival', in Burns (ed.), *The Cambridge history of political thought, 1450–1700*, 132–55. Cambridge 1991.

Burr, D., 'Poverty as a constituent element in Olivi's thought', in D. Flood (ed.), *Poverty in the middle ages*, 71–8. Werl i. W. 1975.

Burrows, M. S., *Jean Gerson and 'De consolatione theologiae' (1418)*. Tübingen 1991.

Calasso, F., *I glossatori e la teoria della sovranità*. 3rd edn, Milan 1957.

Capitani, O. (ed.), *Una economia politica nel medioevo*. Bologna 1987.

Carro, V., *Domingo de Soto y su doctrina jurídica*. Madrid 1943.

La Teología y los teólogos-juristas españoles ante de la conquista de América. Madrid 1944.

Castilla Urbano, F., *El pensamiento de Francisco de Vitoria. Filosofía política e indio americano*. Barcelona 1992.

Coing, H., 'Zur Eigentumslehre des Bartolus', *Zeitschrift der Savigny-Stiftung für Rechtsgeschichte (Römische Abteilung)* 70 (1953), 348–71.

'Zur Geschichte des Begriffs "subjektives Recht"', in Coing, F. H. Lawson and K. Grönfors (eds.), *Das subjektives Recht und der Rechtschutz der Persönlichkeit*. Frankfurt a. M. 1959.

Coleman, J., 'Property and poverty', in J. H. Burns (ed.), *The Cambridge history of medieval political thought, c. 350–c. 1450*, 607–48. Cambridge 1988.

Combes, A., *Jean Gerson commentateur dionysien. Les 'Notulae super quaedam verba Dionysii de Caelesti hierarchia'. Texte inédit*. Paris 1940.

Congar, Y., 'Aspects ecclésiologiques de la querelle entre mendiants et séculiers dans la seconde moitié du XIIIe siècle et le début du XIVe', *Archives d'histoire doctrinale et littéraire du Moyen Age* 36 (1961–2), 35–151.

Connolly, J. L., *Jean Gerson: Reformer and mystic*. Louvain 1928.

Courtenay, W. J., 'Nominalism and late medieval religion', in Trinkaus and Oberman, *Pursuit of holiness*, 26–59.

'Nominalism and late medieval thought', in Courtenay (ed.), *Covenant and causality in medieval thought*, essay XII. London 1984.

Couvreur, G., 'Les pauvres ont-ils des droits? Recherches sur le vol en cas d'extrême nécessité depuis la Concordia de Gratien (1140) jusqu'à Guillaume d'Auxerre (?1231)', *Analecta gregoriana* 111. Rome 1961.

Crowe, M. B., *The changing profile of natural law*. The Hague 1977.

'St Thomas and Ulpian's natural law', in A. A. Maurer (ed.-in-chief), *St Thomas Aquinas, 1274–1974: Commemorative studies*, 2 vols., vol. 1, 261–82. Toronto 1974.

Dagger, R., 'Rights', in T. Ball, J. Farr and R. Hanson (eds.), *Political innovation and conceptual change*, 292–308. Cambridge 1989.

Damiata, M., *Guglielmo d'Ockham. Povertà e potere*. Vol. 1, *Il problema della povertà evangelica e francescana nel secolo XIII e XIV. Origine del pensiero politico di Guglielmo d'Ockham*. Florence 1978.

Darwall, S., *The British moralists and the internal ought: 1640–1740*. Cambridge 1995.

Dawson, J. D., 'Richard Fitzralph and the fourteenth-century poverty controversies', *Journal of Ecclesiastical History* 34 (1983), 315–44.

Deckers, D., *Gerechtigkeit und Recht. Eine historisch-kritische Untersuchung der Gerechtigkeitslehre des Francisco de Vitoria (1483–1546)*. Freiburg 1992.

Dekkers, R., *Bibliotheca belgica juridica*. Brussels 1951.

Dietterle, J., 'Die Summae confessorum (sive de casibus conscientiae) von ihren Anfängen bis zu Silvester Prierias', *Zeitschrift für Kirchengeschichte* 24 (1903), 353–74, 520–48; 25 (1904), 248–72; 26 (1905), 59–81; 27 (1906), 70–83, 166–88; 28 (1907), 401–31.

Dumont, L., *Essays on individualism*. Chicago 1986.

Ehrle, F., *Der Sentenzenkommentar Peters von Candia des Pisaner Papstes Alexanders V*. Münster i. W. 1925.

Eßer, K., 'Die Armutsauffassung des Hl. Franziskus', in D. Flood (ed.), *Poverty in the middle ages*, 60–70. Wern i. W. 1975.

Ewin, R., *Virtues and rights: The moral philosophy of Thomas Hobbes*. Boulder, Colo. and Oxford 1991.

Farrell, W., O. P., *The natural moral law according to St Thomas and Suárez*. Ditchling 1930.

Feenstra, R., 'Der Eigentumsbegriff bei Hugo Grotius im Licht einiger mittelalterlicher und spätscholastiker Quellen', in O. Behrends (ed.), *Festschrift für Franz Wieacker zum 70. Geburtstag*, 209–34. Göttingen 1978.

Fernández-Santamaria, J. A., *The state, war and peace: Spanish political thought in the Renaissance, 1516–1559*. Cambridge 1977.

Ferraro, D., *Itinerari del volontarismo. Teologia e politica al tempo di Luis de León*. Milan 1995.

Finnis, J., *Natural law and natural rights*, Oxford 1980.

'Un ouvrage récent sur Bentham', *Archives de la philosophie du droit* 17 (1972), 423–7.

Finnis, J. (ed.), *Natural law*. Aldershot, Hants. 1991.

Finnis, J. and G. Grisez, 'The basic principles of natural law: A reply to Ralph McInerny', reprinted in Finnis, *Natural law*. Vol. 1, 341–51. Originally published in *American Journal of Jurisprudence* 26 (1981), 21–31.

Gágner, S., 'Vorbemerkungen zum Thema "dominium" bei Ockham', in *Antiqui et moderni. Traditionsbewußtsein und Fortschrittsbewußtsein im späten Mittelalter*, 293–327. Berlin and New York 1974.

Gauthier, R. A. and J. Y. Jolif, *L'Ethique à Nicomaque. Introduction, traduction et commentaire*. Vol. 1. Louvain 1958.

Gerz-von Büren, V. *La tradition de l'oeuvre de Jean Gerson chez les Chartreux. La Chartreuse de Bâle*. Paris 1973.

Gilbert, N. W., 'Ockham, Wyclif and the "Via moderna"', in *Antiqui et moderni. Traditionsbewußtsein und Fortschrittsbewußtsein im späten Mittelalter*, 85–125. Berlin and New York 1974.

Gilson, E., *Jean Duns Scot. Introduction à ses positions fondamentales*. Paris 1952. *La philosophie au moyen âge*. 2nd edn, Paris 1944.

Glorieux, P., 'Les polémiques "contra Geraldinos": Les pièces du dossier', *Recherches de théologie ancienne et médiévale* 6 (1934), 5–41.

Goldsmith, M. M., 'Hobbes on liberty', *Hobbes Studies* 2 (1989), 23–39.

Grabmann, M., 'Einzelgestalten aus der mittelalterlichen Dominikaner- und Thomistenschule. 6: Die Stellung des Kardinals Cajetan in der Geschichte des Thomismus und der Thomistenschule', in Grabmann, *Mittelalterliches Geistesleben*. Vol. II, 602–13. Munich 1936.

'Das Naturrecht in der Scholastik von Gratian bis Thomas von Aquin', in Grabmann, *Mittelalterliches Geistesleben*. Vol. I, 65–103. Munich 1926.

Grossi, P., 'La proprietà nel sistema privatistico della seconda scolastica', in Grossi (ed.), *La seconda scolastica nella formazione del diritto privato moderno. Incontro di studi*, 117–222. Milan 1973.

'*Usus facti*. La nozione di proprietà nell'inaugurazione dell'età nuova', *Quaderni fiorentini* 1 (1972), 287–355.

Gwynn, A., *The English Austin friars in the time of Wycliff*. Oxford 1940.

Hamilton, B., *Political thought in sixteenth-century Spain: A study of the political ideas of Vitoria, De Soto, Suárez and Molina*. Oxford 1963.

Hart, H. L. A., 'Are there any natural rights?', in A. Quinton (ed.), *Political philosophy*. Oxford 1967, 53–66; also in *Philosophical Review* 64 (1955), 175–91.

Heysse, A., 'Ubertini de Casali opusculum "super tribus sceleribus"', *Archivum Franciscanum Historicum* 10 (1917), 103–74.

Hohfeld, W. N., *Fundamental legal conceptions*. New Haven 1919.

Jaffa, H. V., *Thomism and Aristotelianism: A study of the commentary by Thomas Aquinas on the 'Nicomachean Ethics'*. Chicago 1952.

Jedin, H., *A history of the Council of Trent*, trans. by E. Graf. 2 vols. London 1957–61.

Jolowicz, H. F. and B. Nicholas, *A historical introduction to the study of the Roman law*. 3rd edn, Cambridge 1972.

Junghans, H., *Ockham im Lichte der neueren Forschung*. Berlin and Hamburg 1968.

Kalinowski, G., 'Le fondement objectif du droit d'après la "Somme théologique" de saint Thomas d'Aquin', *Archives de la philosophie du droit* 18 (1973), 59–75.

'Sur l'emploi métonymique du terme "ius" par Thomas d'Aquin', *Archives de la philosophie du droit* 18 (1973), 331–9.

Kelley, D., *Foundations of modern historical scholarship: Language, law and history in the French renaissance*. New York and London 1970.

Kenny, A., *Wyclif*. Oxford 1985.

Kölmel, W., 'Das Naturrecht bei Wilhelm Ockham', *Franziskanische Studien* 35 (1953), 39–85.

'Von Ockham zu Gabriel Biel. Zur Naturrechtslehre des 14. und 15. Jhdts', *Franziskanische Studien* 37 (1955), 219–59.

Korolec, J., 'Free will and free choice', in N. Kretzmann, A. Kenny and J. Pinborg (eds.), *The Cambridge history of later medieval philosophy: From the rediscovery of Aristotle to the disintegration of scholasticism, 1100–1600*, 629–41. Cambridge 1982.

Krempel, A., *La doctrine de la relation chez saint Thomas*. Paris 1952.

Kristeller, P. O., *Le thomisme et la pensée italienne de la renaissance*. Montreal 1967.

Lagarde, G. de, *La naissance de l'esprit laïque au déclin du moyen âge*. Vol. VI, *Ockham: La morale et le droit*. 1st edn, Paris 1946.

Lambert, M. D., *Franciscan poverty*. London 1961.

Lang, A., *Heinrich Totting von Oyta. Ein Beitrag zur Entstehungsgeschichte der ersten deutschen Universitäten und zur Problemgeschichte der Spätscholastik*. Münster i. W. 1937.

Leff, G., *The dissolution of the medieval outlook: An essay on intellectual change in the fourteenth century.* New York 1976.

Heresy in the later middle ages. 2 vols. Manchester 1967.

Richard Fitzralph, Commentator of the Sentences: A study in theological orthodoxy. Manchester 1963.

von Leyden, W., *Hobbes and Locke: The politics of freedom and obligation.* London 1982.

Little, A. G., *The grey friars at Oxford.* Oxford 1892.

Little, L. K., *Religious poverty and the profit economy in medieval Europe.* London 1978.

Lottin, O., *Psychologie et morale aux XIIe et XIIIe siècles.* Vol. II, *Problèmes de morale.* Louvain 1948.

Lyons, D., 'The correlativity of rights and duties', *Nous* 4 (1970), 45–55.

McGrade, A. S., 'Ockham and the birth of individual rights', in P. Linehan and B. Tierney (eds.), *Authority and power: Studies in medieval law and thought presented to Walter Ullmann on his seventieth birthday,* 149–60. Cambridge 1980.

The political thought of William of Ockham. Cambridge 1974.

MacIntyre, A., *Three rival versions of moral enquiry: Encyclopaedia, genealogy and tradition.* London 1990.

Maginot, N., *Der actus humanus moralis unter dem Einfluss des heiligen Geistes nach Dionysius Carthusianus.* Munich 1968.

Malcolm, Noel, 'Thomas Hobbes and voluntarist theology', unpublished Ph.D dissertation, Cambridge 1983.

Margiotta Broglio, F., 'Ideali pauperistici e strutture temporali nella canonistica del secolo XIV. Notazioni ed appunti per una edizione del "Liber Minoritarum" di Giovanni da Legnano', *Studia gratiana* 14 (1967), 369–436.

Meynial, E., 'Notes sur la formation de la théorie du domaine divisé (domaine direct et domaine utile) de XIIe au XIVe siècles dans les romanistes', in *Mélanges Fitting,* 409–61. Montpellier 1908.

Miaja de la Muela, A., *Internacionalistas españoles del siglo XVI. Fernando Vázquez de Menchaca, 1512–1569.* Valladolid 1932.

Michaud-Quantin, P., *Sommes de casuistique et manuels de confession au moyen âge (XIIème–XVIème siècles).* Louvain 1962.

Miethke, J., *Ockhams Weg zur Sozialphilosophie.* Berlin 1969.

Miller, F. D., *Nature, justice and rights in Aristotle's 'Politics'.* Oxford 1995.

Morrall, J. B., *Gerson and the great schism.* Manchester 1960.

'Some notes on a recent interpretation of William of Ockham's political philosophy', *Franciscan Studies* 9 (1949), 335–69.

Oakeshott, M., *Hobbes on civil association.* Oxford 1975.

Oakley, F., *Natural law, conciliarism and consent in the later middle ages.* London 1984.

Oberman, H. A., *The harvest of medieval theology.* Cambridge, Mass. 1963.

O'Connor, D. J., *Aquinas and natural law*. London 1967.
Offler, H. S., 'The "influence" of Ockham's political thinking', in W. Vossenkuhl and R. Schönberger (eds.), *Die Gegenwart Ockhams*, 338–65. Weinheim 1990.
'The three modes of natural law in Ockham: A revision of the text', *Franciscan Studies* 37 (1977), 207–18.
Otte, G., *Das Privatrecht bei Francisco de Vitoria*. Cologne and Graz 1964.
Ozment, S., *Homo spiritualis: A comparative study of the anthropology of Johannes Tauler, Jean Gerson and Martin Luther*. Leiden 1969.
Pagden, A. R. D., *The fall of natural man: The American Indian and the origins of comparative ethnology*. Cambridge 1982.
Lords of all the world: Ideologies of empire in Spain, Britain and France, c. 1500–c. 1800. New Haven and London 1995.
Pascoe, L. B., *Jean Gerson: Principles of church reform*. Leiden 1973.
Paulus, N., *Die deutschen Dominikaner im Kampfe gegen Luther*. Freiburg 1903.
Pennock, J. R., 'Hobbes' confusing "clarity" – the case of "liberty"', in K. C. Brown (ed.), *Hobbes studies*, 101–16. Oxford 1965.
Pereña Vicente, L., *La universidad de Salamanca, forja del pensamiento político en el siglo XVI*. Salamanca 1954.
Perry, D., 'Paridis de Puteo: A fifteenth-century civilian's concept of papal sovereignty', in D. Wood (ed.), *The church and sovereignty, c. 590–1918: Essays in honour of Michael Wilks*, 369–92. Oxford 1991.
Pocock, J. G. A., 'The concept of a language and the *métier d'historien*: Some considerations on practice', in A. Pagden (ed.), *The languages of political theory in early modern Europe*, 19–28. Cambridge 1987.
Pugliese, G., ' "Res corporales", "res incorporales" e il problema del diritto soggettivo', in *Studi in onore di V. Arangio-Ruiz*. Vol. III, 223–60. Naples 1953.
Raphael, D. D., 'Hobbes', in Z. Pelczynski and J. Gray (eds.), *Conceptions of liberty in political philosophy*, 27–38. London 1984.
'Human rights', *Aristotelian Society Supplements* 39 (1965), 205–18.
'Obligations and rights in Hobbes', *Philosophy* 37 (1962), 345–52.
Reibstein, E., *Die Anfänge des neueren Natur- und Völkerrechts*. Bern 1949.
Renaudet, A., *Préréforme et humanisme à Paris pendant les guerres d'Italie (1494–1517)*. Paris 1916; 2nd edn, Paris 1953.
de Roover, R., *San Bernardino of Siena and Sant'Antonino of Florence: The two great economic thinkers of the middle ages*. Boston, Mass. 1967.
Schwab, J. B., *Johannes Gerson, Professor der Theologie und Kanzler der Universität Paris*. Würzburg 1858.
Seelmann, K., *Die Lehre des Fernando Vázquez de Menchaca vom 'dominium'*. Cologne and Graz 1979.
Serrano Serrano, J. M., 'Las ideas políticas de Fernando Vázquez de Menchaca', *Revista de estudios políticos* 206–7 (1976), 249–302.
Skinner, Q. R. D., *The foundations of modern political thought*. 2 vols. Cambridge 1978.

'Thomas Hobbes on the proper signification of liberty', *Transactions of the Royal Historical Society* (1992), 121–51.

Söllner, A., 'Die Literatur zum gemeinen und partikularen Recht in Deutschland, Österreich, den Niederlanden und der Schweiz', in H. Coing (ed.), *Handbuch der Quellen und Literatur der neueren europäischen Privatrechtsgeschichte*. Vol. II/1, 501–614. Munich 1977.

Spicciani, A., 'Sant'Antonino, San Bernardino e Pier di Giovanni Olivi nel pensiero economico medievale', in O. Capitani (ed.), *Una economia politica nel medioevo*, 93–120. Bologna 1987.

Stadter, E. *Psychologie und Metaphysik der menschlichen Freiheit. Die ideengeschichtliche Entwicklung zwischen Bonaventura und Duns Scotus*. Munich, Paderborn and Vienna 1971.

Stein, P., *Regulae iuris*. Edinburgh 1966.

Taylor, A. E., 'The ethical doctrine of Hobbes', *Philosophy* 13 (1938), 406–24.

Teetaert, A., 'Deux questions inédites de Gérard d'Abbeville en faveur du clergé séculier', in *Mélanges Auguste Pelzer*, 347–87. Louvain 1947.

'Pierre Auriol', in *Dictionnaire de théologie catholique* 12 (Paris 1933), 1809–1881.

Theiner, J., *Die Entwicklung der Moraltheologie zur eigenständigen Disziplin*. Regensburg 1970.

Tierney, B., 'Aristotle and the American Indians – again: Two critical discussions', *Cristianesimo nella storia* 12 (1991), 295–322.

'Conciliarism, corporatism and individualism: The doctrine of individual rights in Gerson', *Cristianesimo nella storia* 9 (1988), 81–111.

'*Ius* and metonymy in Rufinus', in R. Castillo Lara (ed.), *Studia in honorem eminentissimi Cardinalis Alphonsi M. Stickler*, 549–58. Rome 1992.

'"Ius dictum est a iure possidendo": Law and rights in *Decretales* 5. 40. 12', in D. Wood (ed.), *The church and sovereignty, c. 590–1918: Essays in honour of Michael Wilks*, 457–66. Oxford 1991.

'Ockham, the conciliar theory and the canonists', *Journal of the History of Ideas* 15 (1954), 40–70.

'The origins of natural rights language: Texts and contexts, 1150–1250', *History of Political Thought* 10 (1989), 615–46.

'Tuck on rights: Some medieval problems', *History of Political Thought* 4 (1983), 429–41.

'Villey, Ockham and the origin of individual rights', in J. Witte and F. S. Alexander (eds.), *The weightier matters of the law: Essays on law and religion*, 1–31. Atlanta 1988.

Todeschini, G., ' "Oeconomica franciscana". Proposte di una nuova lettura delle fonti dell'etica economica medievale', *Rivista di storia e letteratura religiosa* 12 (1976), 15–77 and 13 (1977), 461–94.

Un trattato di economia politica francescana: Il 'De emptionibus et venditionibus, de usuris, de restitutionibus' di Pietro di Giovanni Olivi. Rome 1980.

Trinkaus, C. and H. A. Oberman (eds.), *The pursuit of holiness in late medieval and renaissance religion*. Leiden 1974.

Tuck, R., *Natural rights theories: Their origin and development.* Cambridge 1979.
Philosophy and government, 1572–1651. Cambridge 1993.
Tully, J., *An approach to political philosophy: Locke in contexts.* Cambridge 1993.
A discourse on property: John Locke and his adversaries. Cambridge 1980.
Ullmann, W., *Mediaeval papalism: The political theories of the mediaeval canonists.* London 1949.
Van Overbeke, P. M., 'Saint Thomas et le droit. Commentaire de la IIa–II, q. 57', *Revue thomiste* 55 (1955), 519–64.
Villey, M., 'La genèse du droit subjectif chez Guillaume d'Ockham', *Archives de la philosophie du droit* N.S. 9 (1964), 97–127.
Leçons d'histoire de la philosophie du droit. 2nd edn, Paris 1962.
'La promotion de la loi et du droit subjectif dans la seconde scolastique', in P. Grossi, *La seconda scolastica nella formazione del diritto privato moderno. Incontro di studi*, 53–71. Milan 1973.
'Si la théorie générale du droit, pour saint Thomas, est une théorie de la loi', *Archives de la philosophie du droit* 17 (1972), 427–31.
'Sur les essais d'application de la logique déontologique au droit', *Archives de la philosophie du droit* 17 (1972), 407–12.
Villoslada, R. G., *La universidad de Paris durante los estudios de Francisco de Vitoria (1507–1522).* Rome 1938.
Viora, M., 'La "Summa angelica"', *Bollettino storico-bibliografico subalpino* 38 (1936), 443–51.
Walsh, J. J., 'Some relationships between Gerald Odo's and John Buridan's commentaries on Aristotle's "Ethics"', *Franciscan Studies* N.S. 35 (1975), 237–75.
Walsh, K., *A fourteenth-century scholar and primate: Richard Fitzralph in Oxford, Avignon and Armagh.* Oxford 1981.
Waterlow, S., *Nature, change and agency in Aristotle's 'Physics': A philosophical study.* Oxford 1982.
Weiler, A. G., *Heinrich von Gorkum (+ 1431). Seine Stellung in der Philosophie und der Theologie des Spätmittelalters.* Zurich and Cologne 1962.
Wernham, A. G., 'Liberty and obligation in Hobbes', in K. C. Brown (ed.), *Hobbes studies*, 117–39. Oxford 1965.
Wieland, G., 'The reception and interpretation of Aristotle's *Ethics*', in N. Kretzmann, A. Kenny and J. Pinborg (eds.), *The Cambridge history of later medieval philosophy: From the rediscovery of Aristotle to the disintegration of scholasticism, 1100–1600*, 657–72. Cambridge 1982.
Wilks, M., 'Predestination, property and power: Wyclif's theory of dominion and grace', in G. J. Cuming (ed.), *Studies in church history.* Vol. II, 220–36. London and Edinburgh 1965.
The problem of sovereignty in the later middle ages: The papal monarchy with Augustinus Triumphus and the publicists. Cambridge 1963.
Wirszubski, Ch., *Libertas as a political idea at Rome during the late republic and early principate.* Cambridge 1960.
Wolter, A., *Duns Scotus on the will and morality.* Washington, D. C. 1986.

Zuckerman, C., 'The relationship of theories of universals to theories of church government in the middle ages: A critique of previous views', *Journal of the History of Ideas* 36 (1975), 579–94.

Zumkeller, A., 'Die Augustinerschule des Mittelalters: Vertreter and philosophisch-theologische Lehre', *Analecta augustiniana* 27–8 (1964–5), 167–262.

Index

IDEAS IN CONTEXT

Edited by QUENTIN SKINNER (*General Editor*)
LORRAINE DASTON, DOROTHY ROSS and JAMES TULLY

Titles marked with an asterisk are also available in paperback

Lightning Source UK Ltd.
Milton Keynes UK
UKOW04f1917060913

216716UK00001B/92/A